AMBEDKAR
INDIA'S CRUSADER FOR HUMAN RIGHTS

AMBEDKAR
INDIA'S CRUSADER FOR HUMAN RIGHTS

Author   : Kieron Moore

Illustrator : Sachin Nagar

Colourists : Vijay Sharma &
                     Pradeep Sherawat

Editor   : Sourav Dutta

Letterer   : Bhavnath Chaudhary

Designer   : Vijay Sharma

Cover   : Sachin Nagar

Disclaimer

The Author and the Publisher have made every effort to ensure that the information included in this work is correct. This work draws from a variety of sources and is not encyclopaedic. For narrative purposes, dialogues and incidents have been recreated for lack of details.

CAMPFIRE®

www.campfire.co.in

Published by Kalyani Navyug Media Pvt Ltd
101 C, Shiv House, Hari Nagar Ashram,
New Delhi 110014, India

ISBN: 978-93-81182-81-9

Copyright © 2018 Kalyani Navyug Media Pvt Ltd

1 BORN UNTOUCHABLE

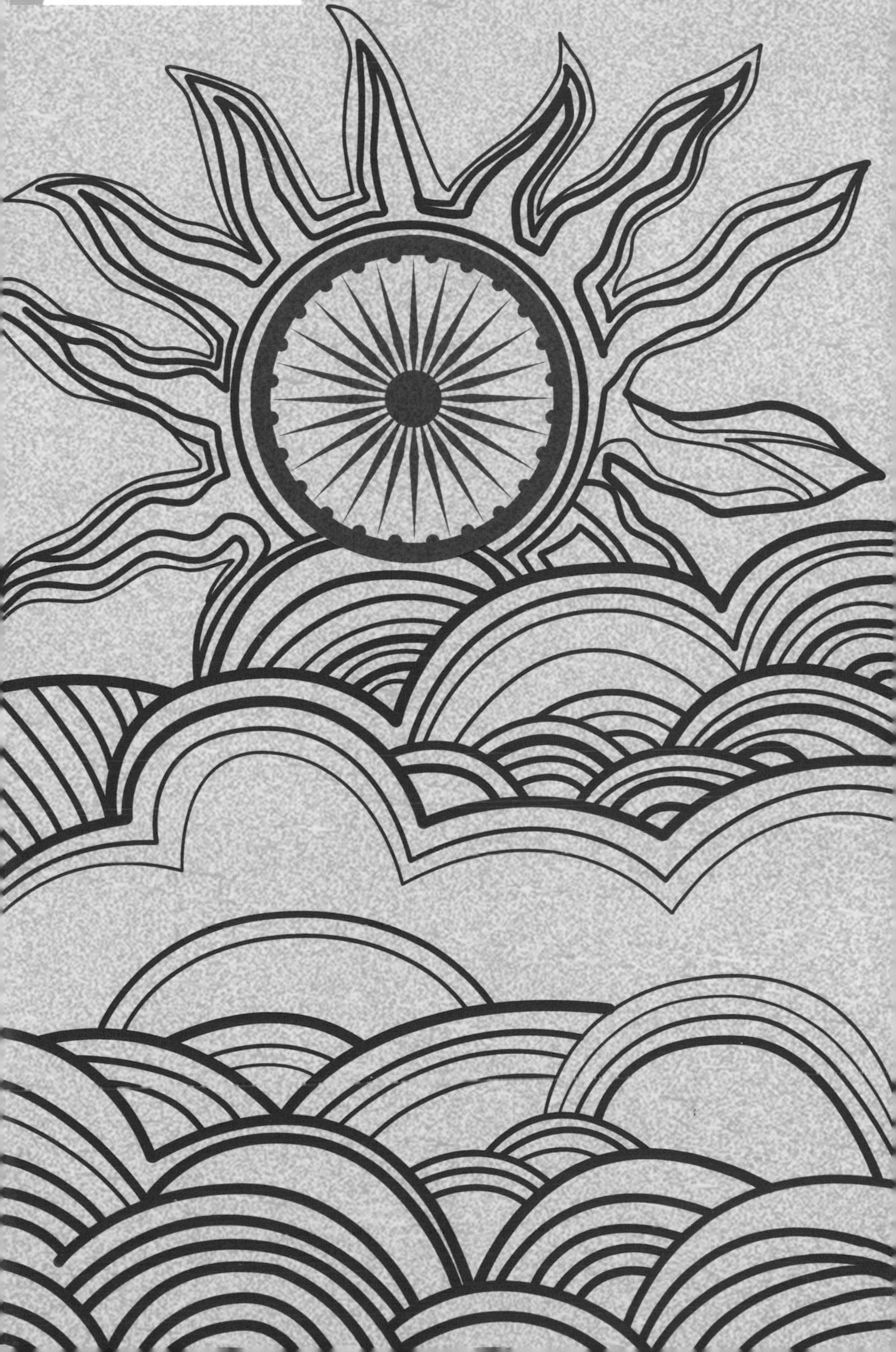

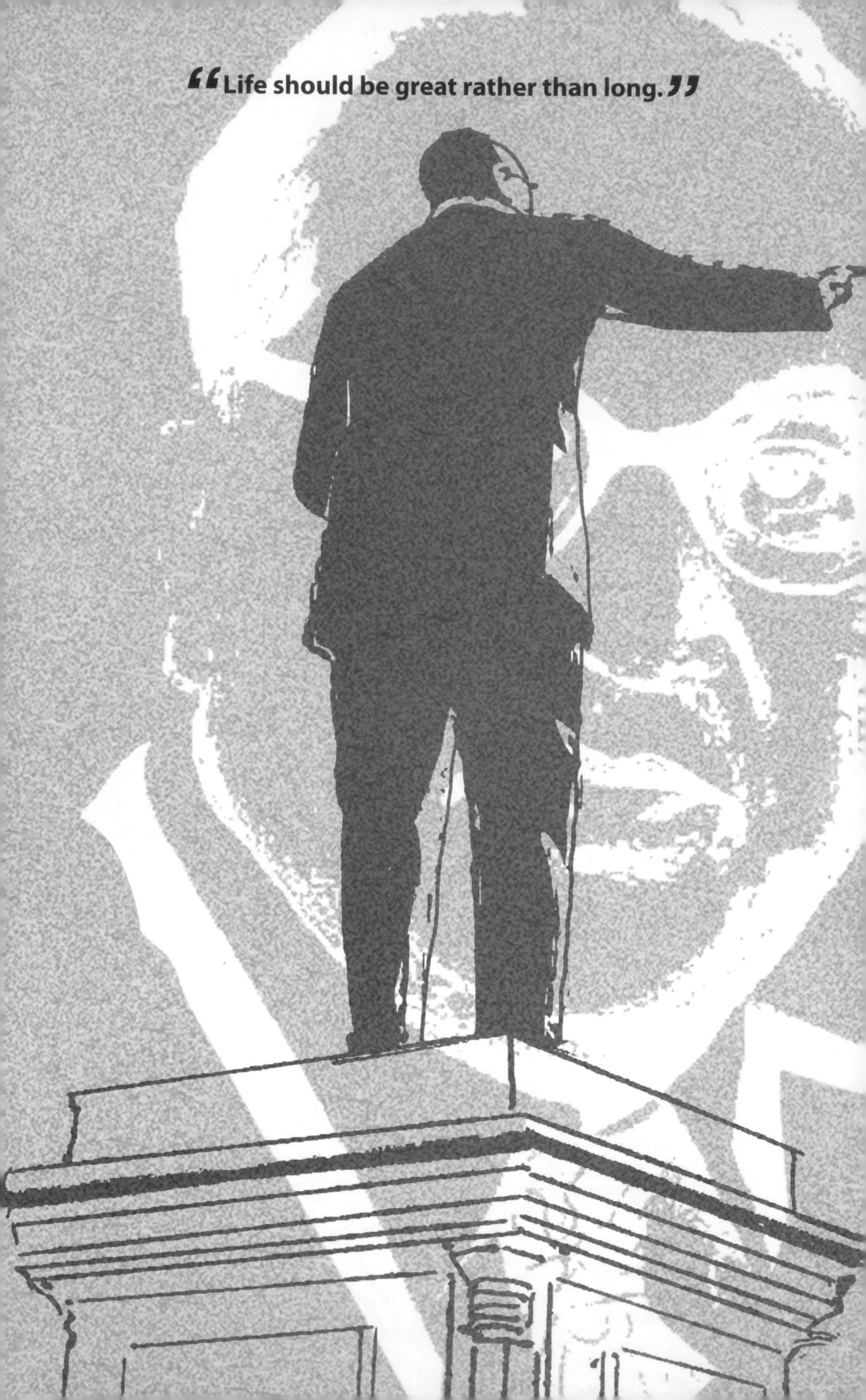
“Life should be great rather than long.”

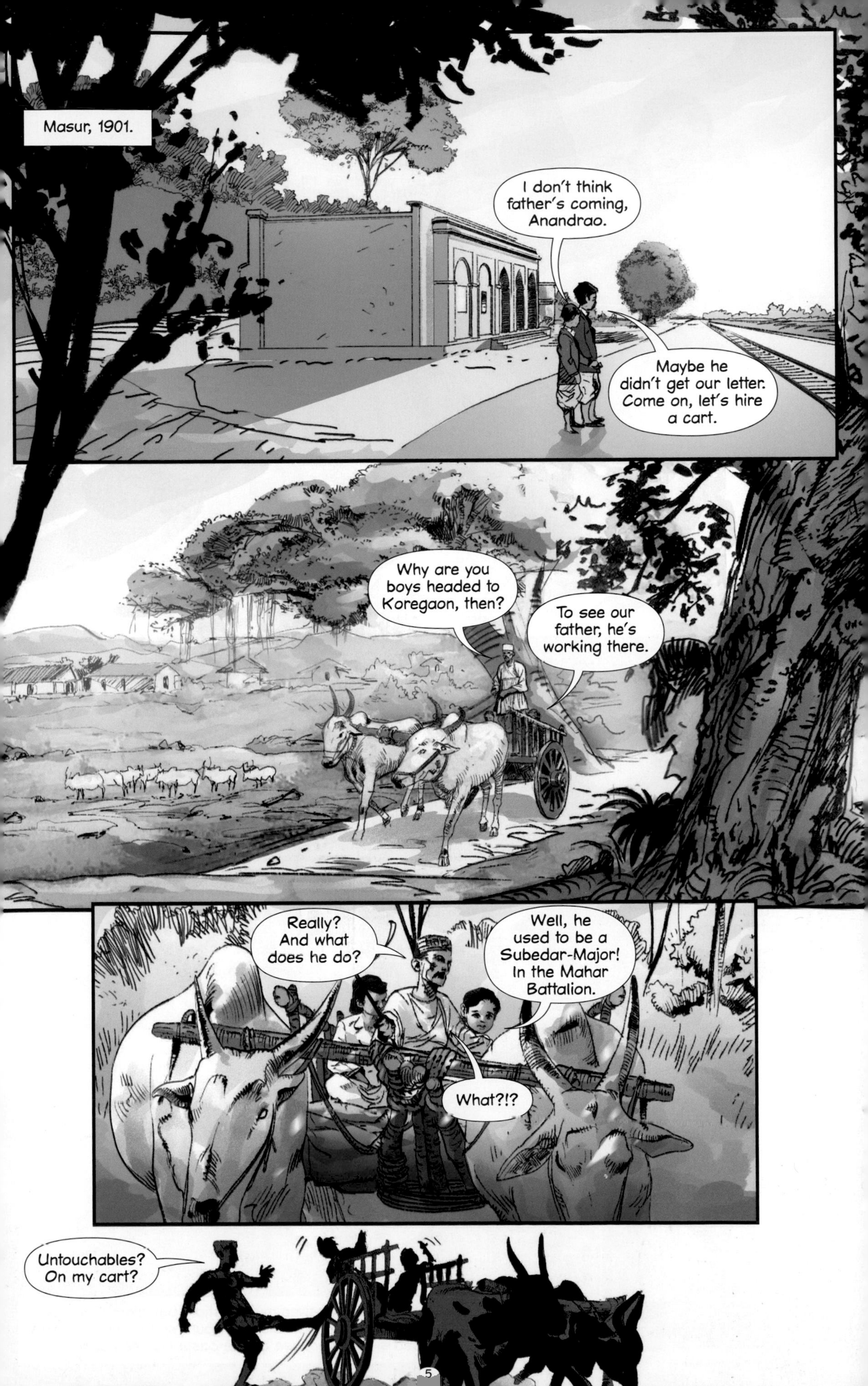
Masur, 1901.
I don't think father's coming, Anandrao.
Maybe he didn't get our letter. Come on, let's hire a cart.
Why are you boys headed to Koregaon, then?
To see our father, he's working there.
Really? And what does he do?
Well, he used to be a Subedar-Major! In the Mahar Battalion.
What?!?
Untouchables? On my cart?

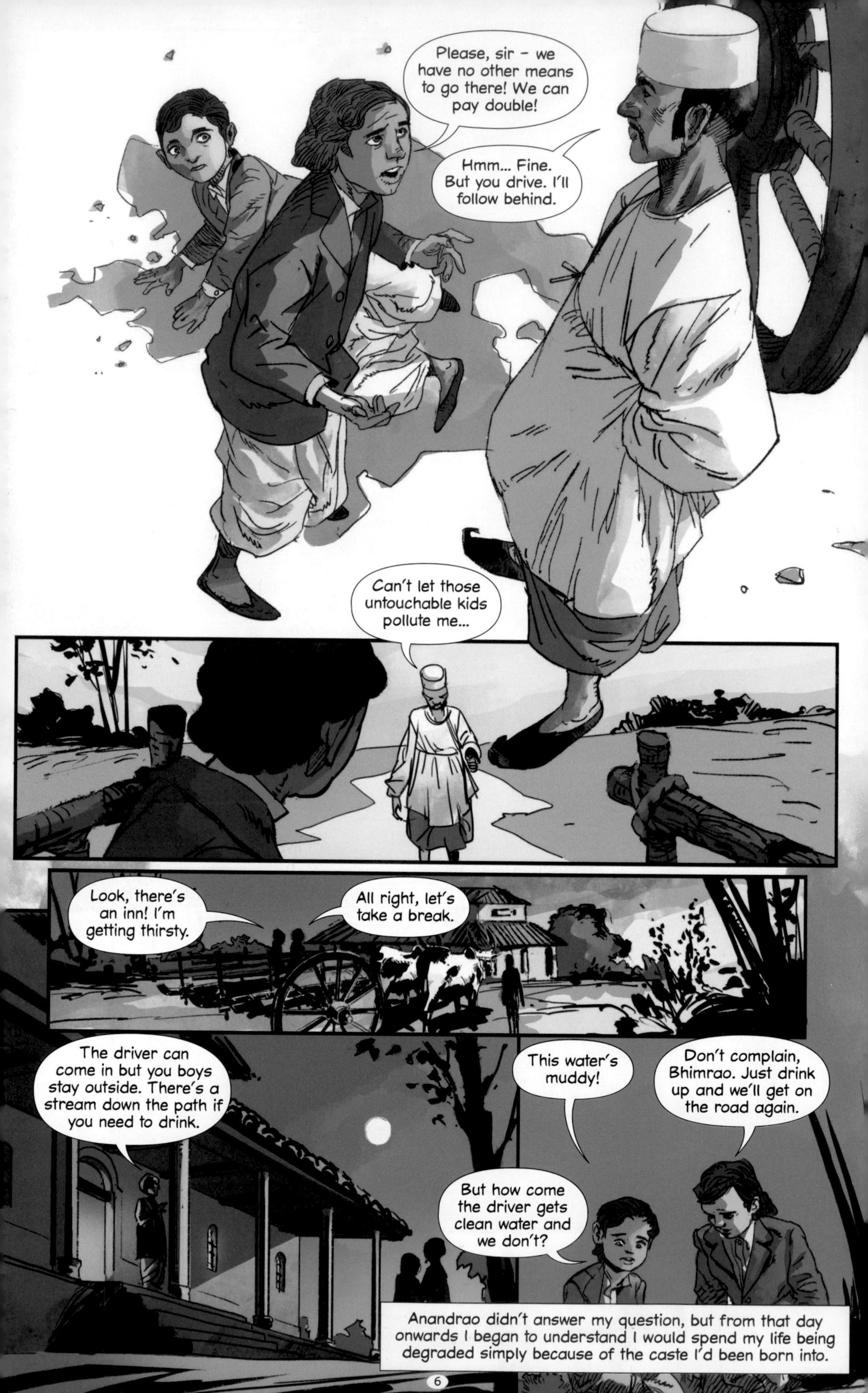

Please, sir – we have no other means to go there! We can pay double!
Hmm... Fine. But you drive. I'll follow behind.
Can't let those untouchable kids pollute me...
Look, there's an inn! I'm getting thirsty.
All right, let's take a break.
The driver can come in but you boys stay outside. There's a stream down the path if you need to drink.
This water's muddy!
Don't complain, Bhimrao. Just drink up and we'll get on the road again.
But how come the driver gets clean water and we don't?
Anandrao didn't answer my question, but from that day onwards I began to understand I would spend my life being degraded simply because of the caste I'd been born into.

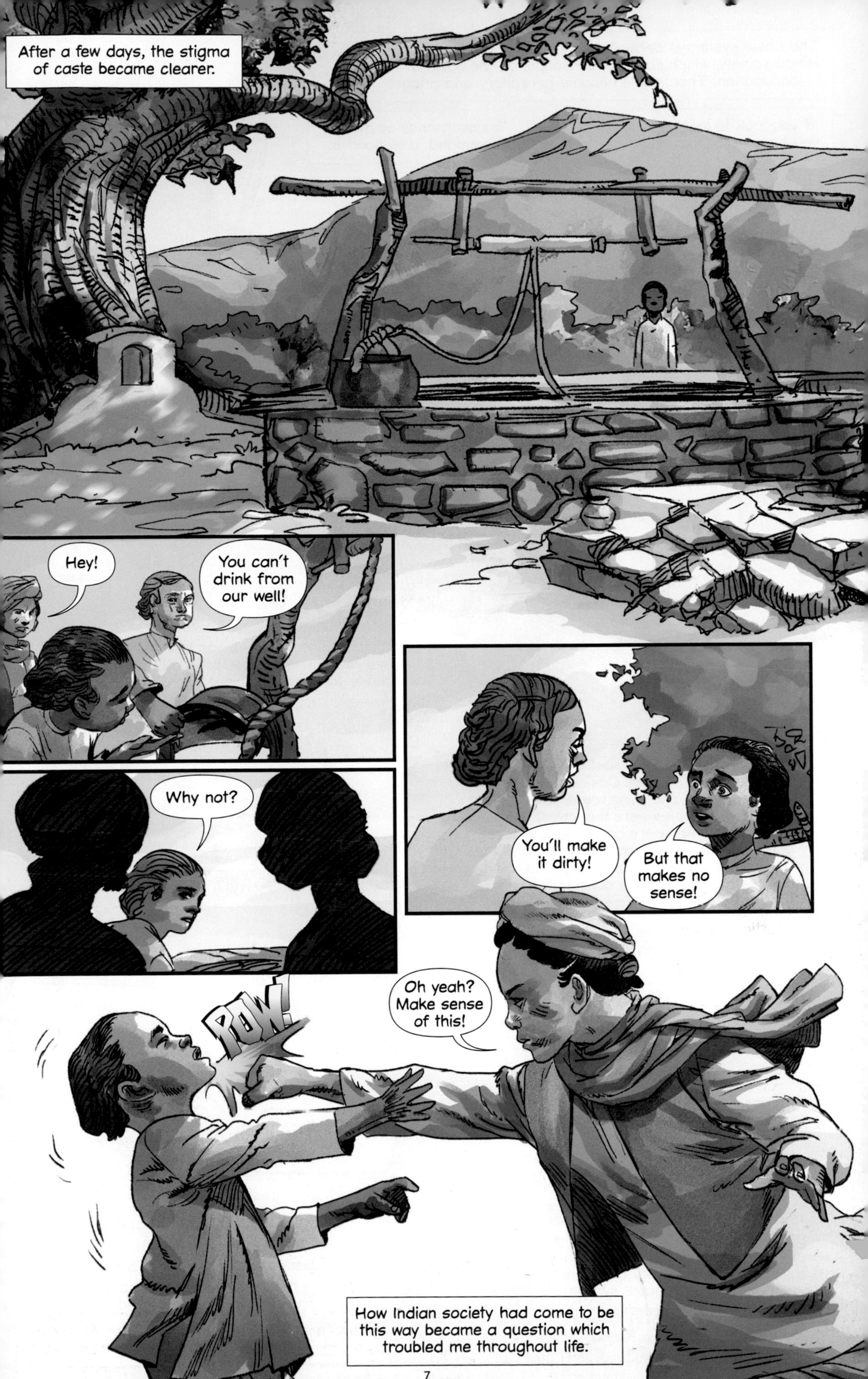

After a few days, the stigma of caste became clearer.
Hey!
You can't drink from our well!
Why not?
You'll make it dirty!
But that makes no sense!
Oh yeah? Make sense of this!
POW!
How Indian society had come to be this way became a question which troubled me throughout life.

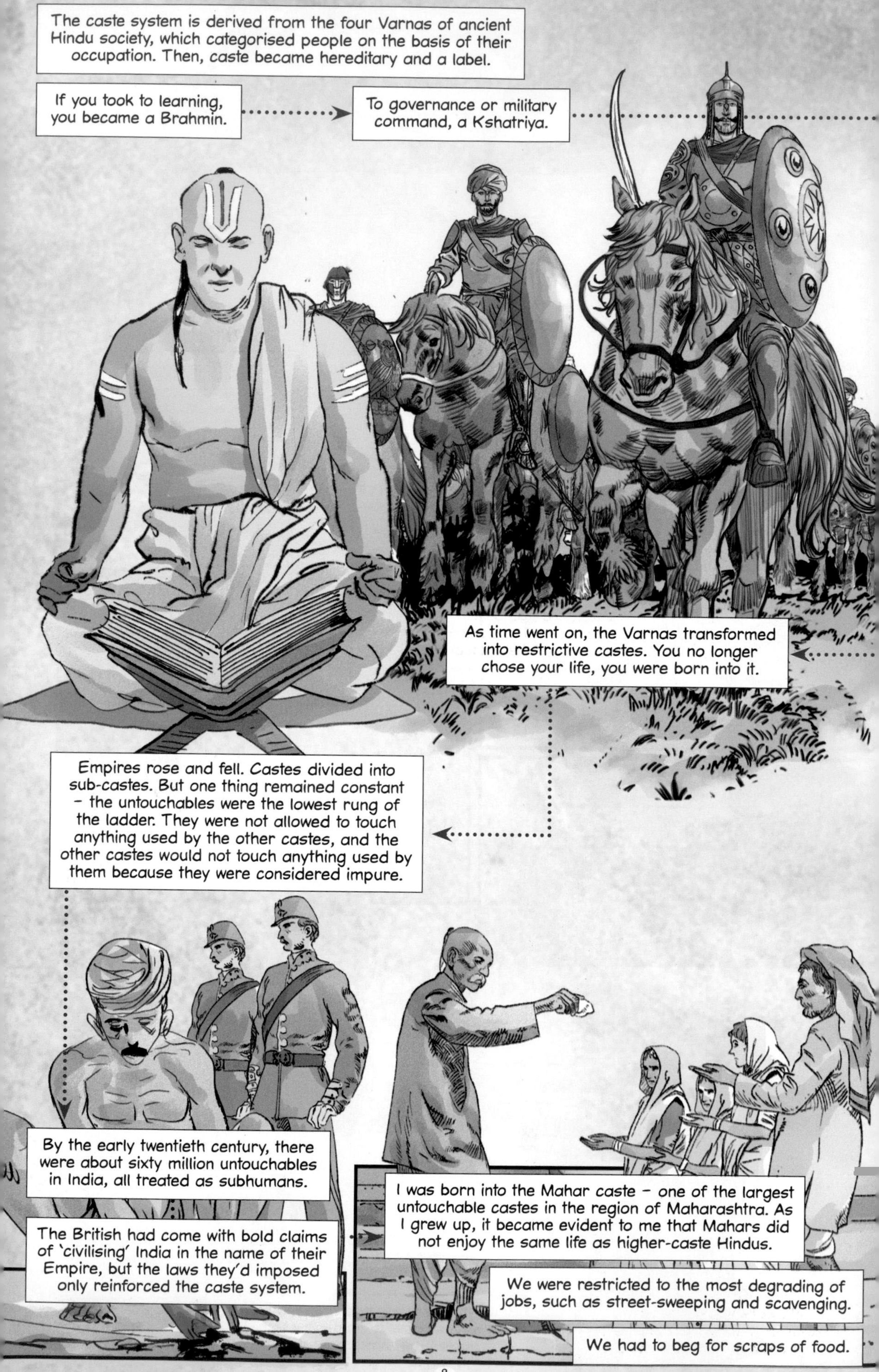
The caste system is derived from the four Varnas of ancient Hindu society, which categorised people on the basis of their occupation. Then, caste became hereditary and a label.
If you took to learning, you became a Brahmin.
To governance or military command, a Kshatriya.
As time went on, the Varnas transformed into restrictive castes. You no longer chose your life, you were born into it.
Empires rose and fell. Castes divided into sub-castes. But one thing remained constant – the untouchables were the lowest rung of the ladder. They were not allowed to touch anything used by the other castes, and the other castes would not touch anything used by them because they were considered impure.
By the early twentieth century, there were about sixty million untouchables in India, all treated as subhumans.
The British had come with bold claims of 'civilising' India in the name of their Empire, but the laws they'd imposed only reinforced the caste system.
I was born into the Mahar caste – one of the largest untouchable castes in the region of Maharashtra. As I grew up, it became evident to me that Mahars did not enjoy the same life as higher-caste Hindus.
We were restricted to the most degrading of jobs, such as street-sweeping and scavenging.
We had to beg for scraps of food.

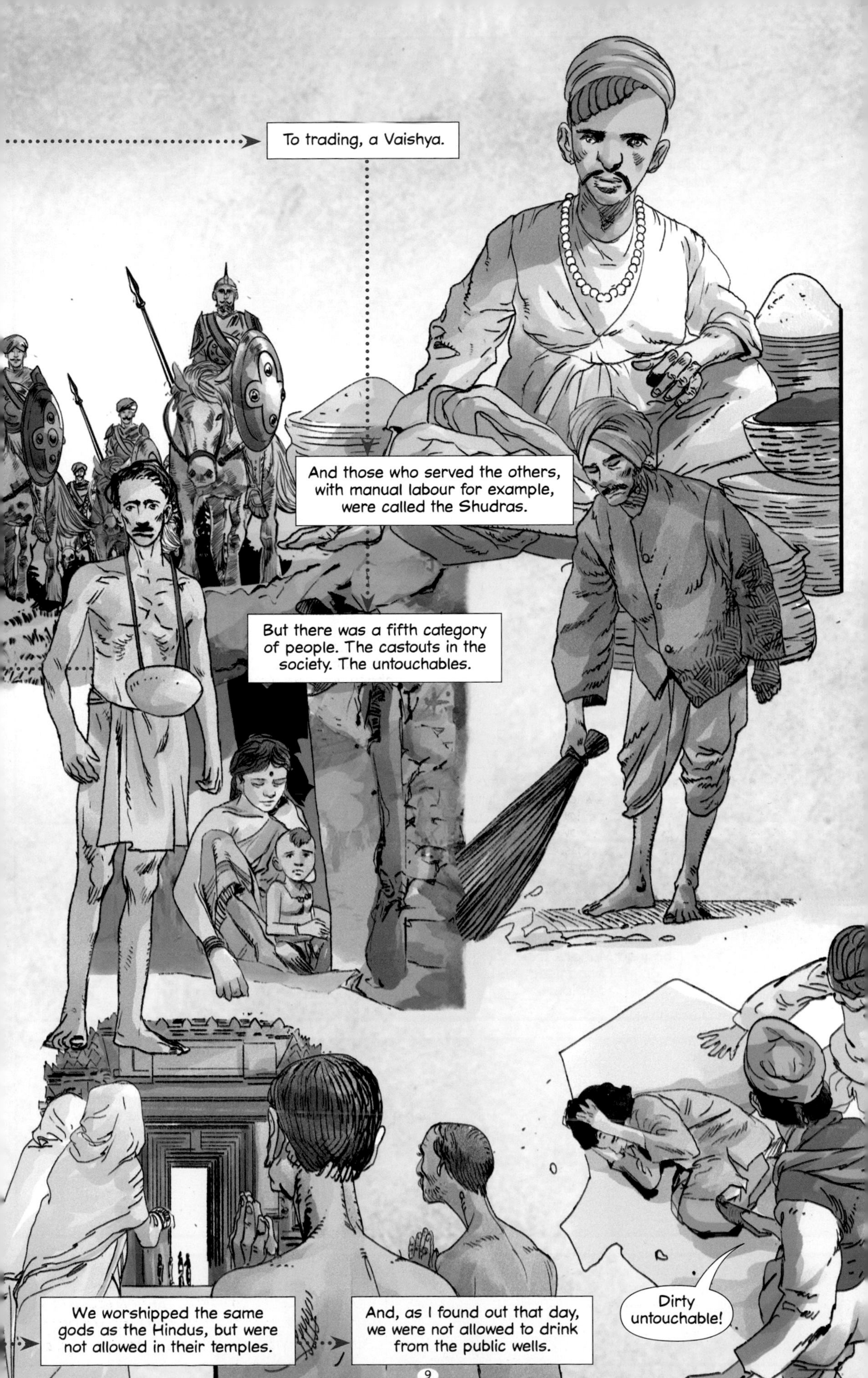
To trading, a Vaishya.
And those who served the others, with manual labour for example, were called the Shudras.
But there was a fifth category of people. The castouts in the society. The untouchables.
We worshipped the same gods as the Hindus, but were not allowed in their temples.
And, as I found out that day, we were not allowed to drink from the public wells.
Dirty untouchable!

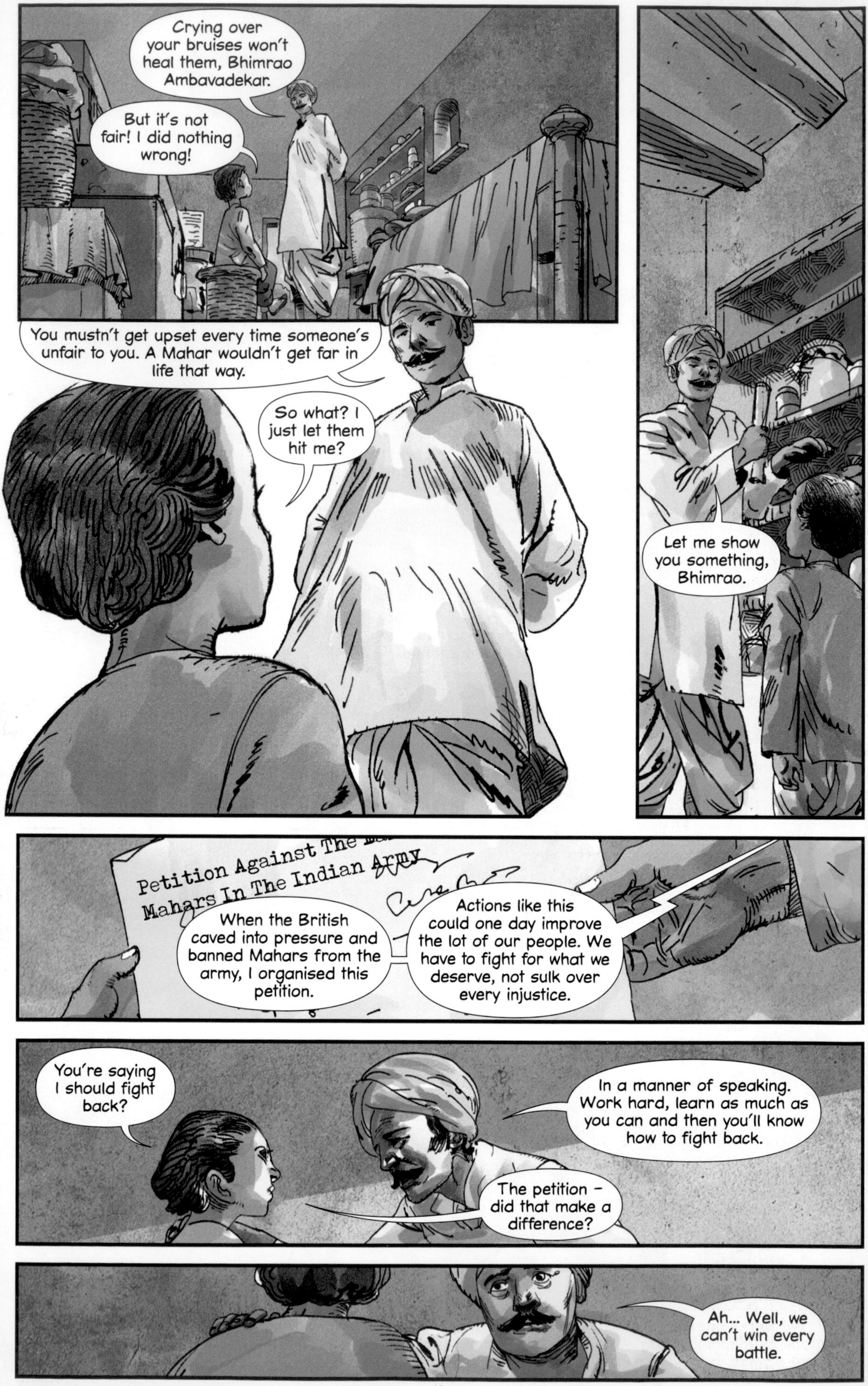
Crying over your bruises won't heal them, Bhimrao Ambavadekar.
But it's not fair! I did nothing wrong!
You mustn't get upset every time someone's unfair to you. A Mahar wouldn't get far in life that way.
So what? I just let them hit me?
Let me show you something, Bhimrao.
Petition Against The
Mahars In The Indian Army
When the British caved into pressure and banned Mahars from the army, I organised this petition.
Actions like this could one day improve the lot of our people. We have to fight for what we deserve, not sulk over every injustice.
You're saying I should fight back?
In a manner of speaking. Work hard, learn as much as you can and then you'll know how to fight back.
The petition – did that make a difference?
Ah... Well, we can't win every battle.

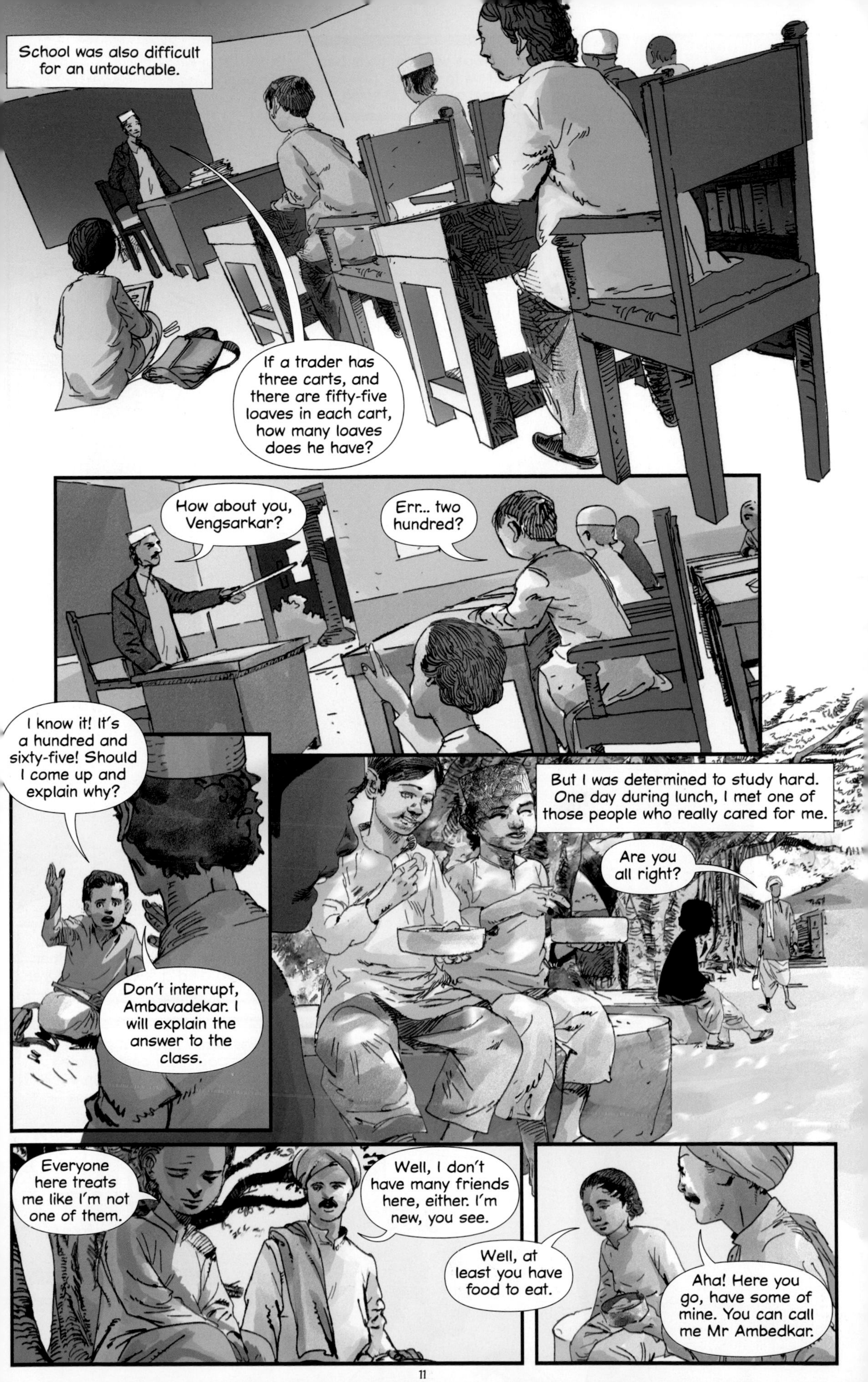
School was also difficult for an untouchable.
If a trader has three carts, and there are fifty-five loaves in each cart, how many loaves does he have?
How about you, Vengsarkar?
Err... two hundred?
I know it! It's a hundred and sixty-five! Should I come up and explain why?
Don't interrupt, Ambavadekar. I will explain the answer to the class.
But I was determined to study hard. One day during lunch, I met one of those people who really cared for me.
Are you all right?
Everyone here treats me like I'm not one of them.
Well, I don't have many friends here, either. I'm new, you see.
Well, at least you have food to eat.
Aha! Here you go, have some of mine. You can call me Mr Ambedkar.

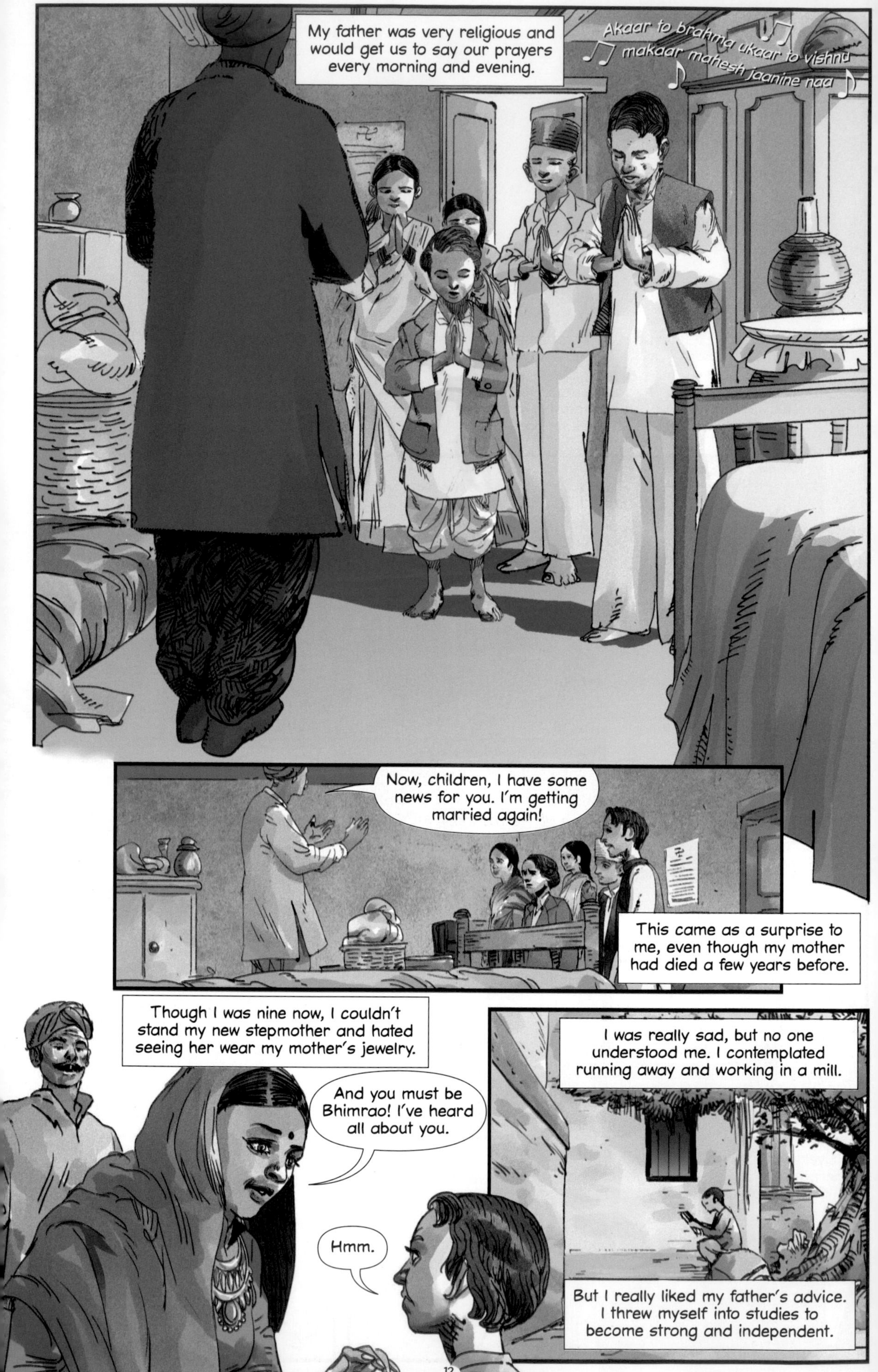

My father was very religious and would get us to say our prayers every morning and evening.
Akaar to brahma ukaar to vishnu makaar mahesh jaanine naa
Now, children, I have some news for you. I'm getting married again!
This came as a surprise to me, even though my mother had died a few years before.
Though I was nine now, I couldn't stand my new stepmother and hated seeing her wear my mother's jewelry.
And you must be Bhimrao! I've heard all about you.
Hmm.
I was really sad, but no one understood me. I contemplated running away and working in a mill.
But I really liked my father's advice. I threw myself into studies to become strong and independent.

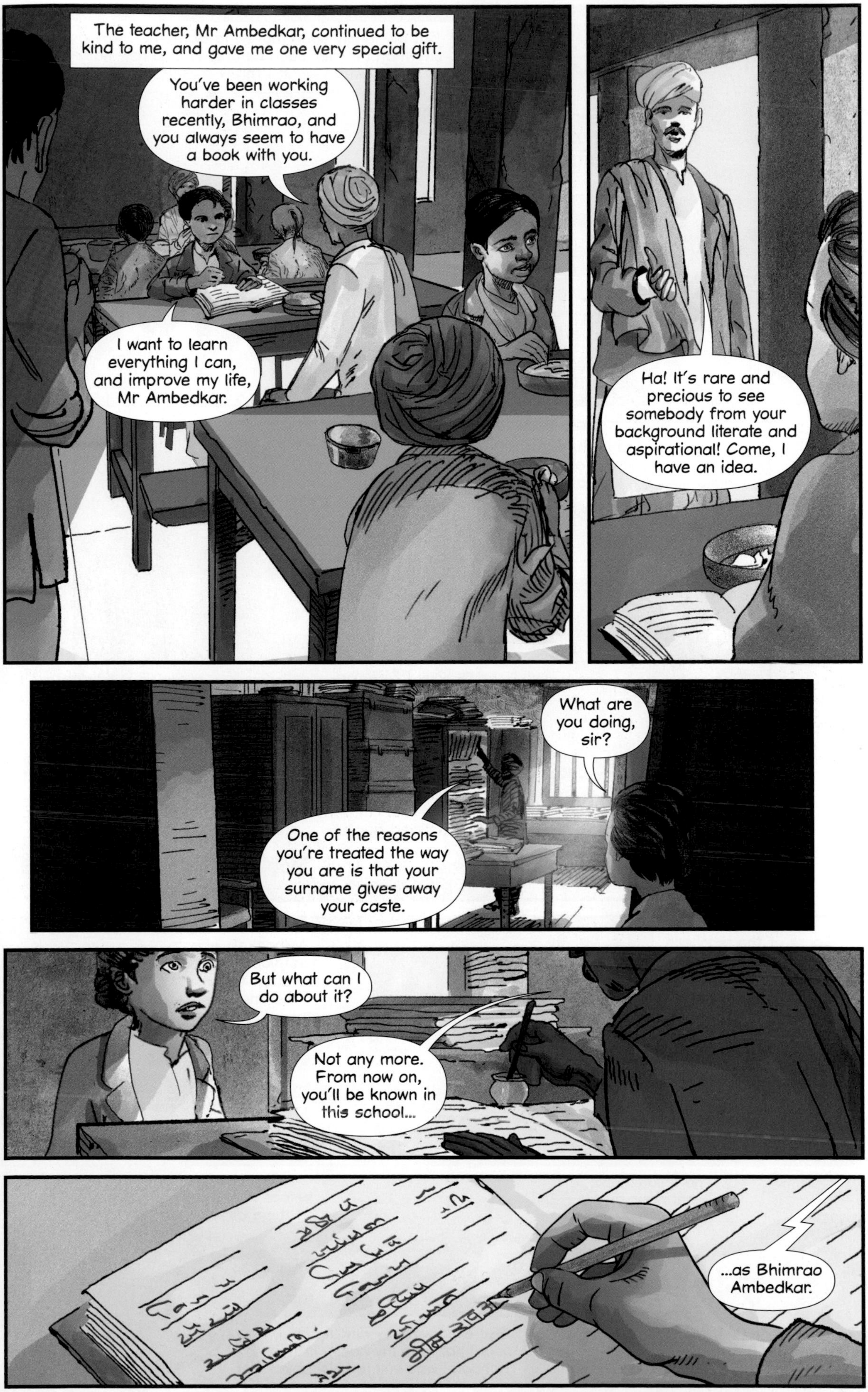

The teacher, Mr Ambedkar, continued to be kind to me, and gave me one very special gift.
You've been working harder in classes recently, Bhimrao, and you always seem to have a book with you.
I want to learn everything I can, and improve my life, Mr Ambedkar.
Ha! It's rare and precious to see somebody from your background literate and aspirational! Come, I have an idea.
What are you doing, sir?
One of the reasons you're treated the way you are is that your surname gives away your caste.
But what can I do about it?
Not any more. From now on, you'll be known in this school...
...as Bhimrao Ambedkar.

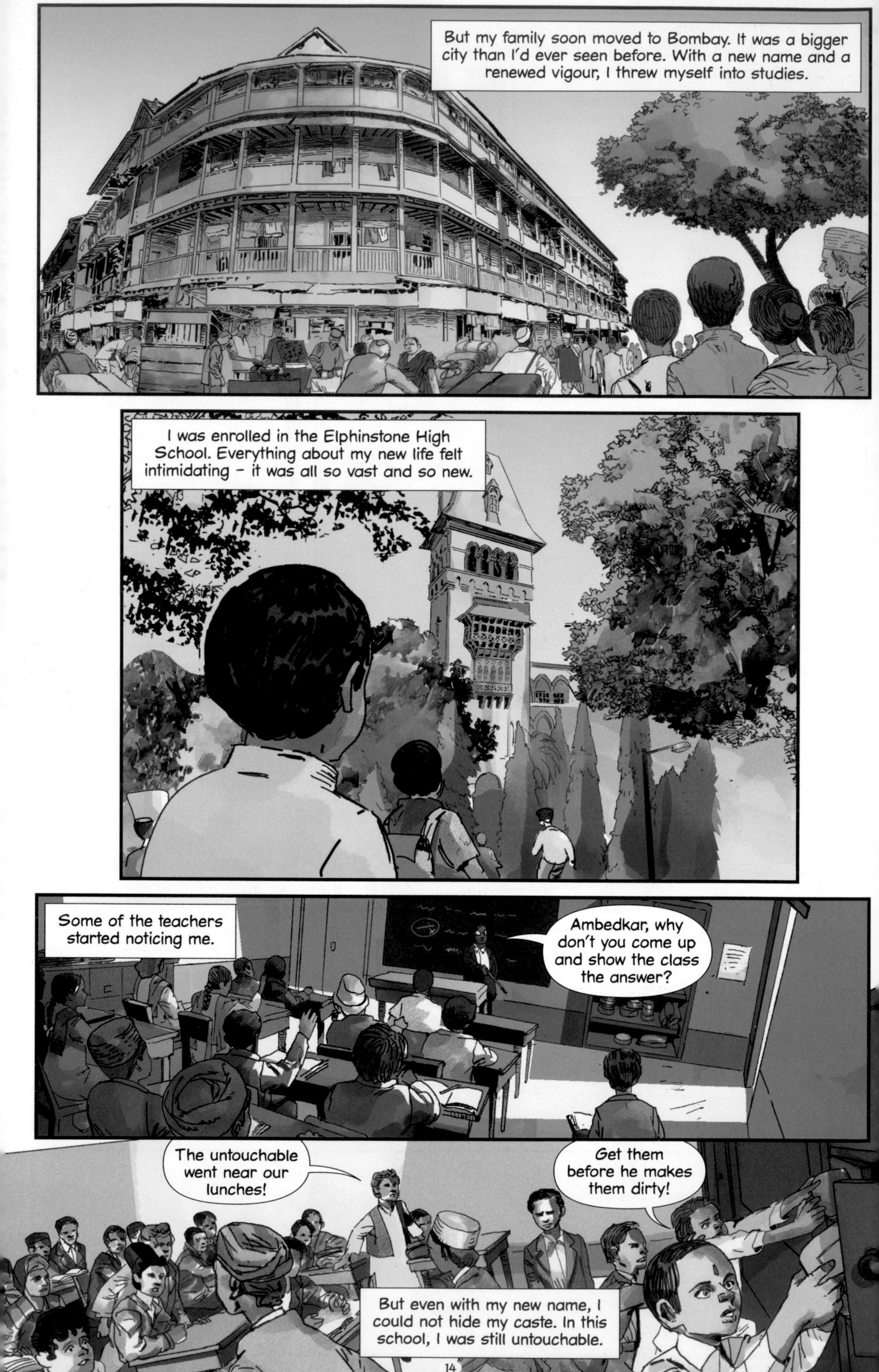
But my family soon moved to Bombay. It was a bigger city than I'd ever seen before. With a new name and a renewed vigour, I threw myself into studies.
I was enrolled in the Elphinstone High School. Everything about my new life felt intimidating – it was all so vast and so new.
Some of the teachers started noticing me.
Ambedkar, why don't you come up and show the class the answer?
The untouchable went near our lunches!
Get them before he makes them dirty!
But even with my new name, I could not hide my caste. In this school, I was still untouchable.

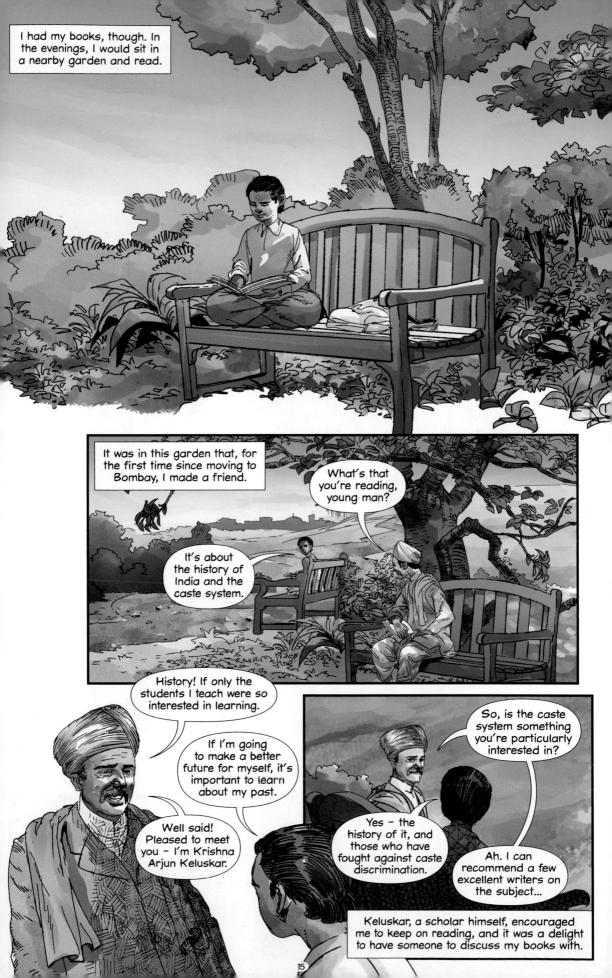

I had my books, though. In the evenings, I would sit in a nearby garden and read.

It was in this garden that, for the first time since moving to Bombay, I made a friend.

What's that you're reading, young man?

It's about the history of India and the caste system.

History! If only the students I teach were so interested in learning.

If I'm going to make a better future for myself, it's important to learn about my past.

Well said! Pleased to meet you – I'm Krishna Arjun Keluskar.

So, is the caste system something you're particularly interested in?

Yes – the history of it, and those who have fought against caste discrimination.

Ah. I can recommend a few excellent writers on the subject...

Keluskar, a scholar himself, encouraged me to keep on reading, and it was a delight to have someone to discuss my books with.

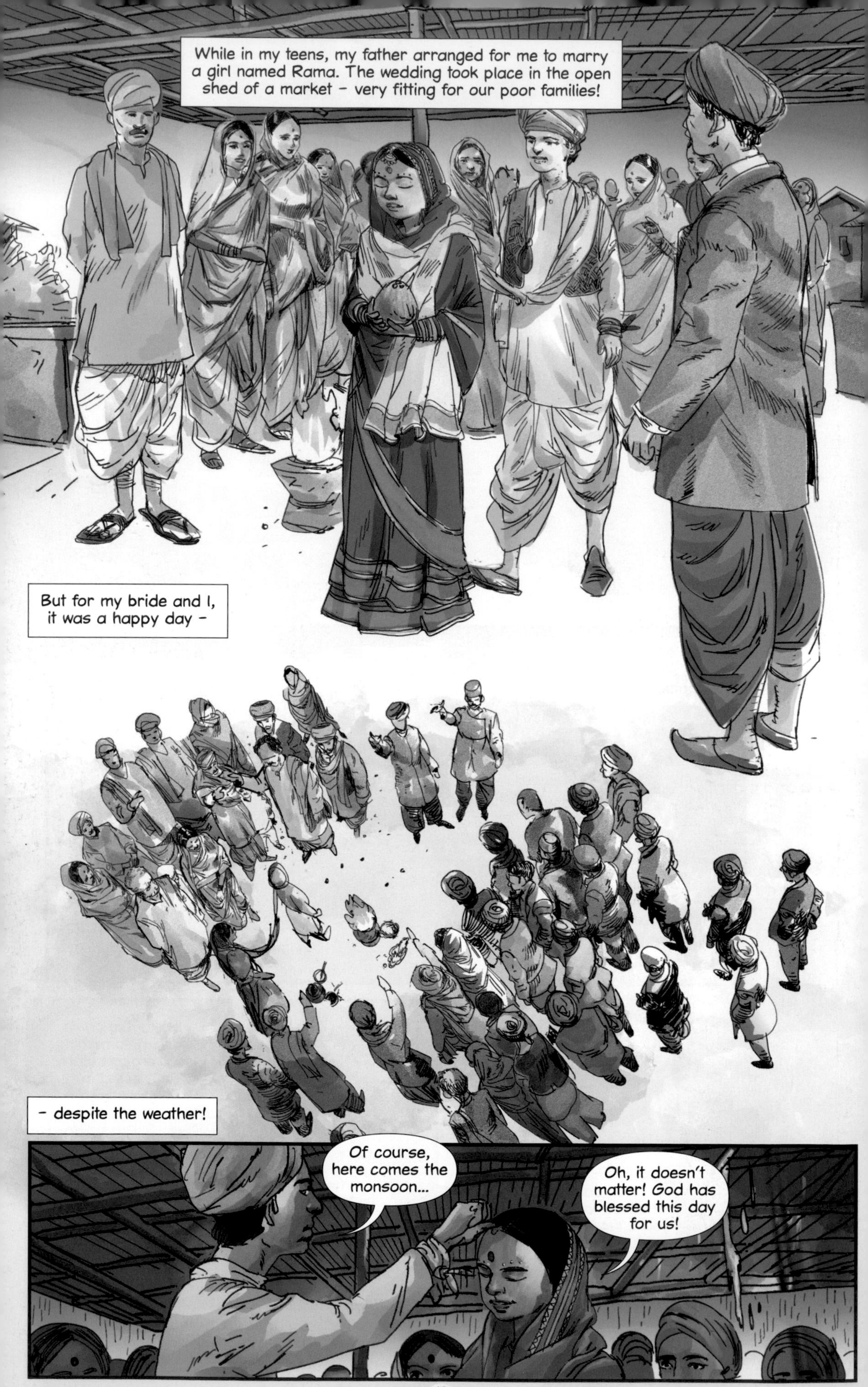
While in my teens, my father arranged for me to marry a girl named Rama. The wedding took place in the open shed of a market – very fitting for our poor families!
But for my bride and I, it was a happy day –
– despite the weather!
Of course, here comes the monsoon...
Oh, it doesn't matter! God has blessed this day for us!

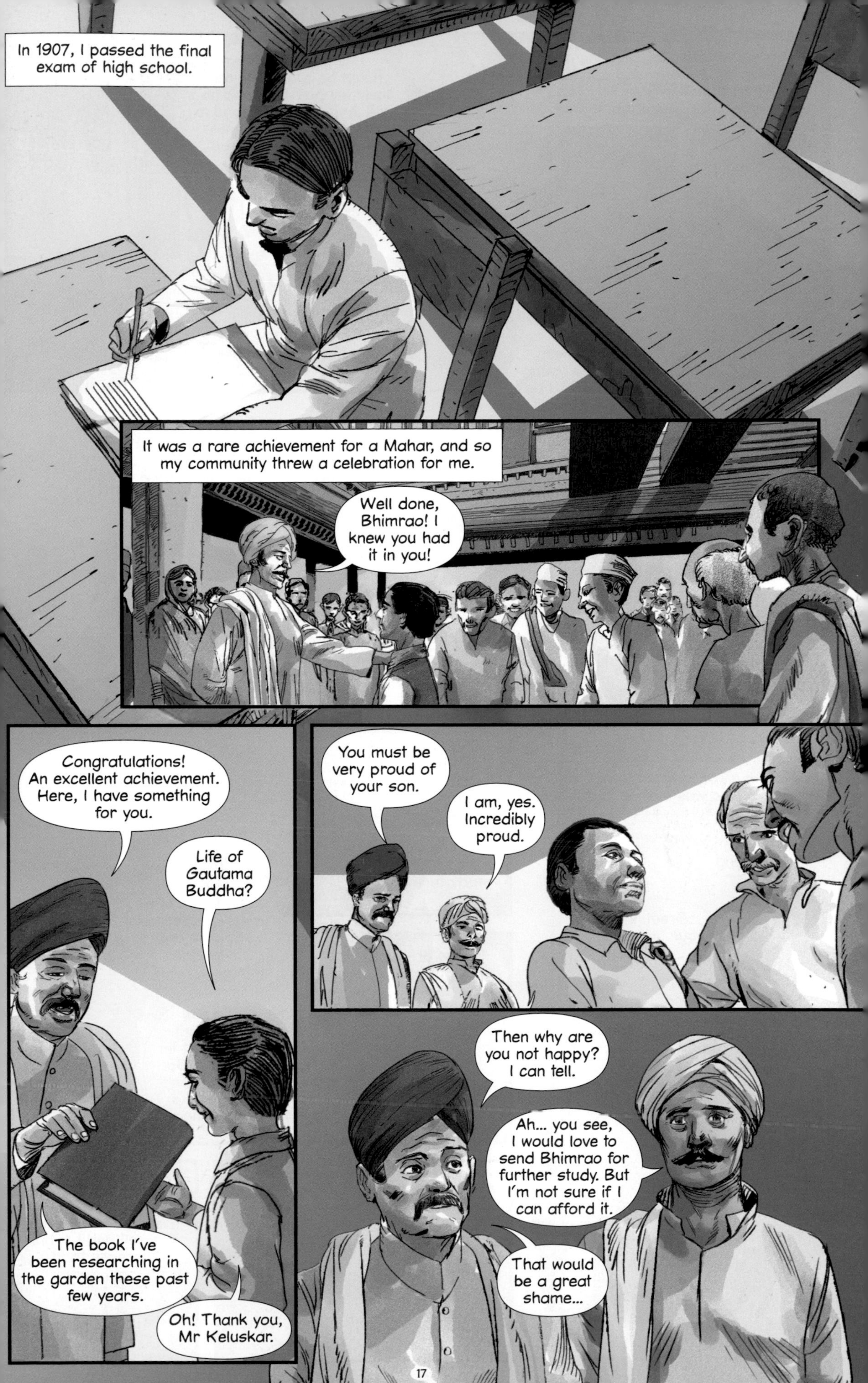
In 1907, I passed the final exam of high school.
It was a rare achievement for a Mahar, and so my community threw a celebration for me.
Well done, Bhimrao! I knew you had it in you!
Congratulations! An excellent achievement. Here, I have something for you.
Life of Gautama Buddha?
The book I've been researching in the garden these past few years.
Oh! Thank you, Mr Keluskar.
You must be very proud of your son.
I am, yes. Incredibly proud.
Then why are you not happy? I can tell.
Ah... you see, I would love to send Bhimrao for further study. But I'm not sure if I can afford it.
That would be a great shame...

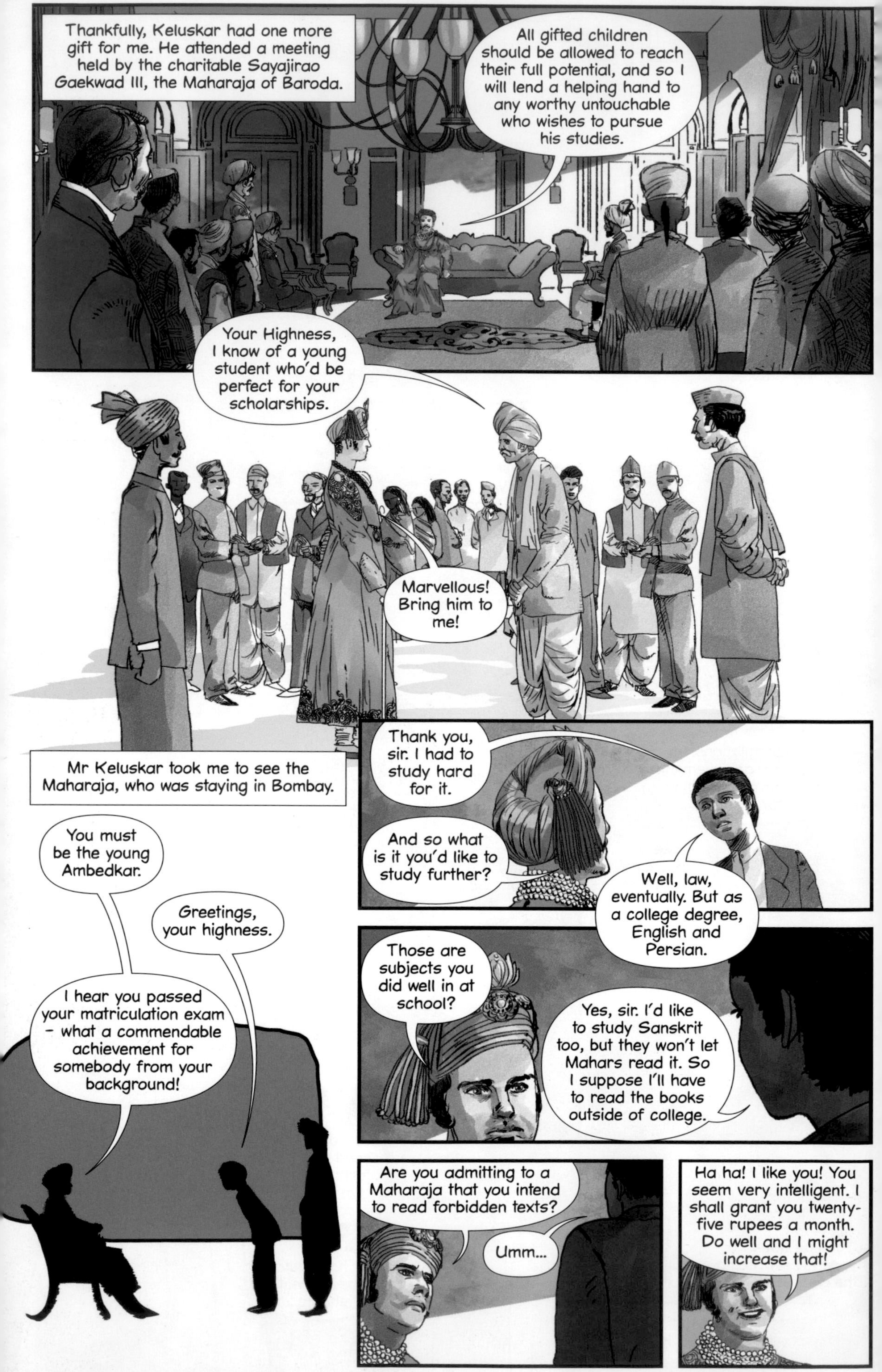
Thankfully, Keluskar had one more gift for me. He attended a meeting held by the charitable Sayajirao Gaekwad III, the Maharaja of Baroda.
All gifted children should be allowed to reach their full potential, and so I will lend a helping hand to any worthy untouchable who wishes to pursue his studies.
Your Highness, I know of a young student who'd be perfect for your scholarships.
Marvellous! Bring him to me!
Mr Keluskar took me to see the Maharaja, who was staying in Bombay.
You must be the young Ambedkar.
Greetings, your highness.
I hear you passed your matriculation exam – what a commendable achievement for somebody from your background!
Thank you, sir. I had to study hard for it.
And so what is it you'd like to study further?
Well, law, eventually. But as a college degree, English and Persian.
Those are subjects you did well in at school?
Yes, sir. I'd like to study Sanskrit too, but they won't let Mahars read it. So I suppose I'll have to read the books outside of college.
Are you admitting to a Maharaja that you intend to read forbidden texts?
Umm...
Ha ha! I like you! You seem very intelligent. I shall grant you twenty-five rupees a month. Do well and I might increase that!

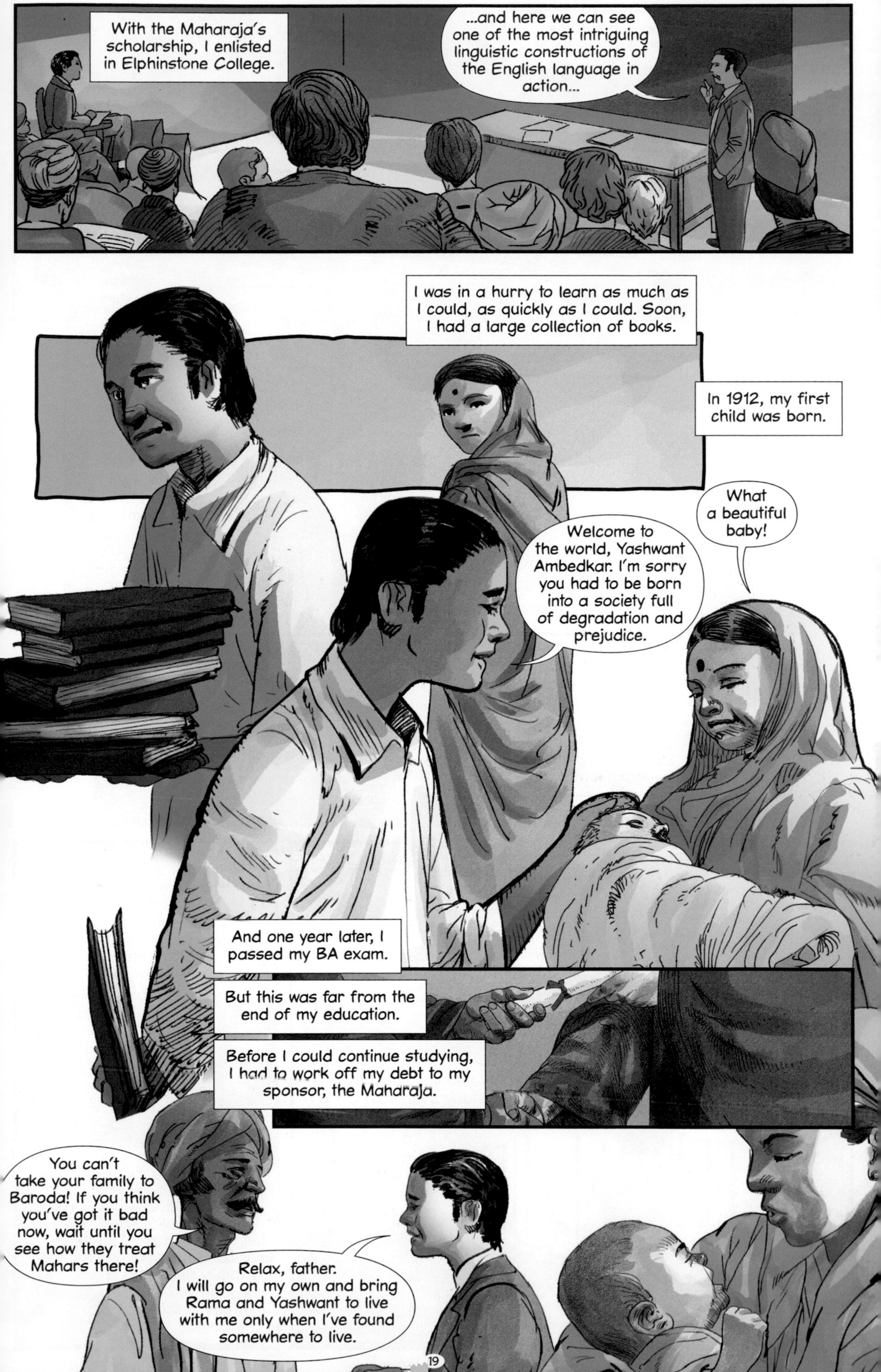
With the Maharaja's scholarship, I enlisted in Elphinstone College.
...and here we can see one of the most intriguing linguistic constructions of the English language in action...
I was in a hurry to learn as much as I could, as quickly as I could. Soon, I had a large collection of books.
In 1912, my first child was born.
What a beautiful baby!
Welcome to the world, Yashwant Ambedkar. I'm sorry you had to be born into a society full of degradation and prejudice.
And one year later, I passed my BA exam.
But this was far from the end of my education.
Before I could continue studying, I had to work off my debt to my sponsor, the Maharaja.
You can't take your family to Baroda! If you think you've got it bad now, wait until you see how they treat Mahars there!
Relax, father. I will go on my own and bring Rama and Yashwant to live with me only when I've found somewhere to live.

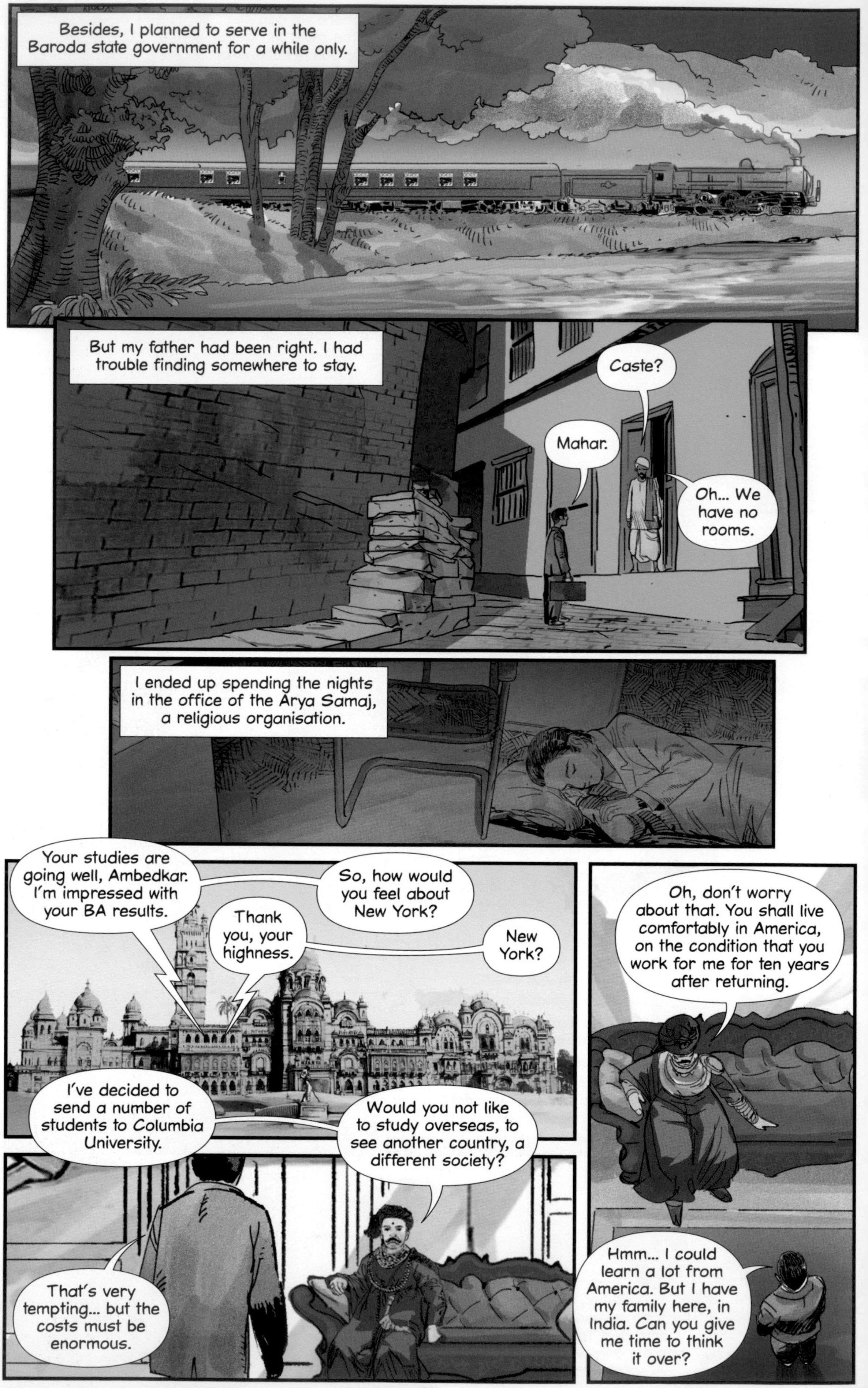
Besides, I planned to serve in the Baroda state government for a while only.
But my father had been right. I had trouble finding somewhere to stay.
Caste?
Mahar.
Oh... We have no rooms.
I ended up spending the nights in the office of the Arya Samaj, a religious organisation.
Your studies are going well, Ambedkar. I'm impressed with your BA results.
Thank you, your highness.
So, how would you feel about New York?
New York?
I've decided to send a number of students to Columbia University.
Would you not like to study overseas, to see another country, a different society?
That's very tempting... but the costs must be enormous.
Oh, don't worry about that. You shall live comfortably in America, on the condition that you work for me for ten years after returning.
Hmm... I could learn a lot from America. But I have my family here, in India. Can you give me time to think it over?

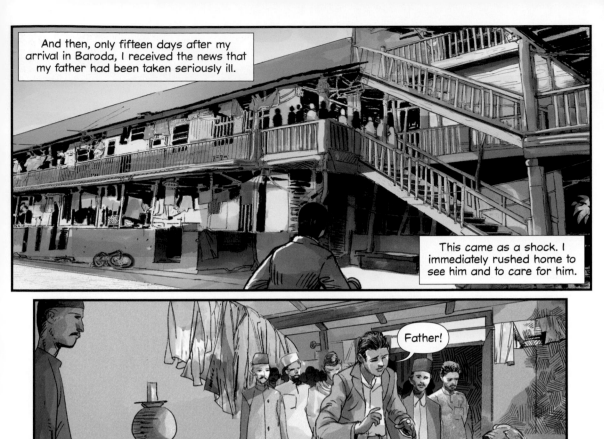

And then, only fifteen days after my arrival in Baroda, I received the news that my father had been taken seriously ill.

This came as a shock. I immediately rushed home to see him and to care for him.

Father!

Father, I came as soon as I heard. You were right about Baroda! And I must tell you about...

Bhimrao...

I felt a great emptiness at my father's passing away.

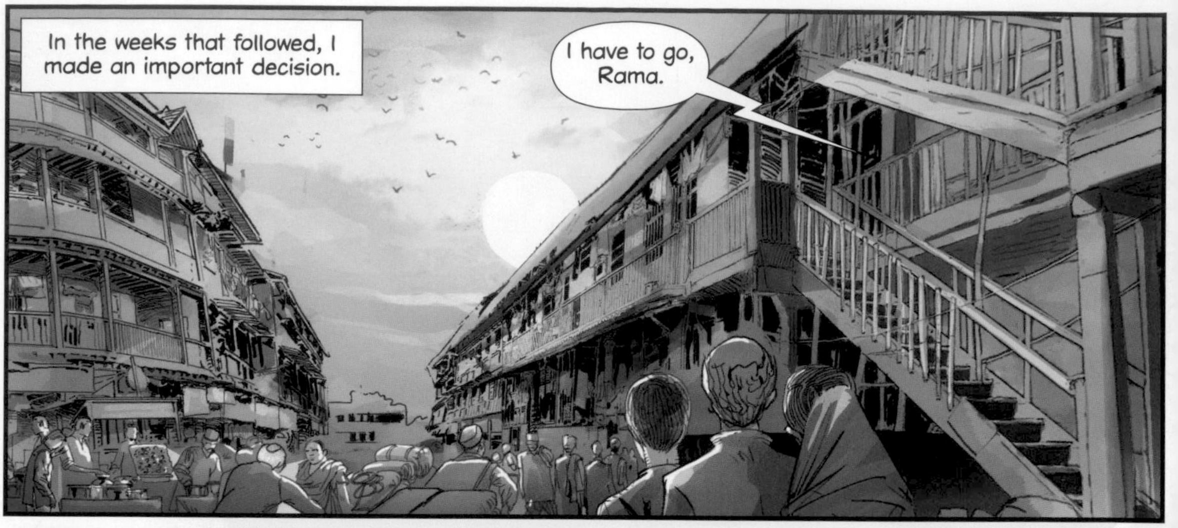
In the weeks that followed, I made an important decision.
I have to go, Rama.

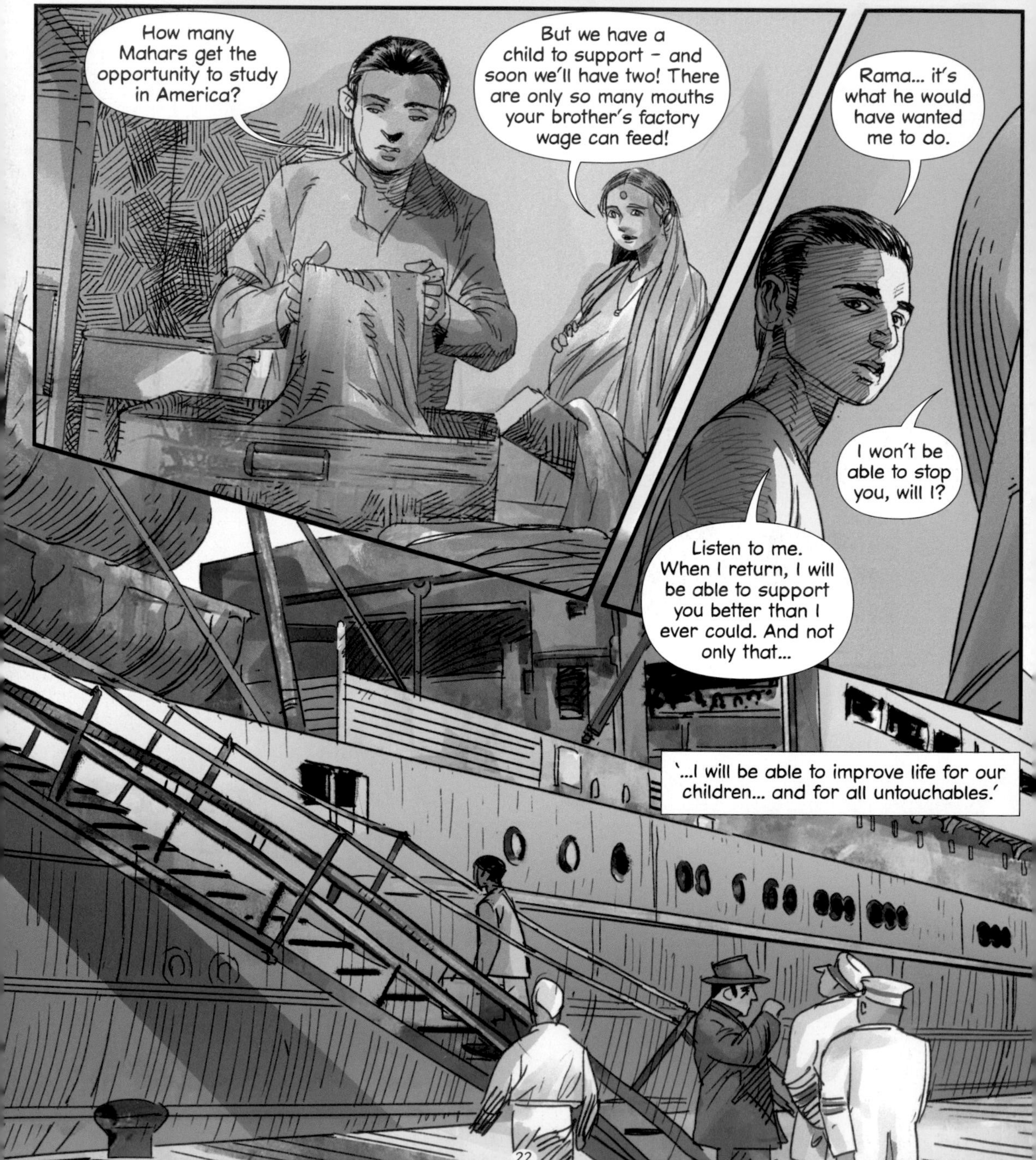
How many Mahars get the opportunity to study in America?
But we have a child to support – and soon we'll have two! There are only so many mouths your brother's factory wage can feed!
Rama... it's what he would have wanted me to do.
I won't be able to stop you, will I?
Listen to me. When I return, I will be able to support you better than I ever could. And not only that...
'...I will be able to improve life for our children... and for all untouchables.'

2 THE STUDENT YEARS

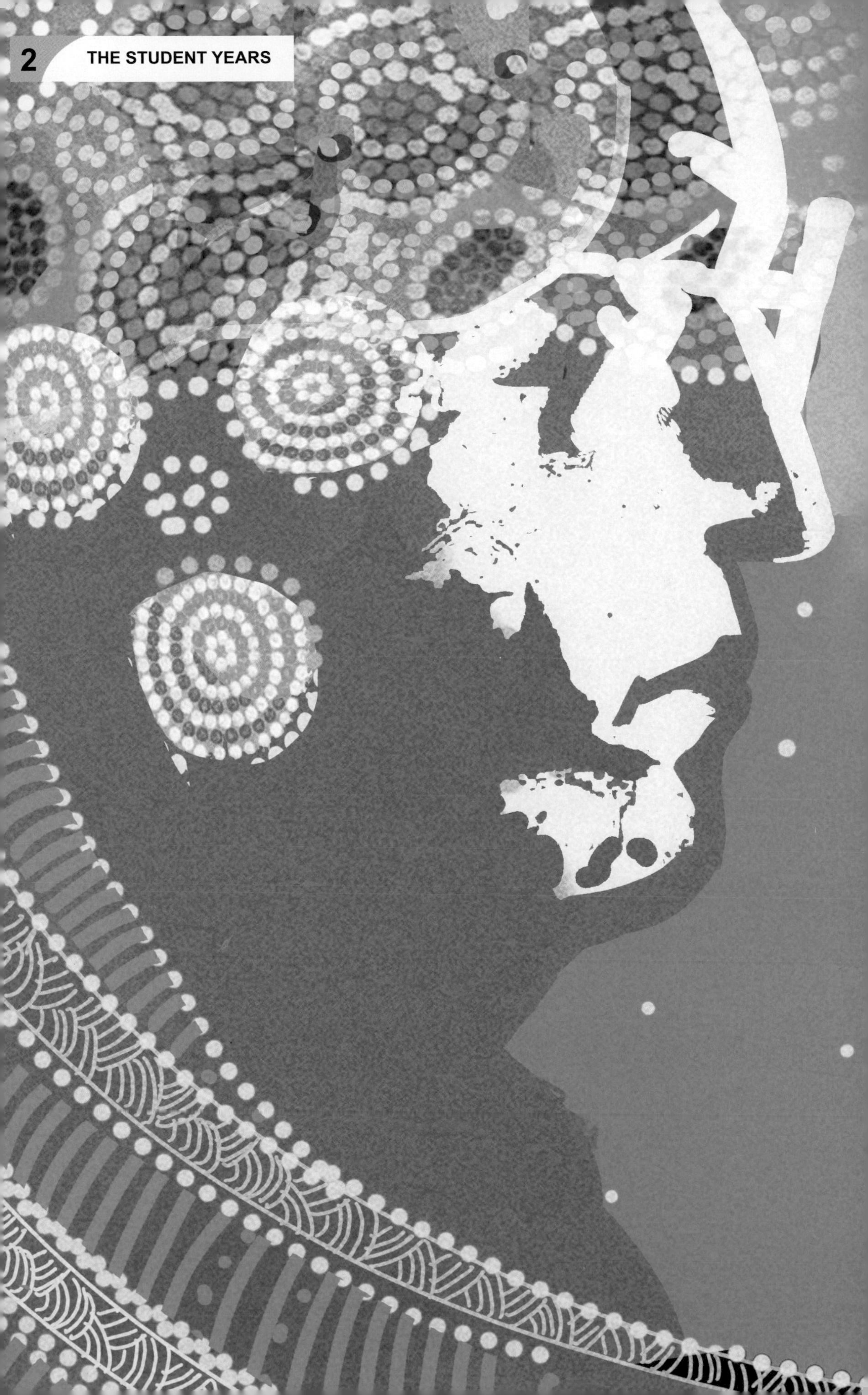

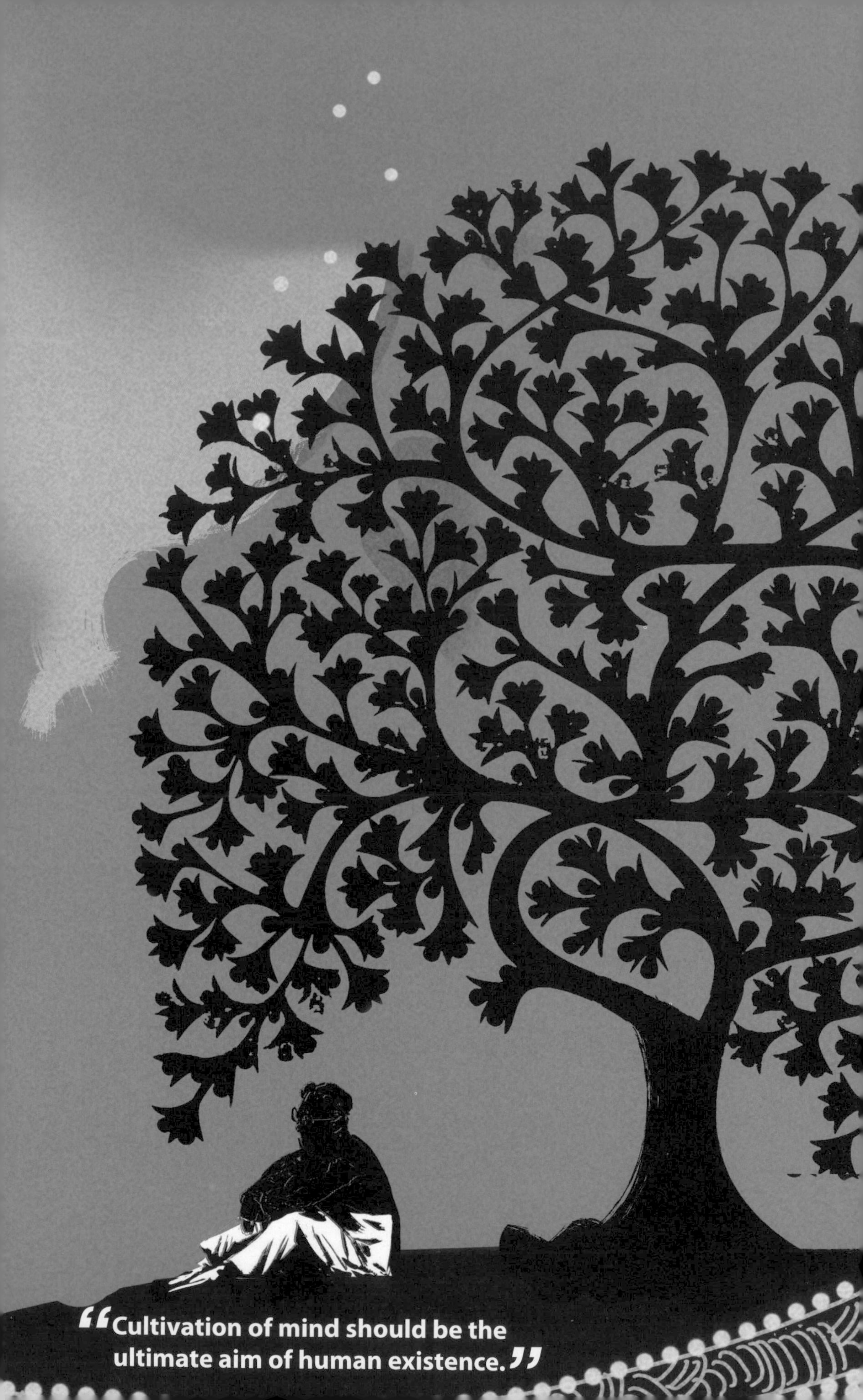

"Cultivation of mind should be the ultimate aim of human existence."

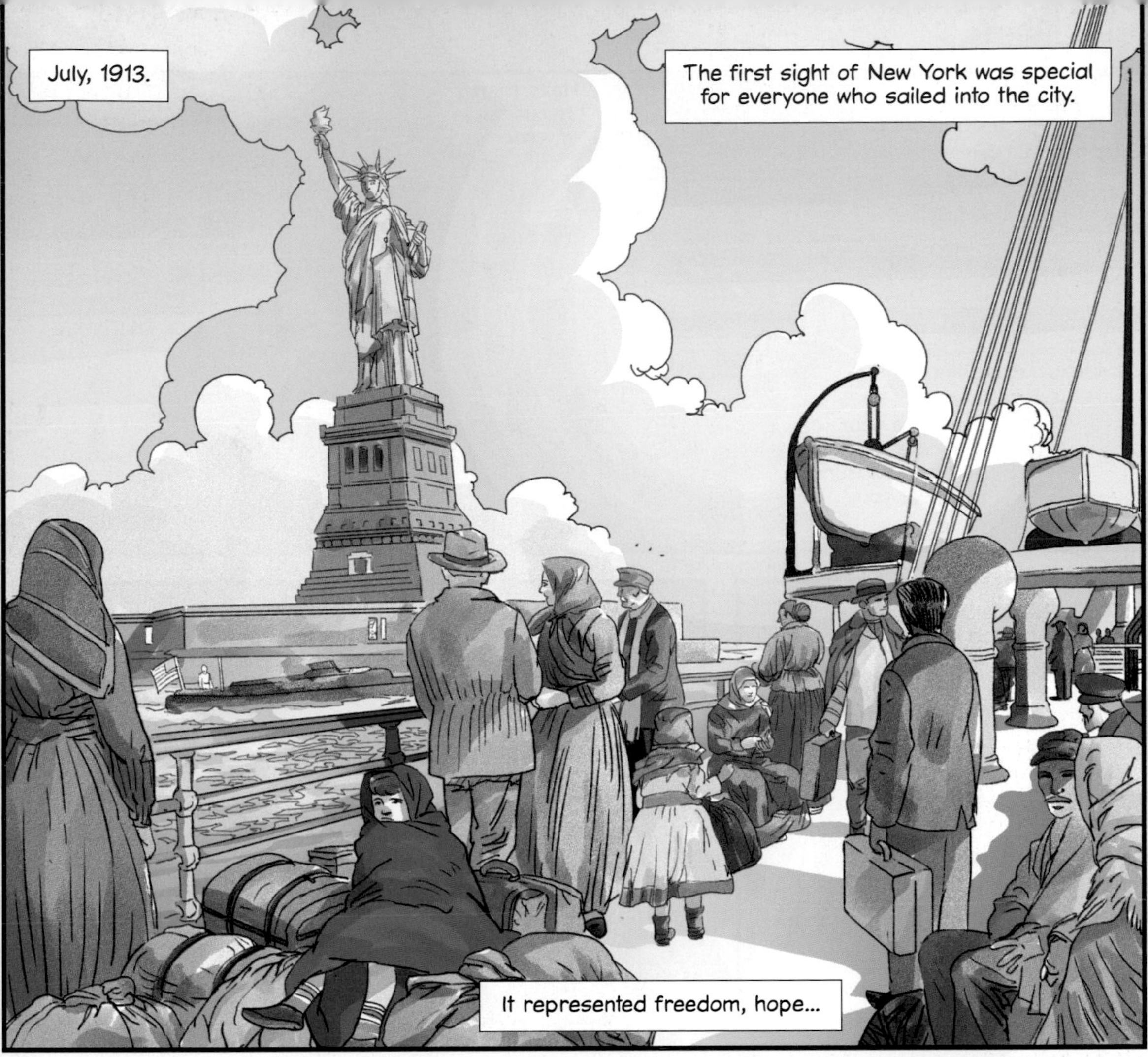
July, 1913.
The first sight of New York was special for everyone who sailed into the city.
It represented freedom, hope...

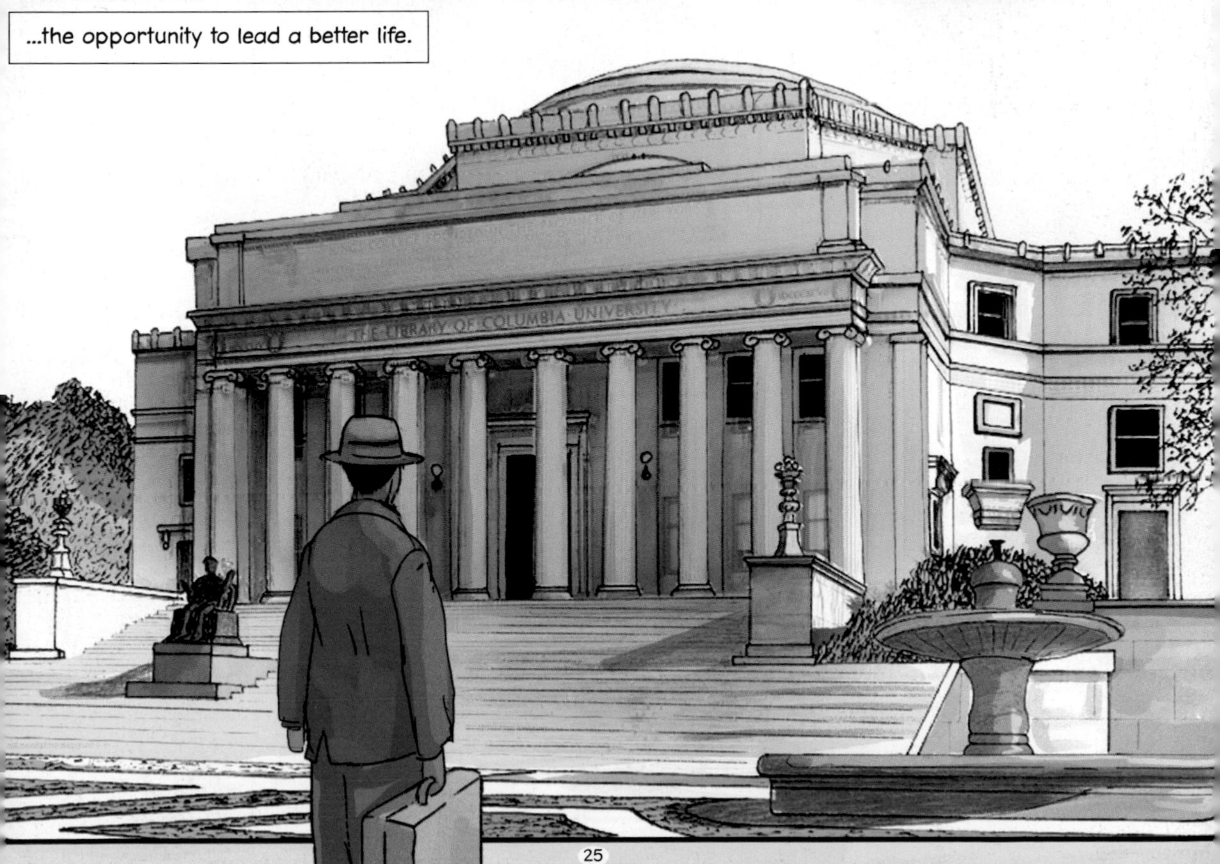
...the opportunity to lead a better life.
THE LIBRARY OF COLUMBIA UNIVERSITY

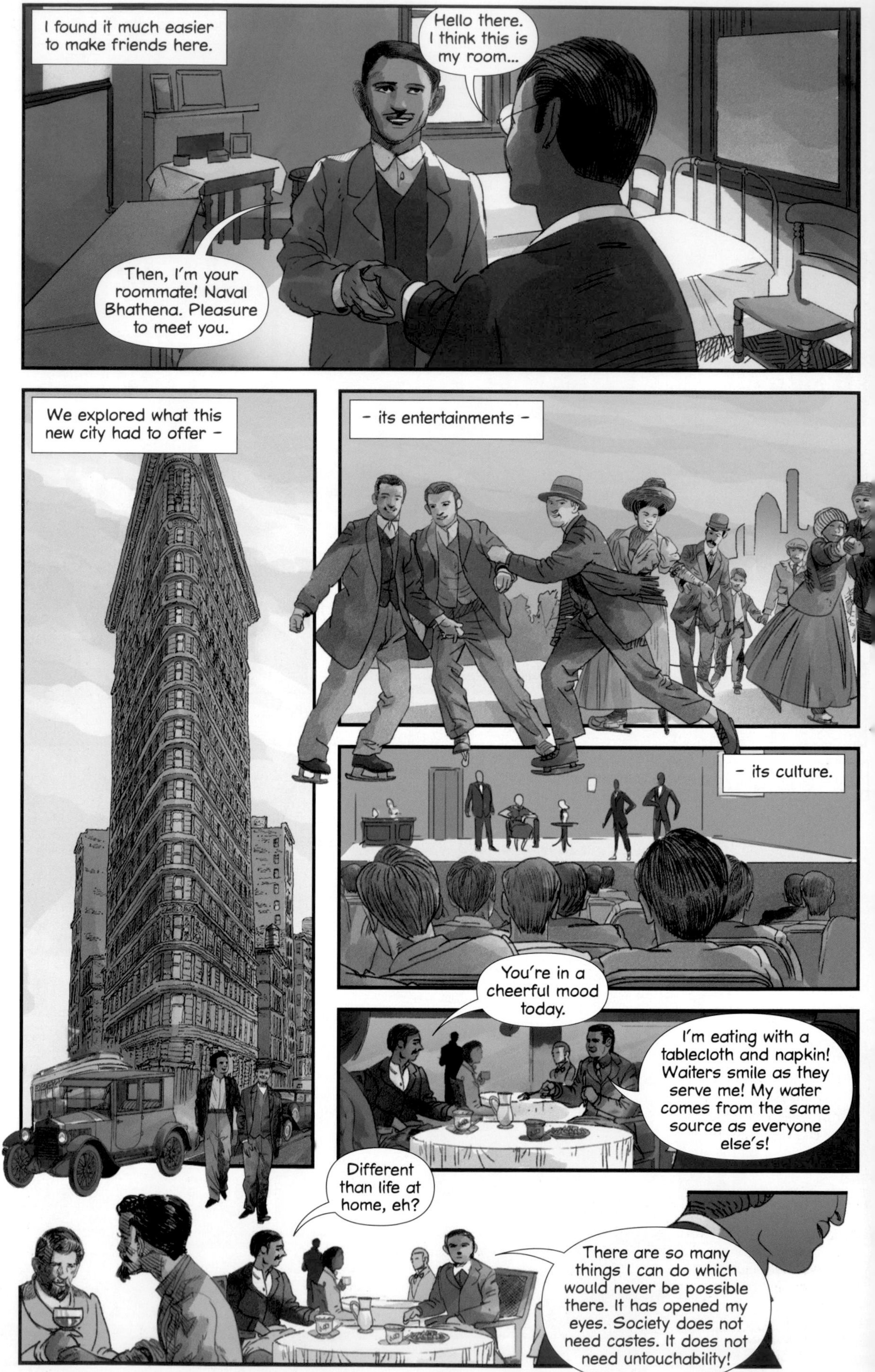
I found it much easier to make friends here.
Hello there. I think this is my room...
Then, I'm your roommate! Naval Bhathena. Pleasure to meet you.
We explored what this new city had to offer –
– its entertainments –
– its culture.
You're in a cheerful mood today.
I'm eating with a tablecloth and napkin! Waiters smile as they serve me! My water comes from the same source as everyone else's!
Different than life at home, eh?
There are so many things I can do which would never be possible there. It has opened my eyes. Society does not need castes. It does not need untouchability!

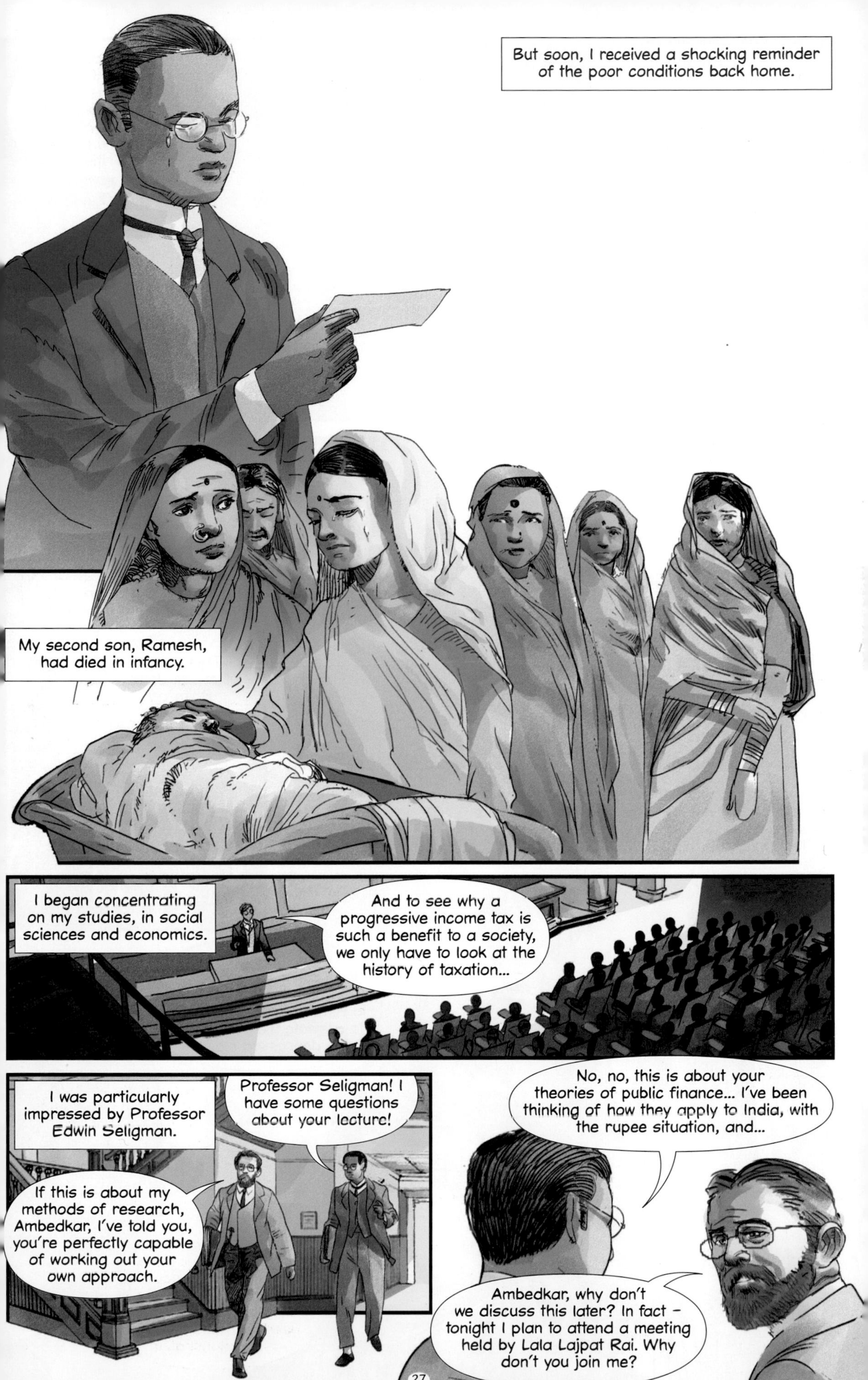

But soon, I received a shocking reminder of the poor conditions back home.
My second son, Ramesh, had died in infancy.
I began concentrating on my studies, in social sciences and economics.
And to see why a progressive income tax is such a benefit to a society, we only have to look at the history of taxation...
I was particularly impressed by Professor Edwin Seligman.
Professor Seligman! I have some questions about your lecture!
If this is about my methods of research, Ambedkar, I've told you, you're perfectly capable of working out your own approach.
No, no, this is about your theories of public finance... I've been thinking of how they apply to India, with the rupee situation, and...
Ambedkar, why don't we discuss this later? In fact – tonight I plan to attend a meeting held by Lala Lajpat Rai. Why don't you join me?

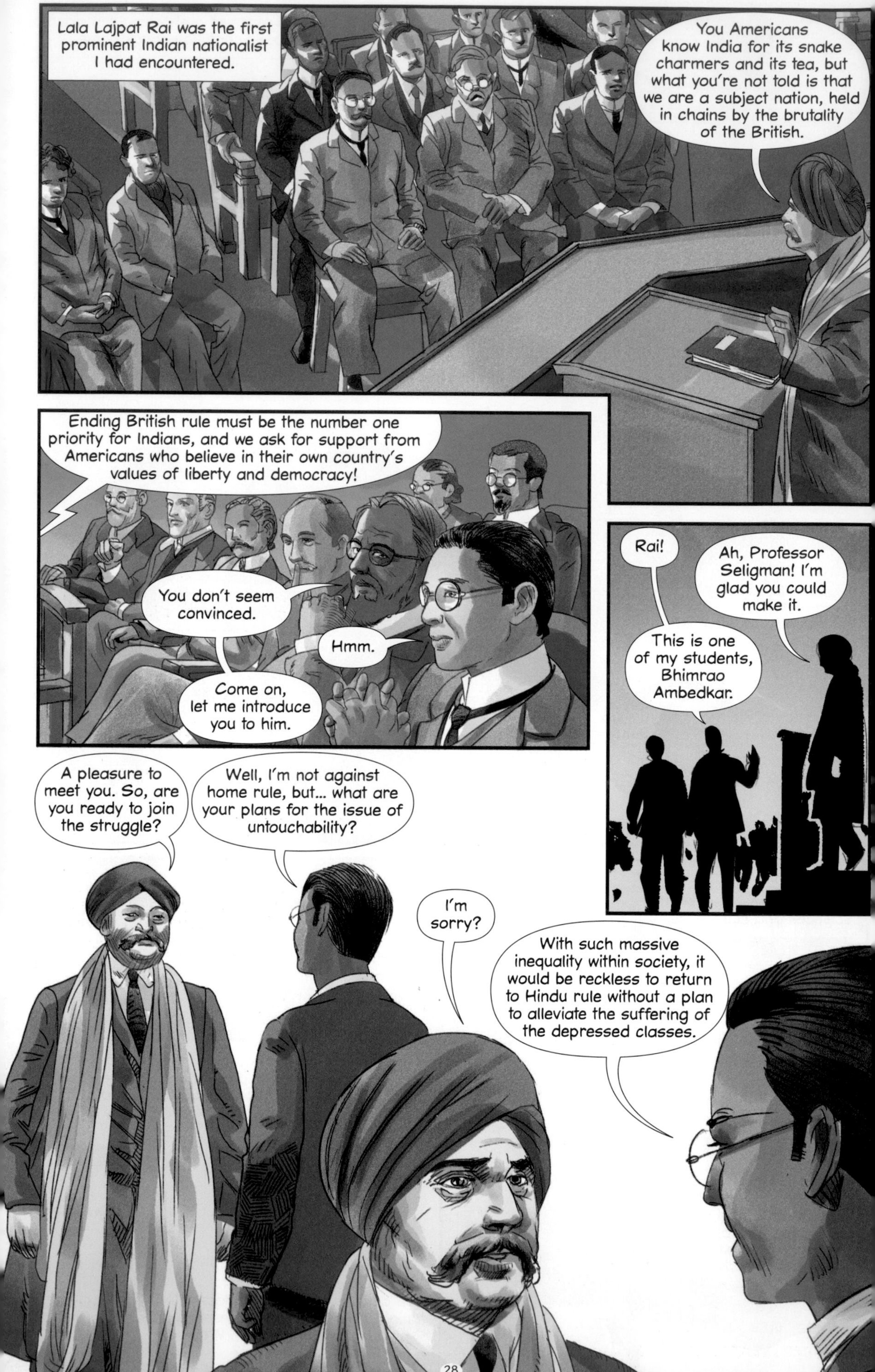

Lala Lajpat Rai was the first prominent Indian nationalist I had encountered.
You Americans know India for its snake charmers and its tea, but what you're not told is that we are a subject nation, held in chains by the brutality of the British.
Ending British rule must be the number one priority for Indians, and we ask for support from Americans who believe in their own country's values of liberty and democracy!
You don't seem convinced.
Hmm.
Come on, let me introduce you to him.
Rai!
Ah, Professor Seligman! I'm glad you could make it.
This is one of my students, Bhimrao Ambedkar.
A pleasure to meet you. So, are you ready to join the struggle?
Well, I'm not against home rule, but... what are your plans for the issue of untouchability?
I'm sorry?
With such massive inequality within society, it would be reckless to return to Hindu rule without a plan to alleviate the suffering of the depressed classes.

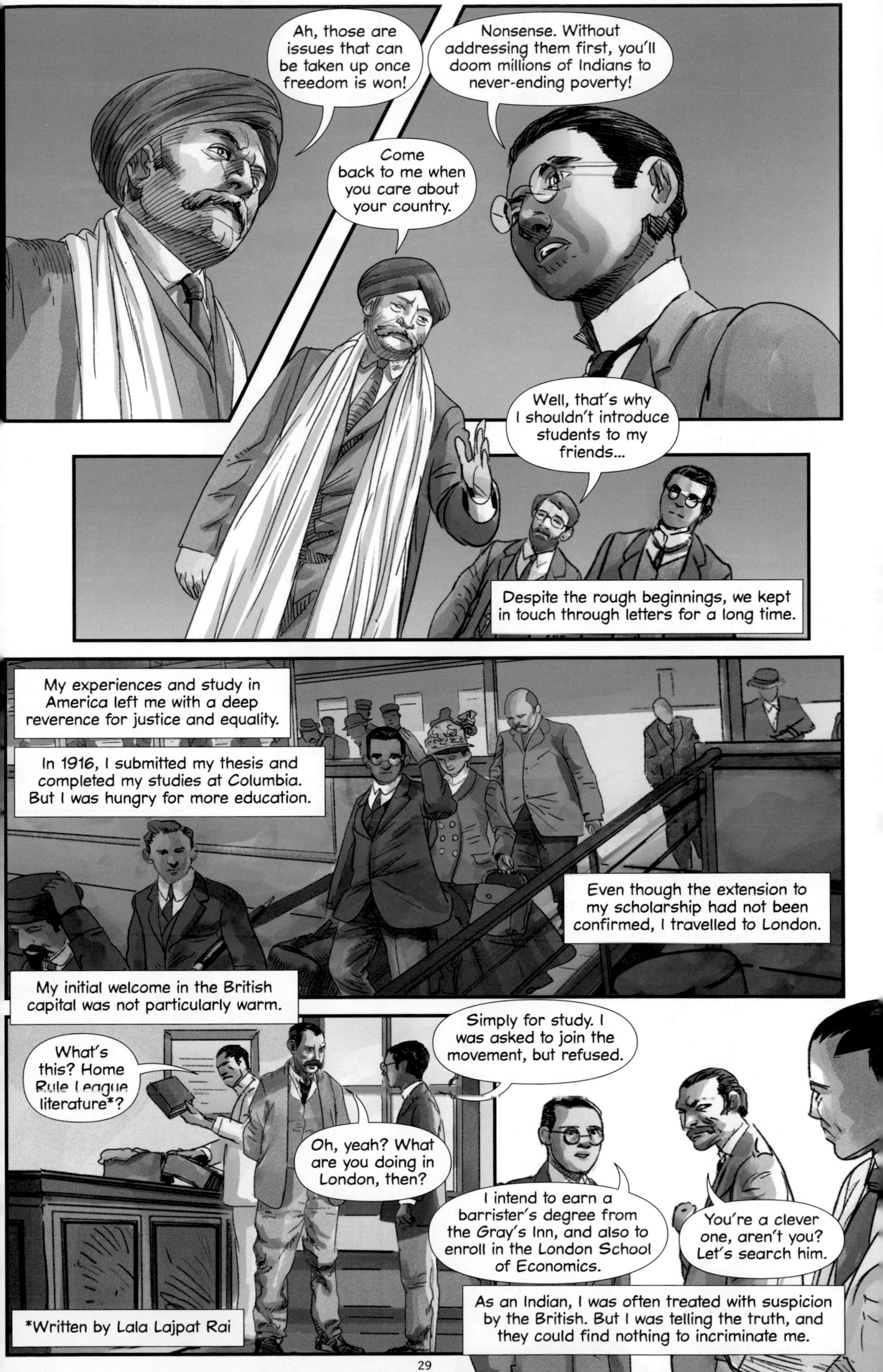
Ah, those are issues that can be taken up once freedom is won!
Nonsense. Without addressing them first, you'll doom millions of Indians to never-ending poverty!
Come back to me when you care about your country.
Well, that's why I shouldn't introduce students to my friends...
Despite the rough beginnings, we kept in touch through letters for a long time.
My experiences and study in America left me with a deep reverence for justice and equality.
In 1916, I submitted my thesis and completed my studies at Columbia. But I was hungry for more education.
Even though the extension to my scholarship had not been confirmed, I travelled to London.
My initial welcome in the British capital was not particularly warm.
What's this? Home Rule League literature*?
Oh, yeah? What are you doing in London, then?
Simply for study. I was asked to join the movement, but refused.
I intend to earn a barrister's degree from the Gray's Inn, and also to enroll in the London School of Economics.
You're a clever one, aren't you? Let's search him.
As an Indian, I was often treated with suspicion by the British. But I was telling the truth, and they could find nothing to incriminate me.
*Written by Lala Lajpat Rai

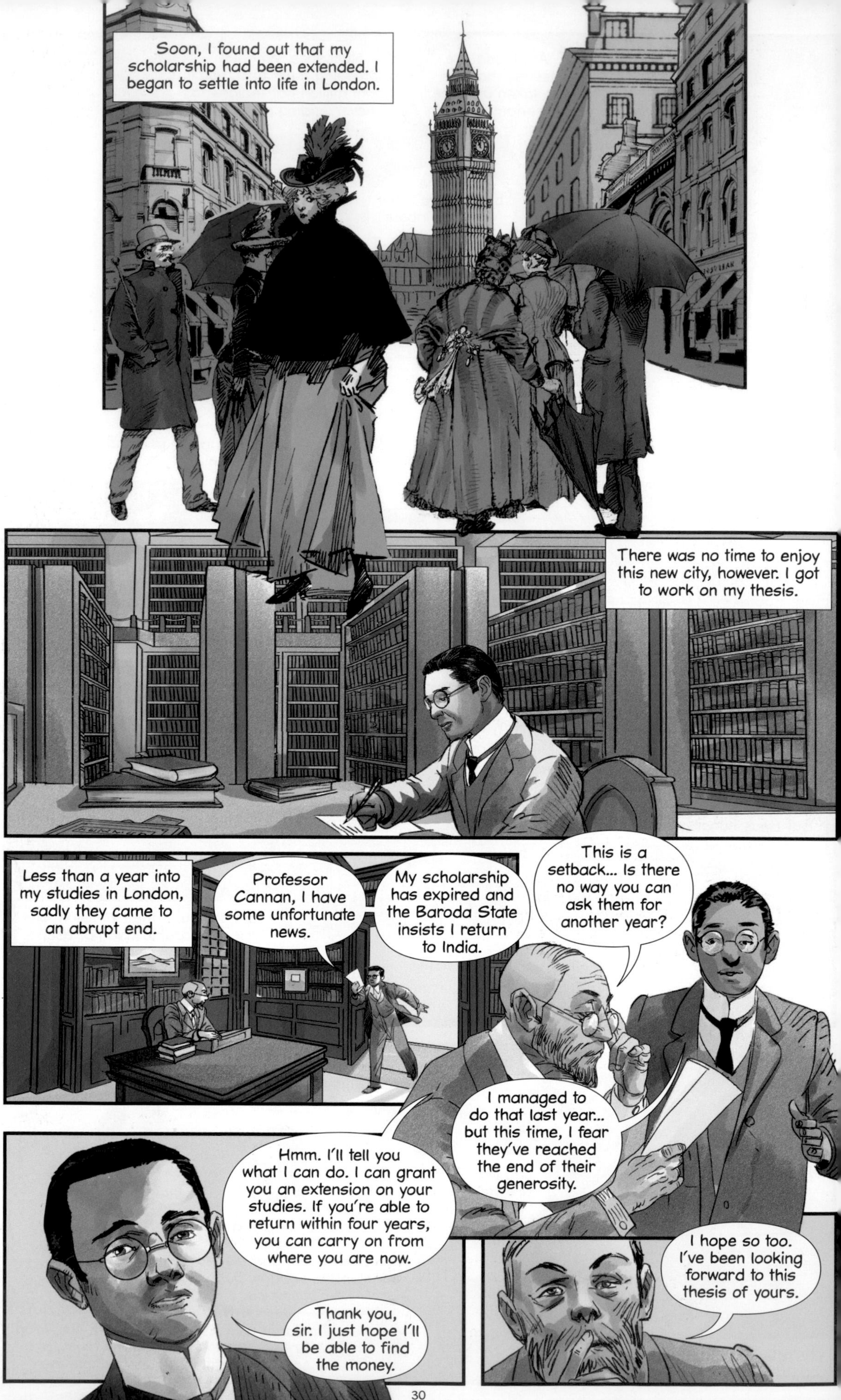
Soon, I found out that my scholarship had been extended. I began to settle into life in London.
There was no time to enjoy this new city, however. I got to work on my thesis.
Less than a year into my studies in London, sadly they came to an abrupt end.
Professor Cannan, I have some unfortunate news.
My scholarship has expired and the Baroda State insists I return to India.
This is a setback... Is there no way you can ask them for another year?
I managed to do that last year... but this time, I fear they've reached the end of their generosity.
Hmm. I'll tell you what I can do. I can grant you an extension on your studies. If you're able to return within four years, you can carry on from where you are now.
Thank you, sir. I just hope I'll be able to find the money.
I hope so too. I've been looking forward to this thesis of yours.

And so, in August 1917, four years after I had left, I returned to India.

I praise the Lord on your safe return, Bhimrao!

Baba!

I hadn't seen my boy since he was an infant. He was eager to hear his father's travel stories.

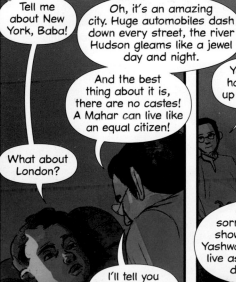

Tell me about New York, Baba!

Oh, it's an amazing city. Huge automobiles dash down every street, the river Hudson gleams like a jewel day and night.

And the best thing about it is, there are no castes! A Mahar can live like an equal citizen!

What about London?

I'll tell you more tomorrow. It's time for you to sleep.

Yashwant has grown up so much.

Rama, you're crying. What's wrong?

He should have a brother... I did everything I could to save Ramesh. But it was so difficult.

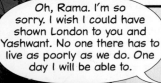

Oh, Rama. I'm so sorry. I wish I could have shown London to you and Yashwant. No one there has to live as poorly as we do. One day I will be able to.

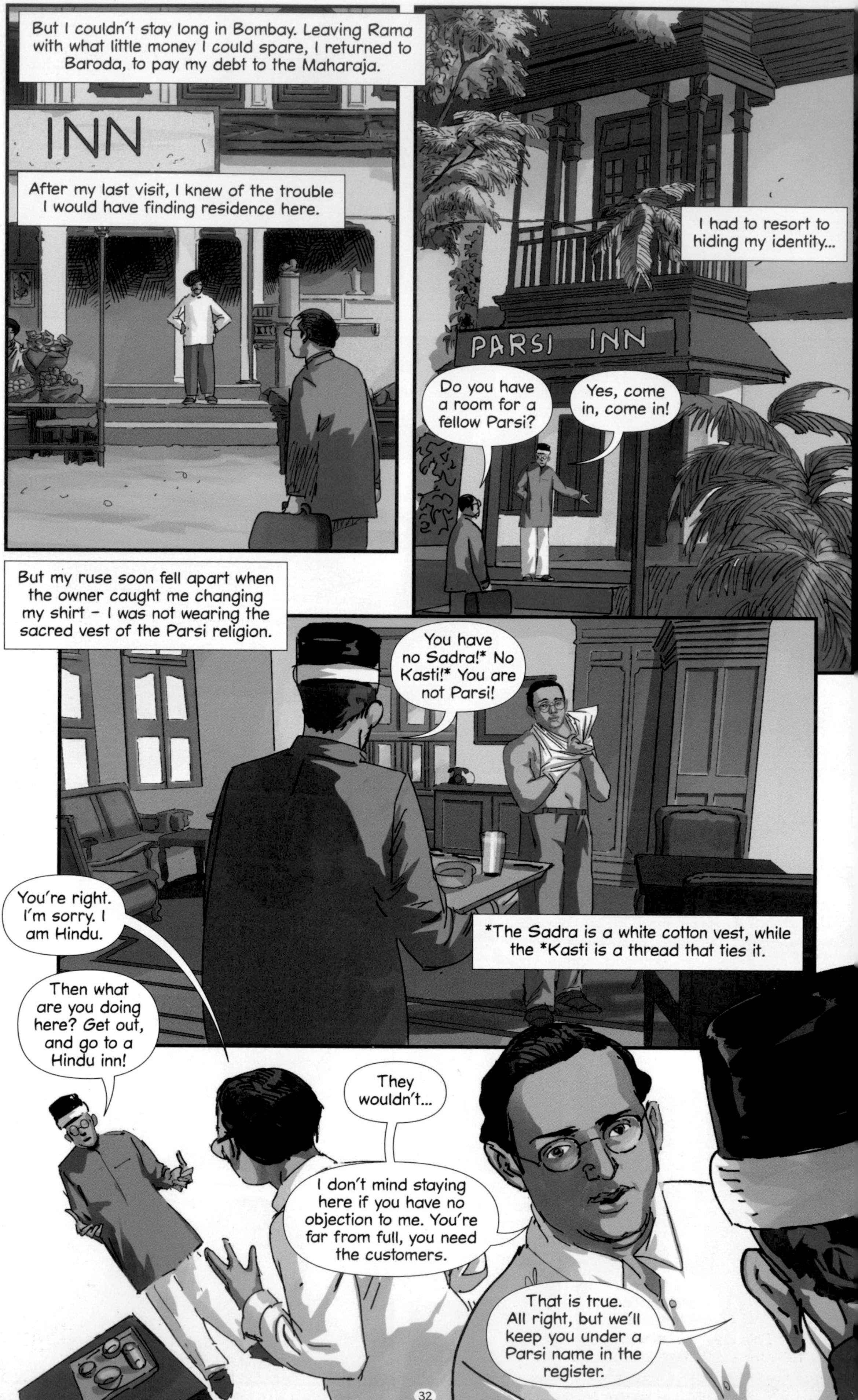

But I couldn't stay long in Bombay. Leaving Rama with what little money I could spare, I returned to Baroda, to pay my debt to the Maharaja.
INN
After my last visit, I knew of the trouble I would have finding residence here.
I had to resort to hiding my identity...
PARSI INN
Do you have a room for a fellow Parsi?
Yes, come in, come in!
But my ruse soon fell apart when the owner caught me changing my shirt – I was not wearing the sacred vest of the Parsi religion.
You have no Sadra!* No Kasti!* You are not Parsi!
You're right. I'm sorry. I am Hindu.
*The Sadra is a white cotton vest, while the *Kasti is a thread that ties it.
Then what are you doing here? Get out, and go to a Hindu inn!
They wouldn't...
I don't mind staying here if you have no objection to me. You're far from full, you need the customers.
That is true. All right, but we'll keep you under a Parsi name in the register.

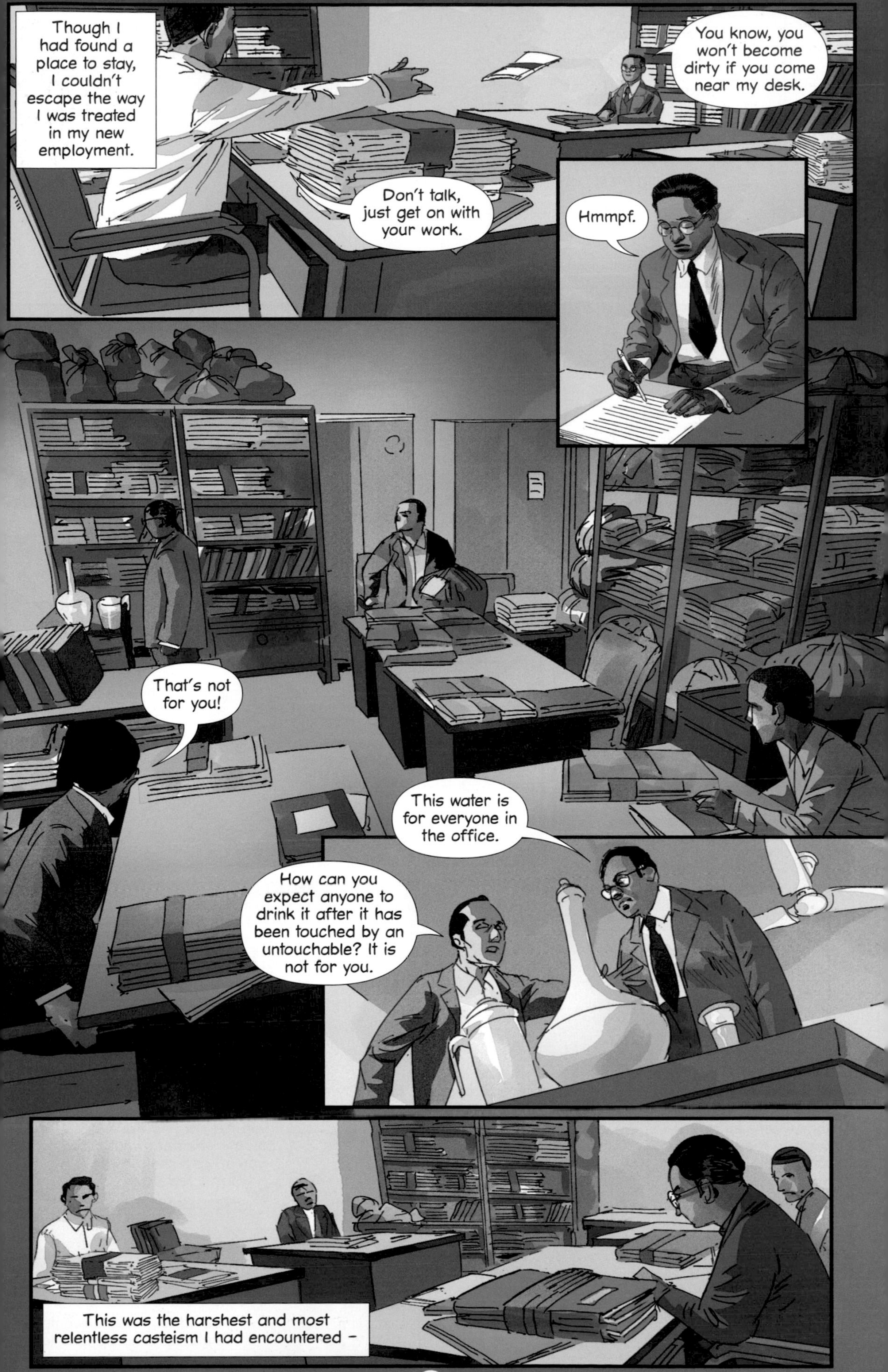
Though I had found a place to stay, I couldn't escape the way I was treated in my new employment.
You know, you won't become dirty if you come near my desk.
Don't talk, just get on with your work.
Hmmpf.
That's not for you!
This water is for everyone in the office.
How can you expect anyone to drink it after it has been touched by an untouchable? It is not for you.
This was the harshest and most relentless casteism I had encountered –

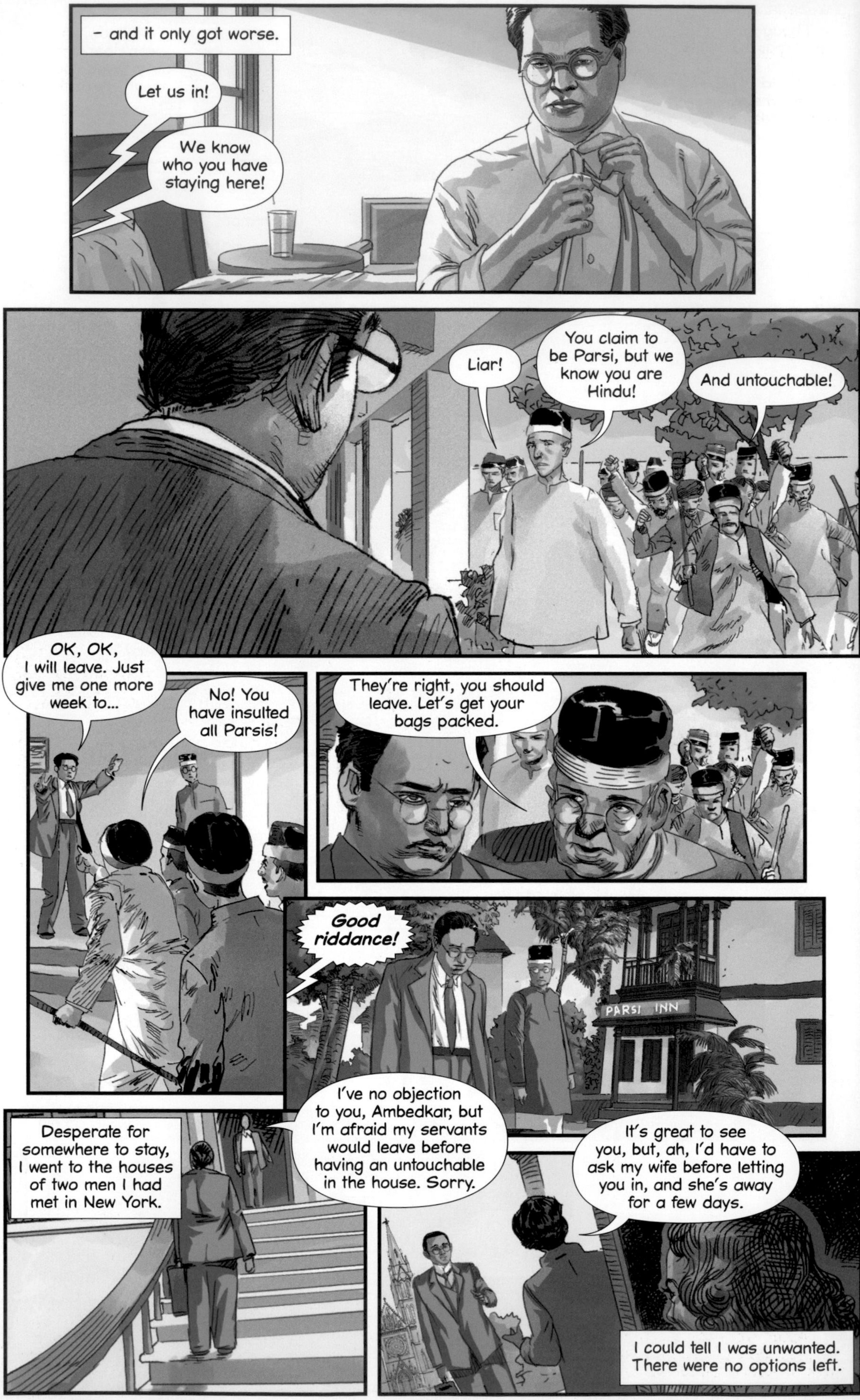
– and it only got worse.
Let us in!
We know who you have staying here!
Liar!
You claim to be Parsi, but we know you are Hindu!
And untouchable!
OK, OK, I will leave. Just give me one more week to...
No! You have insulted all Parsis!
They're right, you should leave. Let's get your bags packed.
Good riddance!
PARSI INN
Desperate for somewhere to stay, I went to the houses of two men I had met in New York.
I've no objection to you, Ambedkar, but I'm afraid my servants would leave before having an untouchable in the house. Sorry.
It's great to see you, but, ah, I'd have to ask my wife before letting you in, and she's away for a few days.
I could tell I was unwanted. There were no options left.

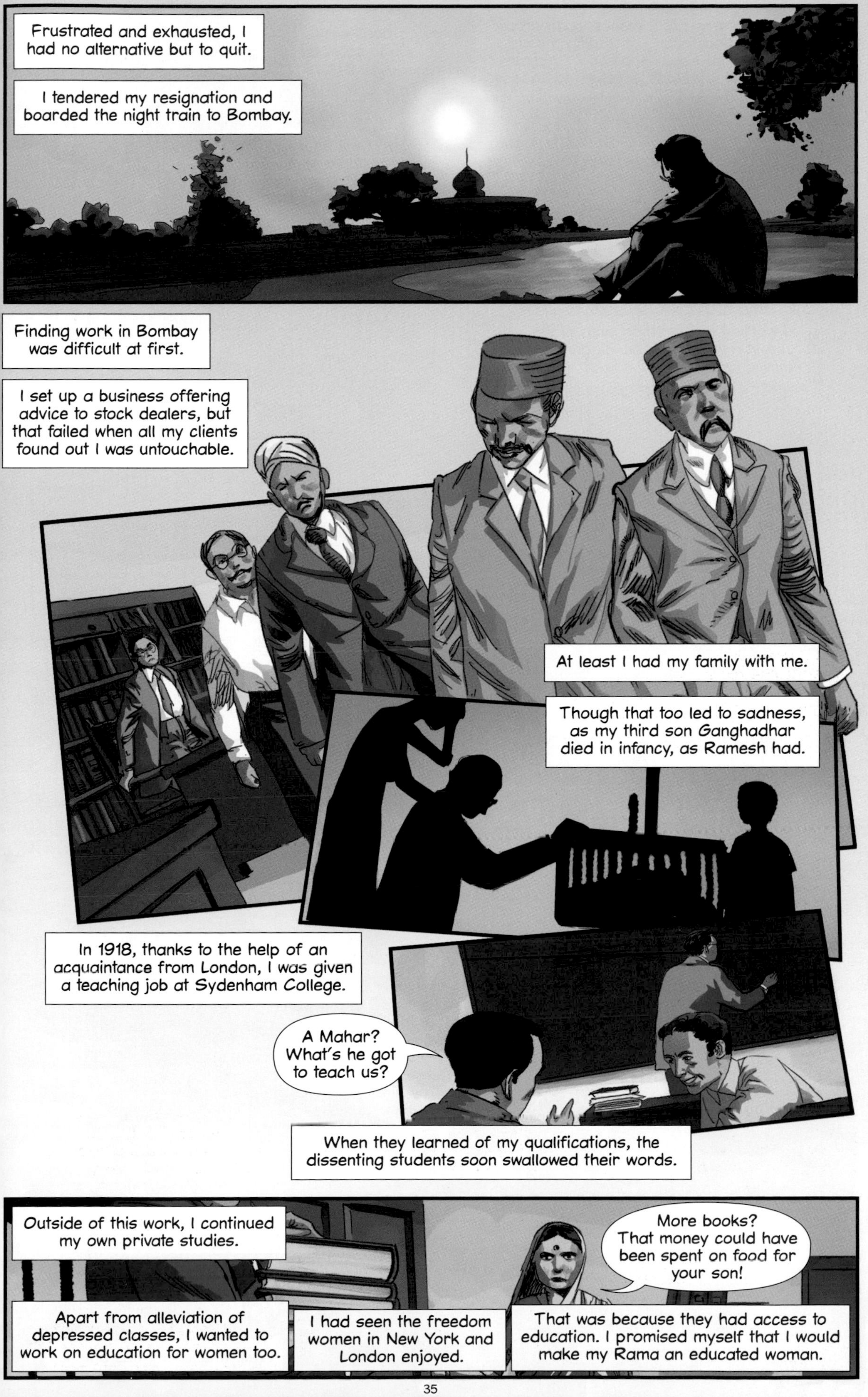
Frustrated and exhausted, I had no alternative but to quit.
I tendered my resignation and boarded the night train to Bombay.
Finding work in Bombay was difficult at first.
I set up a business offering advice to stock dealers, but that failed when all my clients found out I was untouchable.
At least I had my family with me.
Though that too led to sadness, as my third son Ganghadhar died in infancy, as Ramesh had.
In 1918, thanks to the help of an acquaintance from London, I was given a teaching job at Sydenham College.
A Mahar? What's he got to teach us?
When they learned of my qualifications, the dissenting students soon swallowed their words.
Outside of this work, I continued my own private studies.
More books? That money could have been spent on food for your son!
Apart from alleviation of depressed classes, I wanted to work on education for women too.
I had seen the freedom women in New York and London enjoyed.
That was because they had access to education. I promised myself that I would make my Rama an educated woman.

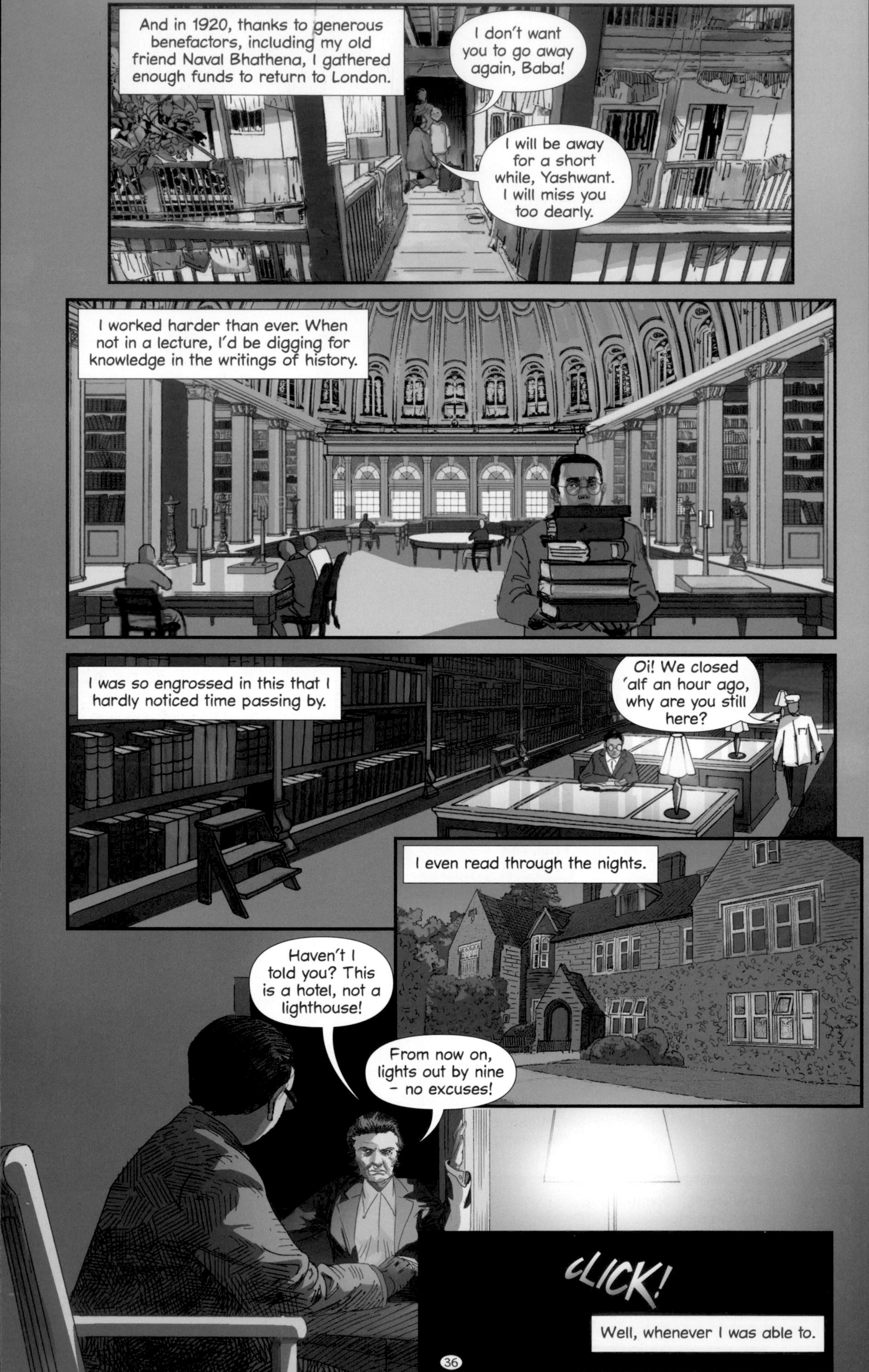
And in 1920, thanks to generous benefactors, including my old friend Naval Bhathena, I gathered enough funds to return to London.
I don't want you to go away again, Baba!
I will be away for a short while, Yashwant. I will miss you too dearly.
I worked harder than ever. When not in a lecture, I'd be digging for knowledge in the writings of history.
I was so engrossed in this that I hardly noticed time passing by.
Oi! We closed 'alf an hour ago, why are you still here?
I even read through the nights.
Haven't I told you? This is a hotel, not a lighthouse!
From now on, lights out by nine - no excuses!
CLICK!
Well, whenever I was able to.

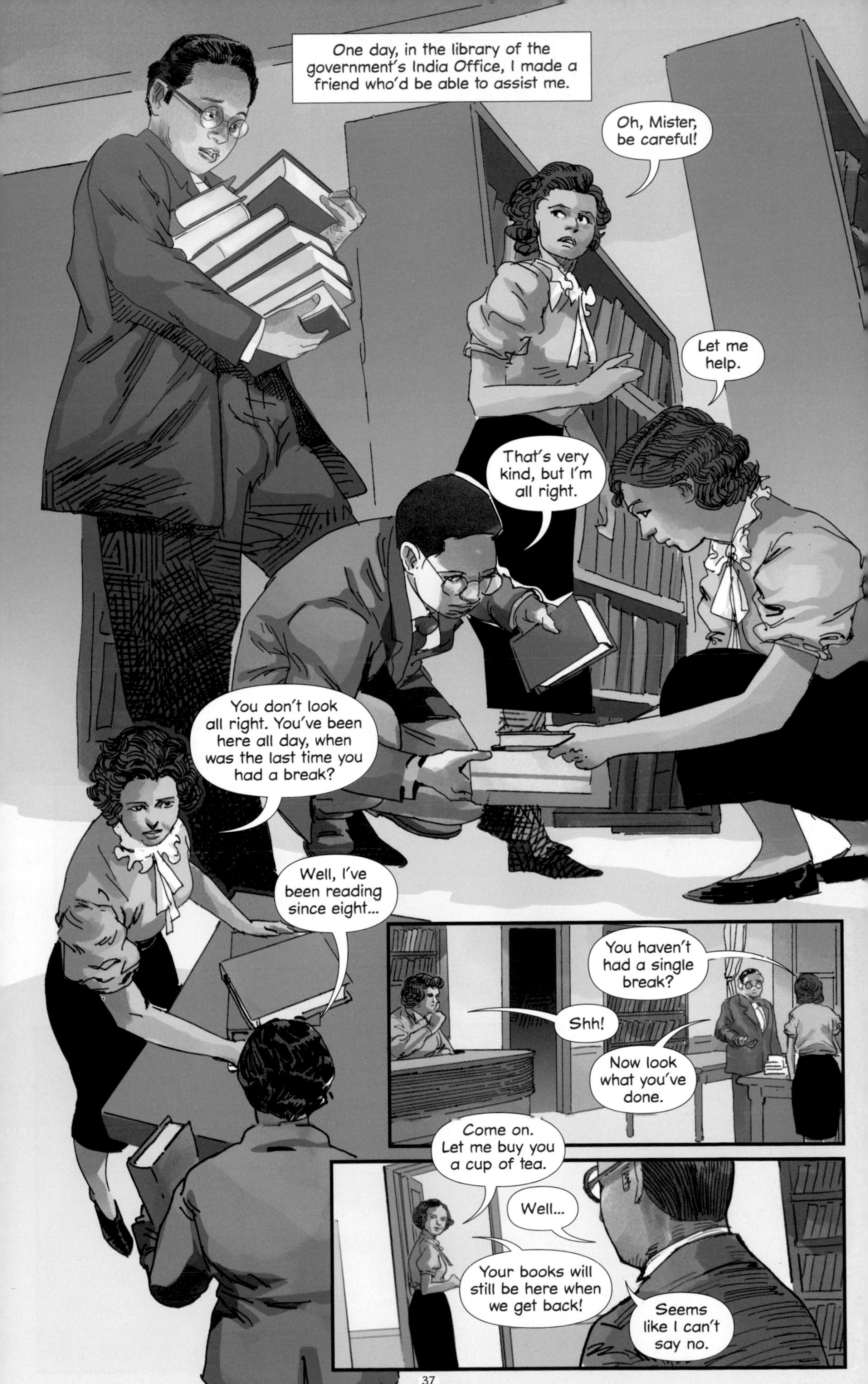
One day, in the library of the government's India Office, I made a friend who'd be able to assist me.
Oh, Mister, be careful!
Let me help.
That's very kind, but I'm all right.
You don't look all right. You've been here all day, when was the last time you had a break?
Well, I've been reading since eight...
You haven't had a single break?
Shh!
Now look what you've done.
Come on. Let me buy you a cup of tea.
Well...
Your books will still be here when we get back!
Seems like I can't say no.

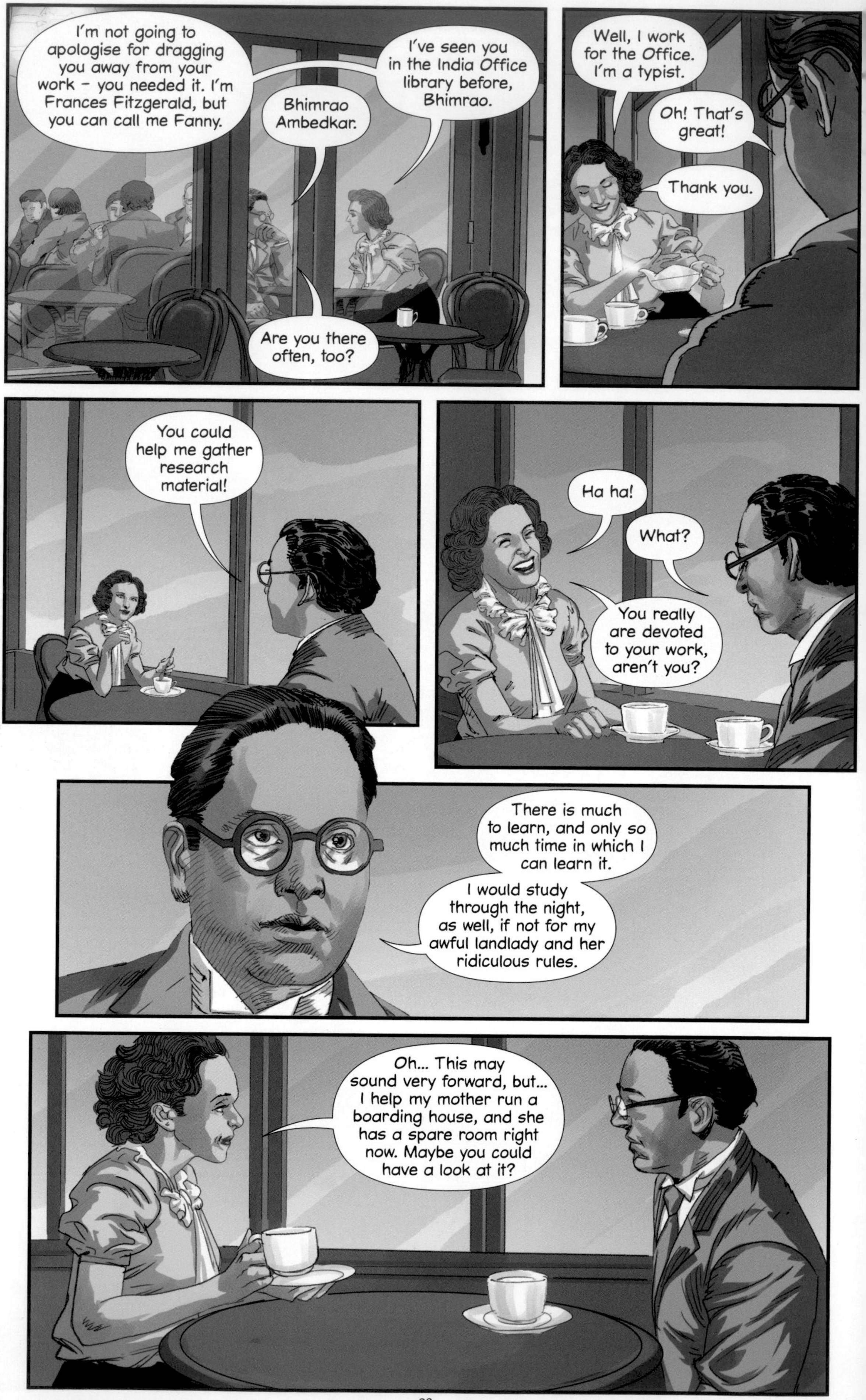
I'm not going to apologise for dragging you away from your work – you needed it. I'm Frances Fitzgerald, but you can call me Fanny.
I've seen you in the India Office library before, Bhimrao.
Bhimrao Ambedkar.
Are you there often, too?
Well, I work for the Office. I'm a typist.
Oh! That's great!
Thank you.
You could help me gather research material!
Ha ha!
What?
You really are devoted to your work, aren't you?
There is much to learn, and only so much time in which I can learn it.
I would study through the night, as well, if not for my awful landlady and her ridiculous rules.
Oh... This may sound very forward, but... I help my mother run a boarding house, and she has a spare room right now. Maybe you could have a look at it?

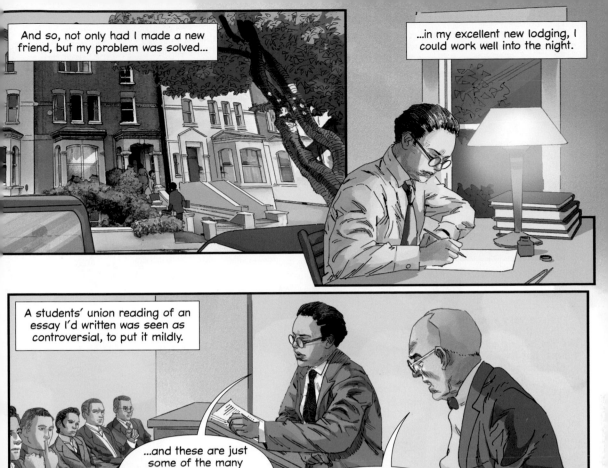

And so, not only had I made a new friend, but my problem was solved...

...in my excellent new lodging, I could work well into the night.

A students' union reading of an essay I'd written was seen as controversial, to put it mildly.

...and these are just some of the many changes a representative government would have to make in order to fulfil their responsibilities to the Indian people.

How dare you spout such revolutionary nonsense? This is London, not Moscow!

But despite my critics, I was successful in my academic life, and soon completed my law degree at Gray's Inn.

I do hereby call you to the bar and do proclaim you barrister.

It was very formal! I was now a qualified lawyer. That just left the economics doctorate...

My freedom to read, however, led to my spending on books going out of control.

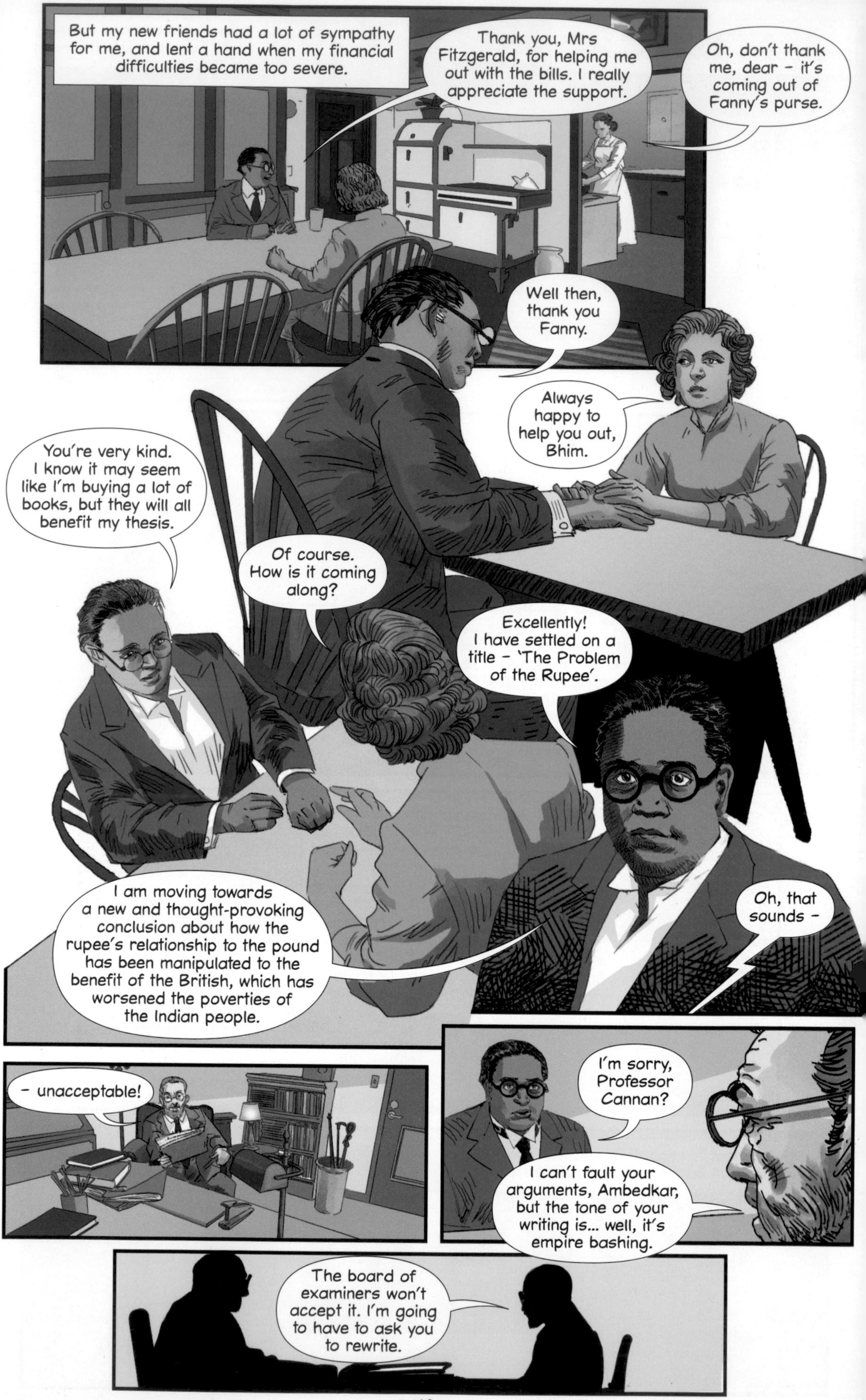

But my new friends had a lot of sympathy for me, and lent a hand when my financial difficulties became too severe.
Thank you, Mrs Fitzgerald, for helping me out with the bills. I really appreciate the support.
Oh, don't thank me, dear – it's coming out of Fanny's purse.
Well then, thank you Fanny.
Always happy to help you out, Bhim.
You're very kind. I know it may seem like I'm buying a lot of books, but they will all benefit my thesis.
Of course. How is it coming along?
Excellently! I have settled on a title – 'The Problem of the Rupee'.
I am moving towards a new and thought-provoking conclusion about how the rupee's relationship to the pound has been manipulated to the benefit of the British, which has worsened the poverties of the Indian people.
Oh, that sounds –
– unacceptable!
I'm sorry, Professor Cannan?
I can't fault your arguments, Ambedkar, but the tone of your writing is... well, it's empire bashing.
The board of examiners won't accept it. I'm going to have to ask you to rewrite.

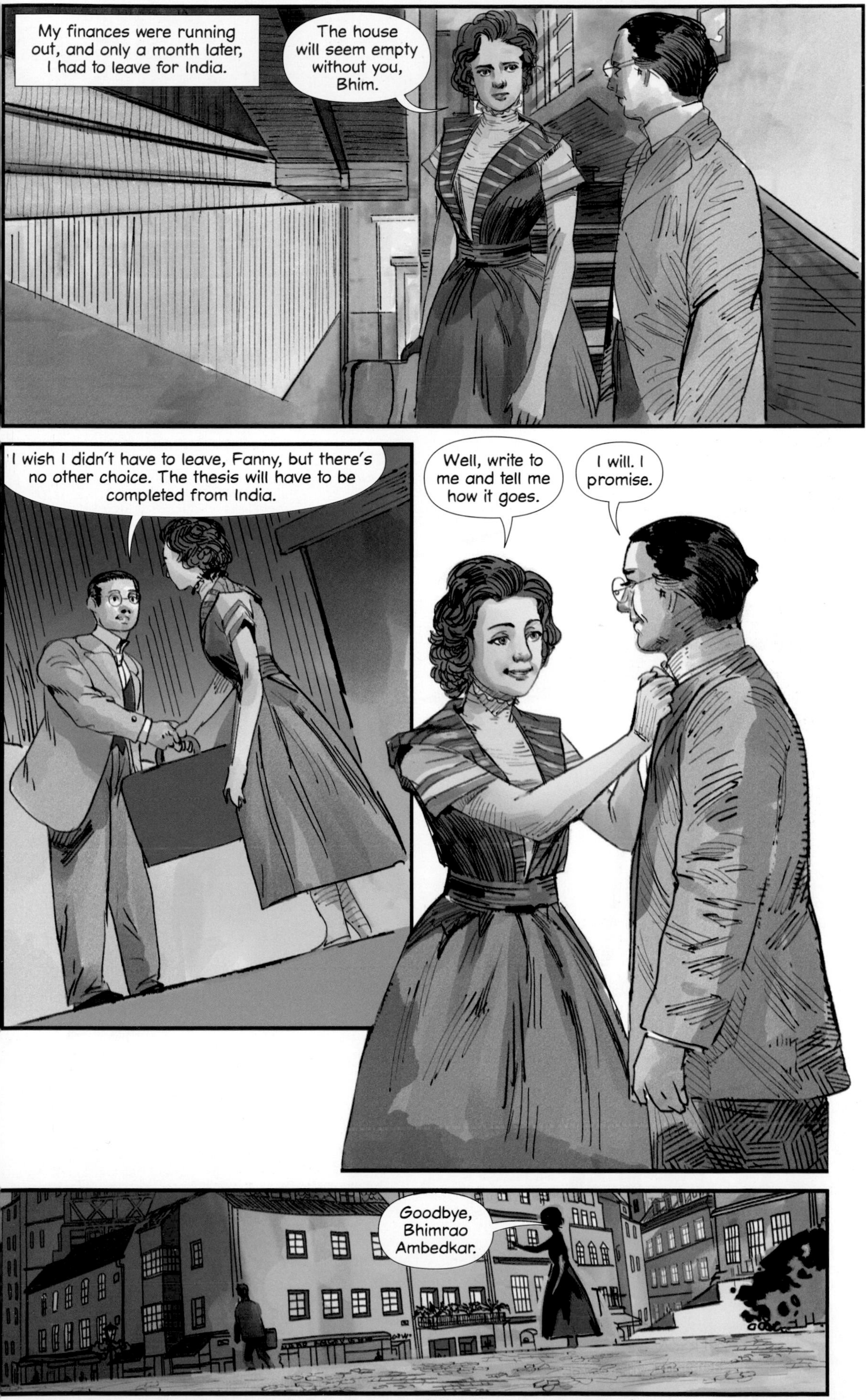
My finances were running out, and only a month later, I had to leave for India.
The house will seem empty without you, Bhim.
I wish I didn't have to leave, Fanny, but there's no other choice. The thesis will have to be completed from India.
Well, write to me and tell me how it goes.
I will. I promise.
Goodbye, Bhimrao Ambedkar.

3 THE STRUGGLE BEGINS

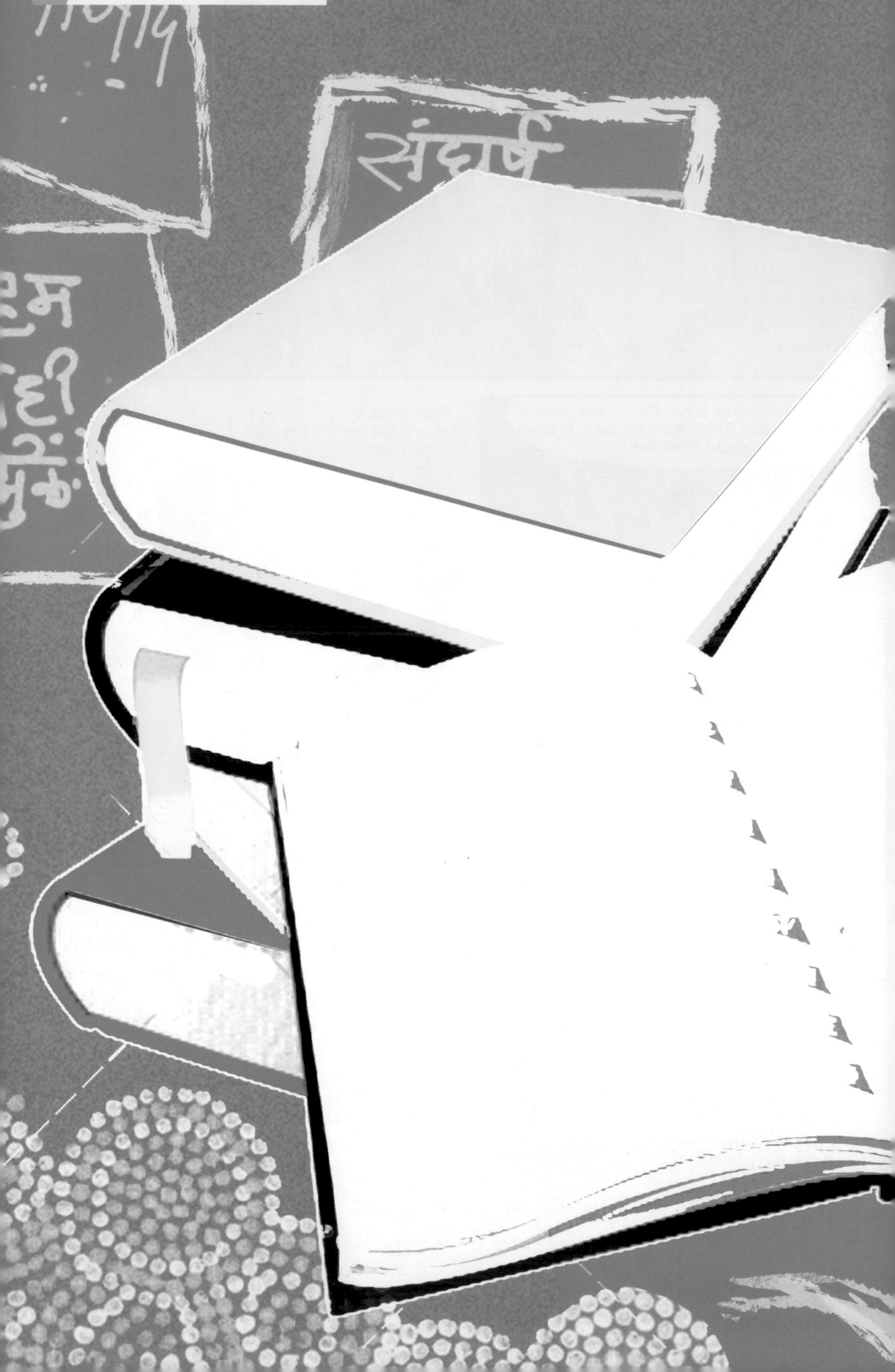
संघर्ष

"Lost rights are never regained by appeals to the conscience of the usurpers, but by relentless struggle.... Goats are used for sacrificial offerings and not lions."

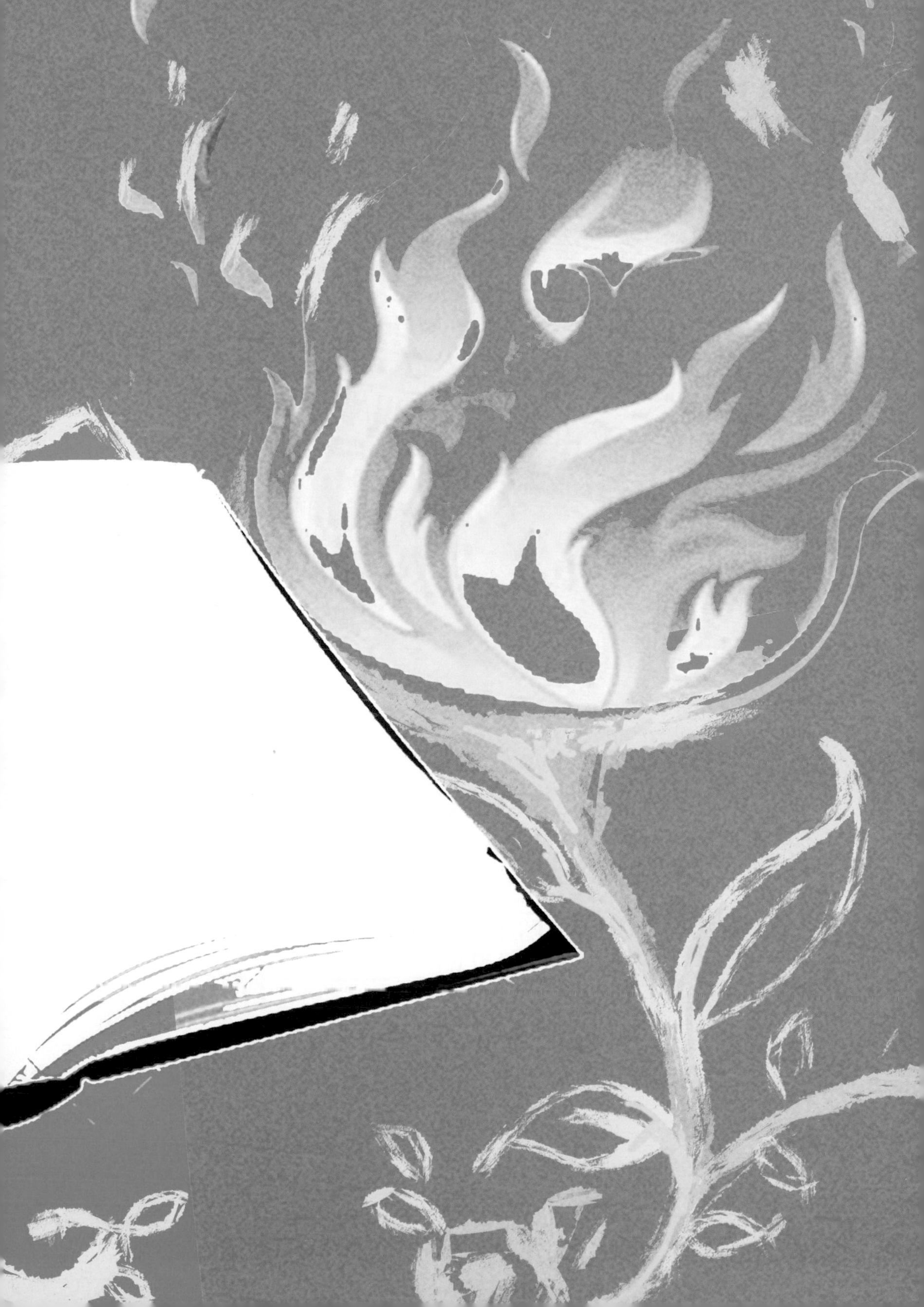

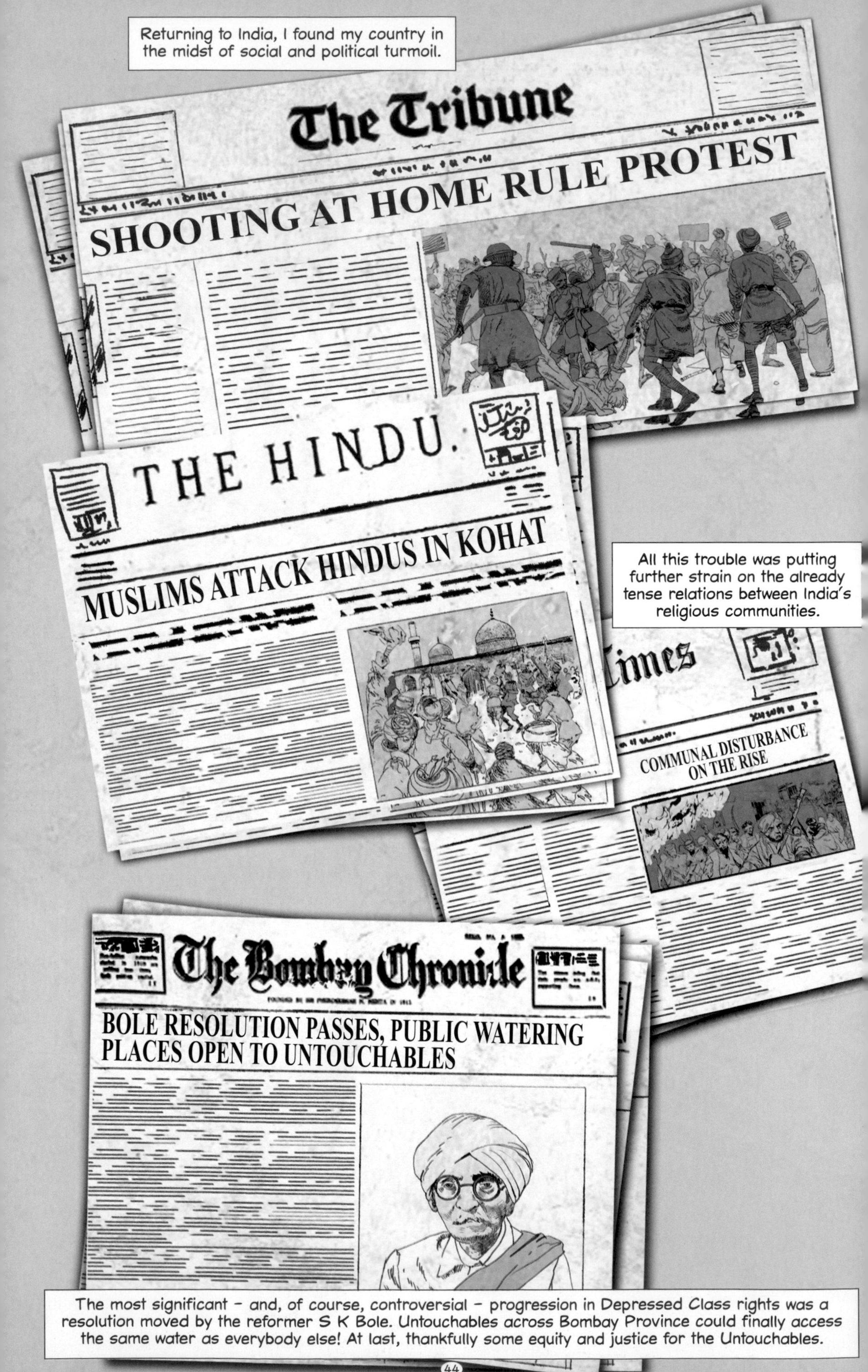

Returning to India, I found my country in the midst of social and political turmoil.
The Tribune
SHOOTING AT HOME RULE PROTEST
THE HINDU.
MUSLIMS ATTACK HINDUS IN KOHAT
All this trouble was putting further strain on the already tense relations between India's religious communities.
COMMUNAL DISTURBANCE ON THE RISE
The Bombay Chronicle
BOLE RESOLUTION PASSES, PUBLIC WATERING PLACES OPEN TO UNTOUCHABLES
The most significant – and, of course, controversial – progression in Depressed Class rights was a resolution moved by the reformer S K Bole. Untouchables across Bombay Province could finally access the same water as everybody else! At last, thankfully some equity and justice for the Untouchables.

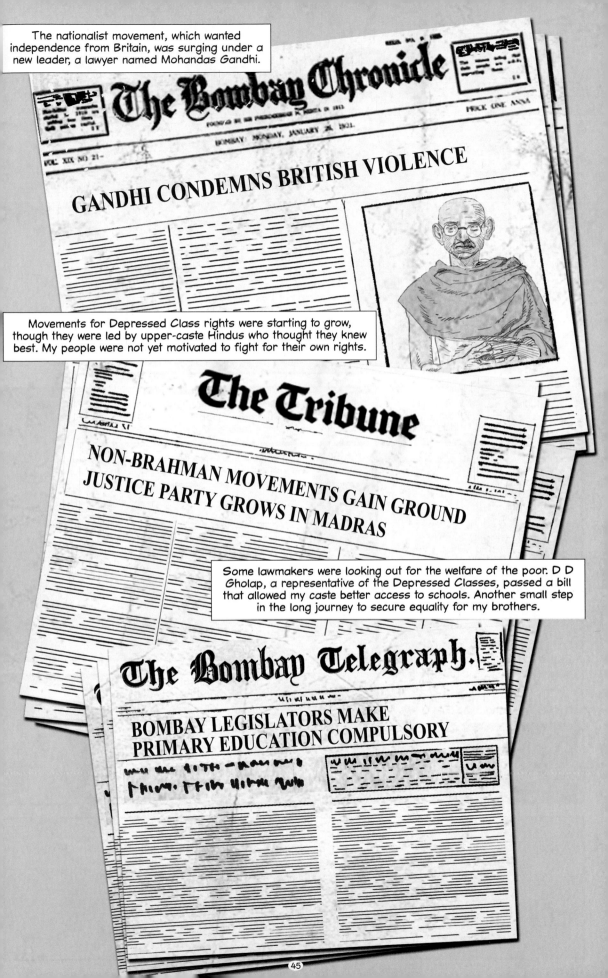

The nationalist movement, which wanted independence from Britain, was surging under a new leader, a lawyer named Mohandas Gandhi.

The Bombay Chronicle

PRICE ONE ANNA

BOMBAY, MONDAY, JANUARY 26, 1921.

VOL. XIX NO 21-

GANDHI CONDEMNS BRITISH VIOLENCE

Movements for Depressed Class rights were starting to grow, though they were led by upper-caste Hindus who thought they knew best. My people were not yet motivated to fight for their own rights.

The Tribune

NON-BRAHMAN MOVEMENTS GAIN GROUND JUSTICE PARTY GROWS IN MADRAS

Some lawmakers were looking out for the welfare of the poor. D D Gholap, a representative of the Depressed Classes, passed a bill that allowed my caste better access to schools. Another small step in the long journey to secure equality for my brothers.

The Bombay Telegraph.

BOMBAY LEGISLATORS MAKE PRIMARY EDUCATION COMPULSORY

Planning to combine my legal career with social activism and economic studies, I immediately made myself busy.

I established a law firm, but had only few clients at first.

My client pleads guilty to stealing the rice, but I ask you to consider that his family was starving. What other choice did he have?

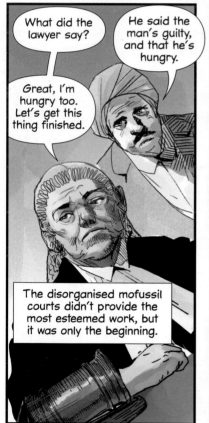

What did the lawyer say?

He said the man's guilty, and that he's hungry.

Great, I'm hungry too. Let's get this thing finished.

The disorganised mofussil courts didn't provide the most esteemed work, but it was only the beginning.

To develop untouchable communities, I set up the Bahishkrit Hitakarini Sabha, which meant 'Association for the Welfare of the Ostracised'.

But this too had a slow start. No one except the organisers attended our first meeting!

Someone will show up soon, right?

Let's give it half an hour.

I cannot hang around another minute! I'm going into the villages to stir up support.

Brothers! I am here to tell you about an organisation which will fight for the rights of our people!

We are counting on your support – it's time for Mahars to get organised!

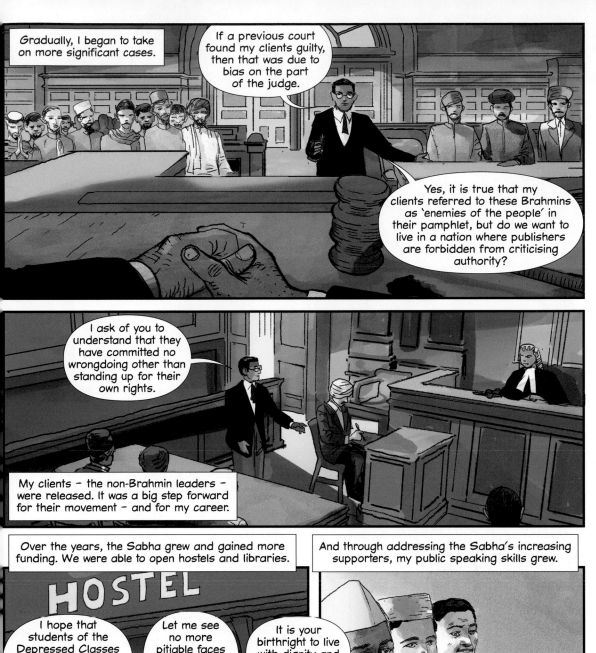

Gradually, I began to take on more significant cases.

If a previous court found my clients guilty, then that was due to bias on the part of the judge.

Yes, it is true that my clients referred to these Brahmins as 'enemies of the people' in their pamphlet, but do we want to live in a nation where publishers are forbidden from criticising authority?

I ask of you to understand that they have committed no wrongdoing other than standing up for their own rights.

My clients − the non-Brahmin leaders − were released. It was a big step forward for their movement − and for my career.

Over the years, the Sabha grew and gained more funding. We were able to open hostels and libraries.

And through addressing the Sabha's increasing supporters, my public speaking skills grew.

HOSTEL

I hope that students of the Depressed Classes will use this establishment in order to better themselves and their castes.

Let me see no more pitiable faces and hear no more sad voices among you.

It is your birthright to live with dignity and equality in the society.

If you believe in living a respectable life, you believe in self-help − which is the best help!

In addition to this, I was working on my writing and had taken up a part-time teaching job at Batliboi's Accounting Training Institute.

Mercantile law is a broad subject...

It's fair to say I was very busy!

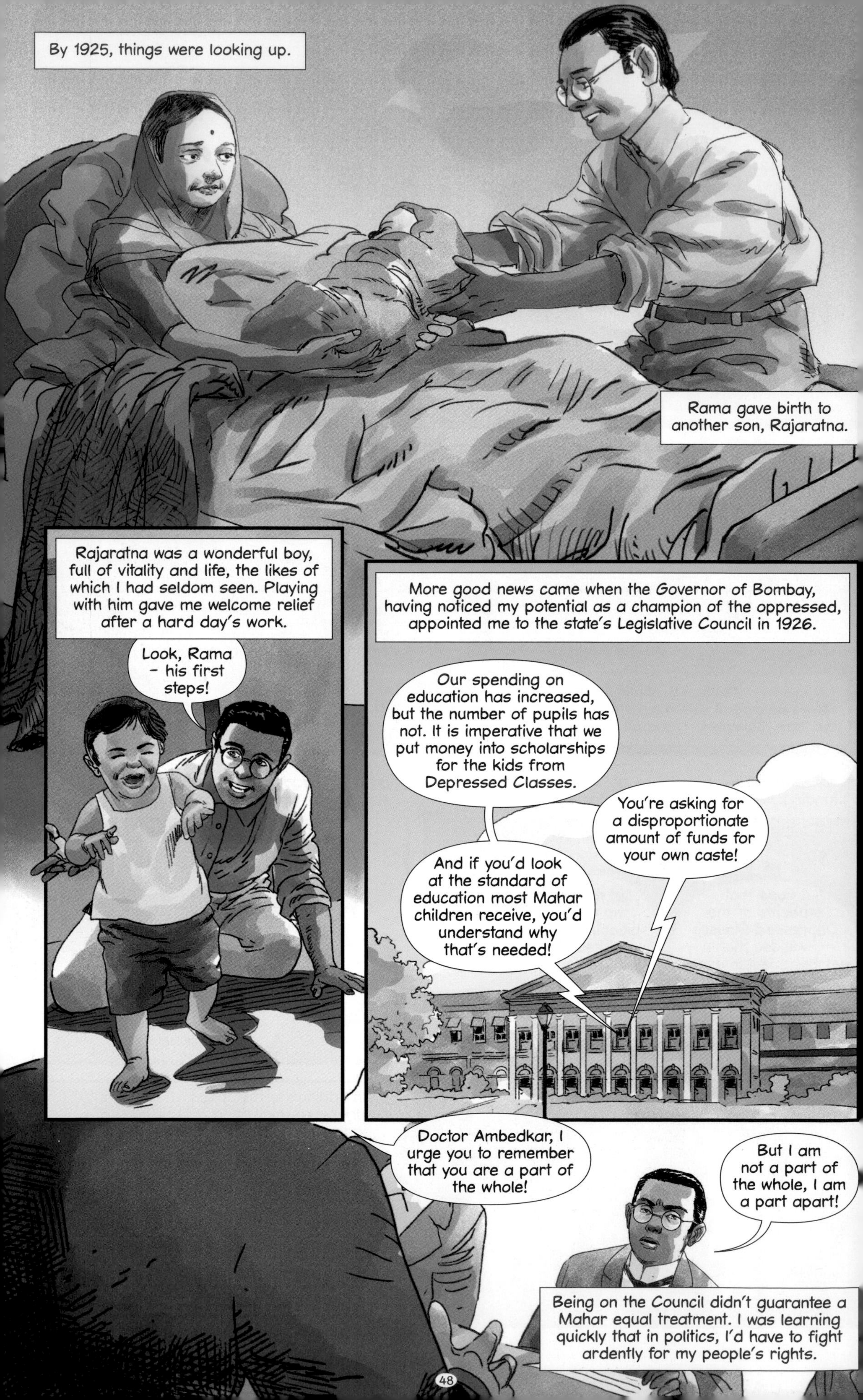
By 1925, things were looking up.
Rama gave birth to another son, Rajaratna.
Rajaratna was a wonderful boy, full of vitality and life, the likes of which I had seldom seen. Playing with him gave me welcome relief after a hard day's work.
Look, Rama – his first steps!
More good news came when the Governor of Bombay, having noticed my potential as a champion of the oppressed, appointed me to the state's Legislative Council in 1926.
Our spending on education has increased, but the number of pupils has not. It is imperative that we put money into scholarships for the kids from Depressed Classes.
You're asking for a disproportionate amount of funds for your own caste!
And if you'd look at the standard of education most Mahar children receive, you'd understand why that's needed!
Doctor Ambedkar, I urge you to remember that you are a part of the whole!
But I am not a part of the whole, I am a part apart!
Being on the Council didn't guarantee a Mahar equal treatment. I was learning quickly that in politics, I'd have to fight ardently for my people's rights.

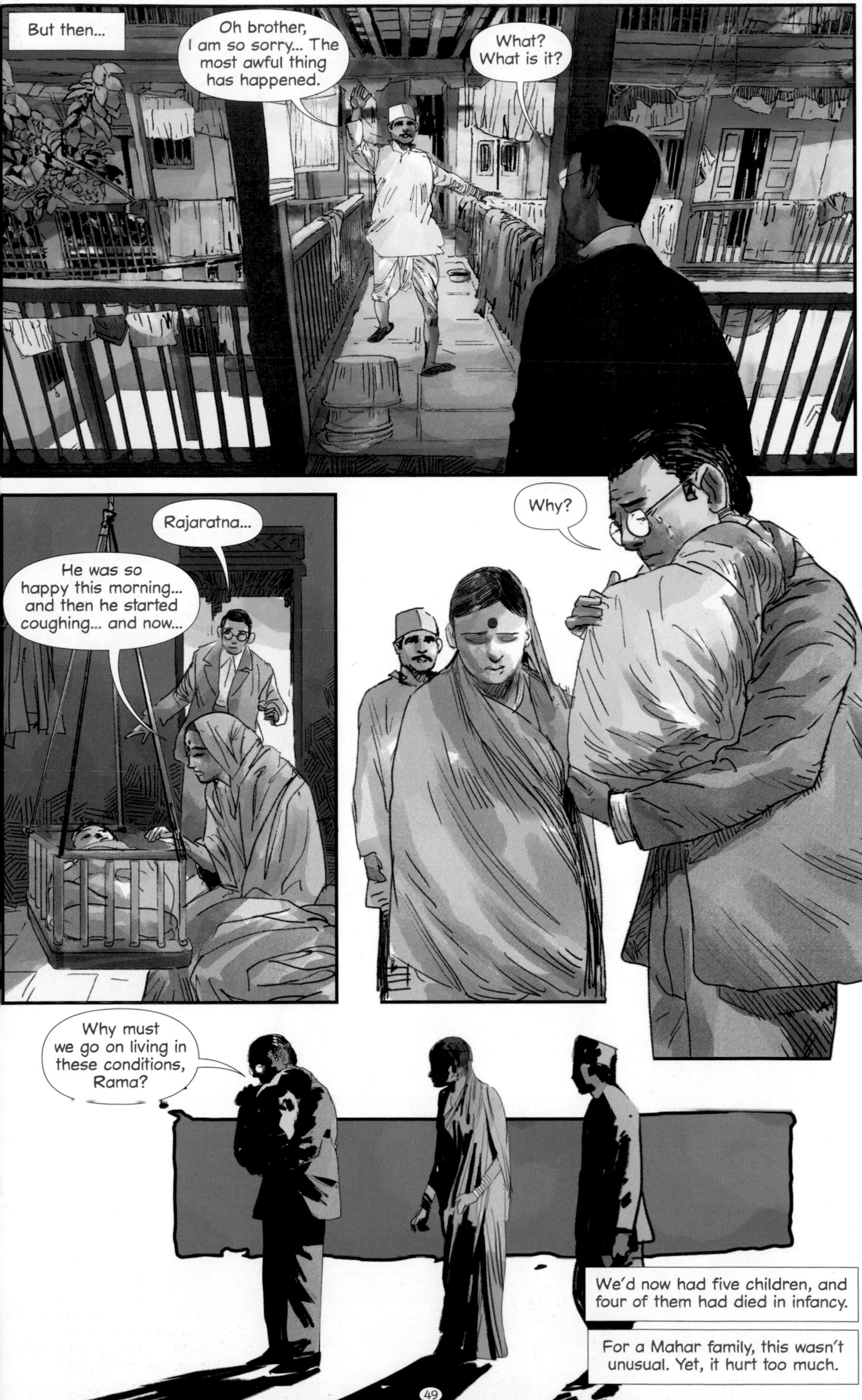

But then...
Oh brother, I am so sorry... The most awful thing has happened.
What? What is it?
Rajaratna...
He was so happy this morning... and then he started coughing... and now...
Why?
Why must we go on living in these conditions, Rama?
We'd now had five children, and four of them had died in infancy.
For a Mahar family, this wasn't unusual. Yet, it hurt too much.

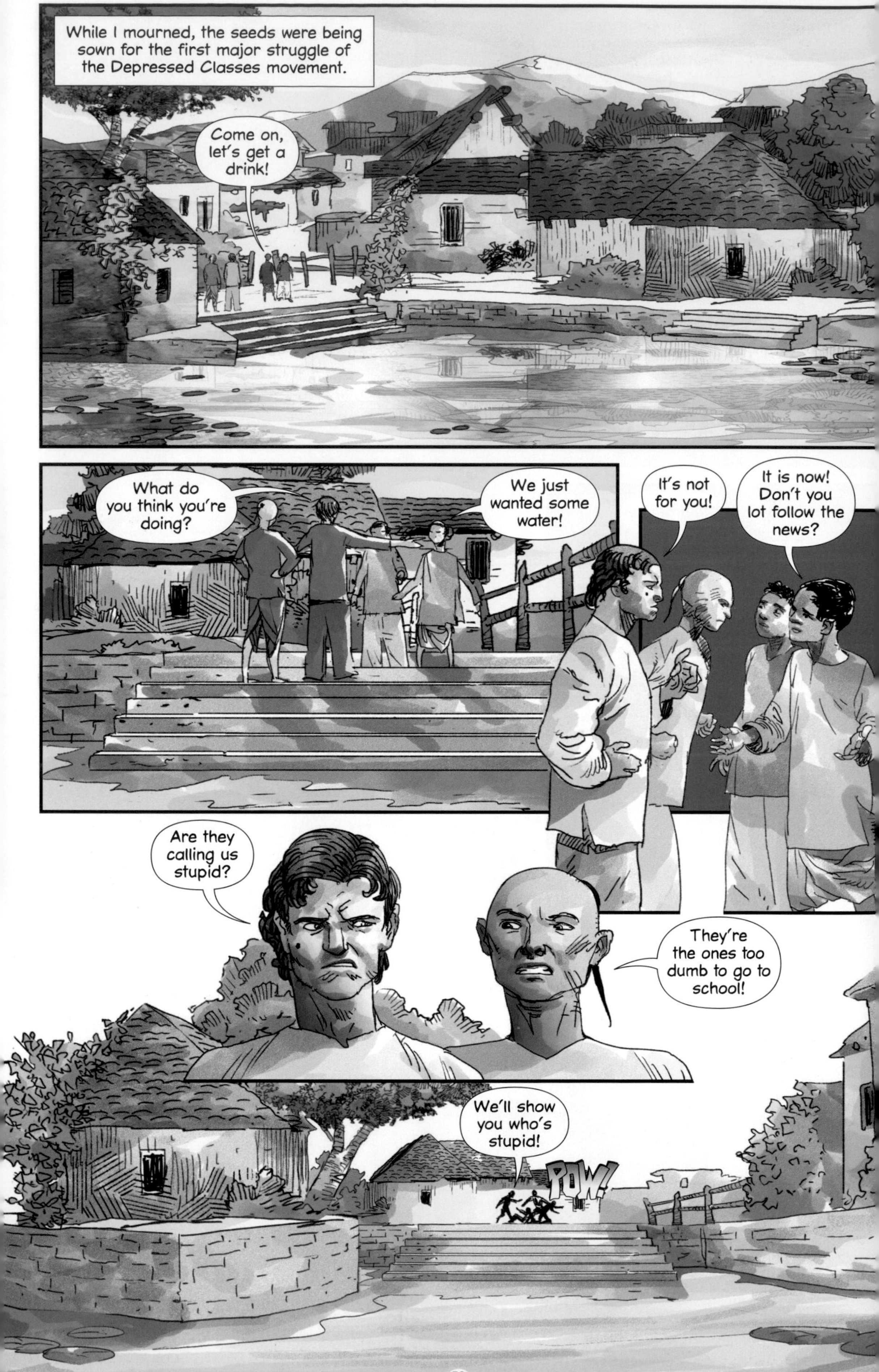
While I mourned, the seeds were being sown for the first major struggle of the Depressed Classes movement.
Come on, let's get a drink!
What do you think you're doing?
We just wanted some water!
It's not for you!
It is now! Don't you lot follow the news?
Are they calling us stupid?
They're the ones too dumb to go to school!
We'll show you who's stupid!
POW!

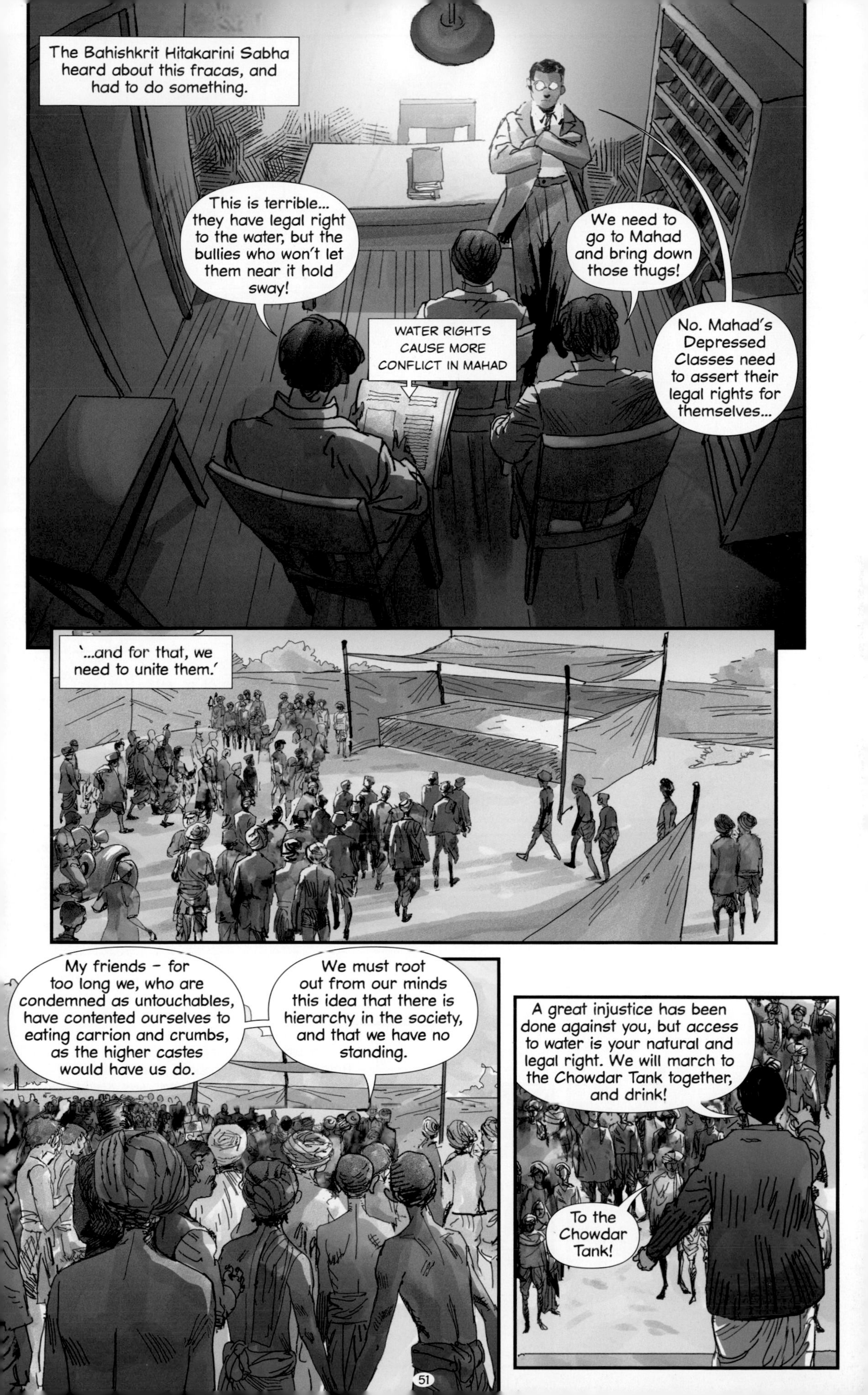
The Bahishkrit Hitakarini Sabha heard about this fracas, and had to do something.
This is terrible... they have legal right to the water, but the bullies who won't let them near it hold sway!
WATER RIGHTS CAUSE MORE CONFLICT IN MAHAD
We need to go to Mahad and bring down those thugs!
No. Mahad's Depressed Classes need to assert their legal rights for themselves...
'...and for that, we need to unite them.'
My friends – for too long we, who are condemned as untouchables, have contented ourselves to eating carrion and crumbs, as the higher castes would have us do.
We must root out from our minds this idea that there is hierarchy in the society, and that we have no standing.
A great injustice has been done against you, but access to water is your natural and legal right. We will march to the Chowdar Tank together, and drink!
To the Chowdar Tank!

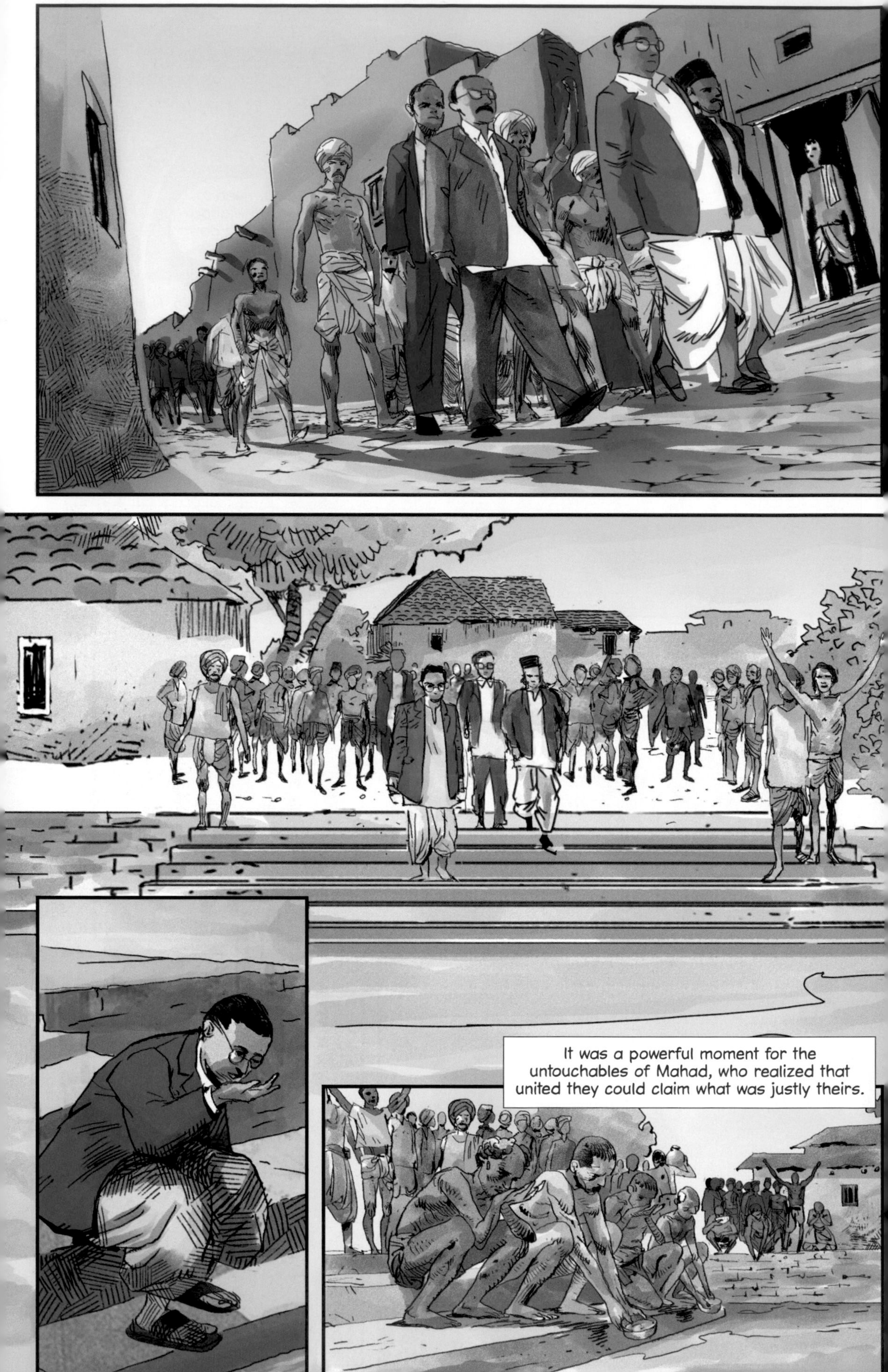
It was a powerful moment for the untouchables of Mahad, who realized that united they could claim what was justly theirs.

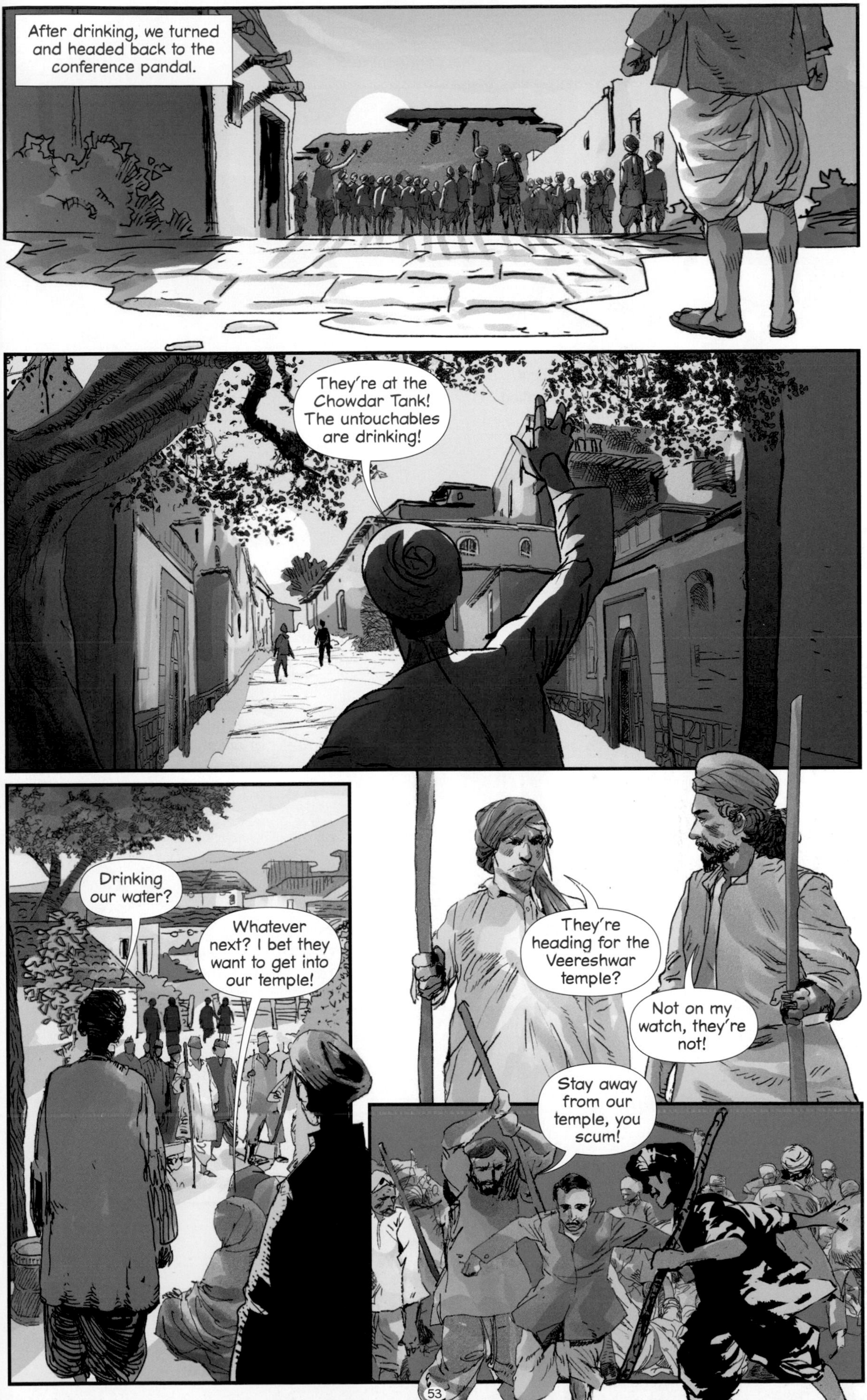
After drinking, we turned and headed back to the conference pandal.
They're at the Chowdar Tank! The untouchables are drinking!
Drinking our water?
Whatever next? I bet they want to get into our temple!
They're heading for the Veereshwar temple?
Not on my watch, they're not!
Stay away from our temple, you scum!

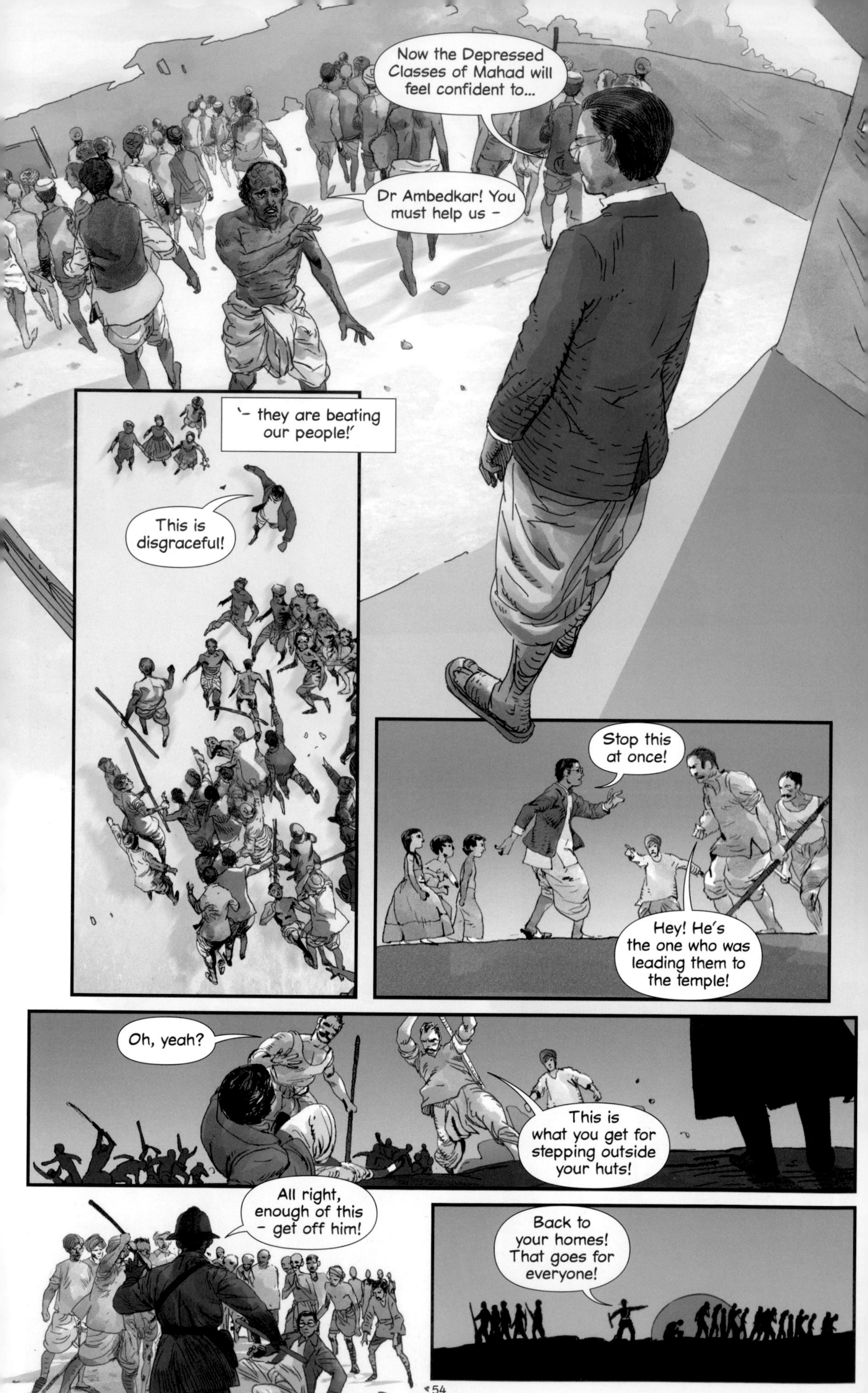
Now the Depressed Classes of Mahad will feel confident to...
Dr Ambedkar! You must help us –
'– they are beating our people!'
This is disgraceful!
Stop this at once!
Hey! He's the one who was leading them to the temple!
Oh, yeah?
This is what you get for stepping outside your huts!
All right, enough of this – get off him!
Back to your homes! That goes for everyone!

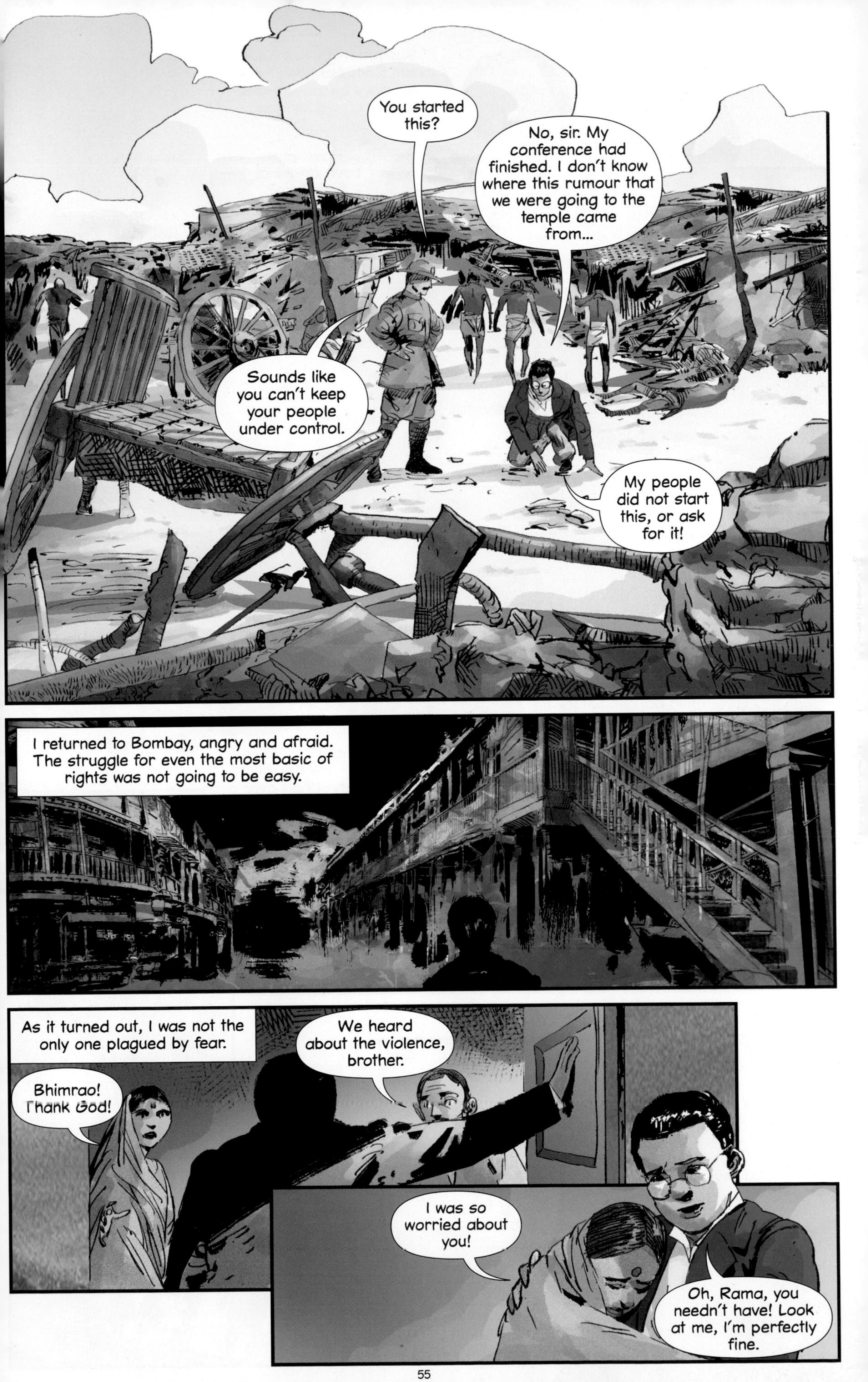
You started this?
No, sir. My conference had finished. I don't know where this rumour that we were going to the temple came from...
Sounds like you can't keep your people under control.
My people did not start this, or ask for it!
I returned to Bombay, angry and afraid. The struggle for even the most basic of rights was not going to be easy.
As it turned out, I was not the only one plagued by fear.
We heard about the violence, brother.
Bhimrao! Thank God!
I was so worried about you!
Oh, Rama, you needn't have! Look at me, I'm perfectly fine.

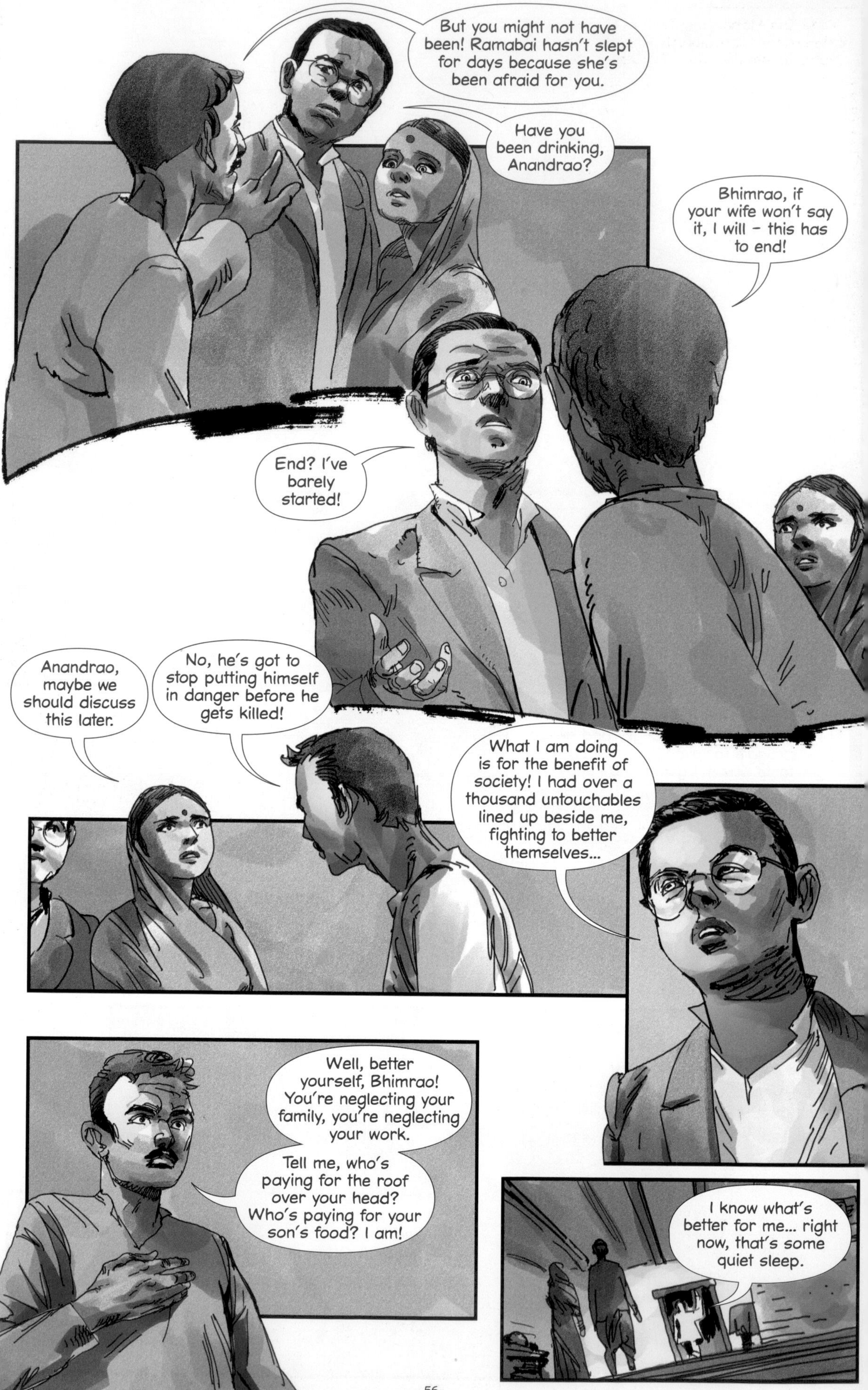
But you might not have been! Ramabai hasn't slept for days because she's been afraid for you.
Have you been drinking, Anandrao?
Bhimrao, if your wife won't say it, I will – this has to end!
End? I've barely started!
Anandrao, maybe we should discuss this later.
No, he's got to stop putting himself in danger before he gets killed!
What I am doing is for the benefit of society! I had over a thousand untouchables lined up beside me, fighting to better themselves...
Well, better yourself, Bhimrao! You're neglecting your family, you're neglecting your work.
Tell me, who's paying for the roof over your head? Who's paying for your son's food? I am!
I know what's better for me... right now, that's some quiet sleep.

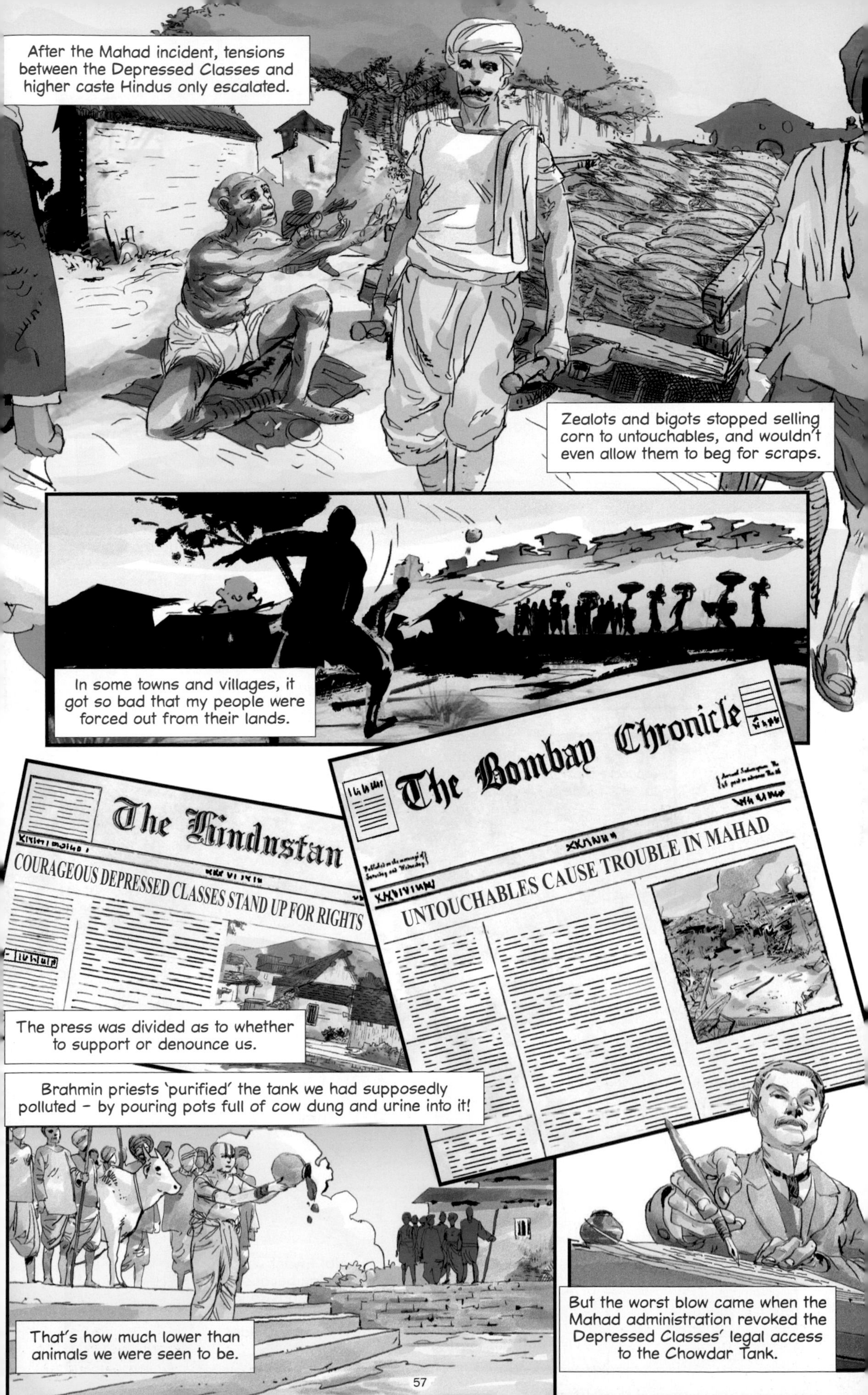
After the Mahad incident, tensions between the Depressed Classes and higher caste Hindus only escalated.
Zealots and bigots stopped selling corn to untouchables, and wouldn't even allow them to beg for scraps.
In some towns and villages, it got so bad that my people were forced out from their lands.
The Hindustan
COURAGEOUS DEPRESSED CLASSES STAND UP FOR RIGHTS
The Bombay Chronicle
UNTOUCHABLES CAUSE TROUBLE IN MAHAD
The press was divided as to whether to support or denounce us.
Brahmin priests 'purified' the tank we had supposedly polluted – by pouring pots full of cow dung and urine into it!
That's how much lower than animals we were seen to be.
But the worst blow came when the Mahad administration revoked the Depressed Classes' legal access to the Chowdar Tank.

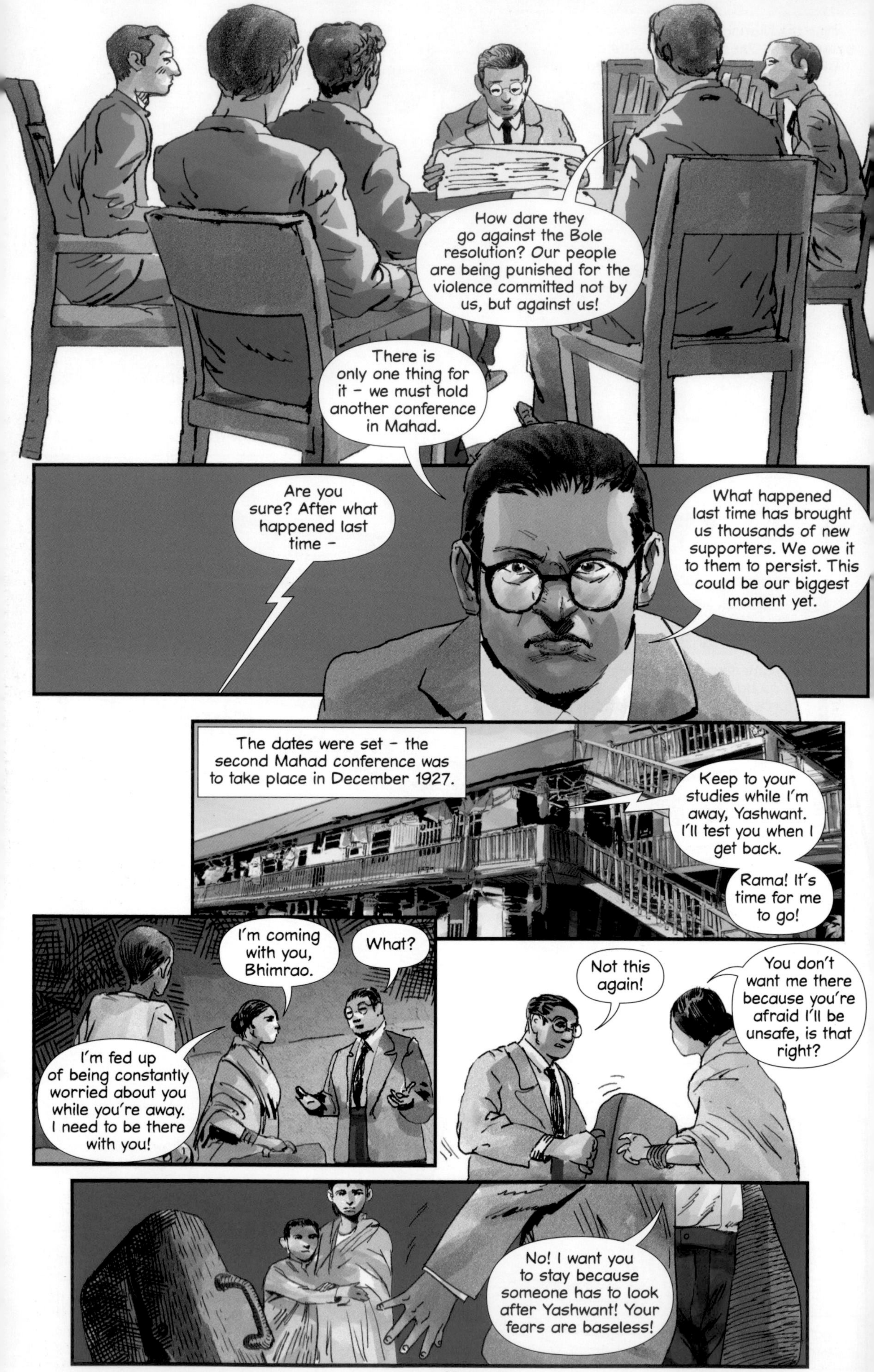
How dare they go against the Bole resolution? Our people are being punished for the violence committed not by us, but against us!
There is only one thing for it – we must hold another conference in Mahad.
Are you sure? After what happened last time –
What happened last time has brought us thousands of new supporters. We owe it to them to persist. This could be our biggest moment yet.
The dates were set – the second Mahad conference was to take place in December 1927.
Keep to your studies while I'm away, Yashwant. I'll test you when I get back.
Rama! It's time for me to go!
I'm coming with you, Bhimrao.
What?
I'm fed up of being constantly worried about you while you're away. I need to be there with you!
Not this again!
You don't want me there because you're afraid I'll be unsafe, is that right?
No! I want you to stay because someone has to look after Yashwant! Your fears are baseless!

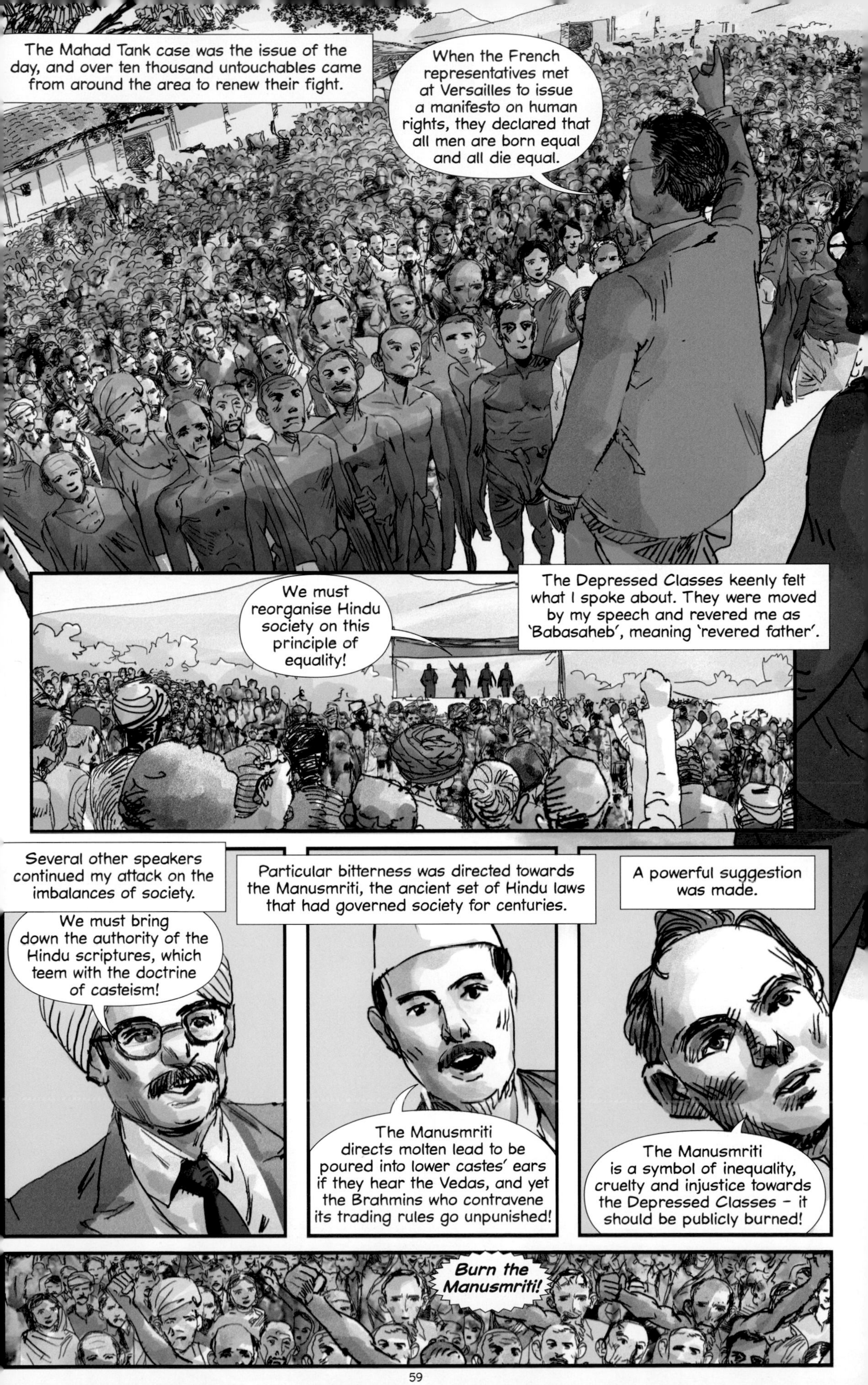

The Mahad Tank case was the issue of the day, and over ten thousand untouchables came from around the area to renew their fight.
When the French representatives met at Versailles to issue a manifesto on human rights, they declared that all men are born equal and all die equal.
We must reorganise Hindu society on this principle of equality!
The Depressed Classes keenly felt what I spoke about. They were moved by my speech and revered me as 'Babasaheb', meaning 'revered father'.
Several other speakers continued my attack on the imbalances of society.
We must bring down the authority of the Hindu scriptures, which teem with the doctrine of casteism!
Particular bitterness was directed towards the Manusmriti, the ancient set of Hindu laws that had governed society for centuries.
The Manusmriti directs molten lead to be poured into lower castes' ears if they hear the Vedas, and yet the Brahmins who contravene its trading rules go unpunished!
A powerful suggestion was made.
The Manusmriti is a symbol of inequality, cruelty and injustice towards the Depressed Classes – it should be publicly burned!
Burn the Manusmriti!

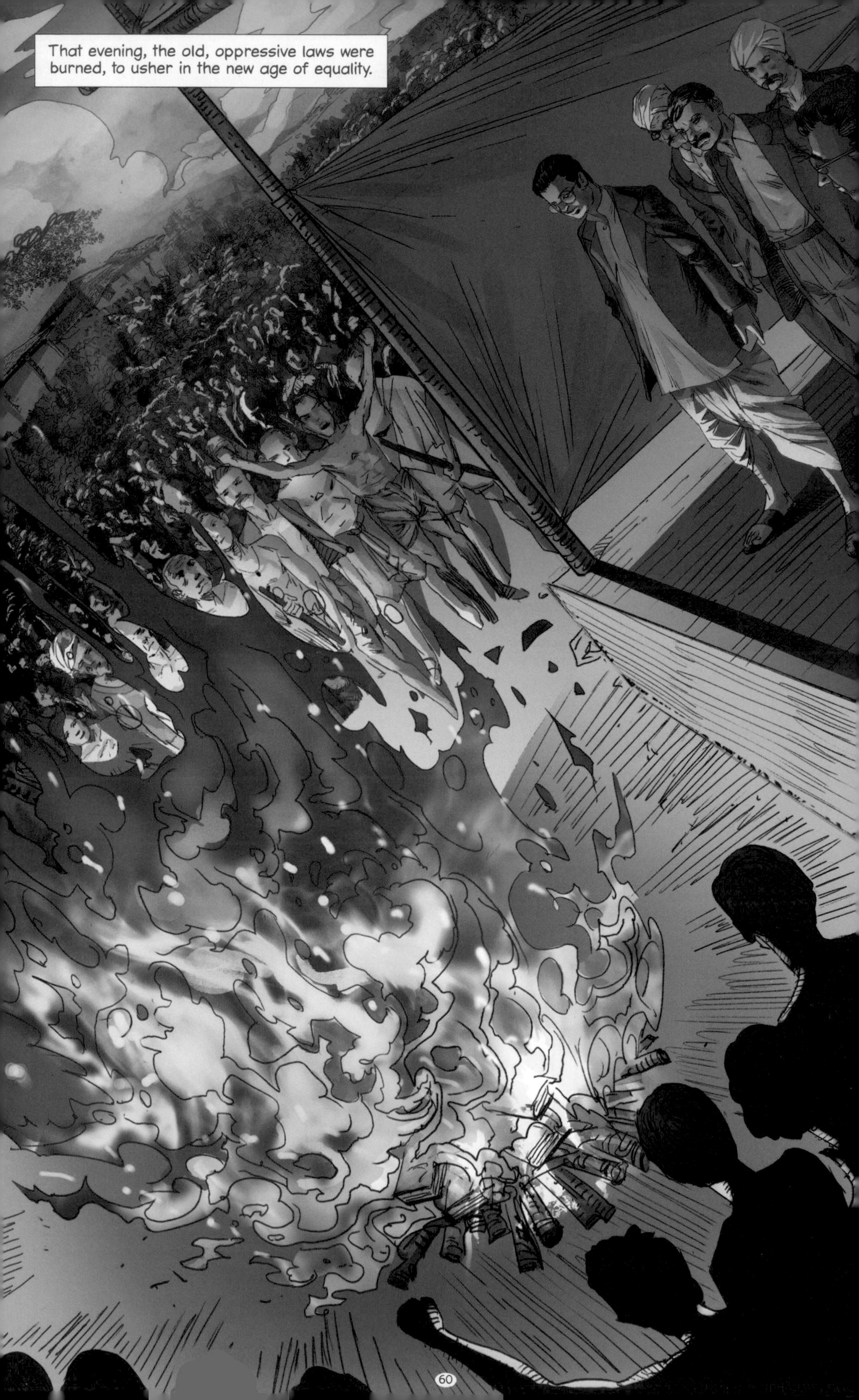
That evening, the old, oppressive laws were burned, to usher in the new age of equality.

4 NO HOMELAND

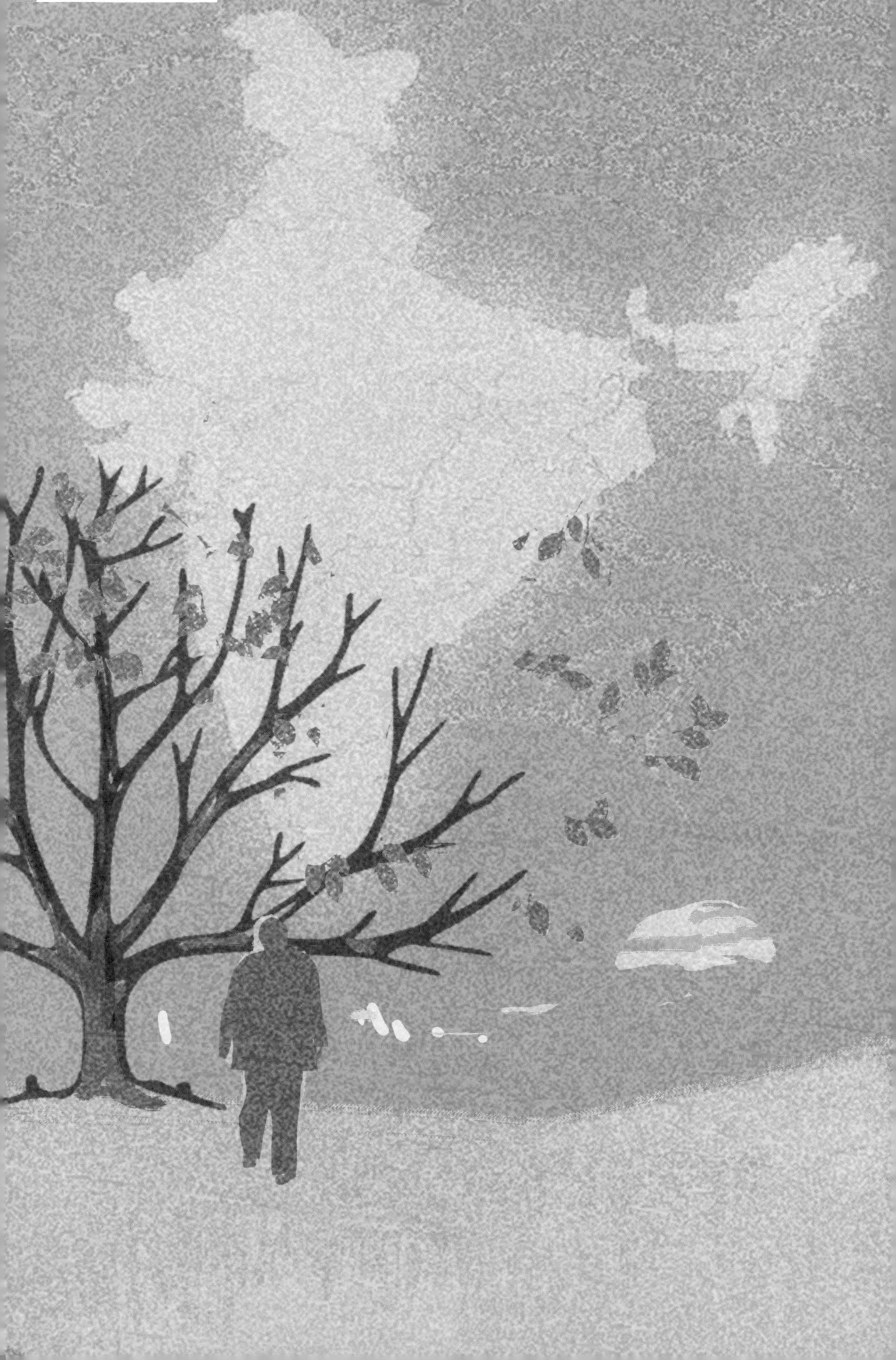

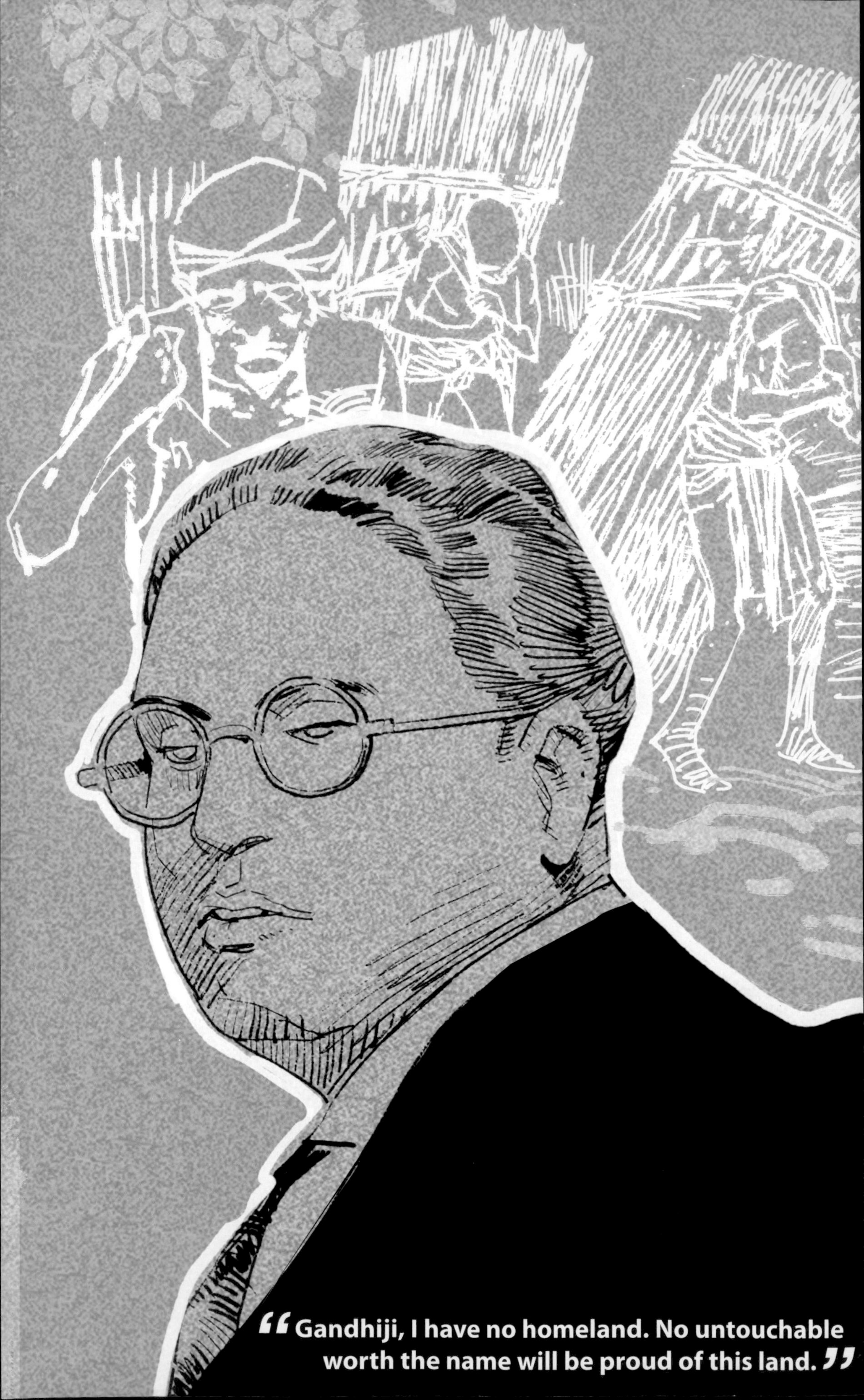
"Gandhiji, I have no homeland. No untouchable worth the name will be proud of this land."

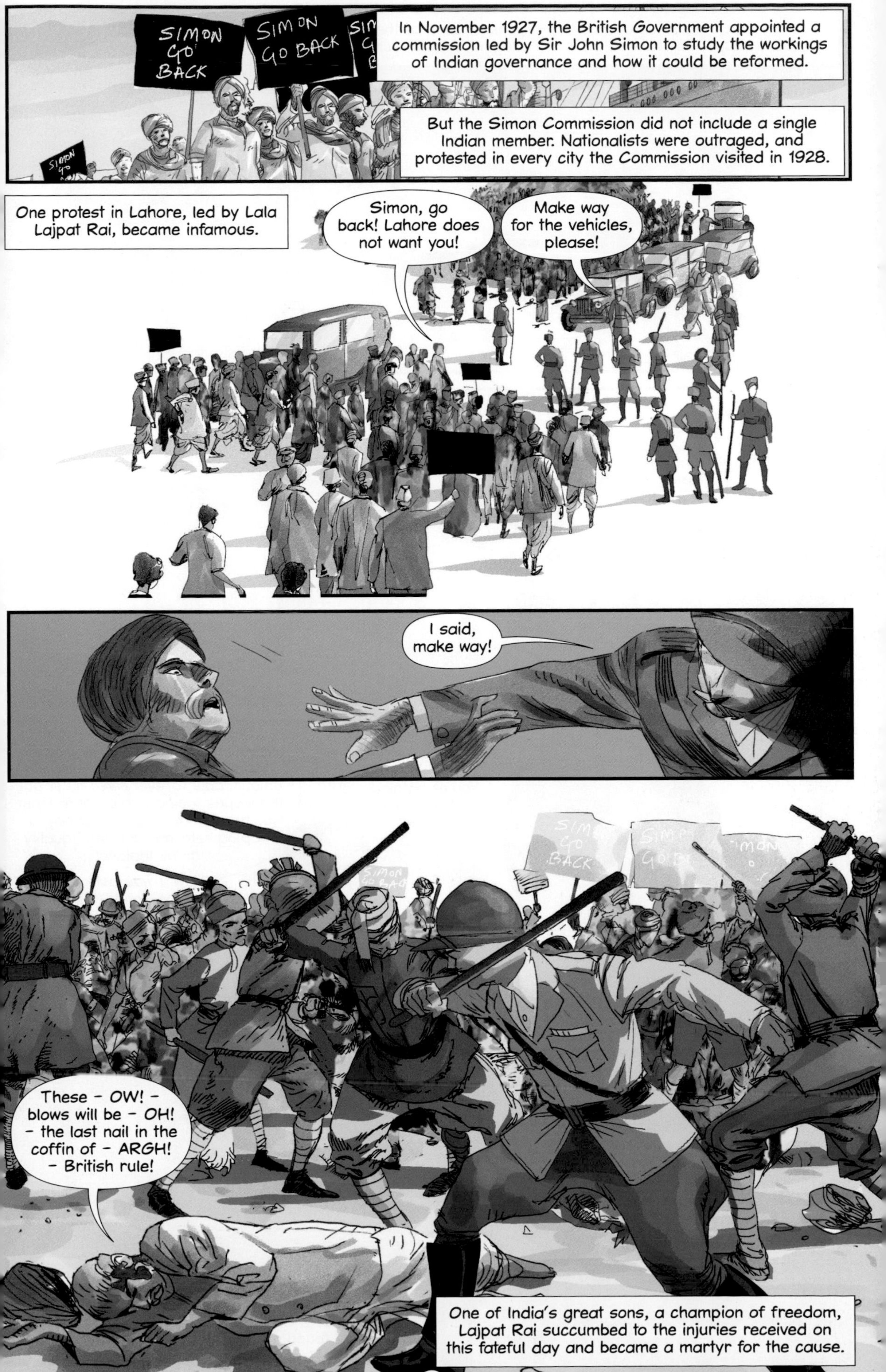
SIMON GO BACK
SIMON GO BACK
In November 1927, the British Government appointed a commission led by Sir John Simon to study the workings of Indian governance and how it could be reformed.
But the Simon Commission did not include a single Indian member. Nationalists were outraged, and protested in every city the Commission visited in 1928.
One protest in Lahore, led by Lala Lajpat Rai, became infamous.
Simon, go back! Lahore does not want you!
Make way for the vehicles, please!
I said, make way!
These – OW! – blows will be – OH! – the last nail in the coffin of – ARGH! – British rule!
One of India's great sons, a champion of freedom, Lajpat Rai succumbed to the injuries received on this fateful day and became a martyr for the cause.

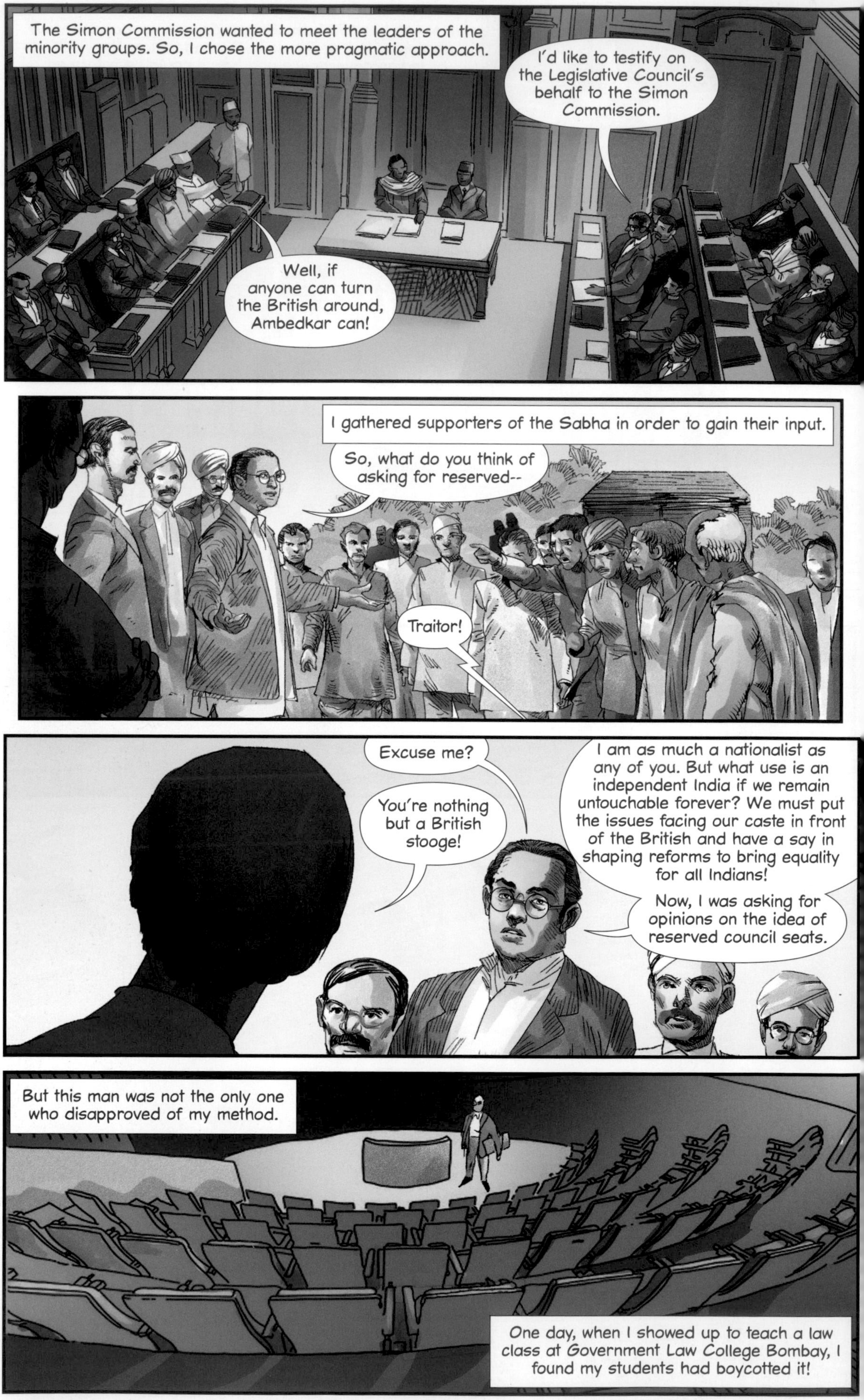

The Simon Commission wanted to meet the leaders of the minority groups. So, I chose the more pragmatic approach.
I'd like to testify on the Legislative Council's behalf to the Simon Commission.
Well, if anyone can turn the British around, Ambedkar can!
I gathered supporters of the Sabha in order to gain their input.
So, what do you think of asking for reserved--
Traitor!
Excuse me?
You're nothing but a British stooge!
I am as much a nationalist as any of you. But what use is an independent India if we remain untouchable forever? We must put the issues facing our caste in front of the British and have a say in shaping reforms to bring equality for all Indians!
Now, I was asking for opinions on the idea of reserved council seats.
But this man was not the only one who disapproved of my method.
One day, when I showed up to teach a law class at Government Law College Bombay, I found my students had boycotted it!

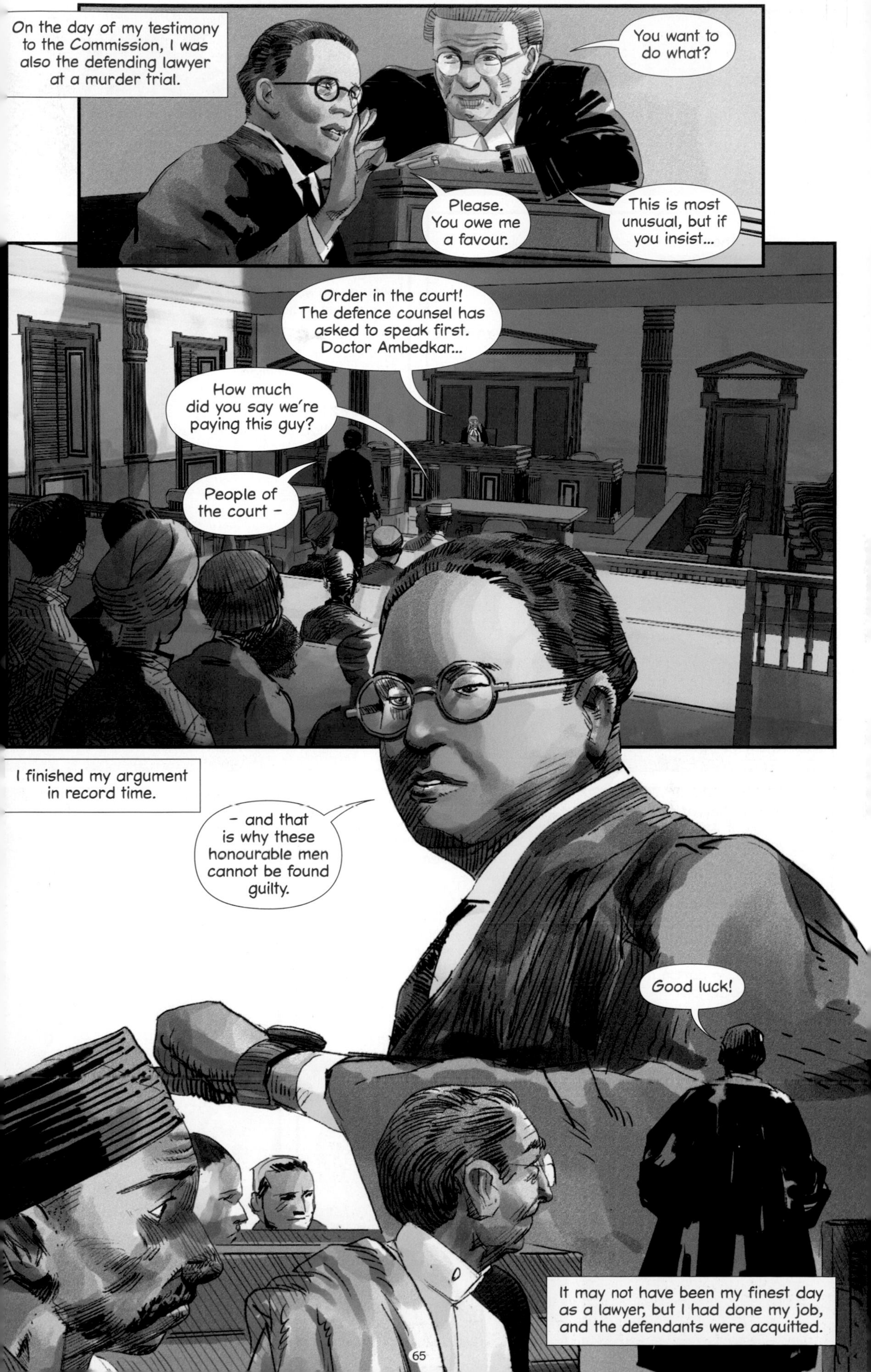
On the day of my testimony to the Commission, I was also the defending lawyer at a murder trial.
You want to do what?
Please. You owe me a favour.
This is most unusual, but if you insist...
Order in the court! The defence counsel has asked to speak first. Doctor Ambedkar...
How much did you say we're paying this guy?
People of the court –
I finished my argument in record time.
– and that is why these honourable men cannot be found guilty.
Good luck!
It may not have been my finest day as a lawyer, but I had done my job, and the defendants were acquitted.

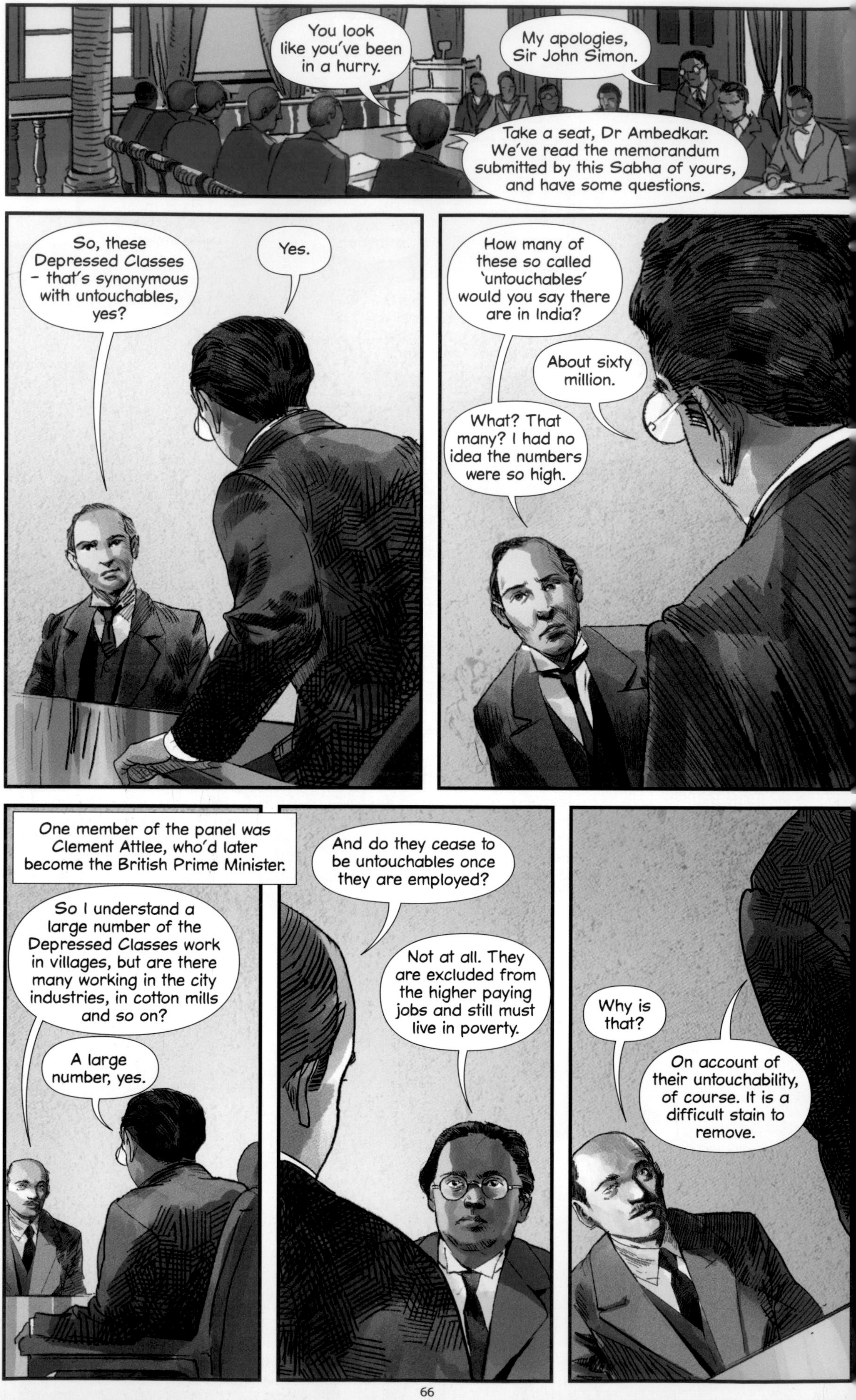

You look like you've been in a hurry.
My apologies, Sir John Simon.
Take a seat, Dr Ambedkar. We've read the memorandum submitted by this Sabha of yours, and have some questions.
So, these Depressed Classes - that's synonymous with untouchables, yes?
Yes.
How many of these so called 'untouchables' would you say there are in India?
About sixty million.
What? That many? I had no idea the numbers were so high.
One member of the panel was Clement Attlee, who'd later become the British Prime Minister.
So I understand a large number of the Depressed Classes work in villages, but are there many working in the city industries, in cotton mills and so on?
A large number, yes.
And do they cease to be untouchables once they are employed?
Not at all. They are excluded from the higher paying jobs and still must live in poverty.
Why is that?
On account of their untouchability, of course. It is a difficult stain to remove.

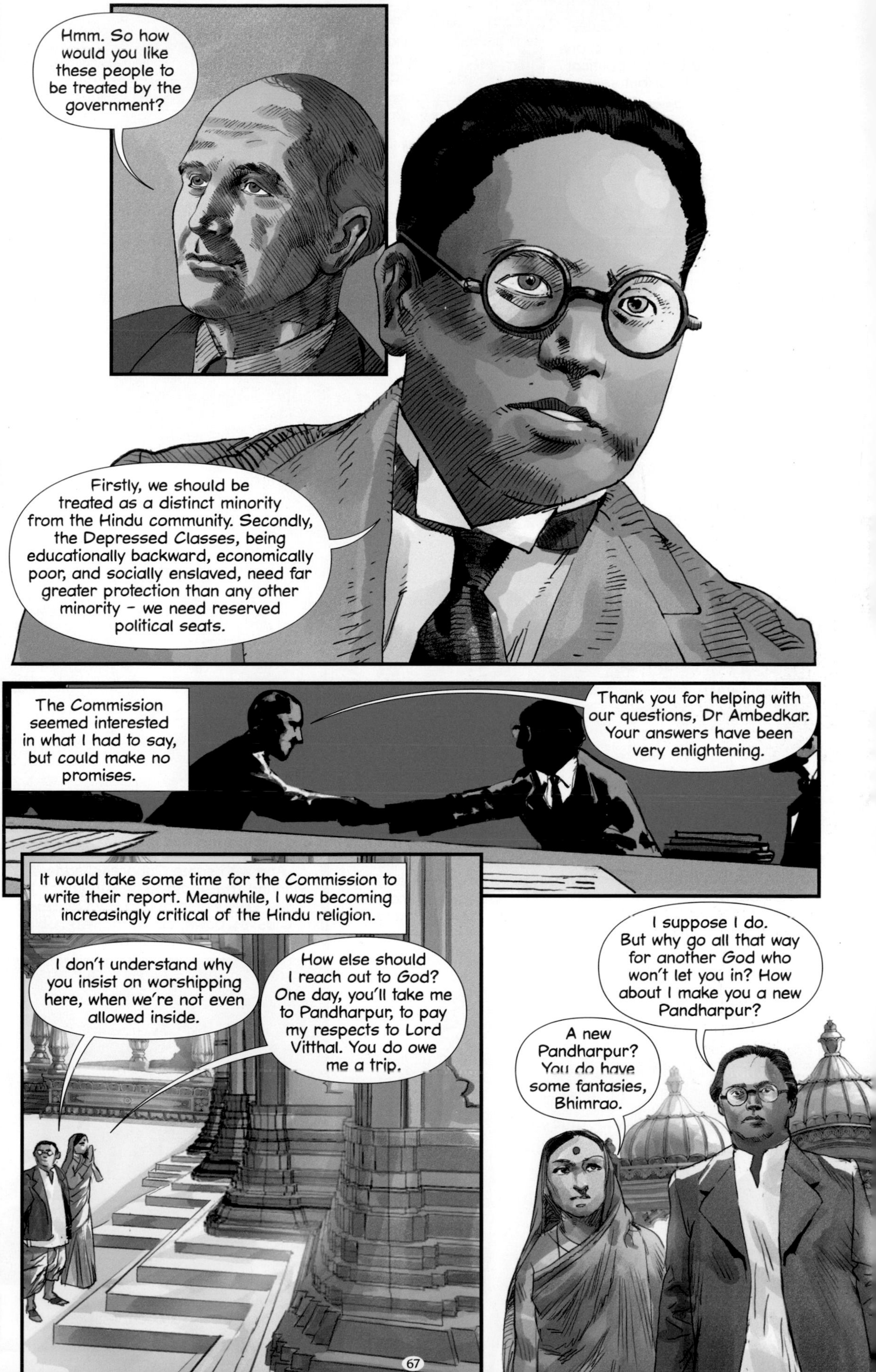
Hmm. So how would you like these people to be treated by the government?
Firstly, we should be treated as a distinct minority from the Hindu community. Secondly, the Depressed Classes, being educationally backward, economically poor, and socially enslaved, need far greater protection than any other minority – we need reserved political seats.
The Commission seemed interested in what I had to say, but could make no promises.
Thank you for helping with our questions, Dr Ambedkar. Your answers have been very enlightening.
It would take some time for the Commission to write their report. Meanwhile, I was becoming increasingly critical of the Hindu religion.
I don't understand why you insist on worshipping here, when we're not even allowed inside.
How else should I reach out to God? One day, you'll take me to Pandharpur, to pay my respects to Lord Vitthal. You do owe me a trip.
I suppose I do. But why go all that way for another God who won't let you in? How about I make you a new Pandharpur?
A new Pandharpur? You do have some fantasies, Bhimrao.

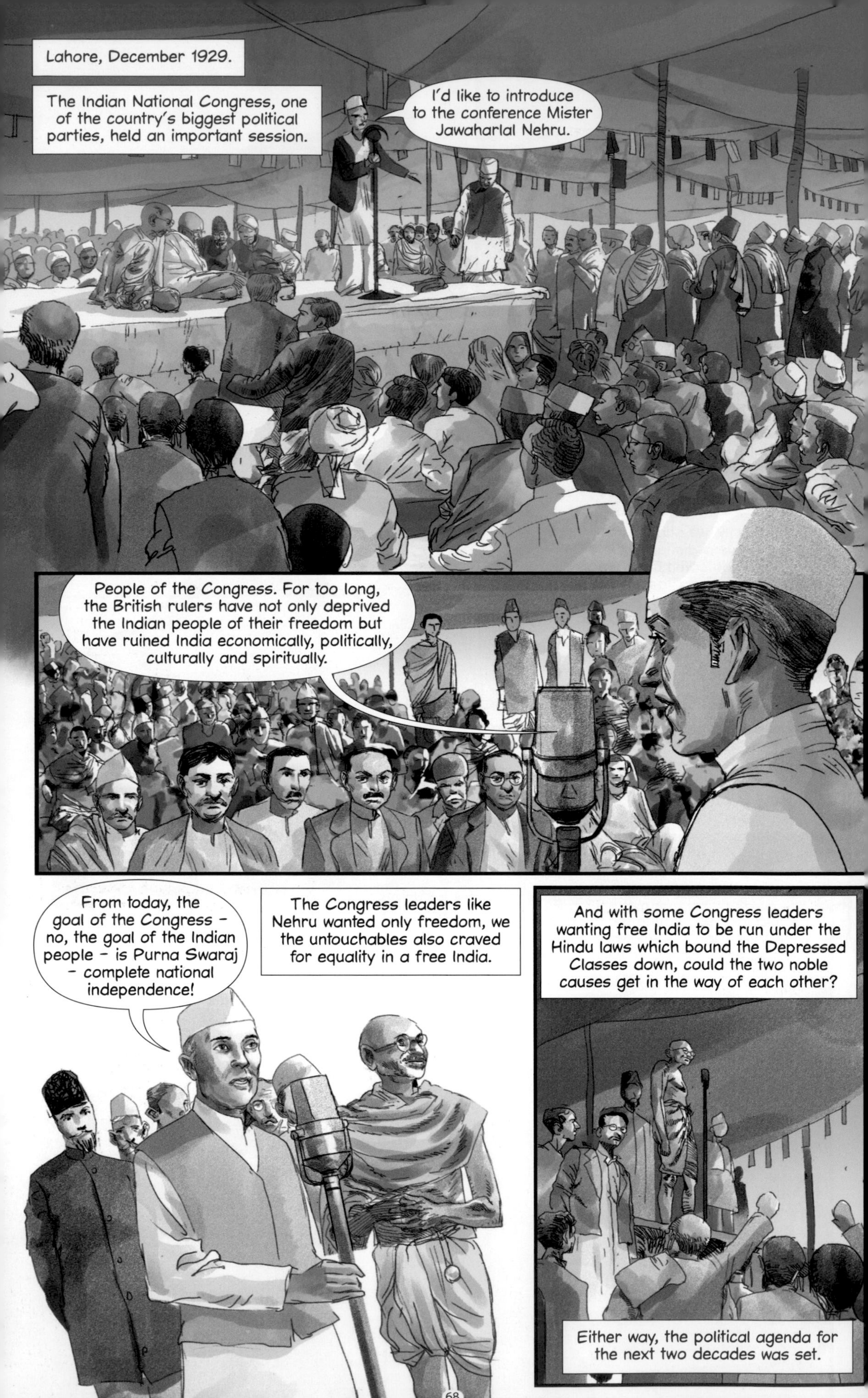

Lahore, December 1929.
The Indian National Congress, one of the country's biggest political parties, held an important session.
I'd like to introduce to the conference Mister Jawaharlal Nehru.
People of the Congress. For too long, the British rulers have not only deprived the Indian people of their freedom but have ruined India economically, politically, culturally and spiritually.
From today, the goal of the Congress – no, the goal of the Indian people – is Purna Swaraj – complete national independence!
The Congress leaders like Nehru wanted only freedom, we the untouchables also craved for equality in a free India.
And with some Congress leaders wanting free India to be run under the Hindu laws which bound the Depressed Classes down, could the two noble causes get in the way of each other?
Either way, the political agenda for the next two decades was set.

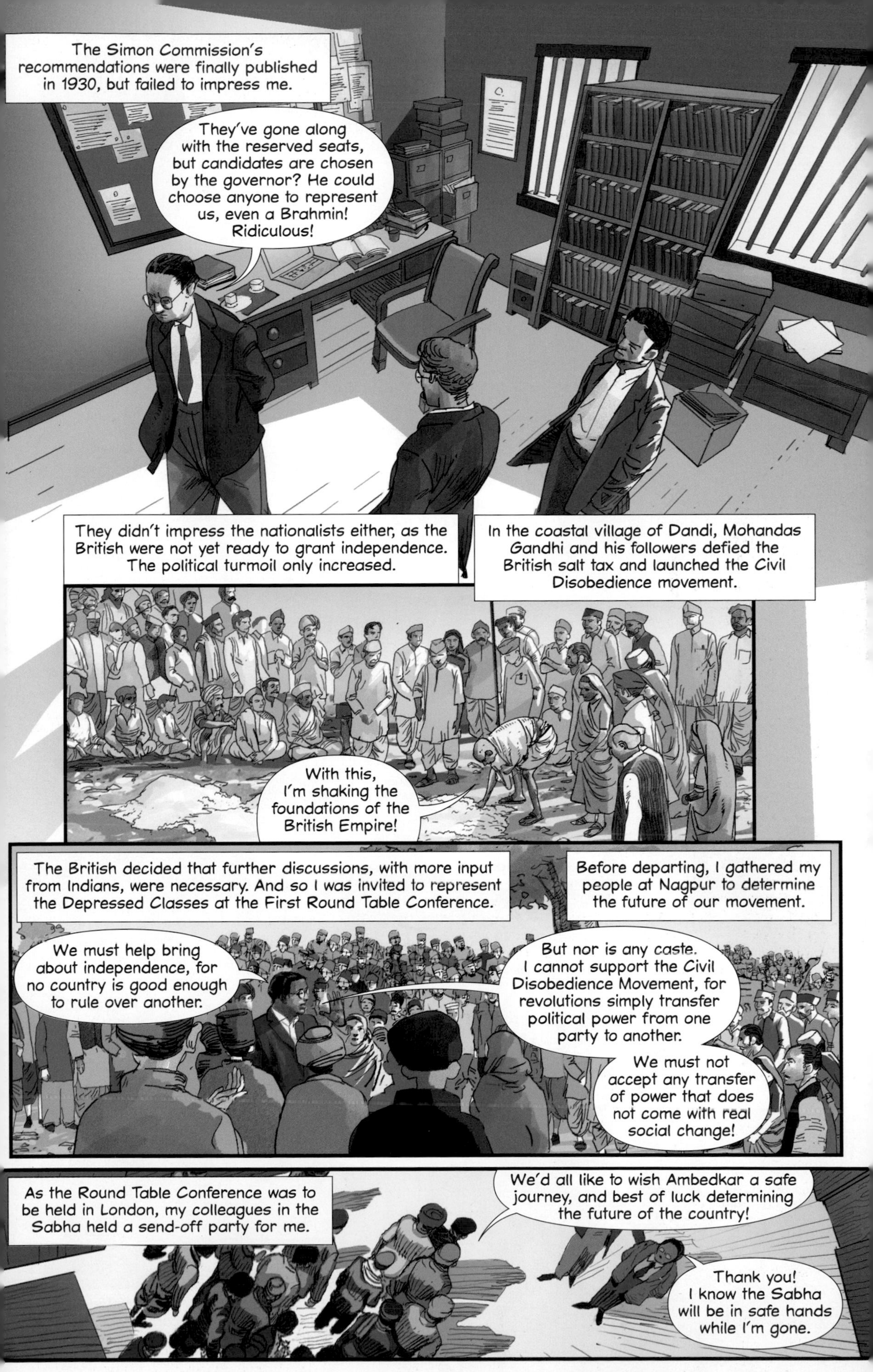
The Simon Commission's recommendations were finally published in 1930, but failed to impress me.
They've gone along with the reserved seats, but candidates are chosen by the governor? He could choose anyone to represent us, even a Brahmin! Ridiculous!
They didn't impress the nationalists either, as the British were not yet ready to grant independence. The political turmoil only increased.
In the coastal village of Dandi, Mohandas Gandhi and his followers defied the British salt tax and launched the Civil Disobedience movement.
With this, I'm shaking the foundations of the British Empire!
The British decided that further discussions, with more input from Indians, were necessary. And so I was invited to represent the Depressed Classes at the First Round Table Conference.
Before departing, I gathered my people at Nagpur to determine the future of our movement.
We must help bring about independence, for no country is good enough to rule over another.
But nor is any caste. I cannot support the Civil Disobedience Movement, for revolutions simply transfer political power from one party to another.
We must not accept any transfer of power that does not come with real social change!
As the Round Table Conference was to be held in London, my colleagues in the Sabha held a send-off party for me.
We'd all like to wish Ambedkar a safe journey, and best of luck determining the future of the country!
Thank you! I know the Sabha will be in safe hands while I'm gone.

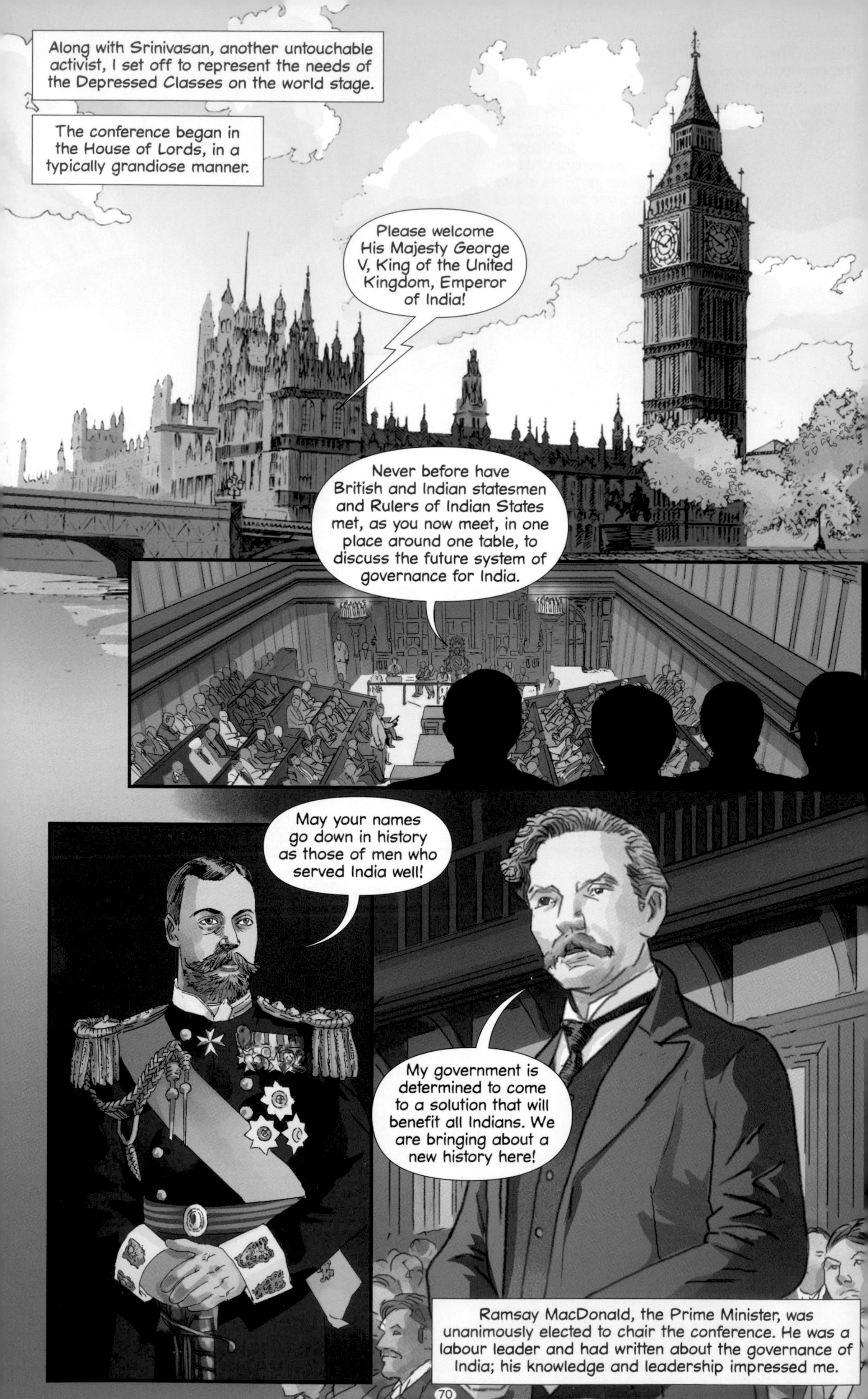

Along with Srinivasan, another untouchable activist, I set off to represent the needs of the Depressed Classes on the world stage.
The conference began in the House of Lords, in a typically grandiose manner.
Please welcome His Majesty George V, King of the United Kingdom, Emperor of India!
Never before have British and Indian statesmen and Rulers of Indian States met, as you now meet, in one place around one table, to discuss the future system of governance for India.
May your names go down in history as those of men who served India well!
My government is determined to come to a solution that will benefit all Indians. We are bringing about a new history here!
Ramsay MacDonald, the Prime Minister, was unanimously elected to chair the conference. He was a labour leader and had written about the governance of India; his knowledge and leadership impressed me.

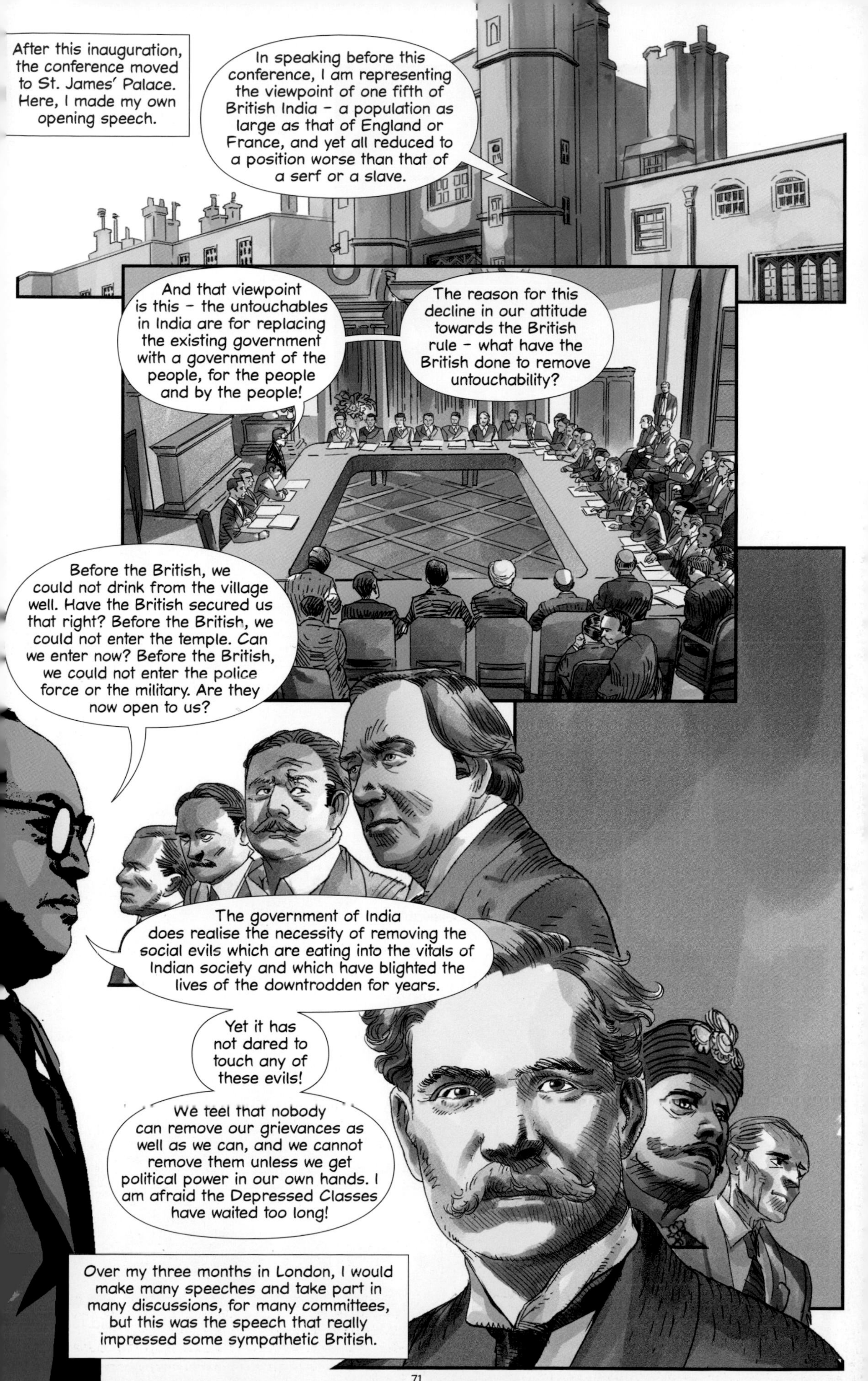
After this inauguration, the conference moved to St. James' Palace. Here, I made my own opening speech.
In speaking before this conference, I am representing the viewpoint of one fifth of British India – a population as large as that of England or France, and yet all reduced to a position worse than that of a serf or a slave.
And that viewpoint is this – the untouchables in India are for replacing the existing government with a government of the people, for the people and by the people!
The reason for this decline in our attitude towards the British rule – what have the British done to remove untouchability?
Before the British, we could not drink from the village well. Have the British secured us that right? Before the British, we could not enter the temple. Can we enter now? Before the British, we could not enter the police force or the military. Are they now open to us?
The government of India does realise the necessity of removing the social evils which are eating into the vitals of Indian society and which have blighted the lives of the downtrodden for years.
Yet it has not dared to touch any of these evils!
We feel that nobody can remove our grievances as well as we can, and we cannot remove them unless we get political power in our own hands. I am afraid the Depressed Classes have waited too long!
Over my three months in London, I would make many speeches and take part in many discussions, for many committees, but this was the speech that really impressed some sympathetic British.

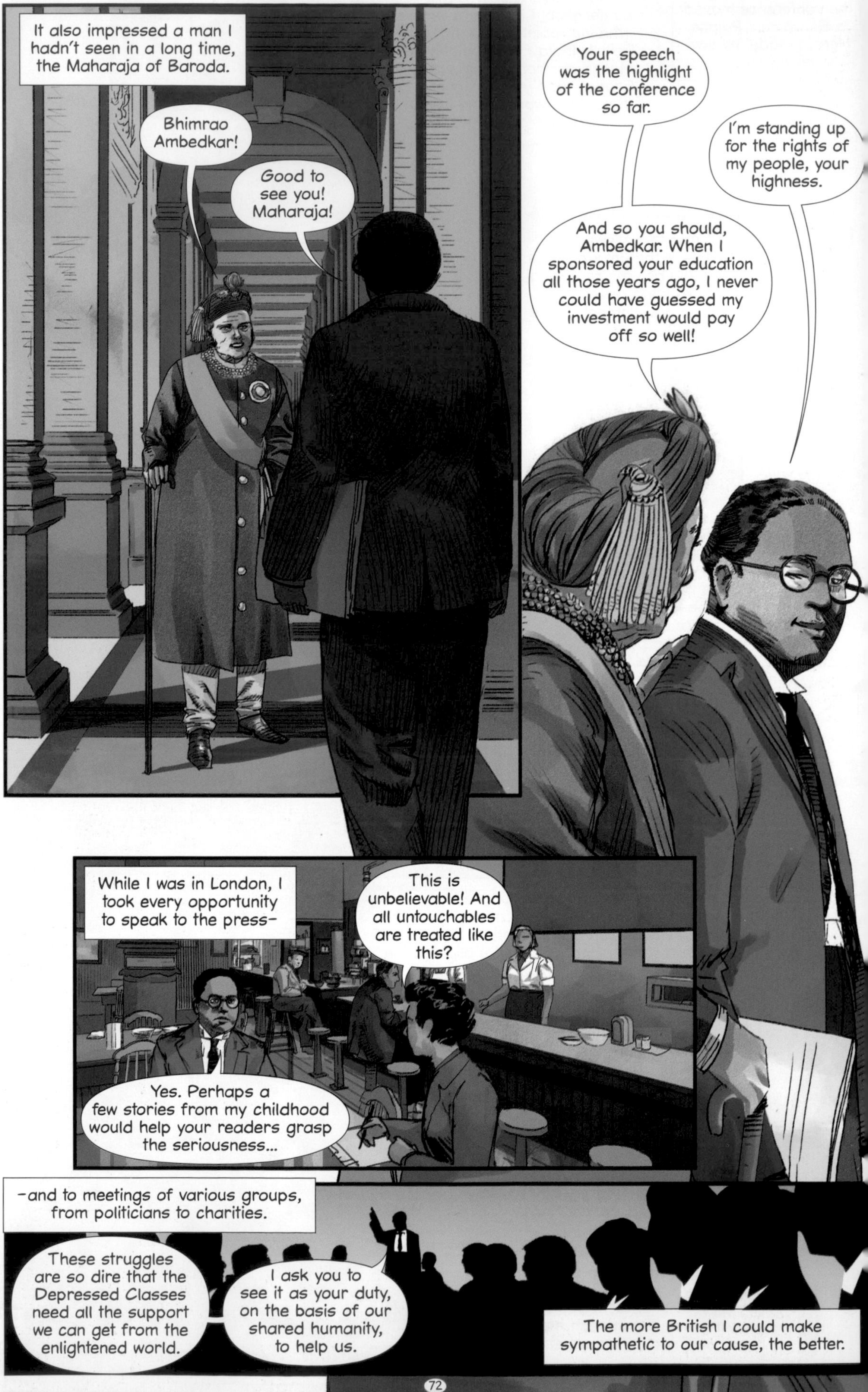
It also impressed a man I hadn't seen in a long time, the Maharaja of Baroda.
Bhimrao Ambedkar!
Good to see you! Maharaja!
Your speech was the highlight of the conference so far.
I'm standing up for the rights of my people, your highness.
And so you should, Ambedkar. When I sponsored your education all those years ago, I never could have guessed my investment would pay off so well!
While I was in London, I took every opportunity to speak to the press–
This is unbelievable! And all untouchables are treated like this?
Yes. Perhaps a few stories from my childhood would help your readers grasp the seriousness...
–and to meetings of various groups, from politicians to charities.
These struggles are so dire that the Depressed Classes need all the support we can get from the enlightened world.
I ask you to see it as your duty, on the basis of our shared humanity, to help us.
The more British I could make sympathetic to our cause, the better.

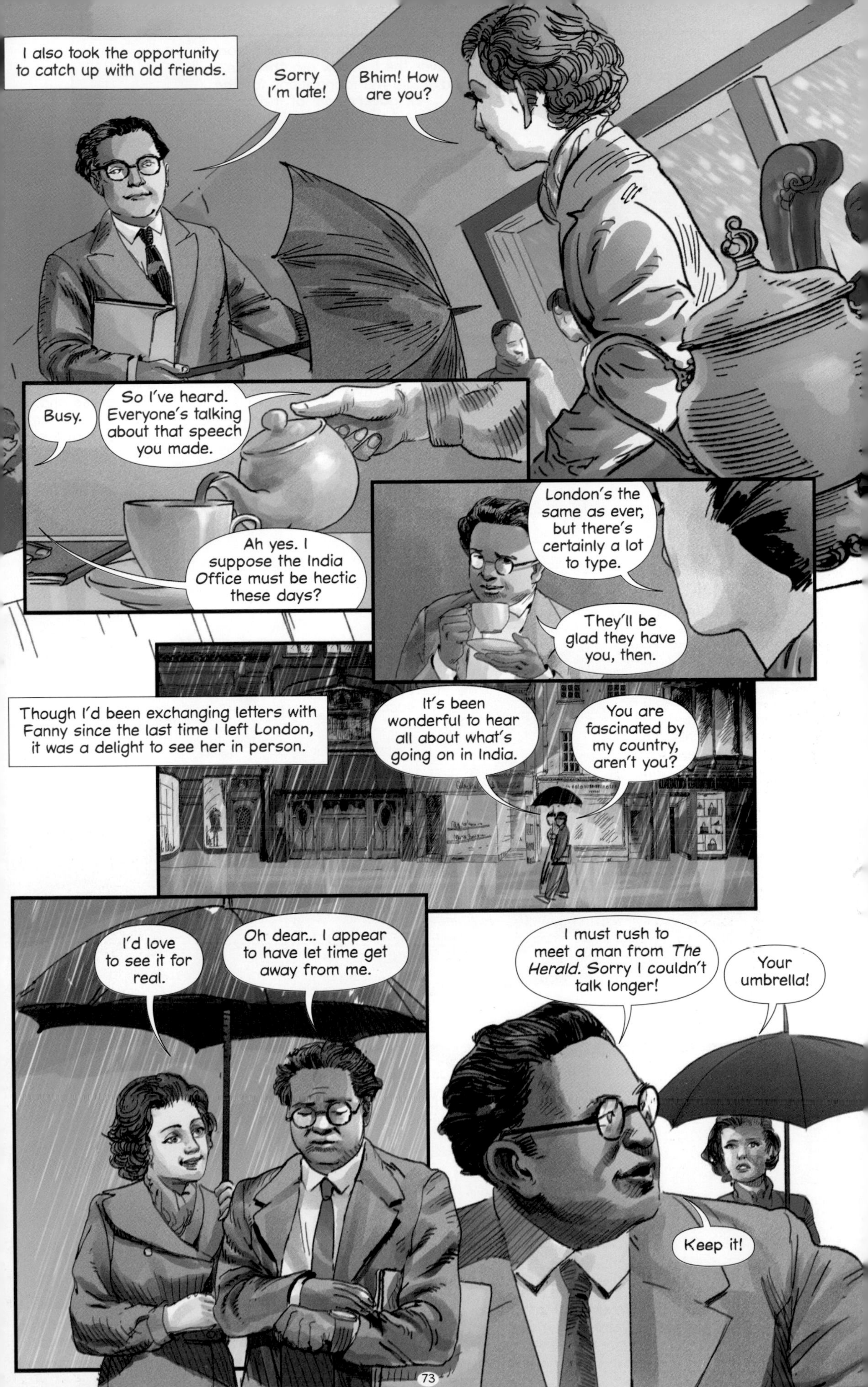

I also took the opportunity to catch up with old friends.
Sorry I'm late!
Bhim! How are you?
Busy.
So I've heard. Everyone's talking about that speech you made.
Ah yes. I suppose the India Office must be hectic these days?
London's the same as ever, but there's certainly a lot to type.
They'll be glad they have you, then.
Though I'd been exchanging letters with Fanny since the last time I left London, it was a delight to see her in person.
It's been wonderful to hear all about what's going on in India.
You are fascinated by my country, aren't you?
I'd love to see it for real.
Oh dear... I appear to have let time get away from me.
I must rush to meet a man from *The Herald*. Sorry I couldn't talk longer!
Your umbrella!
Keep it!

In January 1931, the conference was adjourned.

Thank you all for your hard work over the last few months. We have laid the foundations for the self-government of India!

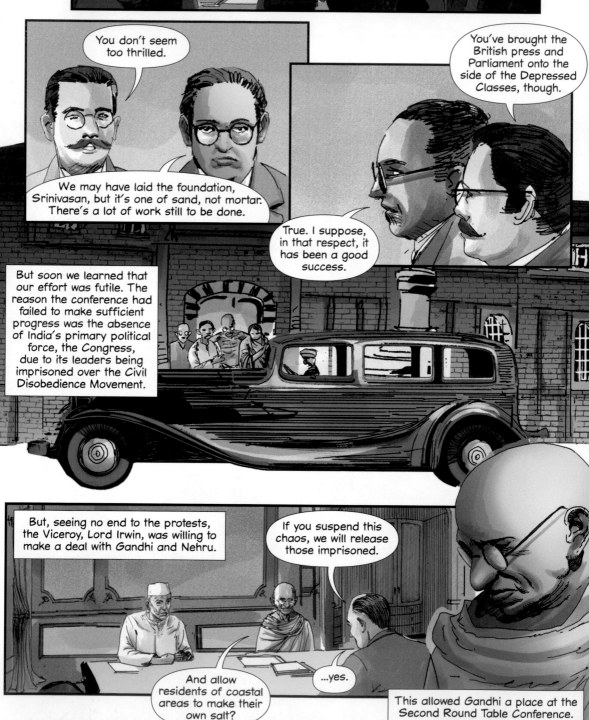

You don't seem too thrilled.

We may have laid the foundation, Srinivasan, but it's one of sand, not mortar. There's a lot of work still to be done.

You've brought the British press and Parliament onto the side of the Depressed Classes, though.

True. I suppose, in that respect, it has been a good success.

But soon we learned that our effort was futile. The reason the conference had failed to make sufficient progress was the absence of India's primary political force, the Congress, due to its leaders being imprisoned over the Civil Disobedience Movement.

But, seeing no end to the protests, the Viceroy, Lord Irwin, was willing to make a deal with Gandhi and Nehru.

If you suspend this chaos, we will release those imprisoned.

And allow residents of coastal areas to make their own salt?

...yes.

This allowed Gandhi a place at the Second Round Table Conference.

74

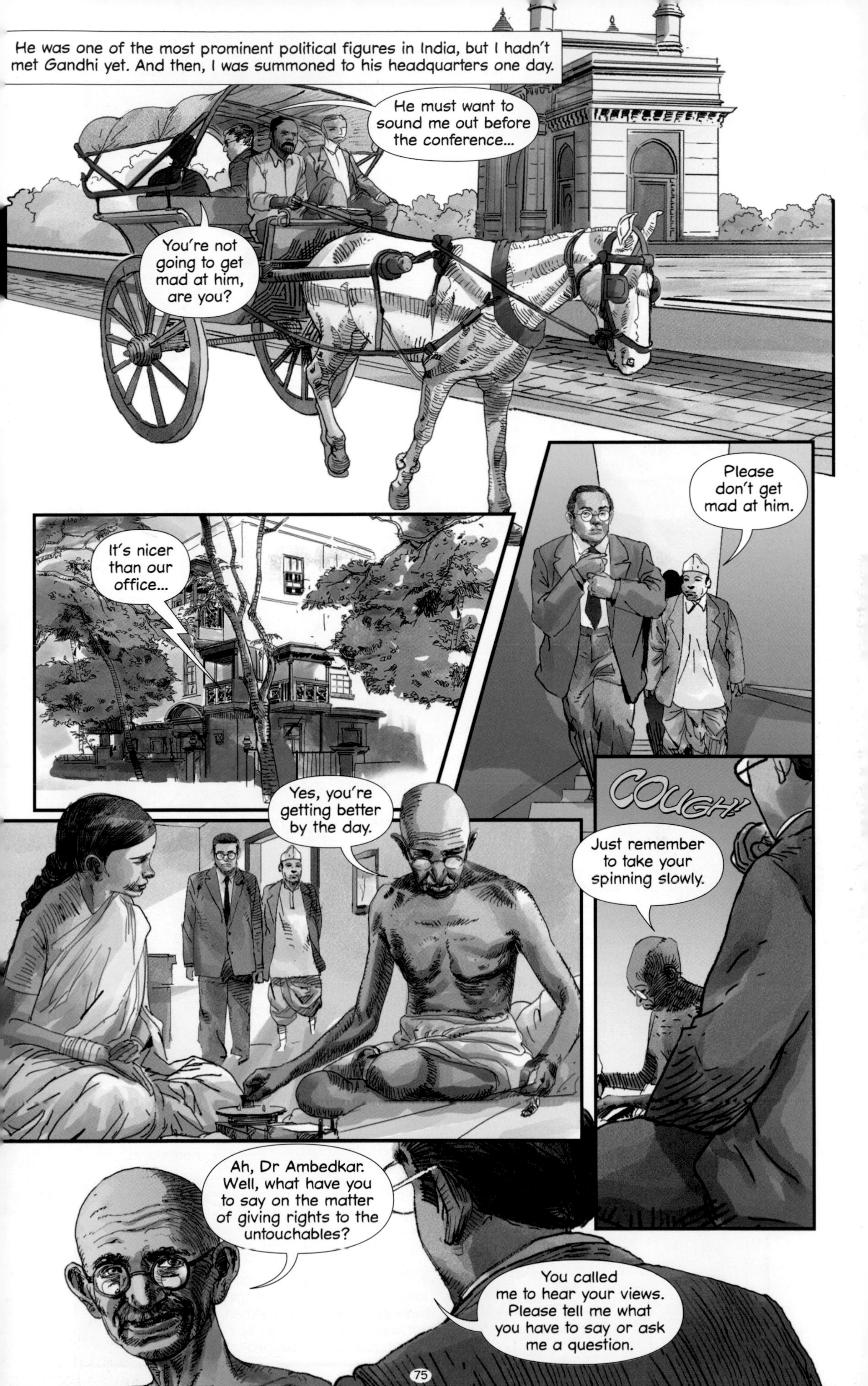
He was one of the most prominent political figures in India, but I hadn't met Gandhi yet. And then, I was summoned to his headquarters one day.
He must want to sound me out before the conference...
You're not going to get mad at him, are you?
It's nicer than our office...
Please don't get mad at him.
Yes, you're getting better by the day.
COUGH!
Just remember to take your spinning slowly.
Ah, Dr Ambedkar. Well, what have you to say on the matter of giving rights to the untouchables?
You called me to hear your views. Please tell me what you have to say or ask me a question.

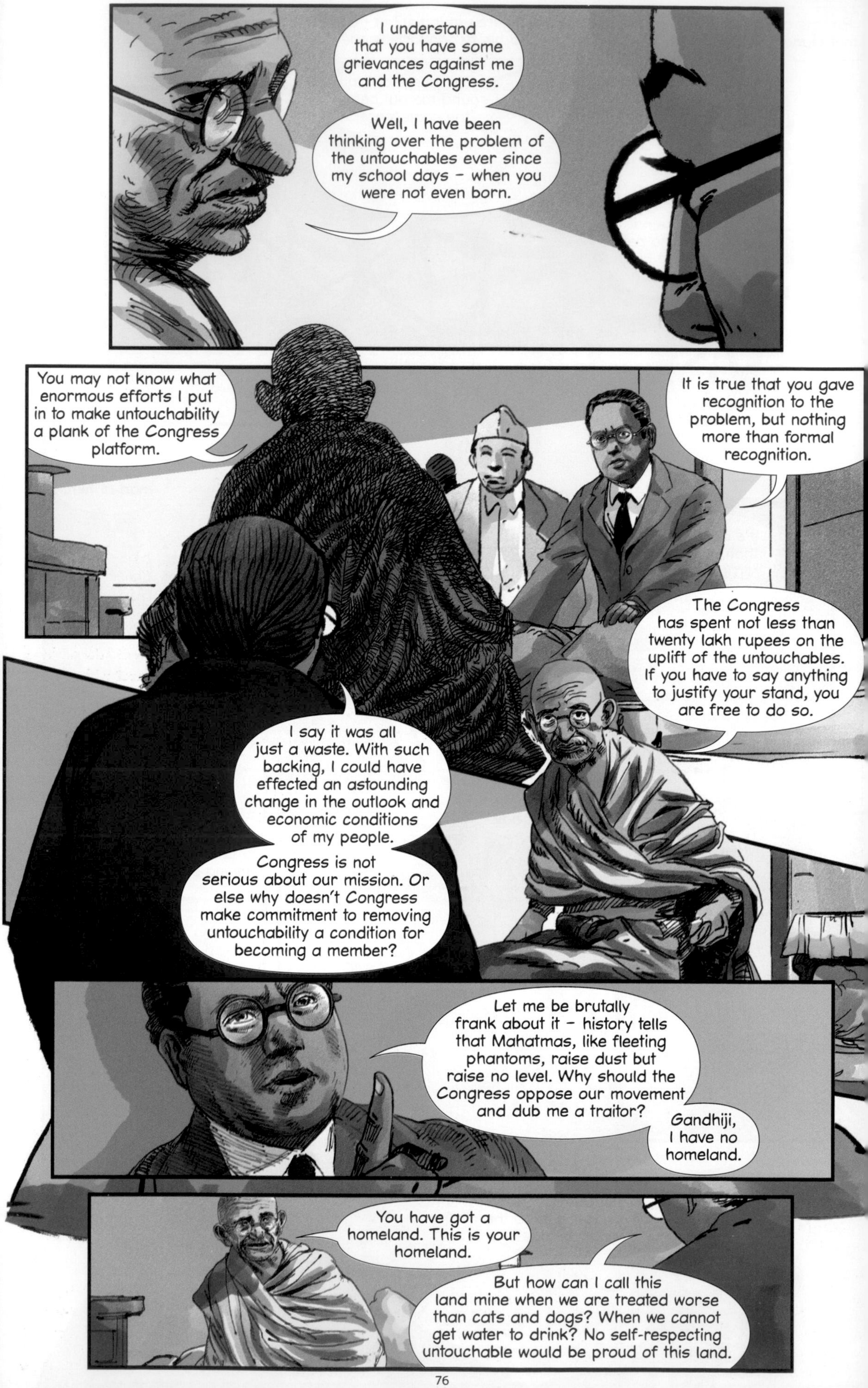
I understand that you have some grievances against me and the Congress.
Well, I have been thinking over the problem of the untouchables ever since my school days – when you were not even born.
You may not know what enormous efforts I put in to make untouchability a plank of the Congress platform.
It is true that you gave recognition to the problem, but nothing more than formal recognition.
The Congress has spent not less than twenty lakh rupees on the uplift of the untouchables. If you have to say anything to justify your stand, you are free to do so.
I say it was all just a waste. With such backing, I could have effected an astounding change in the outlook and economic conditions of my people.
Congress is not serious about our mission. Or else why doesn't Congress make commitment to removing untouchability a condition for becoming a member?
Let me be brutally frank about it – history tells that Mahatmas, like fleeting phantoms, raise dust but raise no level. Why should the Congress oppose our movement and dub me a traitor?
Gandhiji, I have no homeland.
You have got a homeland. This is your homeland.
But how can I call this land mine when we are treated worse than cats and dogs? When we cannot get water to drink? No self-respecting untouchable would be proud of this land.

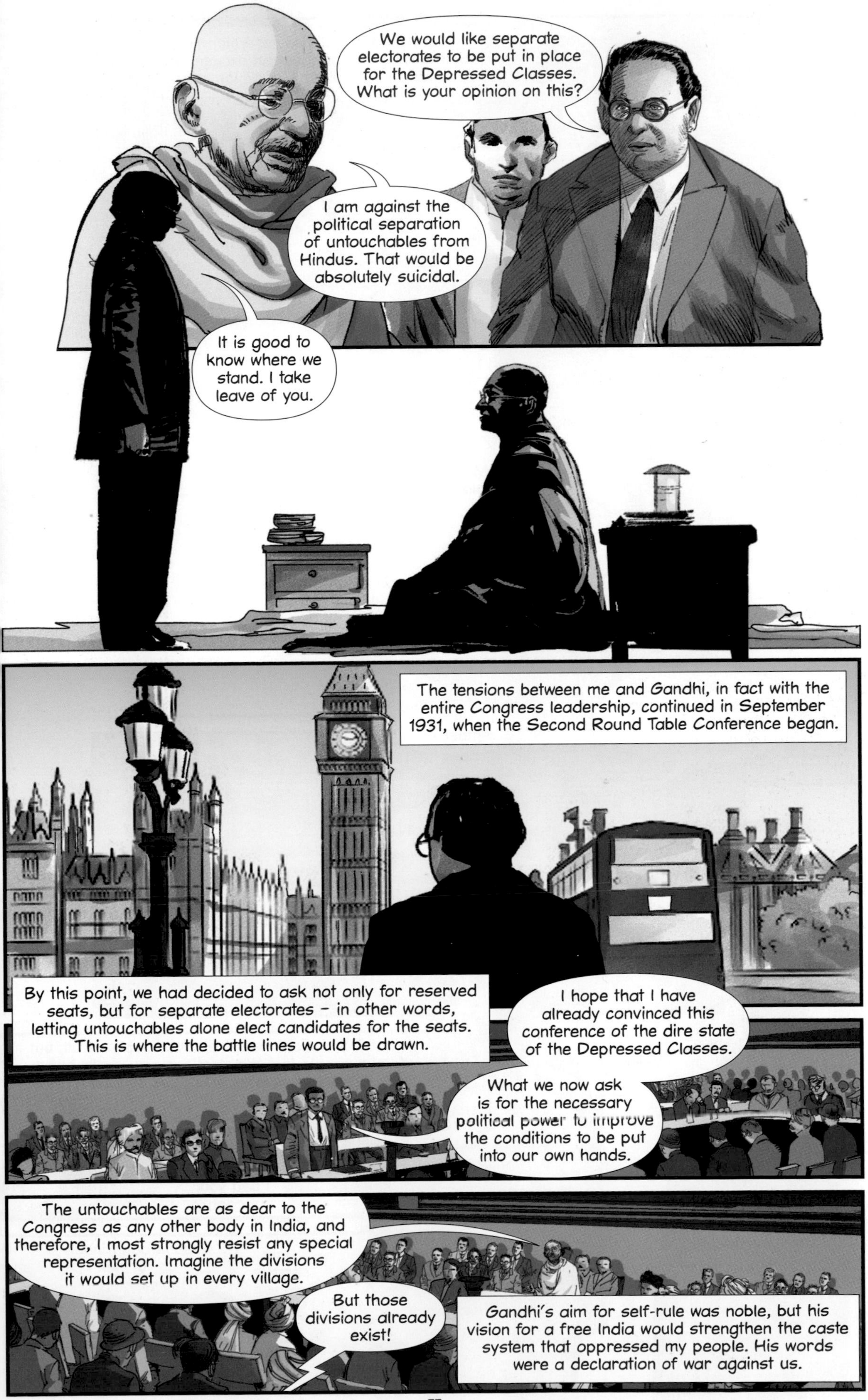

We would like separate electorates to be put in place for the Depressed Classes. What is your opinion on this?
I am against the political separation of untouchables from Hindus. That would be absolutely suicidal.
It is good to know where we stand. I take leave of you.
The tensions between me and Gandhi, in fact with the entire Congress leadership, continued in September 1931, when the Second Round Table Conference began.
By this point, we had decided to ask not only for reserved seats, but for separate electorates – in other words, letting untouchables alone elect candidates for the seats. This is where the battle lines would be drawn.
I hope that I have already convinced this conference of the dire state of the Depressed Classes.
What we now ask is for the necessary political power to improve the conditions to be put into our own hands.
The untouchables are as dear to the Congress as any other body in India, and therefore, I most strongly resist any special representation. Imagine the divisions it would set up in every village.
But those divisions already exist!
Gandhi's aim for self-rule was noble, but his vision for a free India would strengthen the caste system that oppressed my people. His words were a declaration of war against us.

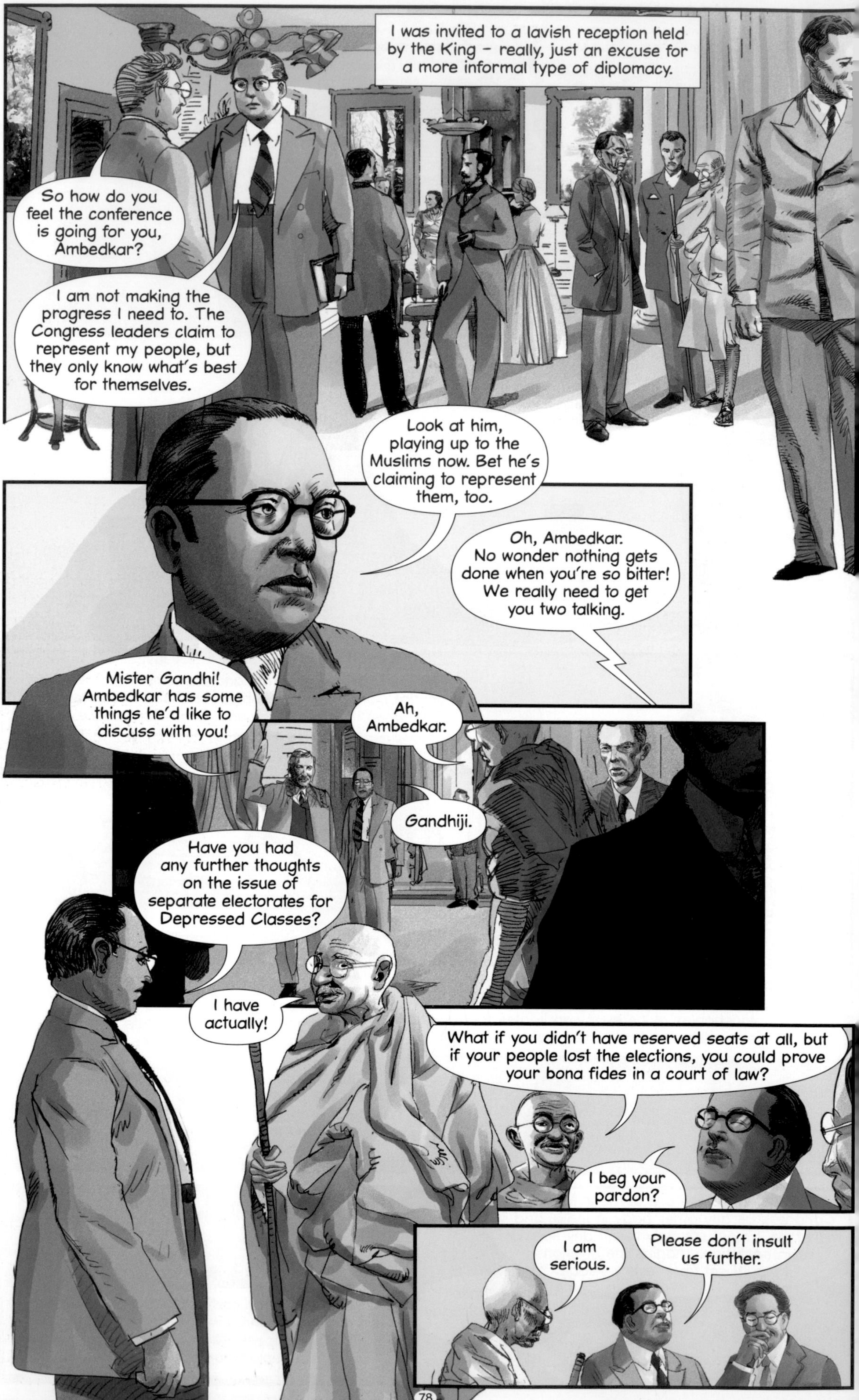
I was invited to a lavish reception held by the King – really, just an excuse for a more informal type of diplomacy.
So how do you feel the conference is going for you, Ambedkar?
I am not making the progress I need to. The Congress leaders claim to represent my people, but they only know what's best for themselves.
Look at him, playing up to the Muslims now. Bet he's claiming to represent them, too.
Oh, Ambedkar. No wonder nothing gets done when you're so bitter! We really need to get you two talking.
Mister Gandhi! Ambedkar has some things he'd like to discuss with you!
Ah, Ambedkar.
Gandhiji.
Have you had any further thoughts on the issue of separate electorates for Depressed Classes?
I have actually!
What if you didn't have reserved seats at all, but if your people lost the elections, you could prove your bona fides in a court of law?
I beg your pardon?
I am serious.
Please don't insult us further.

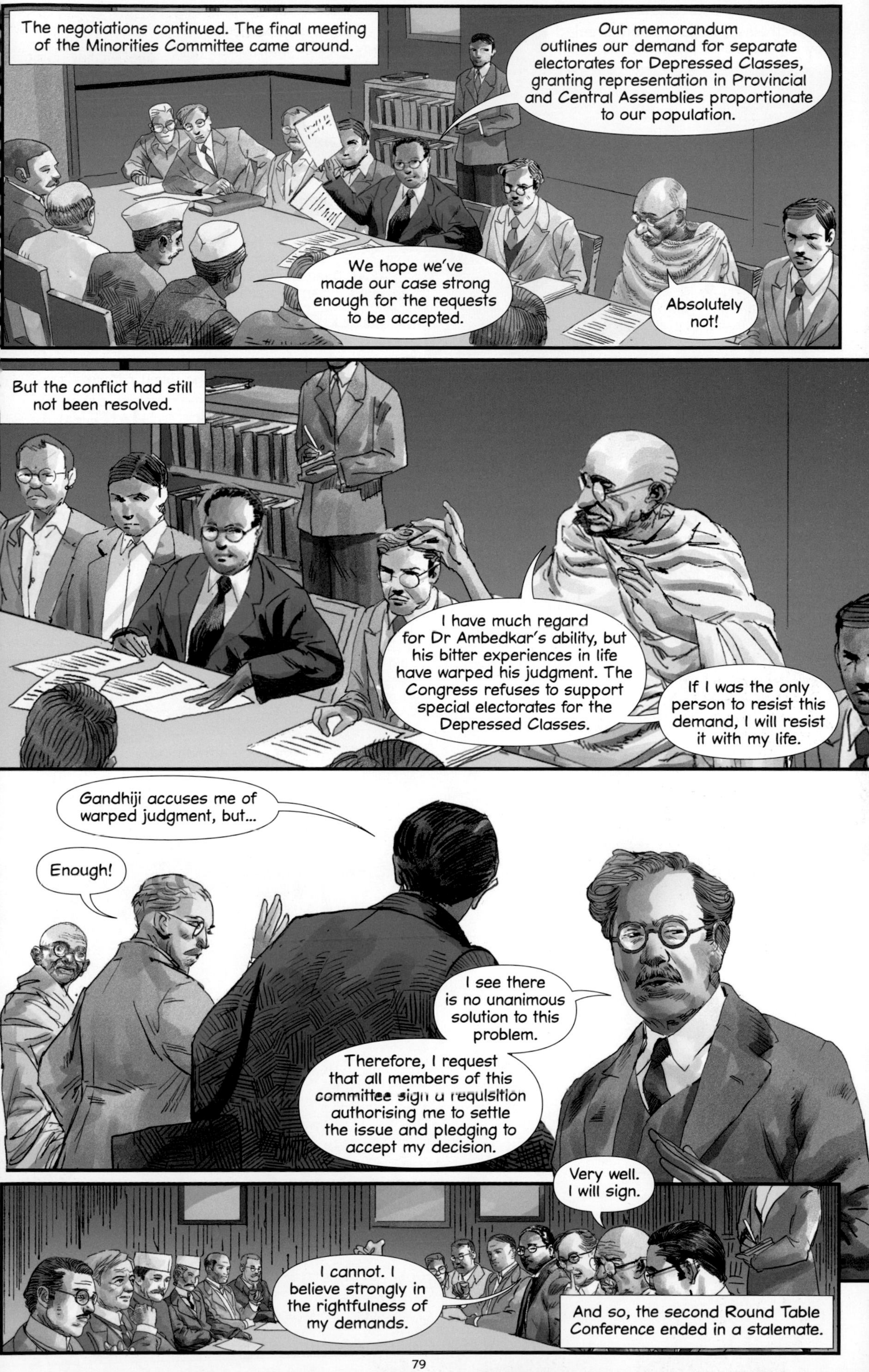

The negotiations continued. The final meeting of the Minorities Committee came around.
Our memorandum outlines our demand for separate electorates for Depressed Classes, granting representation in Provincial and Central Assemblies proportionate to our population.
We hope we've made our case strong enough for the requests to be accepted.
Absolutely not!
But the conflict had still not been resolved.
I have much regard for Dr Ambedkar's ability, but his bitter experiences in life have warped his judgment. The Congress refuses to support special electorates for the Depressed Classes.
If I was the only person to resist this demand, I will resist it with my life.
Gandhiji accuses me of warped judgment, but...
Enough!
I see there is no unanimous solution to this problem.
Therefore, I request that all members of this committee sign a requisition authorising me to settle the issue and pledging to accept my decision.
Very well. I will sign.
I cannot. I believe strongly in the rightfulness of my demands.
And so, the second Round Table Conference ended in a stalemate.

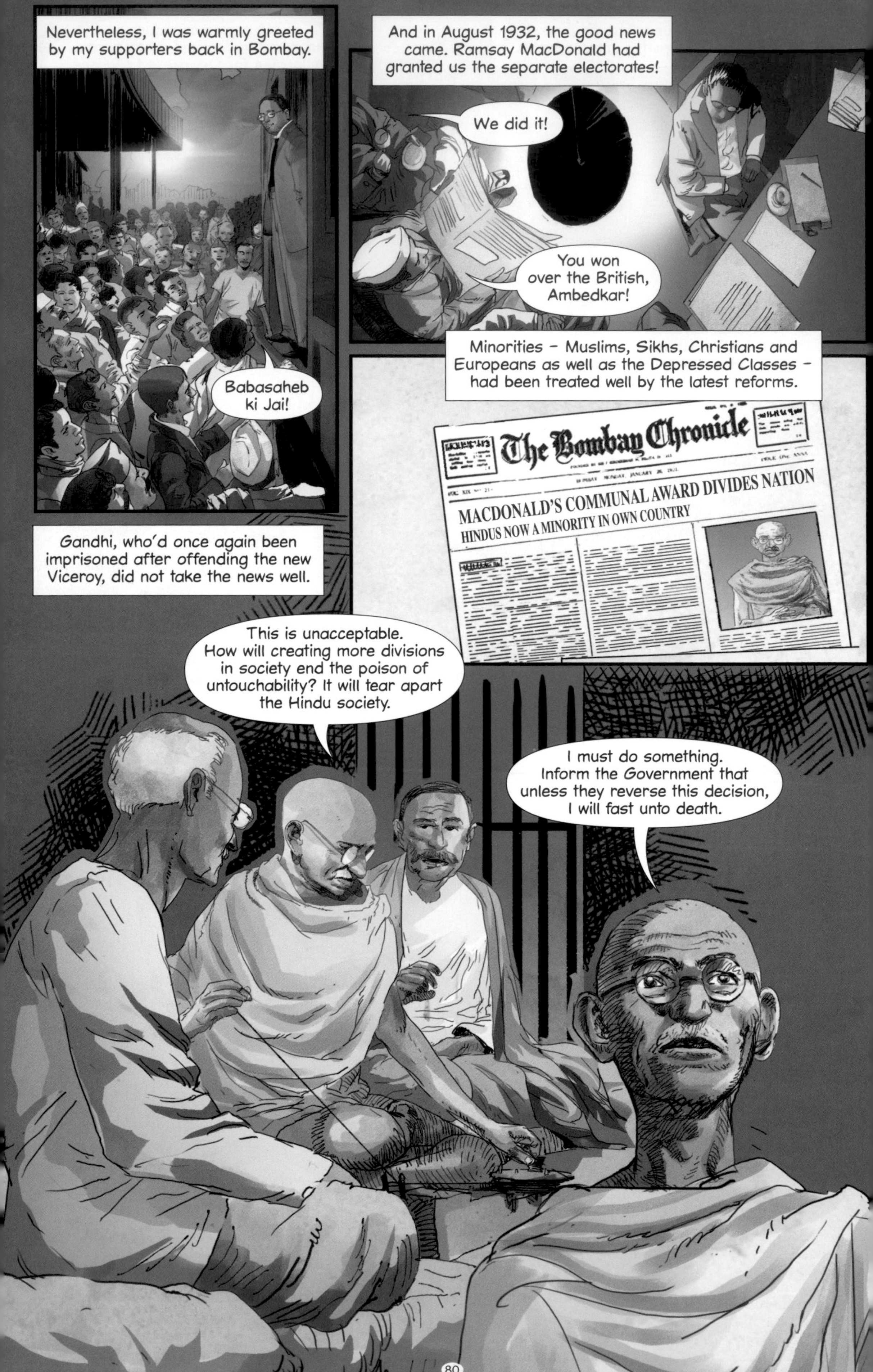

Nevertheless, I was warmly greeted by my supporters back in Bombay.
Babasaheb ki Jai!
And in August 1932, the good news came. Ramsay MacDonald had granted us the separate electorates!
We did it!
You won over the British, Ambedkar!
Minorities – Muslims, Sikhs, Christians and Europeans as well as the Depressed Classes – had been treated well by the latest reforms.
The Bombay Chronicle
MACDONALD'S COMMUNAL AWARD DIVIDES NATION
HINDUS NOW A MINORITY IN OWN COUNTRY
Gandhi, who'd once again been imprisoned after offending the new Viceroy, did not take the news well.
This is unacceptable. How will creating more divisions in society end the poison of untouchability? It will tear apart the Hindu society.
I must do something. Inform the Government that unless they reverse this decision, I will fast unto death.

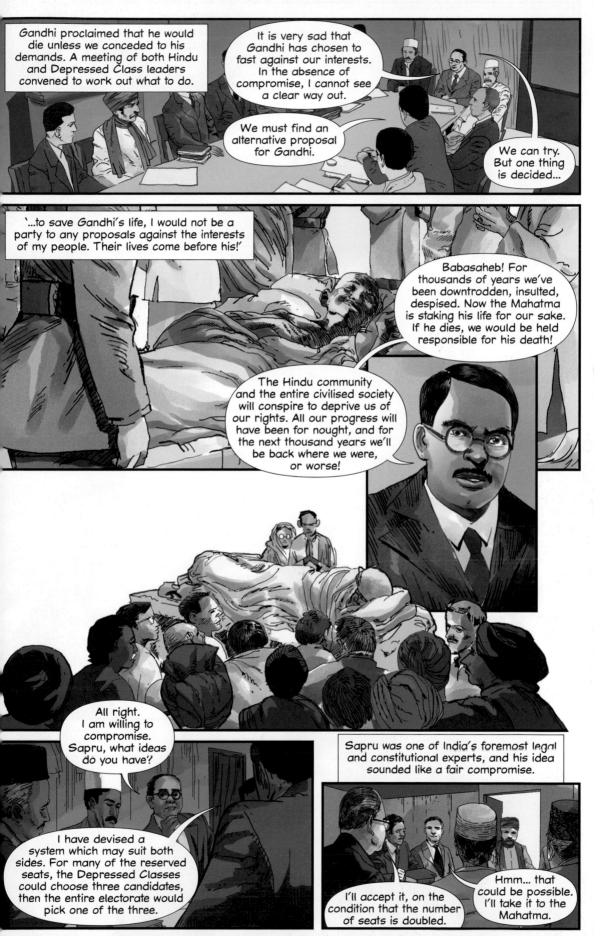

Gandhi proclaimed that he would die unless we conceded to his demands. A meeting of both Hindu and Depressed Class leaders convened to work out what to do.

It is very sad that Gandhi has chosen to fast against our interests. In the absence of compromise, I cannot see a clear way out.

We must find an alternative proposal for Gandhi.

We can try. But one thing is decided...

'...to save Gandhi's life, I would not be a party to any proposals against the interests of my people. Their lives come before his!'

Babasaheb! For thousands of years we've been downtrodden, insulted, despised. Now the Mahatma is staking his life for our sake. If he dies, we would be held responsible for his death!

The Hindu community and the entire civilised society will conspire to deprive us of our rights. All our progress will have been for nought, and for the next thousand years we'll be back where we were, or worse!

All right. I am willing to compromise. Sapru, what ideas do you have?

Sapru was one of India's foremost legal and constitutional experts, and his idea sounded like a fair compromise.

I have devised a system which may suit both sides. For many of the reserved seats, the Depressed Classes could choose three candidates, then the entire electorate would pick one of the three.

I'll accept it, on the condition that the number of seats is doubled.

Hmm... that could be possible. I'll take it to the Mahatma.

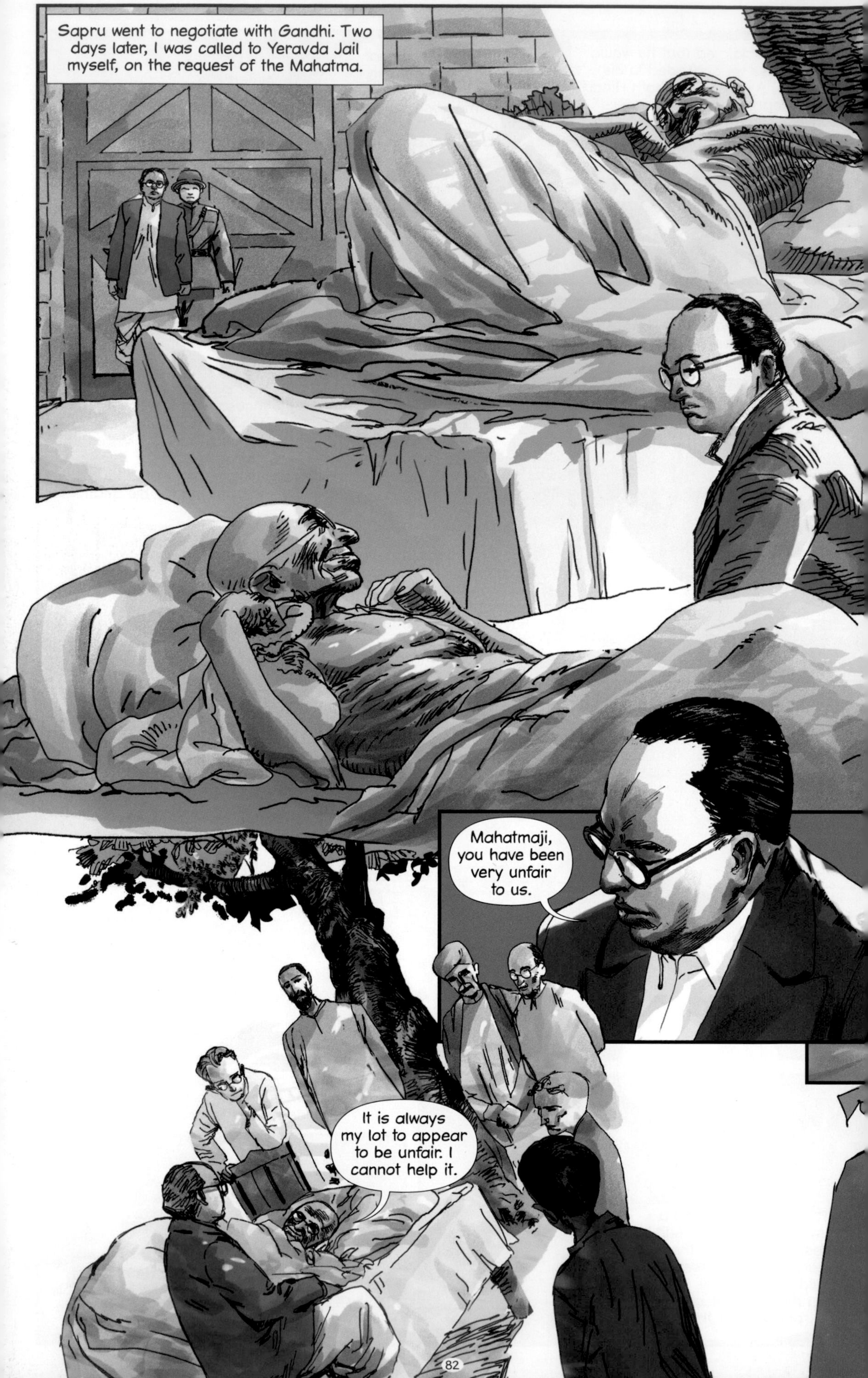
Sapru went to negotiate with Gandhi. Two days later, I was called to Yeravda Jail myself, on the request of the Mahatma.
Mahatmaji, you have been very unfair to us.
It is always my lot to appear to be unfair. I cannot help it.

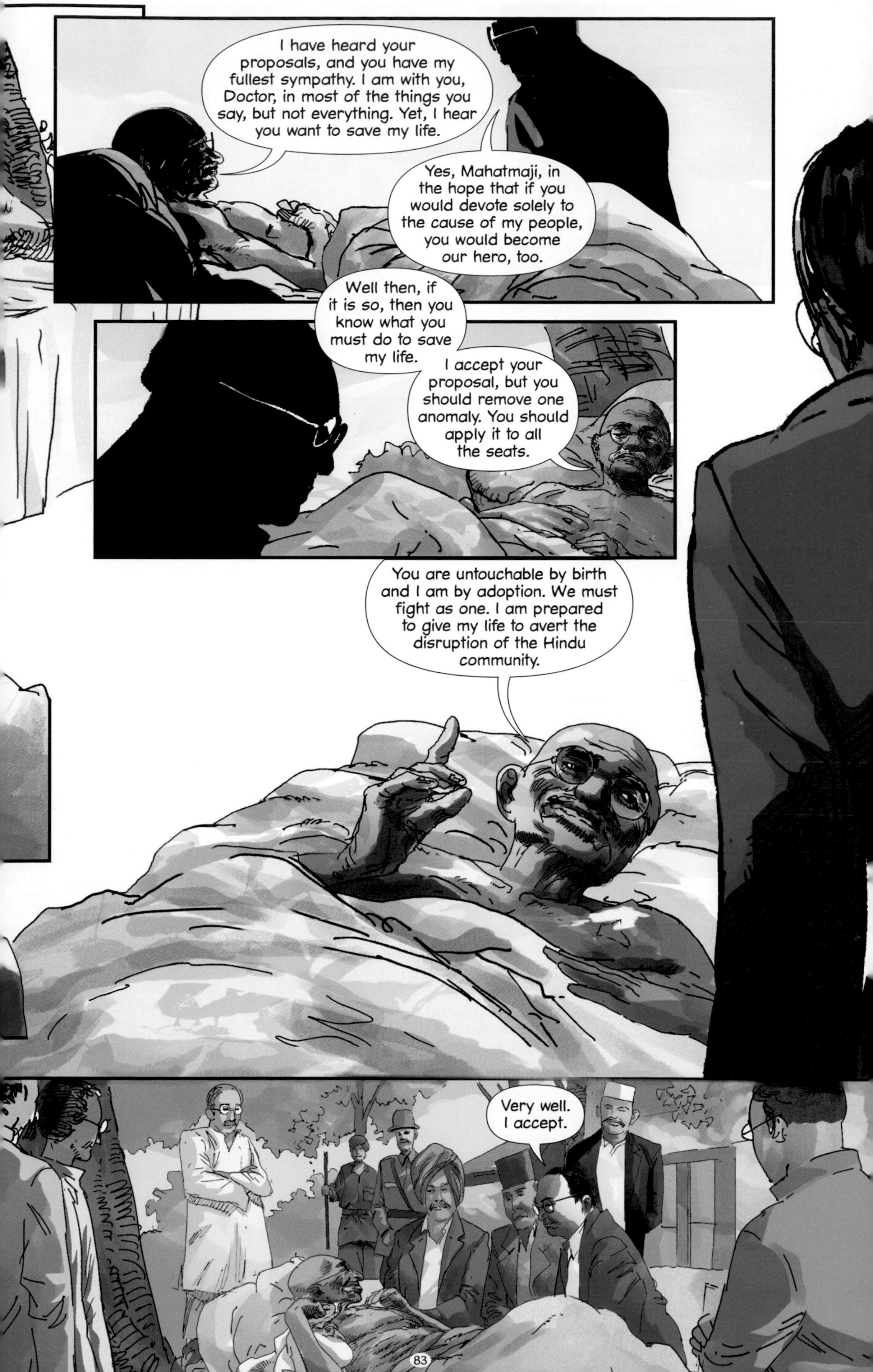
I have heard your proposals, and you have my fullest sympathy. I am with you, Doctor, in most of the things you say, but not everything. Yet, I hear you want to save my life.
Yes, Mahatmaji, in the hope that if you would devote solely to the cause of my people, you would become our hero, too.
Well then, if it is so, then you know what you must do to save my life.
I accept your proposal, but you should remove one anomaly. You should apply it to all the seats.
You are untouchable by birth and I am by adoption. We must fight as one. I am prepared to give my life to avert the disruption of the Hindu community.
Very well. I accept.

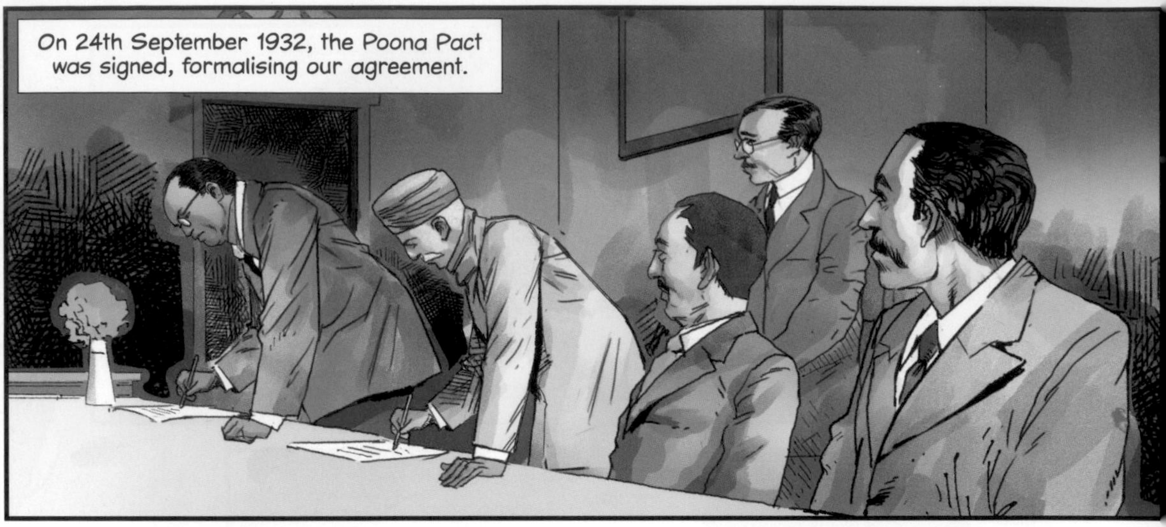
On 24th September 1932, the Poona Pact was signed, formalising our agreement.

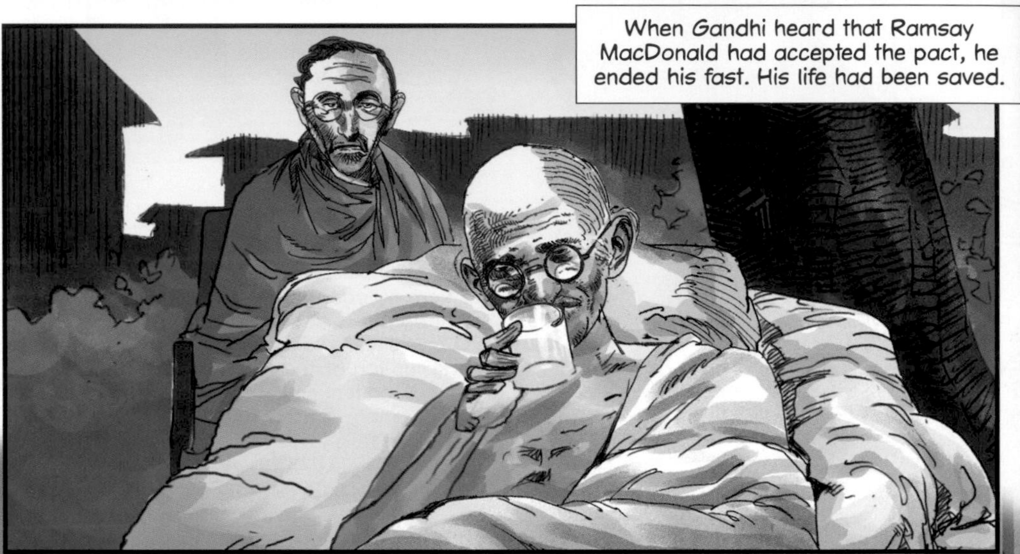
When Gandhi heard that Ramsay MacDonald had accepted the pact, he ended his fast. His life had been saved.

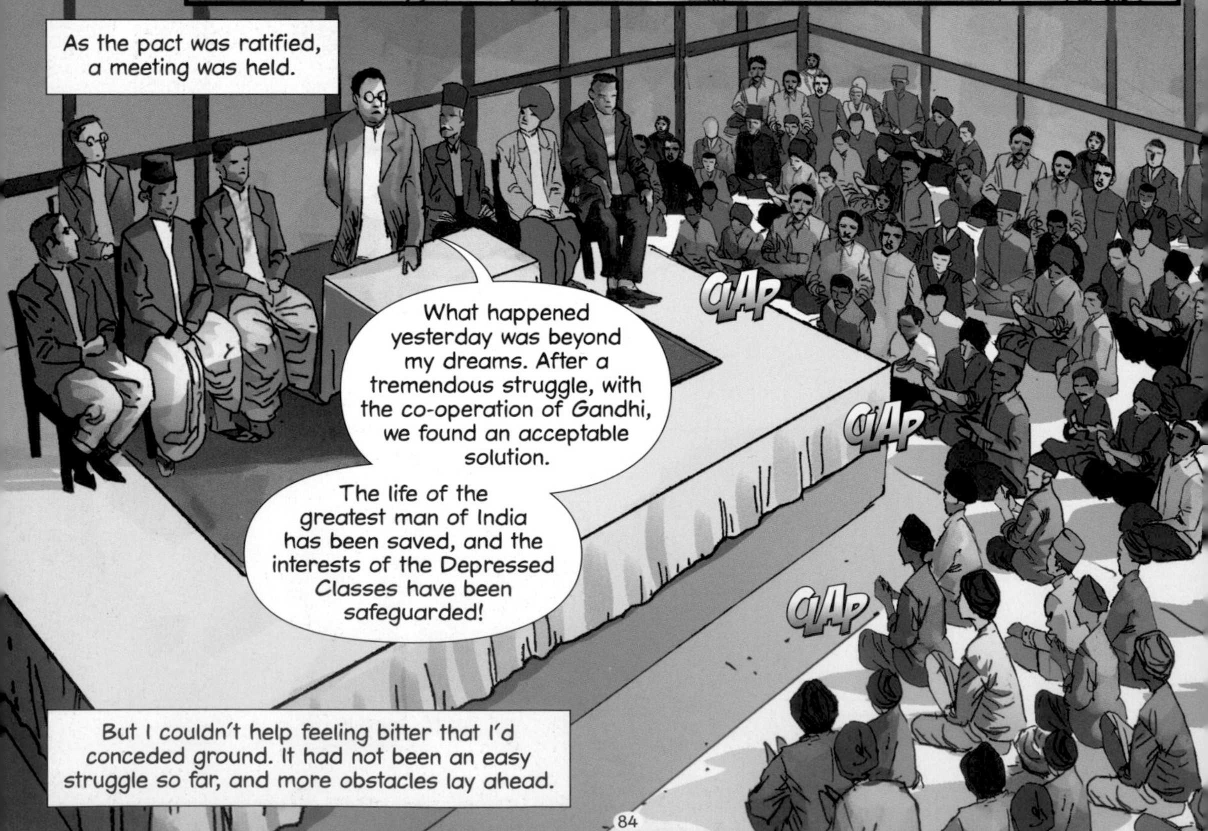
As the pact was ratified, a meeting was held.
What happened yesterday was beyond my dreams. After a tremendous struggle, with the co-operation of Gandhi, we found an acceptable solution.
The life of the greatest man of India has been saved, and the interests of the Depressed Classes have been safeguarded!
CLAP
CLAP
CLAP
But I couldn't help feeling bitter that I'd conceded ground. It had not been an easy struggle so far, and more obstacles lay ahead.

5 I WILL NOT DIE A HINDU

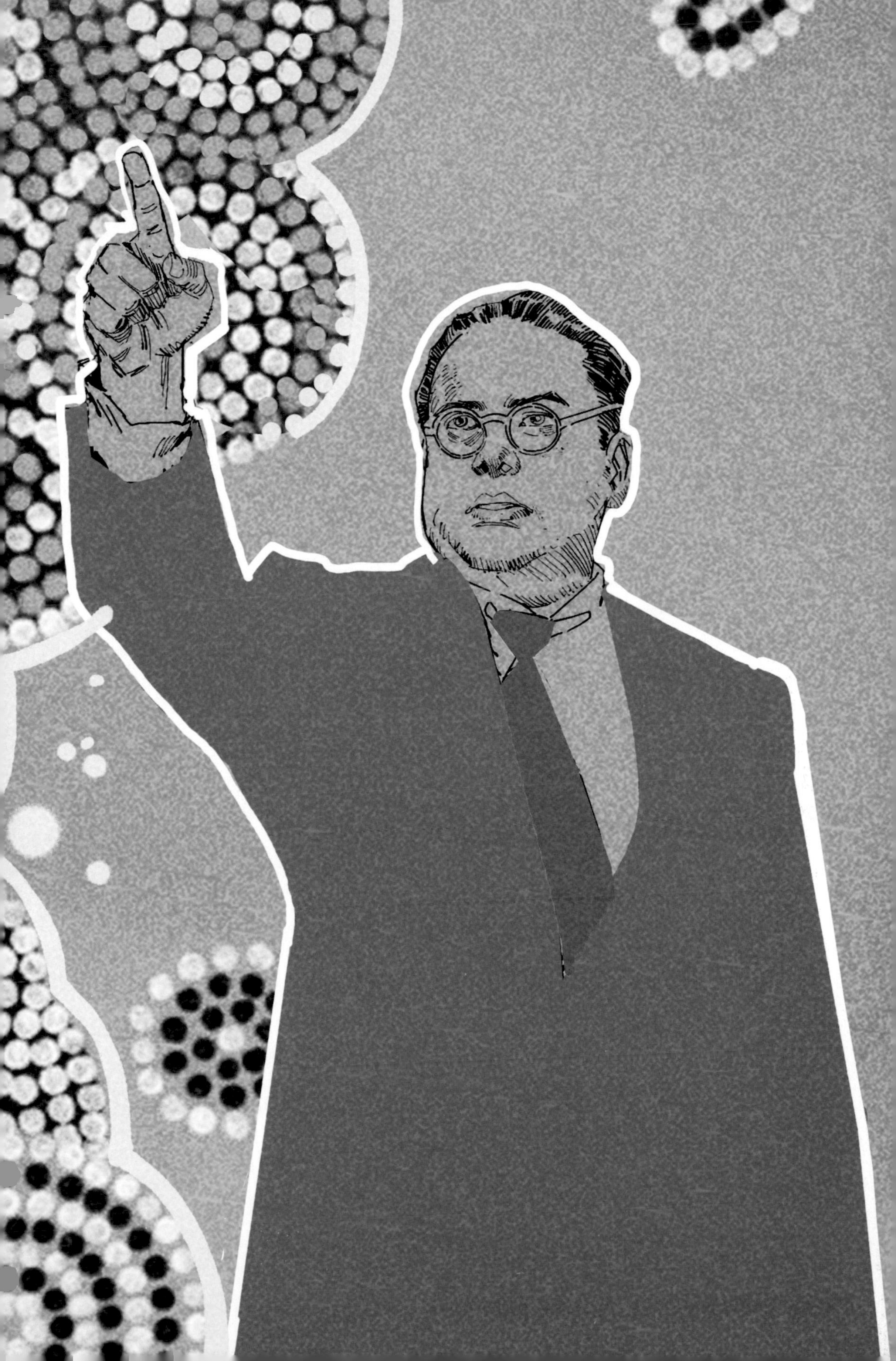

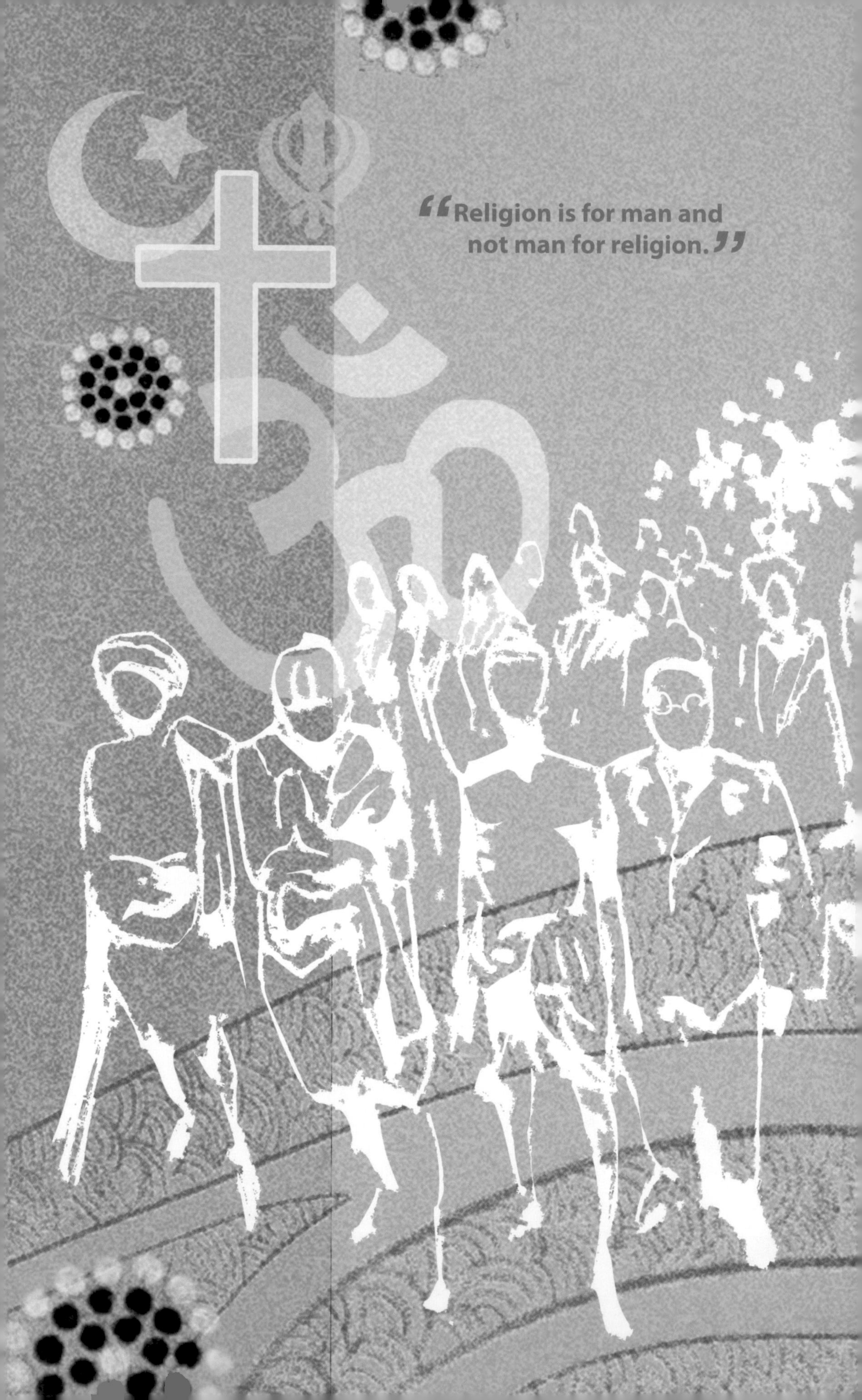
"Religion is for man and
not man for religion."

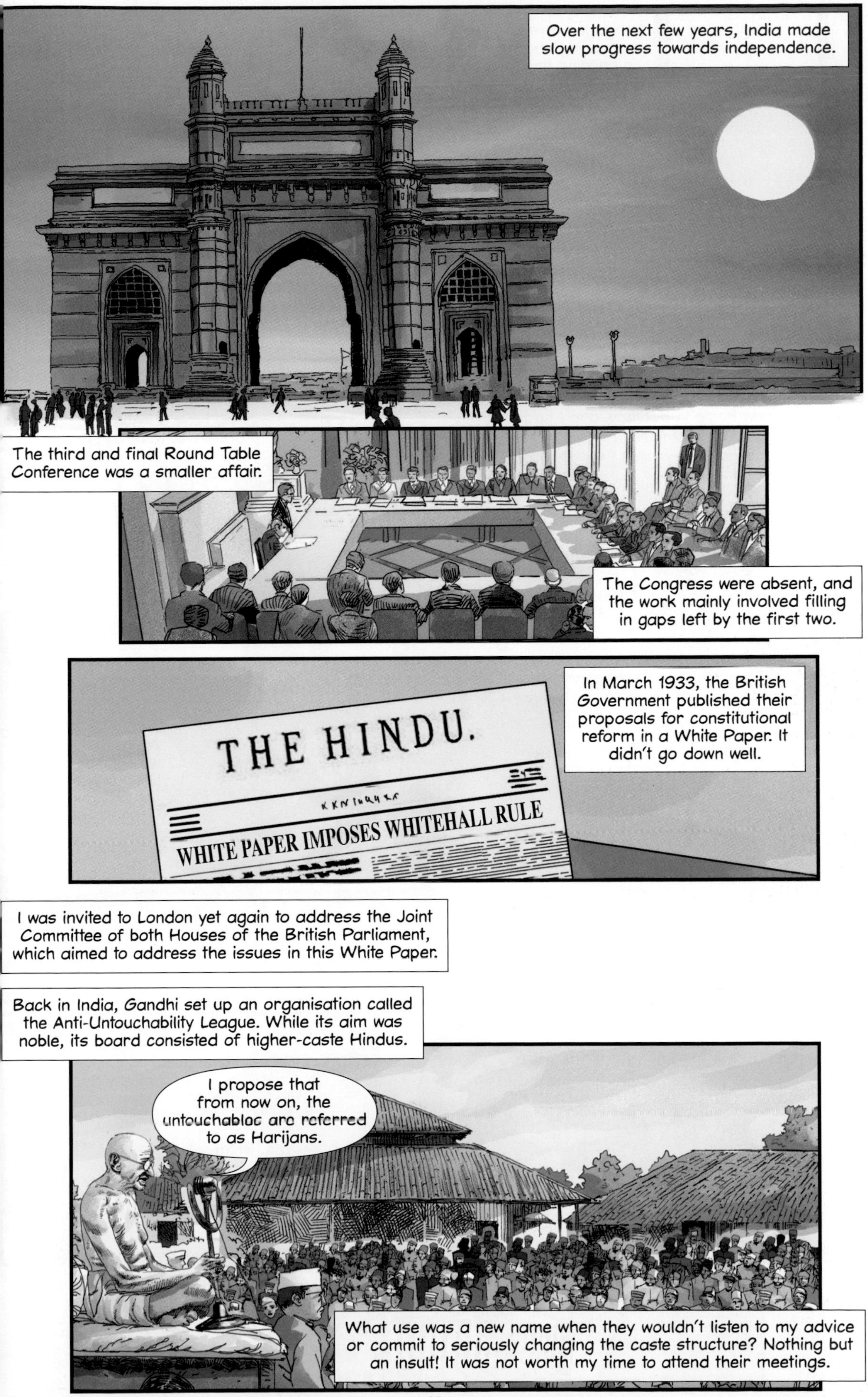

Over the next few years, India made slow progress towards independence.
The third and final Round Table Conference was a smaller affair.
The Congress were absent, and the work mainly involved filling in gaps left by the first two.
THE HINDU.
WHITE PAPER IMPOSES WHITEHALL RULE
In March 1933, the British Government published their proposals for constitutional reform in a White Paper. It didn't go down well.
I was invited to London yet again to address the Joint Committee of both Houses of the British Parliament, which aimed to address the issues in this White Paper.
Back in India, Gandhi set up an organisation called the Anti-Untouchability League. While its aim was noble, its board consisted of higher-caste Hindus.
I propose that from now on, the untouchables are referred to as Harijans.
What use was a new name when they wouldn't listen to my advice or commit to seriously changing the caste structure? Nothing but an insult! It was not worth my time to attend their meetings.

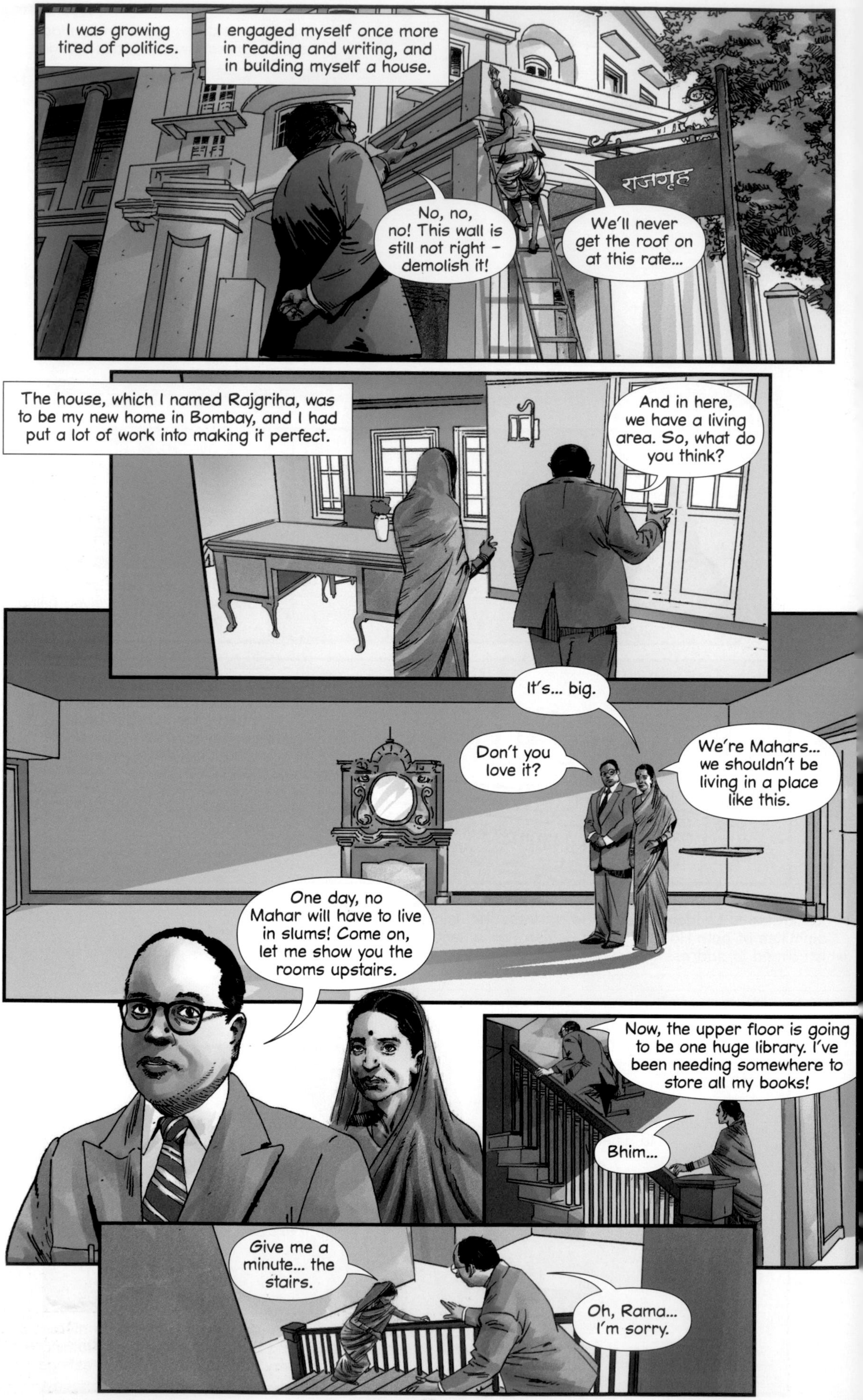

I was growing tired of politics.
I engaged myself once more in reading and writing, and in building myself a house.
राजगृह
No, no, no! This wall is still not right – demolish it!
We'll never get the roof on at this rate...
The house, which I named Rajgriha, was to be my new home in Bombay, and I had put a lot of work into making it perfect.
And in here, we have a living area. So, what do you think?
It's... big.
Don't you love it?
We're Mahars... we shouldn't be living in a place like this.
One day, no Mahar will have to live in slums! Come on, let me show you the rooms upstairs.
Now, the upper floor is going to be one huge library. I've been needing somewhere to store all my books!
Bhim...
Give me a minute... the stairs.
Oh, Rama... I'm sorry.

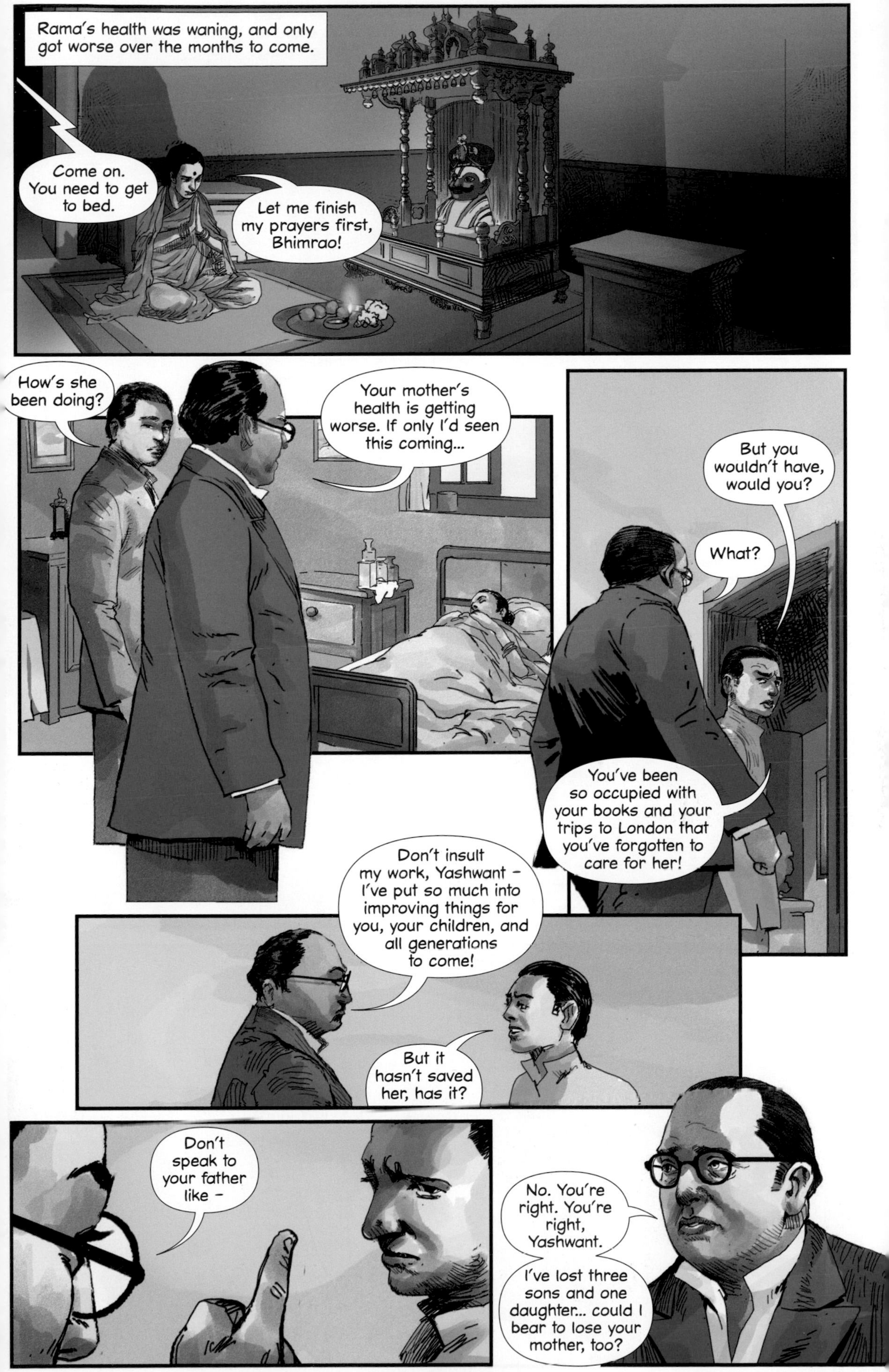

Rama's health was waning, and only got worse over the months to come.
Come on. You need to get to bed.
Let me finish my prayers first, Bhimrao!
How's she been doing?
Your mother's health is getting worse. If only I'd seen this coming...
But you wouldn't have, would you?
What?
You've been so occupied with your books and your trips to London that you've forgotten to care for her!
Don't insult my work, Yashwant – I've put so much into improving things for you, your children, and all generations to come!
But it hasn't saved her, has it?
Don't speak to your father like –
No. You're right. You're right, Yashwant.
I've lost three sons and one daughter... could I bear to lose your mother, too?

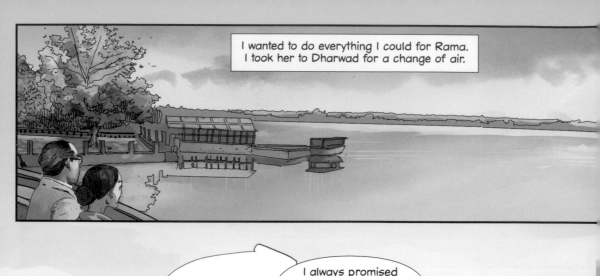

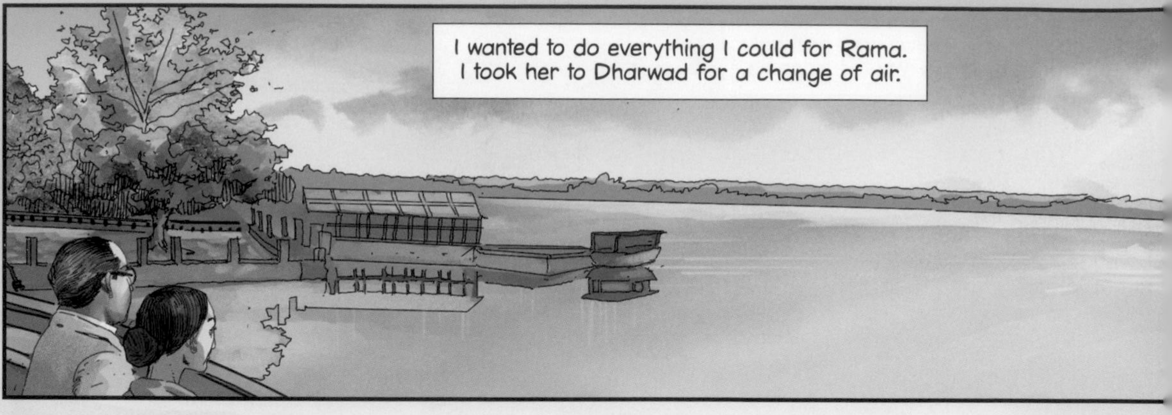
I wanted to do everything I could for Rama. I took her to Dharwad for a change of air.

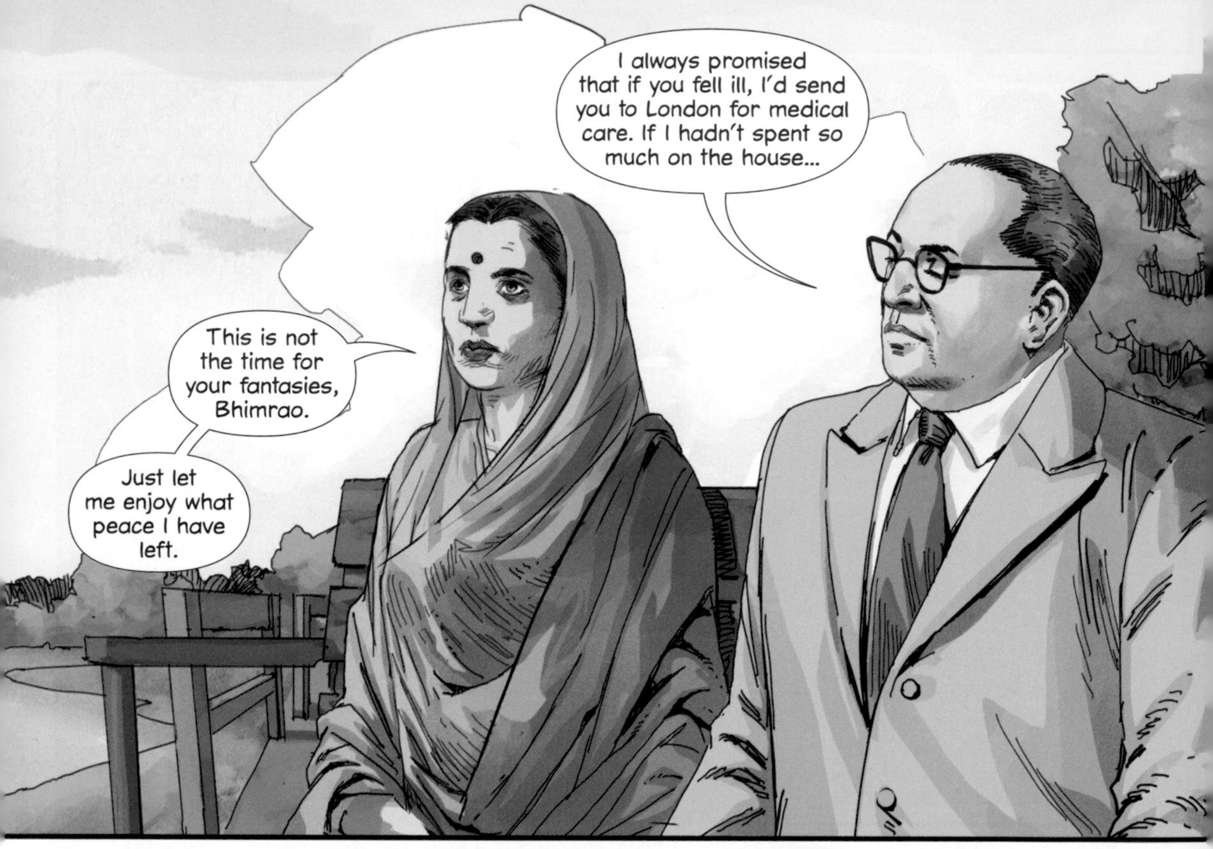
I always promised that if you fell ill, I'd send you to London for medical care. If I hadn't spent so much on the house...
This is not the time for your fantasies, Bhimrao.
Just let me enjoy what peace I have left.

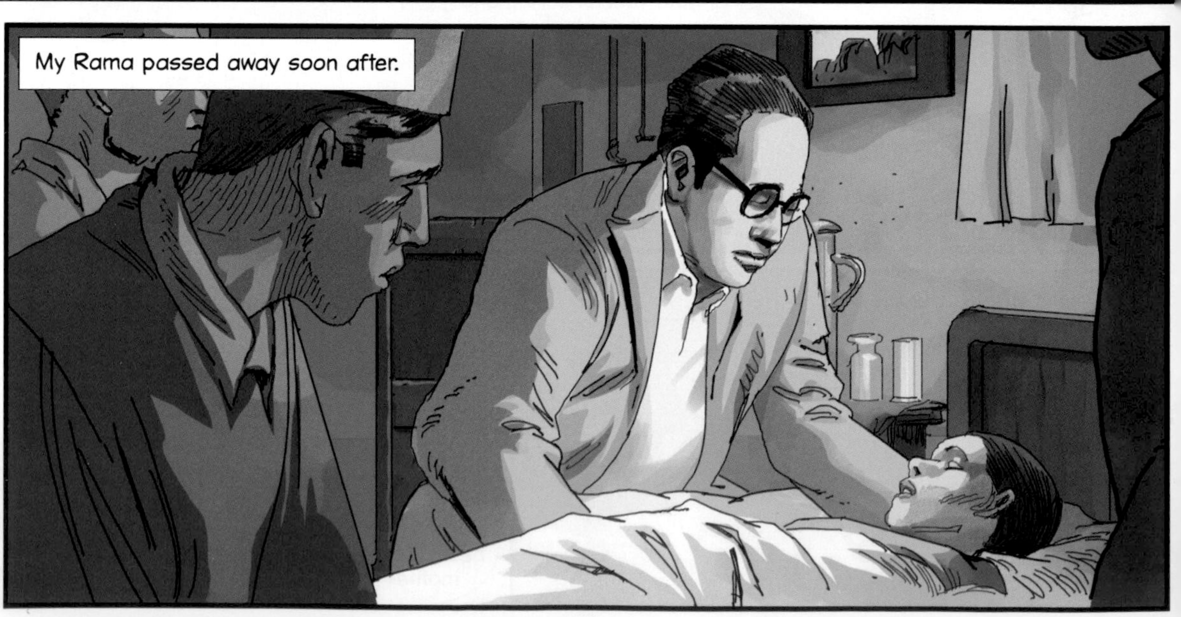
My Rama passed away soon after.

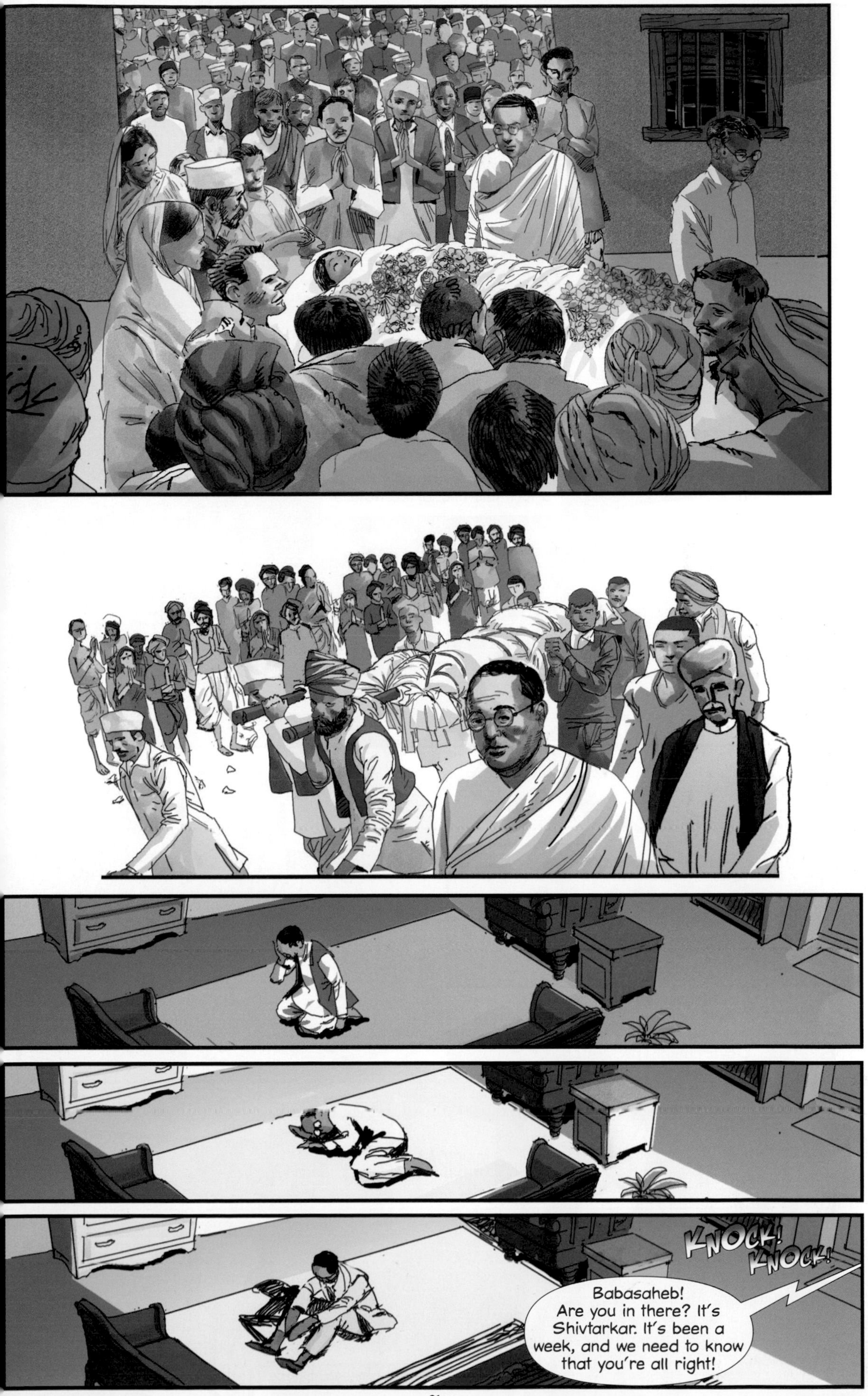
KNOCK! KNOCK!
Babasaheb! Are you in there? It's Shivtarkar. It's been a week, and we need to know that you're all right!

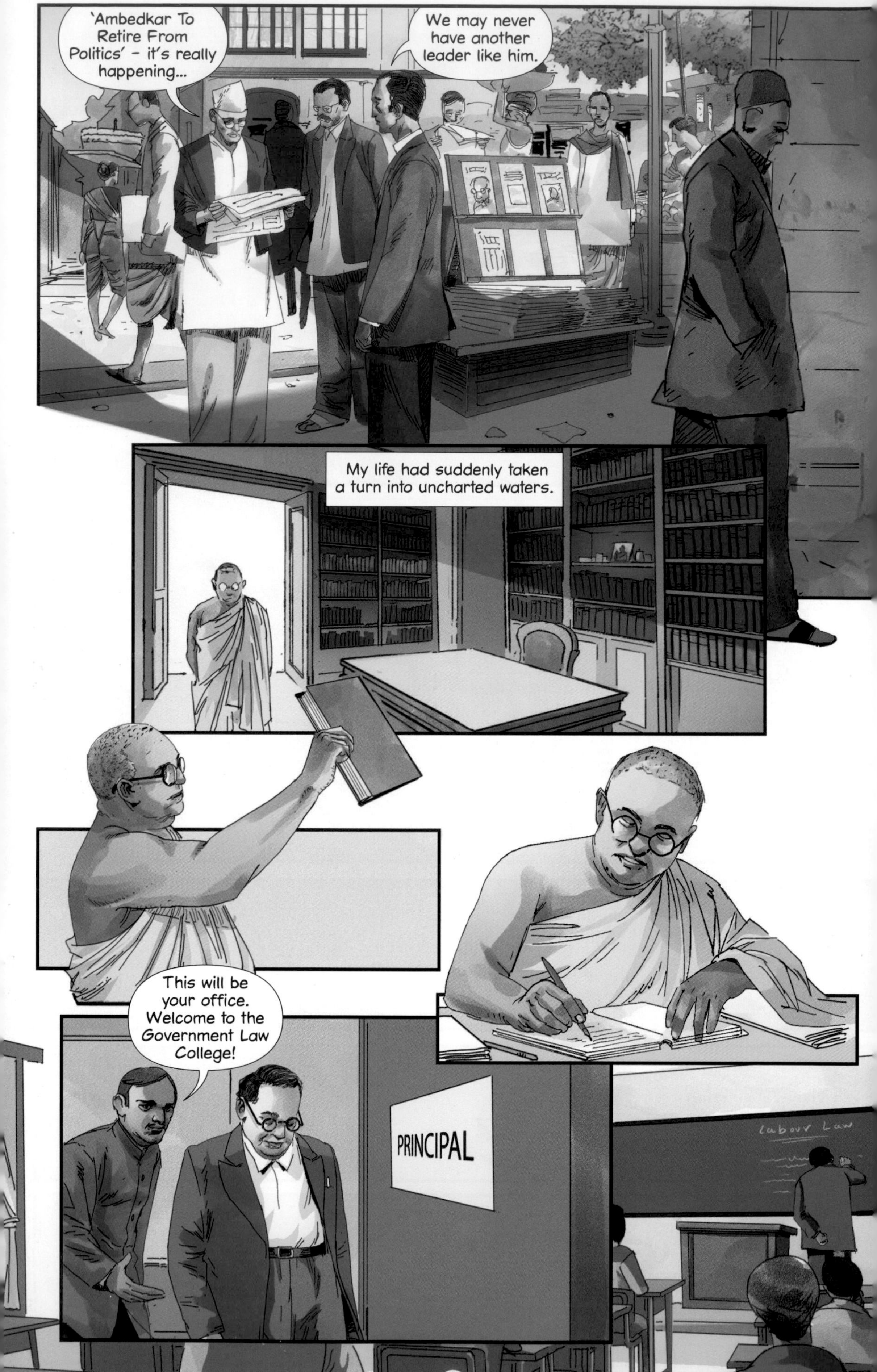
'Ambedkar To Retire From Politics' - it's really happening...
We may never have another leader like him.
My life had suddenly taken a turn into uncharted waters.
This will be your office. Welcome to the Government Law College!
PRINCIPAL
Labour Law

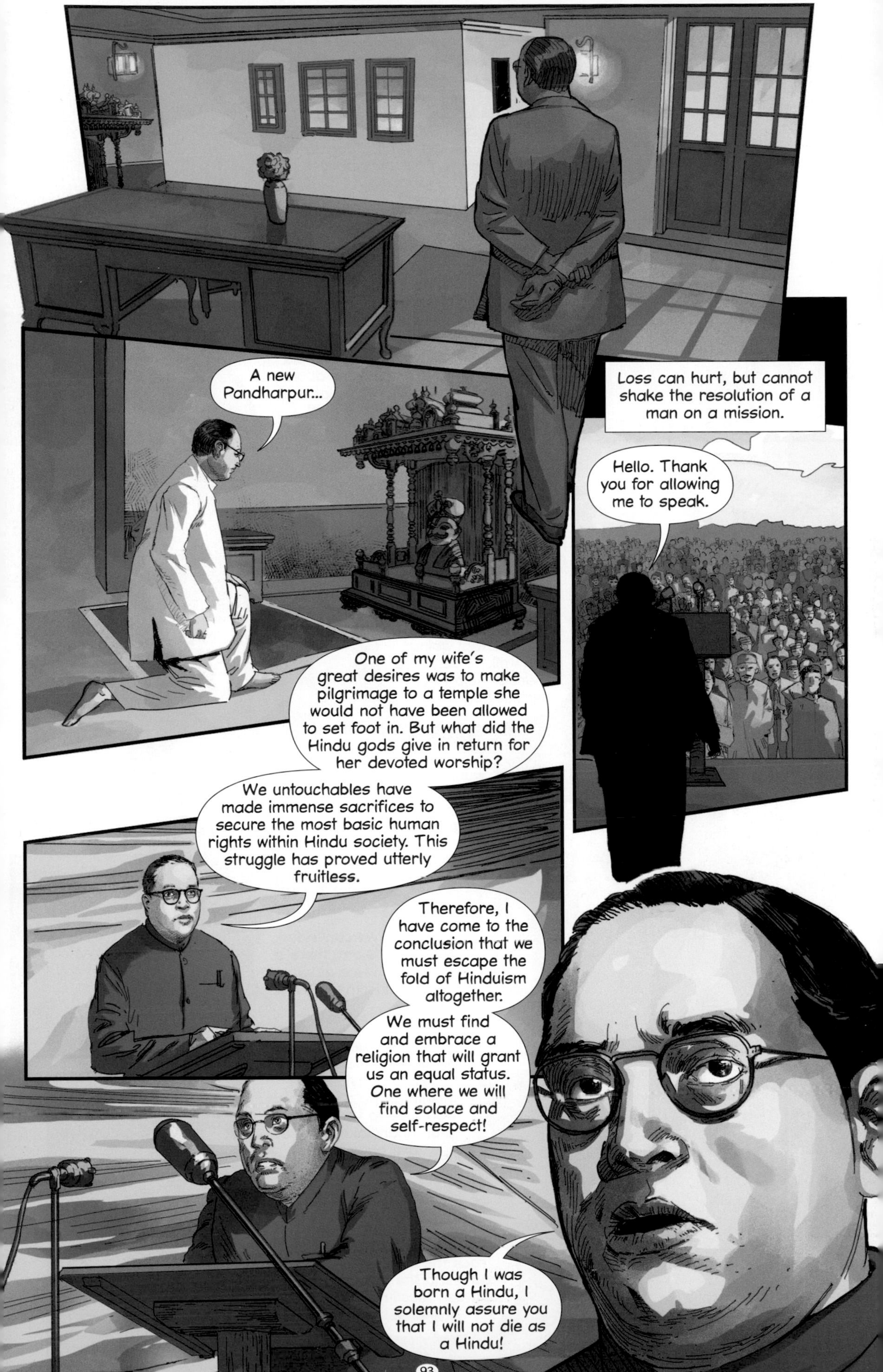
A new Pandharpur...
Loss can hurt, but cannot shake the resolution of a man on a mission.
Hello. Thank you for allowing me to speak.
One of my wife's great desires was to make pilgrimage to a temple she would not have been allowed to set foot in. But what did the Hindu gods give in return for her devoted worship?
We untouchables have made immense sacrifices to secure the most basic human rights within Hindu society. This struggle has proved utterly fruitless.
Therefore, I have come to the conclusion that we must escape the fold of Hinduism altogether.
We must find and embrace a religion that will grant us an equal status. One where we will find solace and self-respect!
Though I was born a Hindu, I solemnly assure you that I will not die as a Hindu!

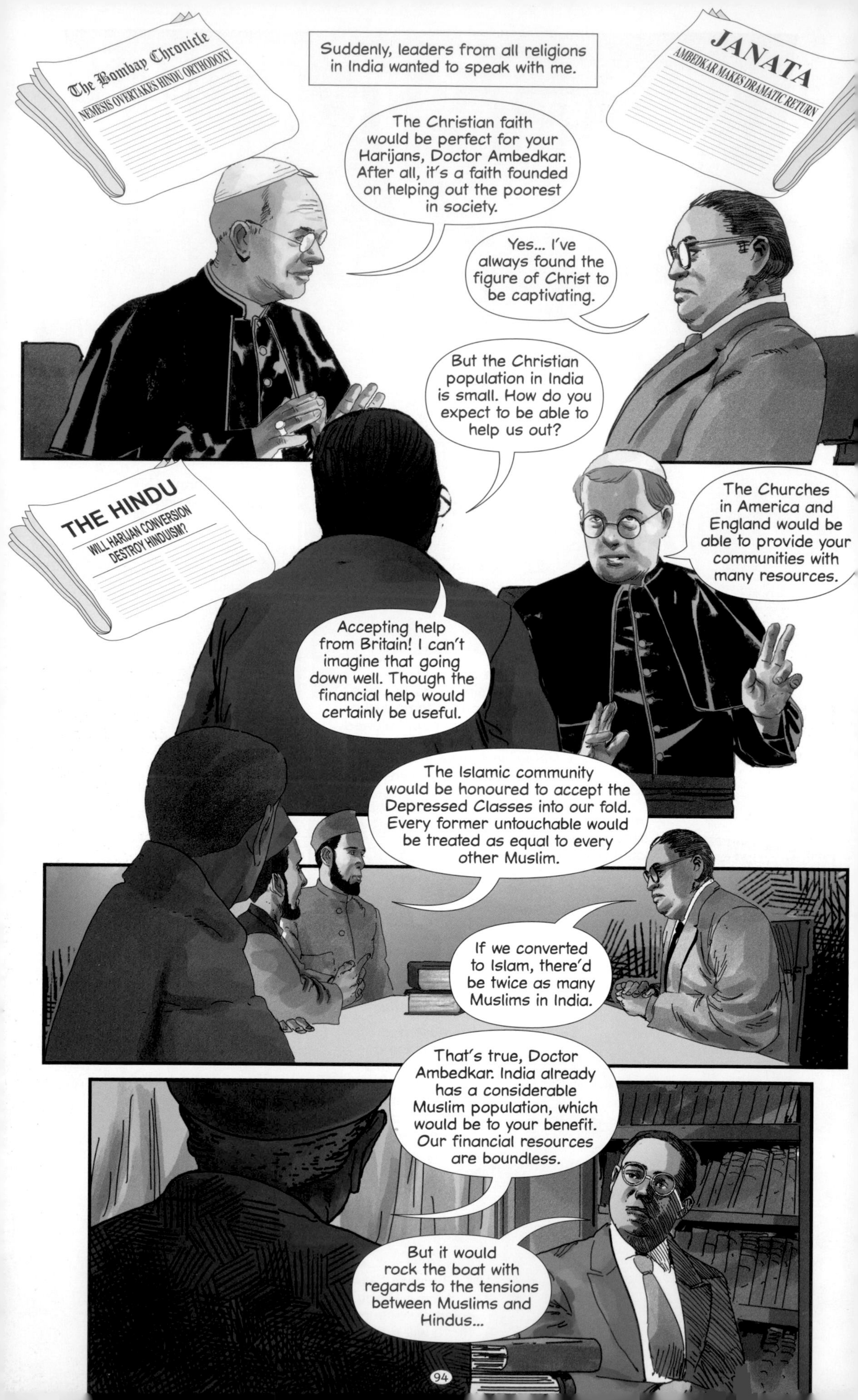
The Bombay Chronicle
NEMESIS OVERTAKES HINDU ORTHODOXY
Suddenly, leaders from all religions in India wanted to speak with me.
JANATA
AMBEDKAR MAKES DRAMATIC RETURN
The Christian faith would be perfect for your Harijans, Doctor Ambedkar. After all, it's a faith founded on helping out the poorest in society.
Yes... I've always found the figure of Christ to be captivating.
But the Christian population in India is small. How do you expect to be able to help us out?
THE HINDU
WILL HARIJAN CONVERSION DESTROY HINDUISM?
The Churches in America and England would be able to provide your communities with many resources.
Accepting help from Britain! I can't imagine that going down well. Though the financial help would certainly be useful.
The Islamic community would be honoured to accept the Depressed Classes into our fold. Every former untouchable would be treated as equal to every other Muslim.
If we converted to Islam, there'd be twice as many Muslims in India.
That's true, Doctor Ambedkar. India already has a considerable Muslim population, which would be to your benefit. Our financial resources are boundless.
But it would rock the boat with regards to the tensions between Muslims and Hindus...

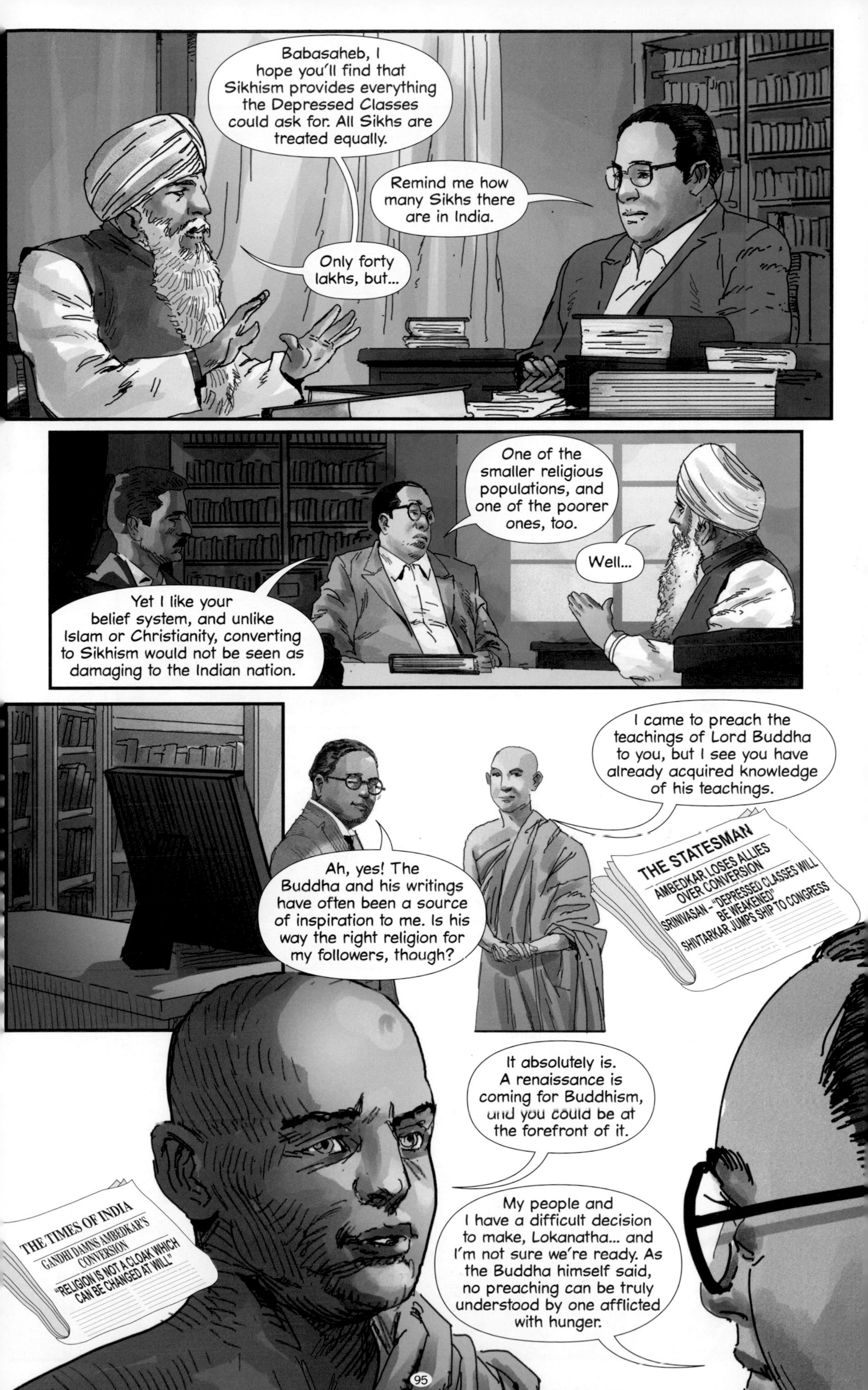
Babasaheb, I hope you'll find that Sikhism provides everything the Depressed Classes could ask for. All Sikhs are treated equally.
Remind me how many Sikhs there are in India.
Only forty lakhs, but...
One of the smaller religious populations, and one of the poorer ones, too.
Well...
Yet I like your belief system, and unlike Islam or Christianity, converting to Sikhism would not be seen as damaging to the Indian nation.
I came to preach the teachings of Lord Buddha to you, but I see you have already acquired knowledge of his teachings.
Ah, yes! The Buddha and his writings have often been a source of inspiration to me. Is his way the right religion for my followers, though?
THE STATESMAN
AMBEDKAR LOSES ALLIES OVER CONVERSION
SRINIVASAN - "DEPRESSED CLASSES WILL BE WEAKENED"
SHIVTARKAR JUMPS SHIP TO CONGRESS
It absolutely is. A renaissance is coming for Buddhism, and you could be at the forefront of it.
THE TIMES OF INDIA
GANDHI DAMNS AMBEDKAR'S CONVERSION
"RELIGION IS NOT A CLOAK WHICH CAN BE CHANGED AT WILL"
My people and I have a difficult decision to make, Lokanatha... and I'm not sure we're ready. As the Buddha himself said, no preaching can be truly understood by one afflicted with hunger.

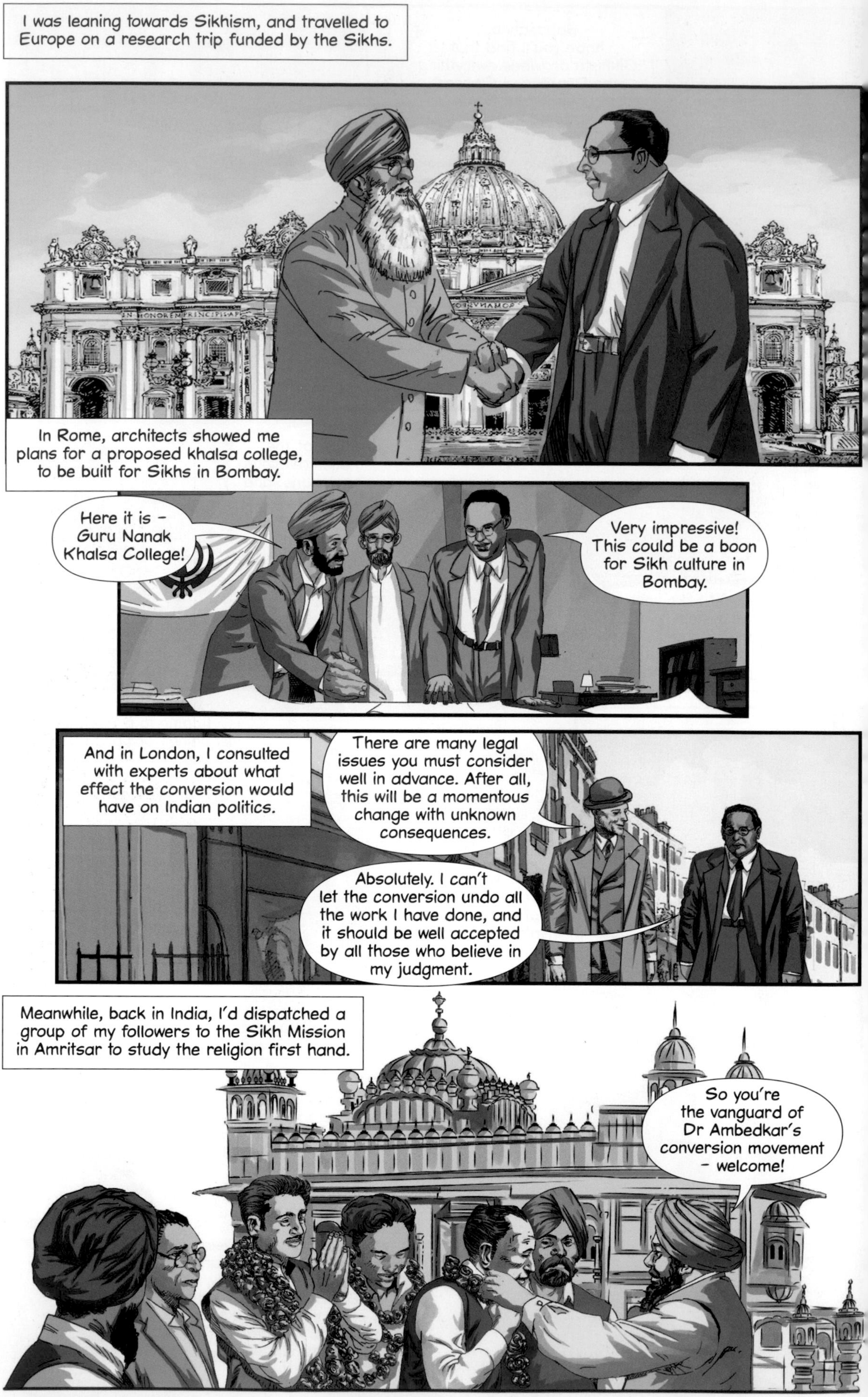
I was leaning towards Sikhism, and travelled to Europe on a research trip funded by the Sikhs.
In Rome, architects showed me plans for a proposed khalsa college, to be built for Sikhs in Bombay.
Here it is – Guru Nanak Khalsa College!
Very impressive! This could be a boon for Sikh culture in Bombay.
And in London, I consulted with experts about what effect the conversion would have on Indian politics.
There are many legal issues you must consider well in advance. After all, this will be a momentous change with unknown consequences.
Absolutely. I can't let the conversion undo all the work I have done, and it should be well accepted by all those who believe in my judgment.
Meanwhile, back in India, I'd dispatched a group of my followers to the Sikh Mission in Amritsar to study the religion first hand.
So you're the vanguard of Dr Ambedkar's conversion movement – welcome!

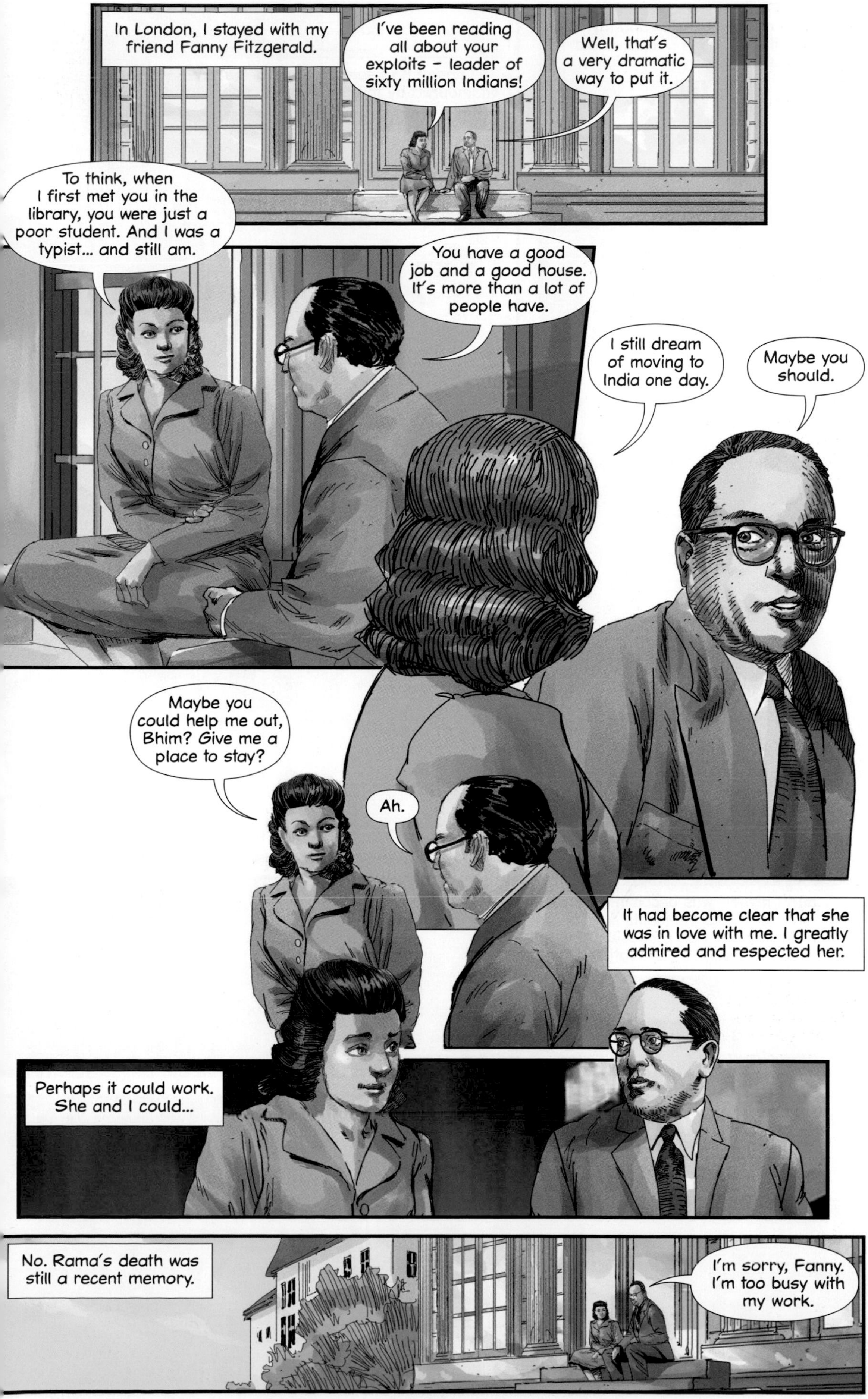
In London, I stayed with my friend Fanny Fitzgerald.
I've been reading all about your exploits – leader of sixty million Indians!
Well, that's a very dramatic way to put it.
To think, when I first met you in the library, you were just a poor student. And I was a typist... and still am.
You have a good job and a good house. It's more than a lot of people have.
I still dream of moving to India one day.
Maybe you should.
Maybe you could help me out, Bhim? Give me a place to stay?
Ah.
It had become clear that she was in love with me. I greatly admired and respected her.
Perhaps it could work. She and I could...
No. Rama's death was still a recent memory.
I'm sorry, Fanny. I'm too busy with my work.

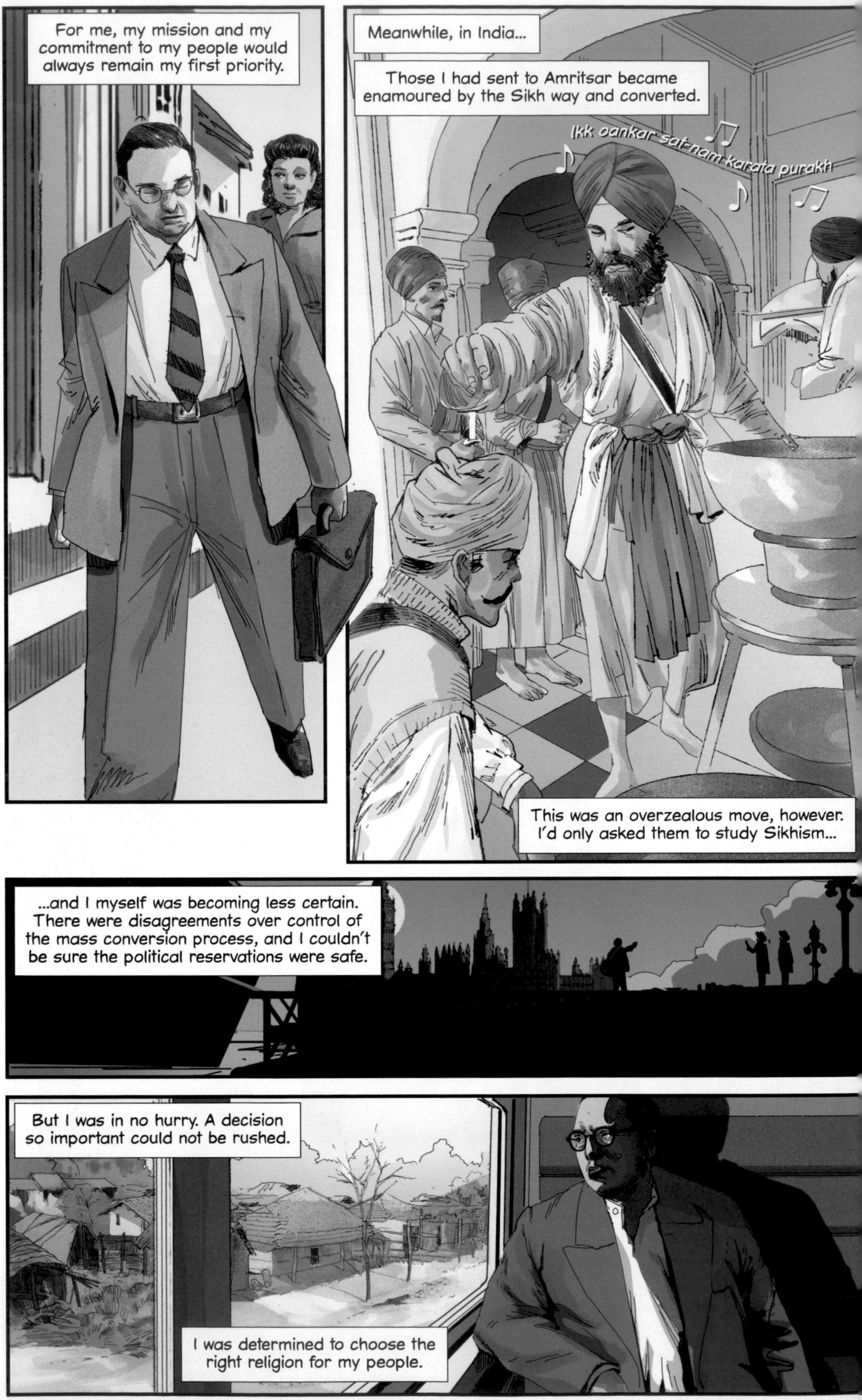
For me, my mission and my commitment to my people would always remain my first priority.
Meanwhile, in India...
Those I had sent to Amritsar became enamoured by the Sikh way and converted.
Ikk oankar sat-nam karata purakh
This was an overzealous move, however. I'd only asked them to study Sikhism...
...and I myself was becoming less certain. There were disagreements over control of the mass conversion process, and I couldn't be sure the political reservations were safe.
But I was in no hurry. A decision so important could not be rushed.
I was determined to choose the right religion for my people.

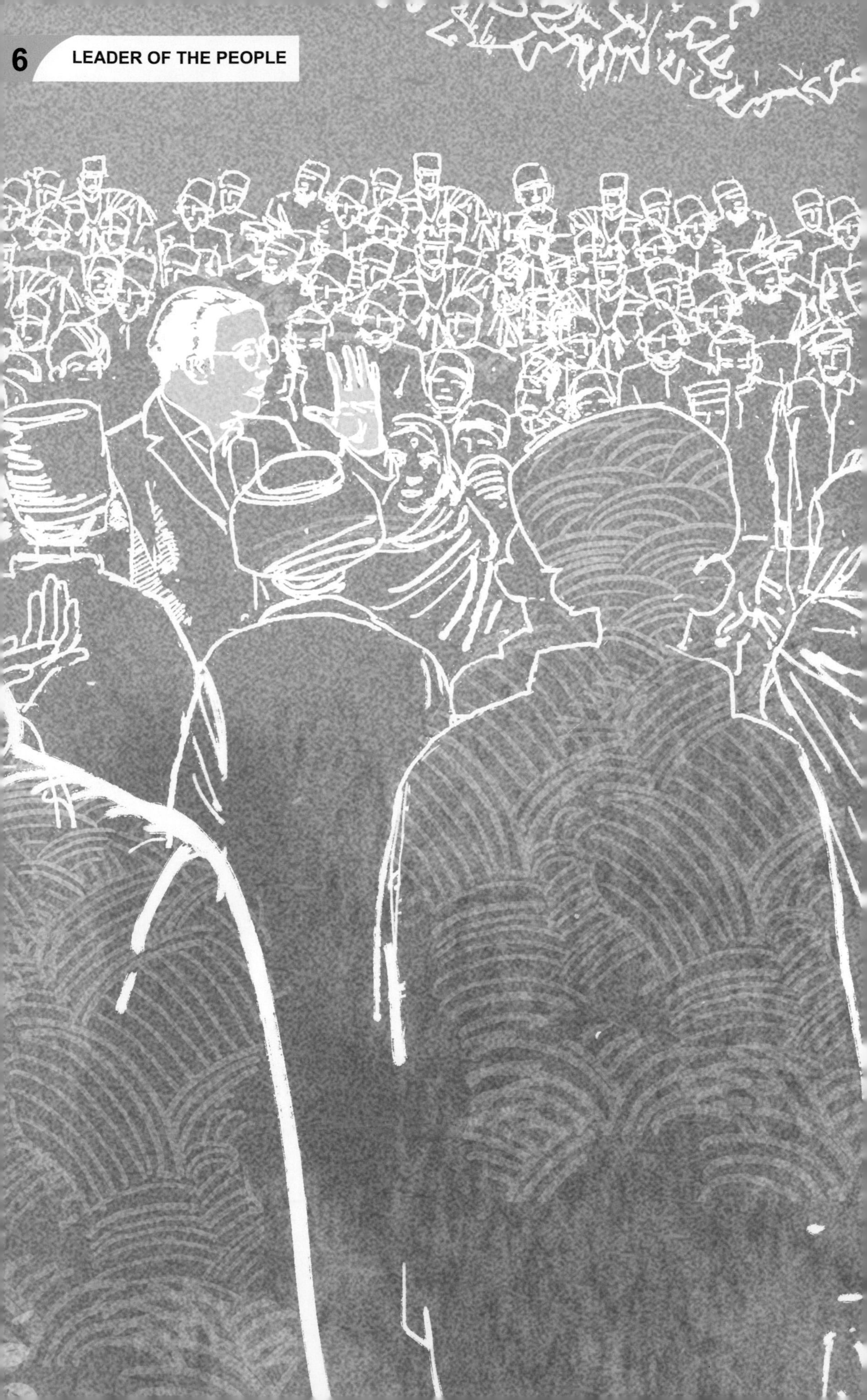

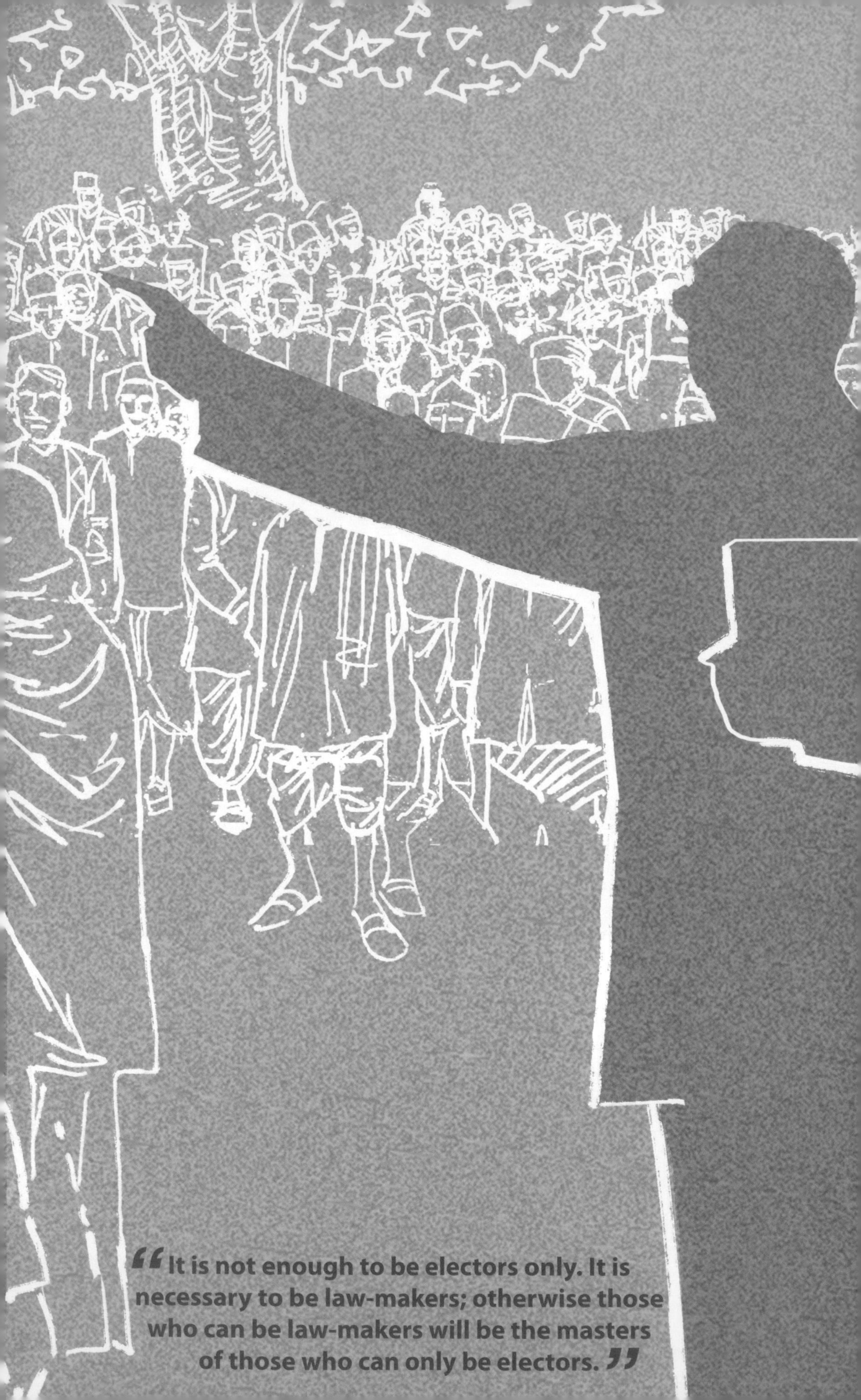

"It is not enough to be electors only. It is necessary to be law-makers; otherwise those who can be law-makers will be the masters of those who can only be electors."

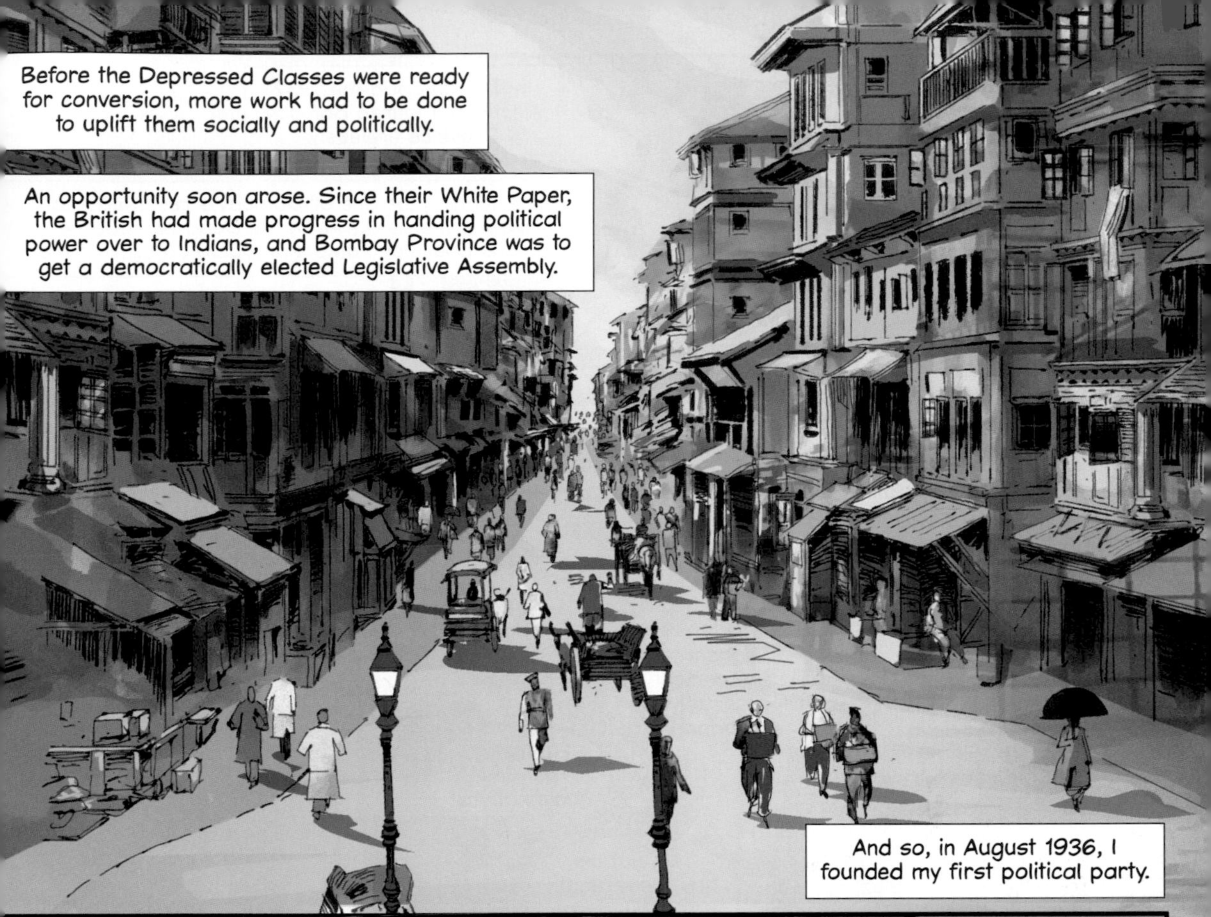
Before the Depressed Classes were ready for conversion, more work had to be done to uplift them socially and politically.
An opportunity soon arose. Since their White Paper, the British had made progress in handing political power over to Indians, and Bombay Province was to get a democratically elected Legislative Assembly.
And so, in August 1936, I founded my first political party.

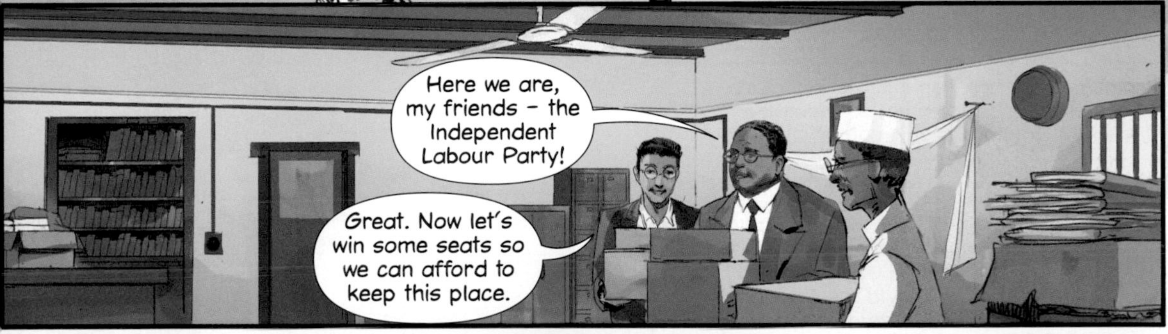
Here we are, my friends – the Independent Labour Party!
Great. Now let's win some seats so we can afford to keep this place.

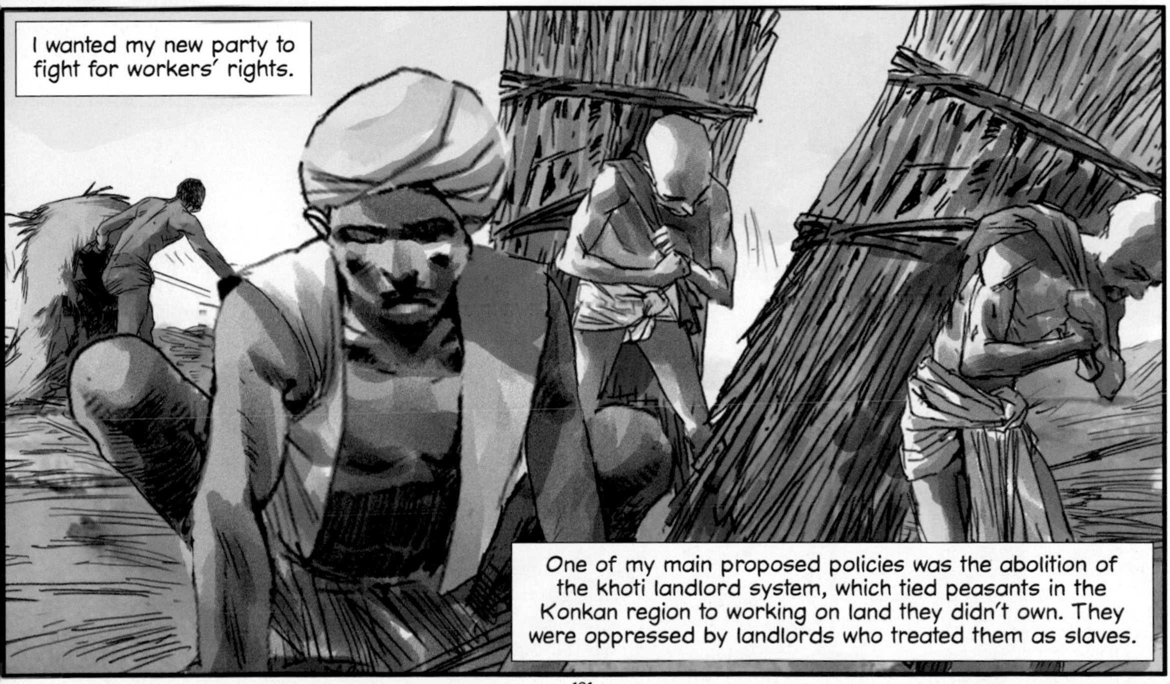
I wanted my new party to fight for workers' rights.
One of my main proposed policies was the abolition of the khoti landlord system, which tied peasants in the Konkan region to working on land they didn't own. They were oppressed by landlords who treated them as slaves.

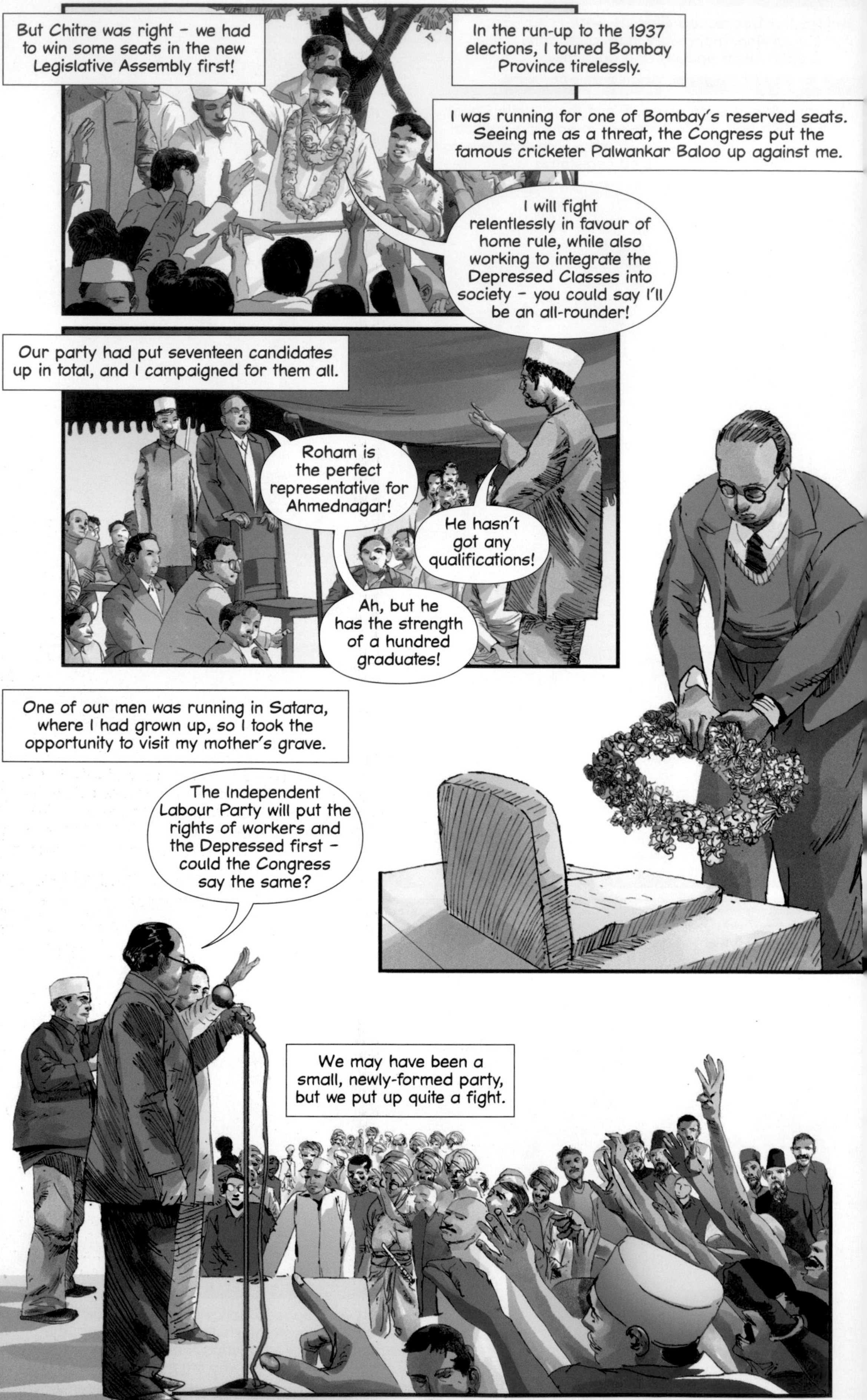
But Chitre was right – we had to win some seats in the new Legislative Assembly first!
In the run-up to the 1937 elections, I toured Bombay Province tirelessly.
I was running for one of Bombay's reserved seats. Seeing me as a threat, the Congress put the famous cricketer Palwankar Baloo up against me.
I will fight relentlessly in favour of home rule, while also working to integrate the Depressed Classes into society – you could say I'll be an all-rounder!
Our party had put seventeen candidates up in total, and I campaigned for them all.
Roham is the perfect representative for Ahmednagar!
He hasn't got any qualifications!
Ah, but he has the strength of a hundred graduates!
One of our men was running in Satara, where I had grown up, so I took the opportunity to visit my mother's grave.
The Independent Labour Party will put the rights of workers and the Depressed first – could the Congress say the same?
We may have been a small, newly-formed party, but we put up quite a fight.

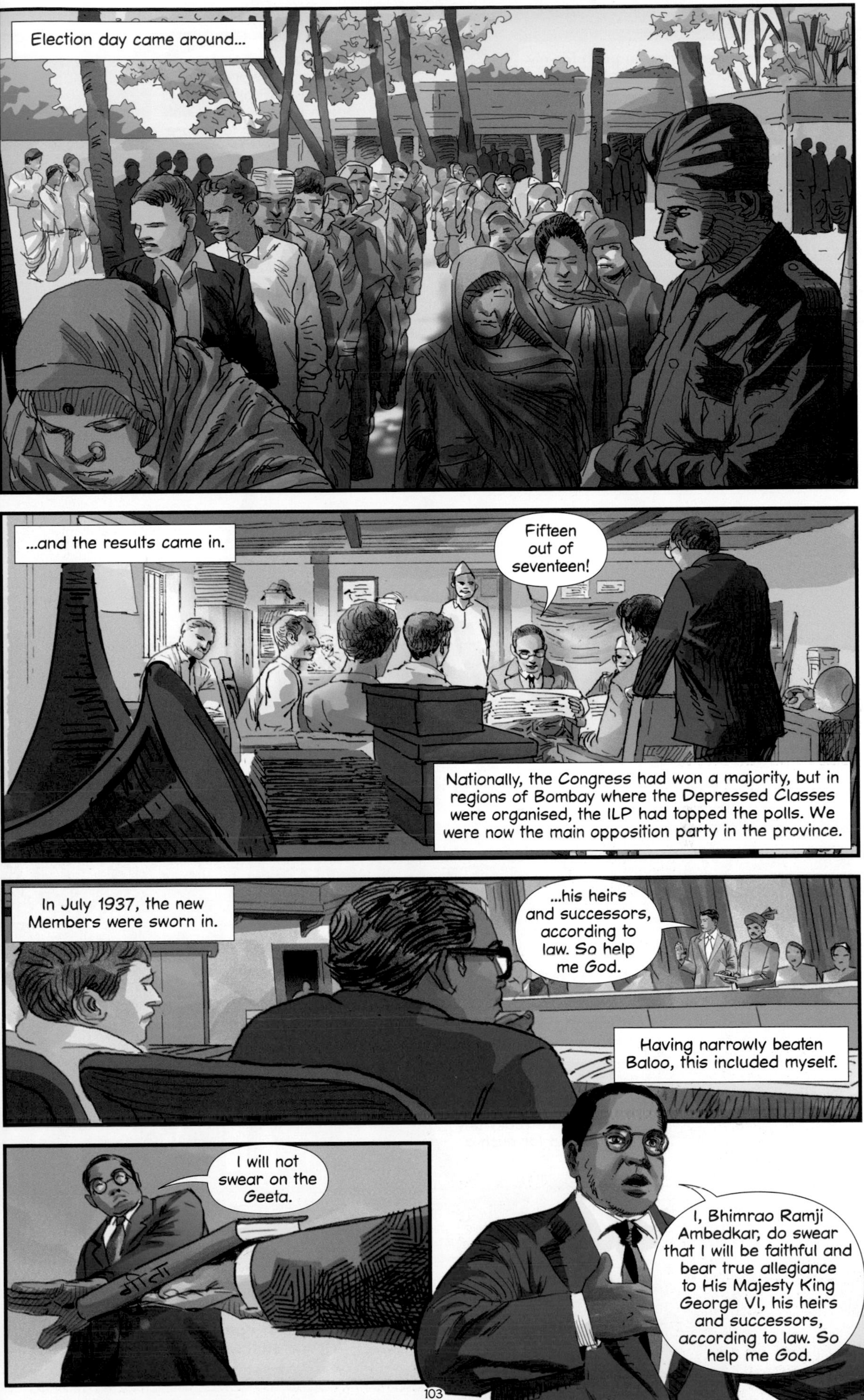

Election day came around...
...and the results came in.
Fifteen out of seventeen!
Nationally, the Congress had won a majority, but in regions of Bombay where the Depressed Classes were organised, the ILP had topped the polls. We were now the main opposition party in the province.
In July 1937, the new Members were sworn in.
...his heirs and successors, according to law. So help me God.
Having narrowly beaten Baloo, this included myself.
I will not swear on the Geeta.
I, Bhimrao Ramji Ambedkar, do swear that I will be faithful and bear true allegiance to His Majesty King George VI, his heirs and successors, according to law. So help me God.

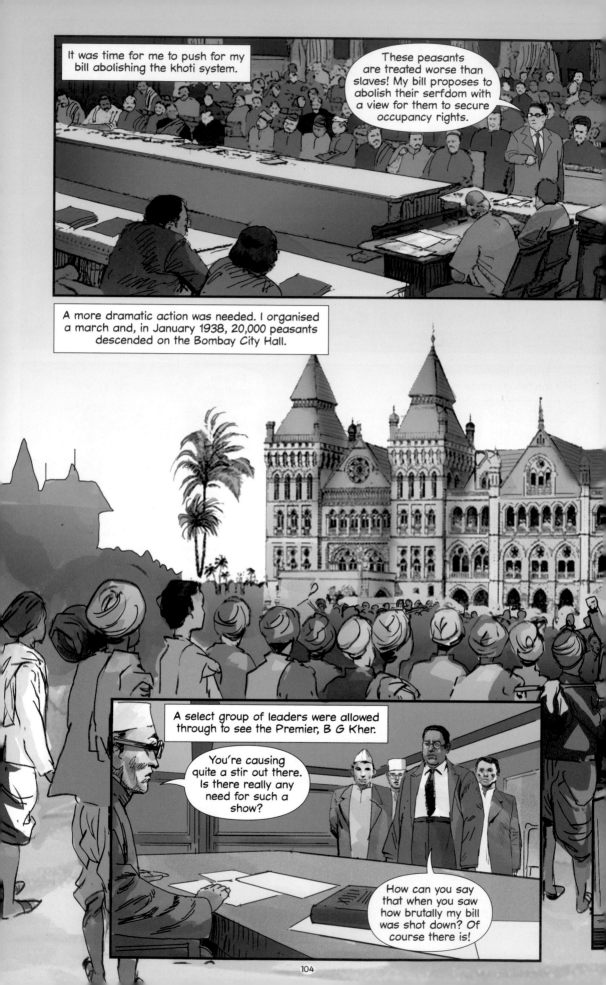

It was time for me to push for my bill abolishing the khoti system.

These peasants are treated worse than slaves! My bill proposes to abolish their serfdom with a view for them to secure occupancy rights.

A more dramatic action was needed. I organised a march and, in January 1938, 20,000 peasants descended on the Bombay City Hall.

A select group of leaders were allowed through to see the Premier, B G Kher.

You're causing quite a stir out there. Is there really any need for such a show?

How can you say that when you saw how brutally my bill was shot down? Of course there is!

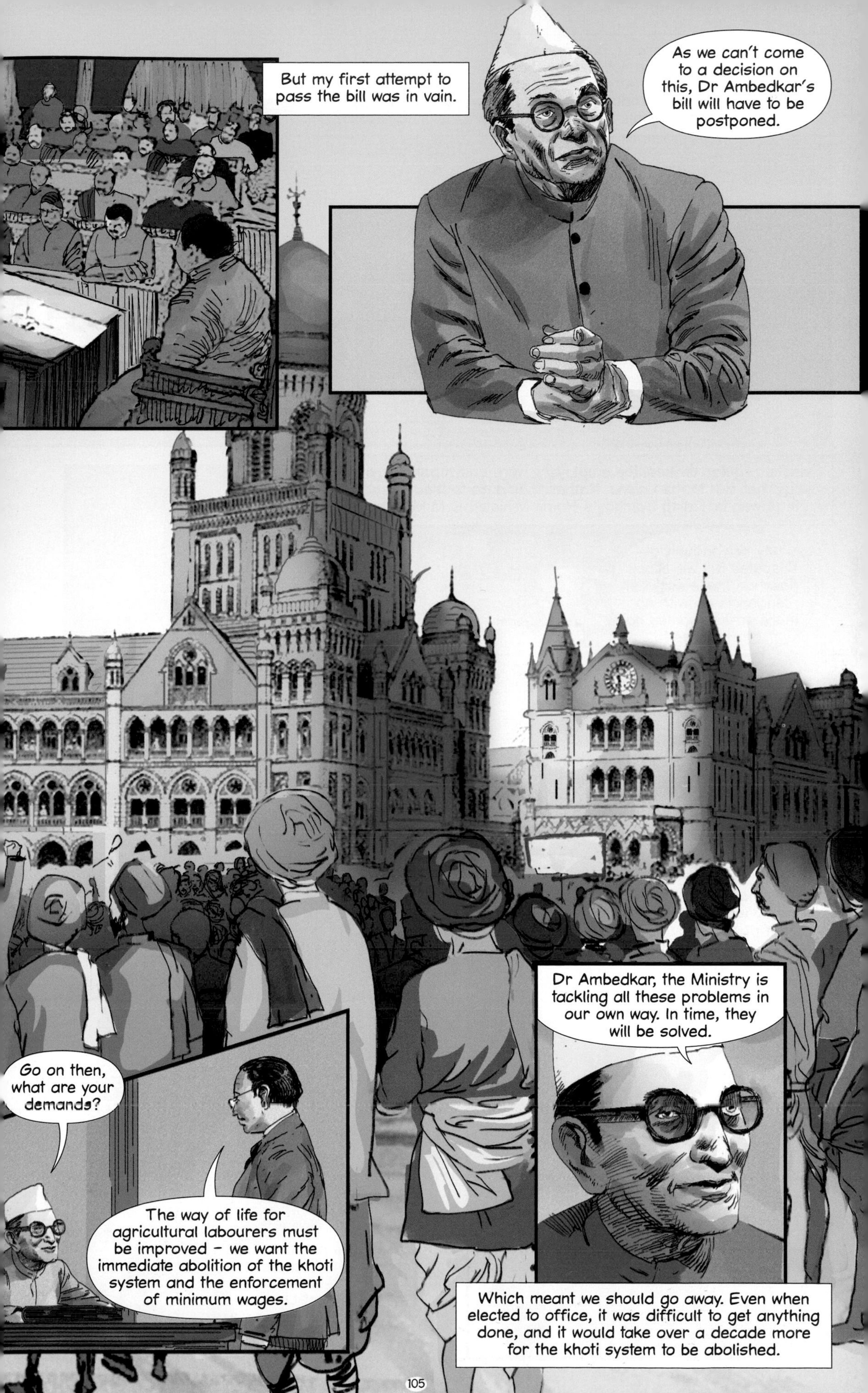
But my first attempt to pass the bill was in vain.
As we can't come to a decision on this, Dr Ambedkar's bill will have to be postponed.
Go on then, what are your demands?
The way of life for agricultural labourers must be improved – we want the immediate abolition of the khoti system and the enforcement of minimum wages.
Dr Ambedkar, the Ministry is tackling all these problems in our own way. In time, they will be solved.
Which meant we should go away. Even when elected to office, it was difficult to get anything done, and it would take over a decade more for the khoti system to be abolished.

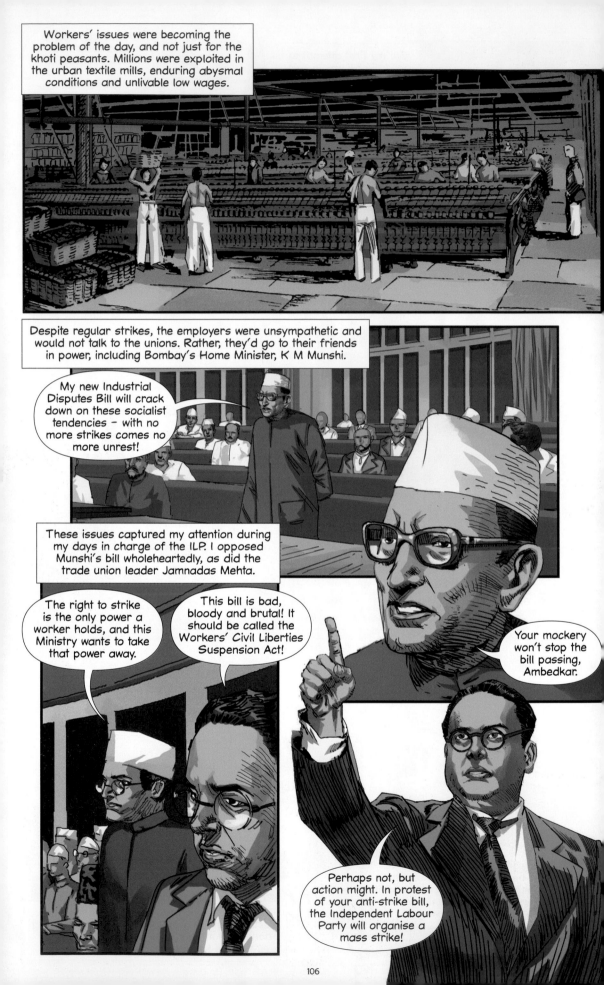

Workers' issues were becoming the problem of the day, and not just for the khoti peasants. Millions were exploited in the urban textile mills, enduring abysmal conditions and unlivable low wages.

Despite regular strikes, the employers were unsympathetic and would not talk to the unions. Rather, they'd go to their friends in power, including Bombay's Home Minister, K M Munshi.

My new Industrial Disputes Bill will crack down on these socialist tendencies – with no more strikes comes no more unrest!

These issues captured my attention during my days in charge of the ILP. I opposed Munshi's bill wholeheartedly, as did the trade union leader Jamnadas Mehta.

The right to strike is the only power a worker holds, and this Ministry wants to take that power away.

This bill is bad, bloody and brutal! It should be called the Workers' Civil Liberties Suspension Act!

Your mockery won't stop the bill passing, Ambedkar.

Perhaps not, but action might. In protest of your anti-strike bill, the Independent Labour Party will organise a mass strike!

106

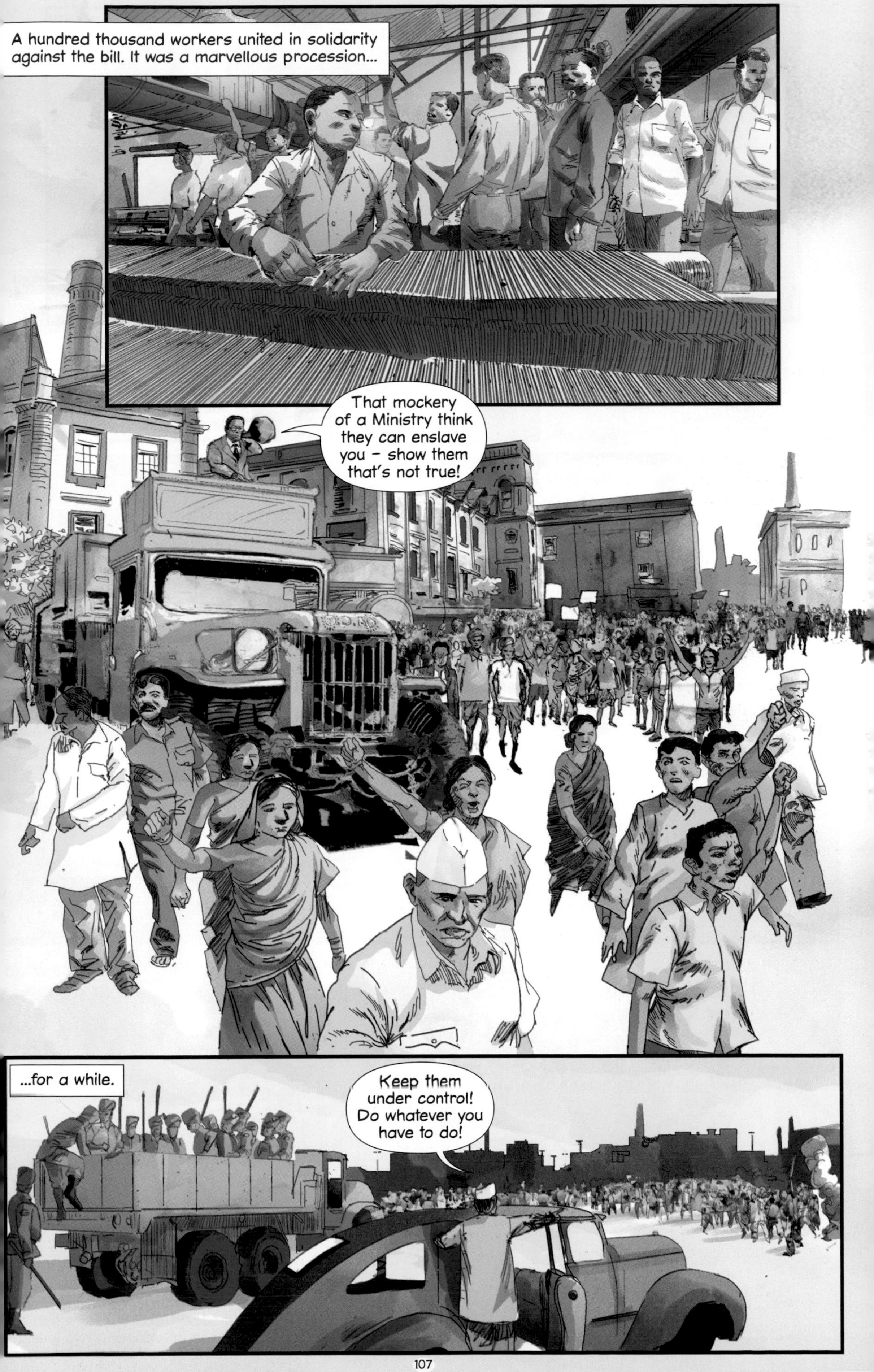
A hundred thousand workers united in solidarity against the bill. It was a marvellous procession...
That mockery of a Ministry think they can enslave you – show them that's not true!
...for a while.
Keep them under control! Do whatever you have to do!

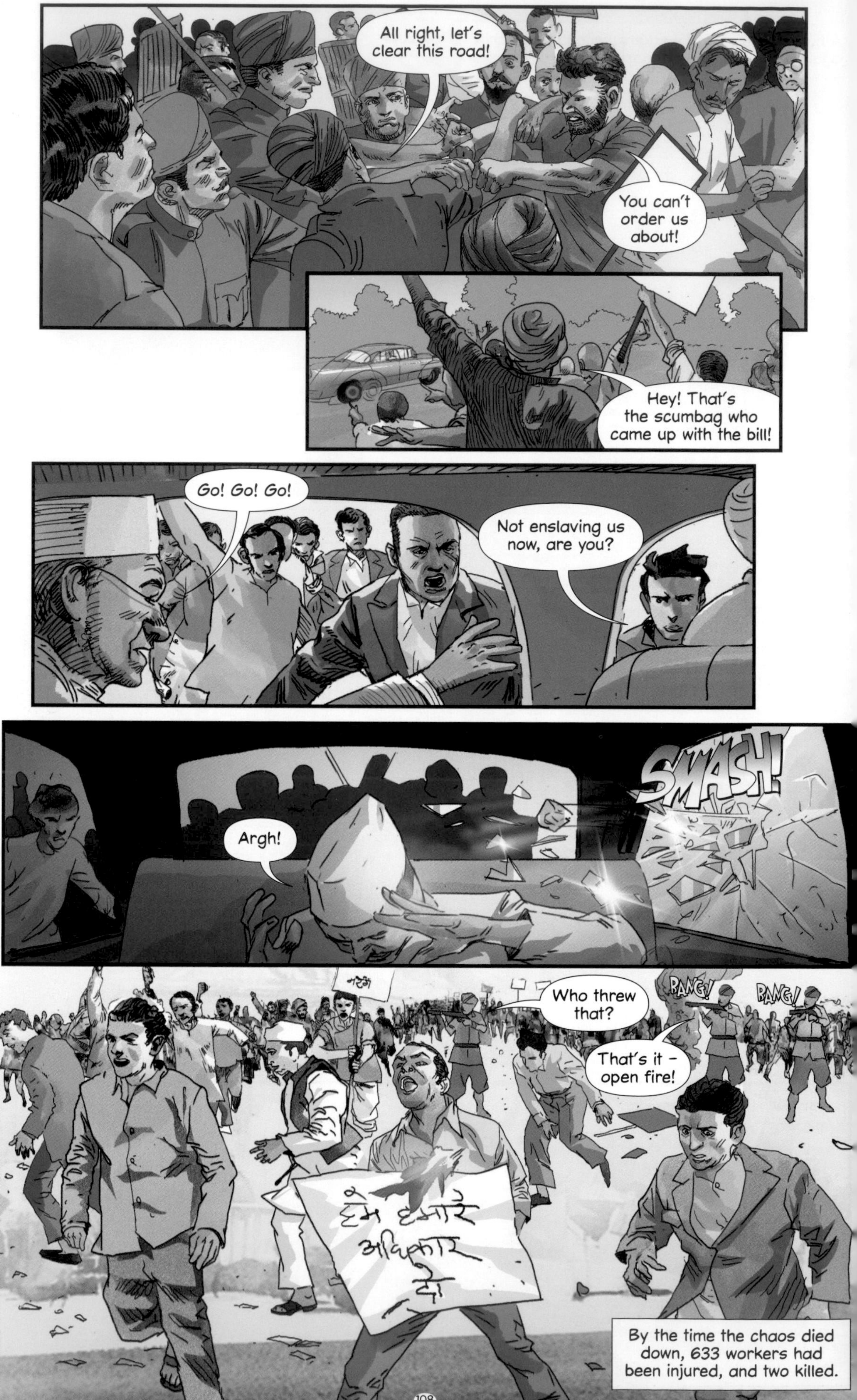
All right, let's clear this road!
You can't order us about!
Hey! That's the scumbag who came up with the bill!
Go! Go! Go!
Not enslaving us now, are you?
SMASH!
Argh!
BANG!
BANG!
Who threw that?
That's it - open fire!
By the time the chaos died down, 633 workers had been injured, and two killed.

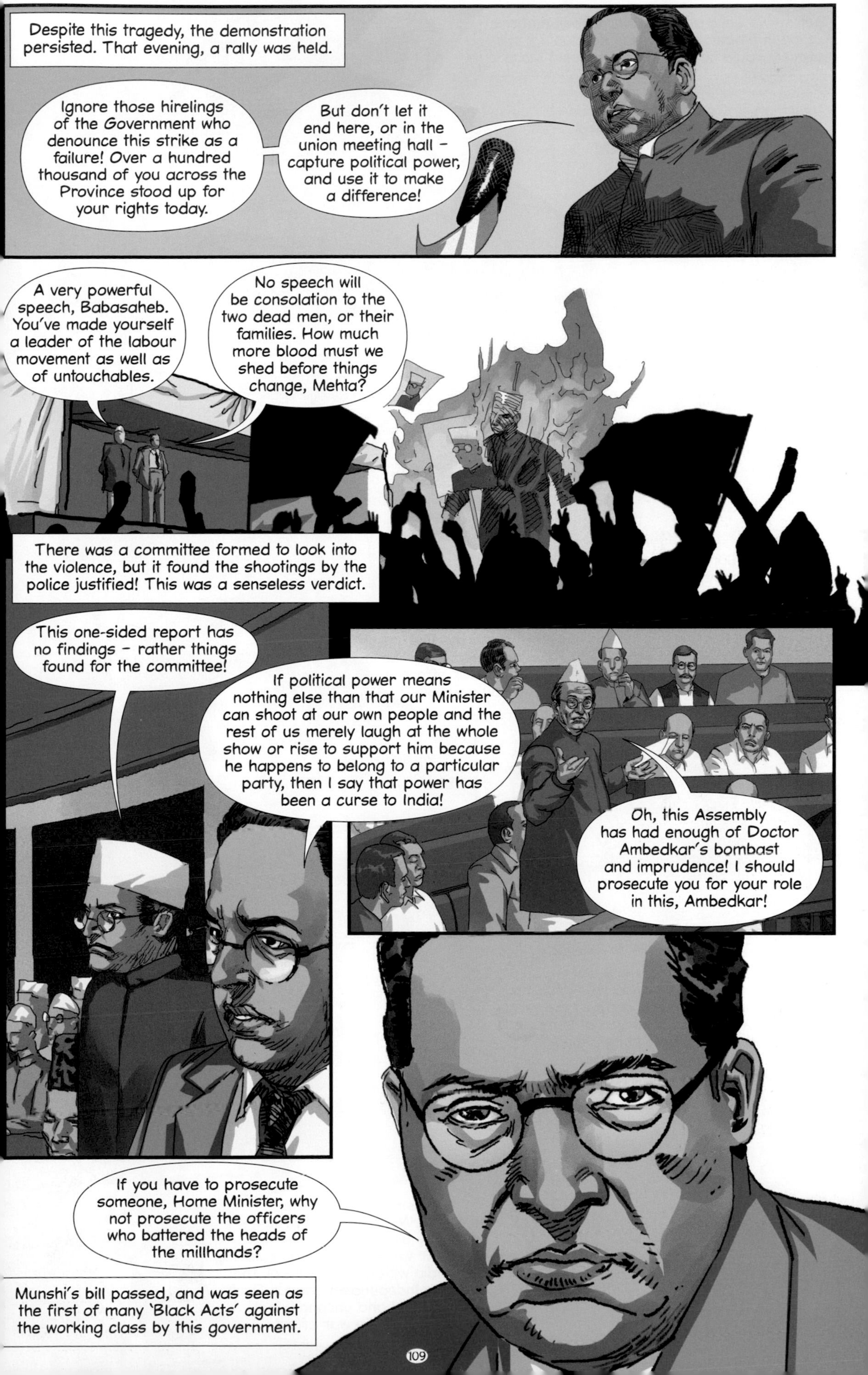
Despite this tragedy, the demonstration persisted. That evening, a rally was held.
Ignore those hirelings of the Government who denounce this strike as a failure! Over a hundred thousand of you across the Province stood up for your rights today.
But don't let it end here, or in the union meeting hall – capture political power, and use it to make a difference!
A very powerful speech, Babasaheb. You've made yourself a leader of the labour movement as well as of untouchables.
No speech will be consolation to the two dead men, or their families. How much more blood must we shed before things change, Mehta?
There was a committee formed to look into the violence, but it found the shootings by the police justified! This was a senseless verdict.
This one-sided report has no findings – rather things found for the committee!
If political power means nothing else than that our Minister can shoot at our own people and the rest of us merely laugh at the whole show or rise to support him because he happens to belong to a particular party, then I say that power has been a curse to India!
Oh, this Assembly has had enough of Doctor Ambedkar's bombast and imprudence! I should prosecute you for your role in this, Ambedkar!
If you have to prosecute someone, Home Minister, why not prosecute the officers who battered the heads of the millhands?
Munshi's bill passed, and was seen as the first of many 'Black Acts' against the working class by this government.

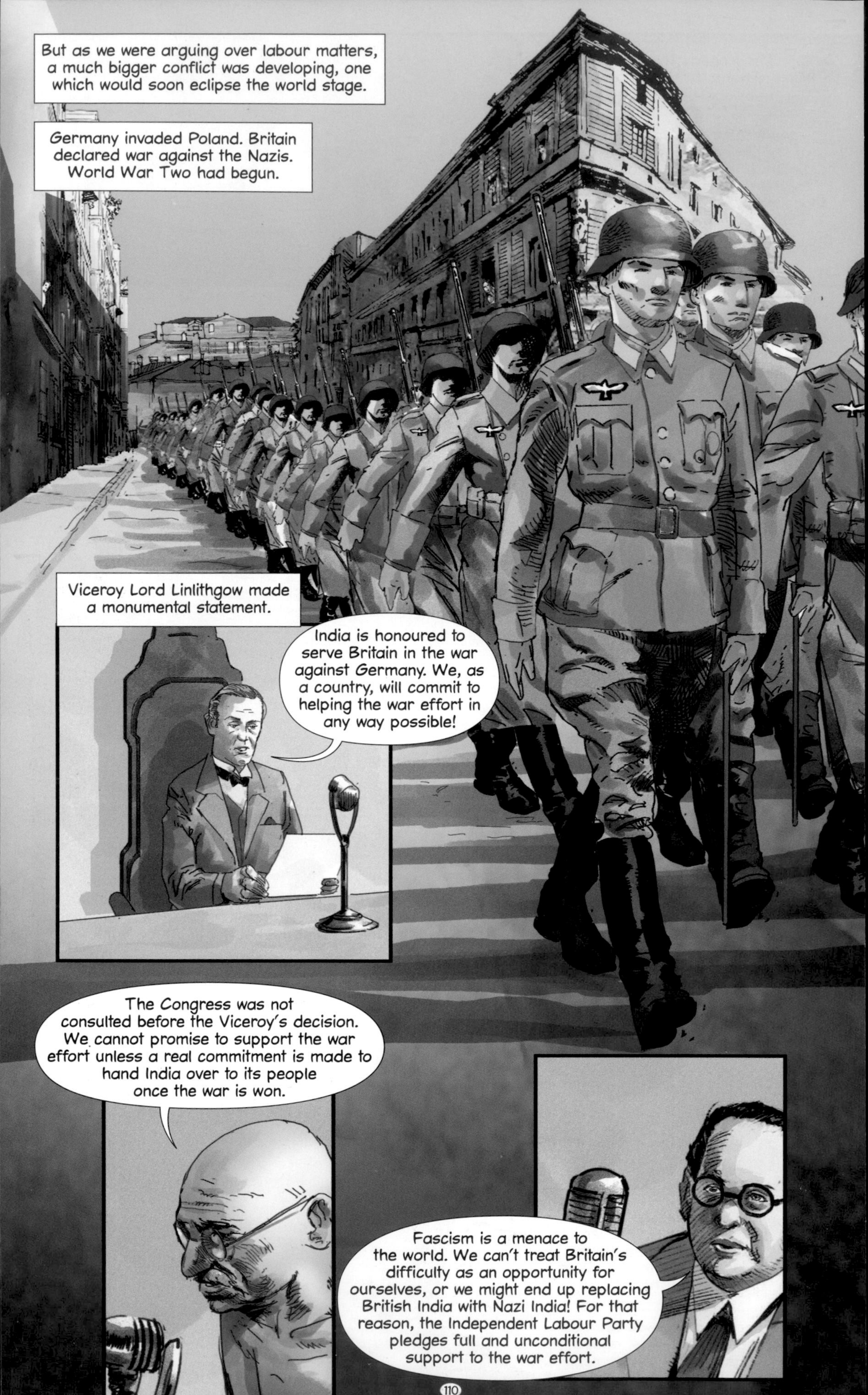

But as we were arguing over labour matters, a much bigger conflict was developing, one which would soon eclipse the world stage.
Germany invaded Poland. Britain declared war against the Nazis. World War Two had begun.
Viceroy Lord Linlithgow made a monumental statement.
India is honoured to serve Britain in the war against Germany. We, as a country, will commit to helping the war effort in any way possible!
The Congress was not consulted before the Viceroy's decision. We cannot promise to support the war effort unless a real commitment is made to hand India over to its people once the war is won.
Fascism is a menace to the world. We can't treat Britain's difficulty as an opportunity for ourselves, or we might end up replacing British India with Nazi India! For that reason, the Independent Labour Party pledges full and unconditional support to the war effort.

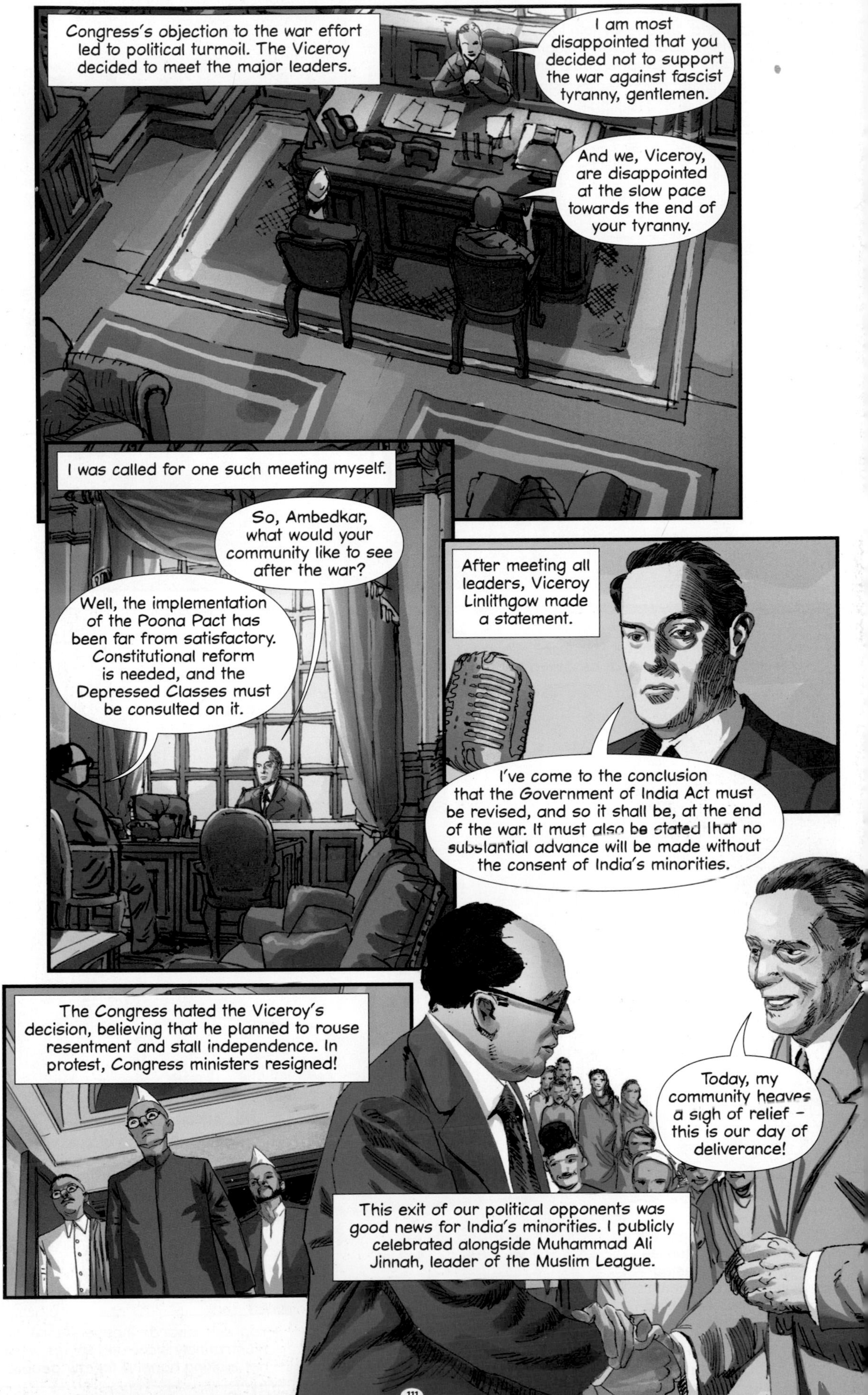

Congress's objection to the war effort led to political turmoil. The Viceroy decided to meet the major leaders.
I am most disappointed that you decided not to support the war against fascist tyranny, gentlemen.
And we, Viceroy, are disappointed at the slow pace towards the end of your tyranny.
I was called for one such meeting myself.
So, Ambedkar, what would your community like to see after the war?
Well, the implementation of the Poona Pact has been far from satisfactory. Constitutional reform is needed, and the Depressed Classes must be consulted on it.
After meeting all leaders, Viceroy Linlithgow made a statement.
I've come to the conclusion that the Government of India Act must be revised, and so it shall be, at the end of the war. It must also be stated that no substantial advance will be made without the consent of India's minorities.
The Congress hated the Viceroy's decision, believing that he planned to rouse resentment and stall independence. In protest, Congress ministers resigned!
Today, my community heaves a sigh of relief – this is our day of deliverance!
This exit of our political opponents was good news for India's minorities. I publicly celebrated alongside Muhammad Ali Jinnah, leader of the Muslim League.

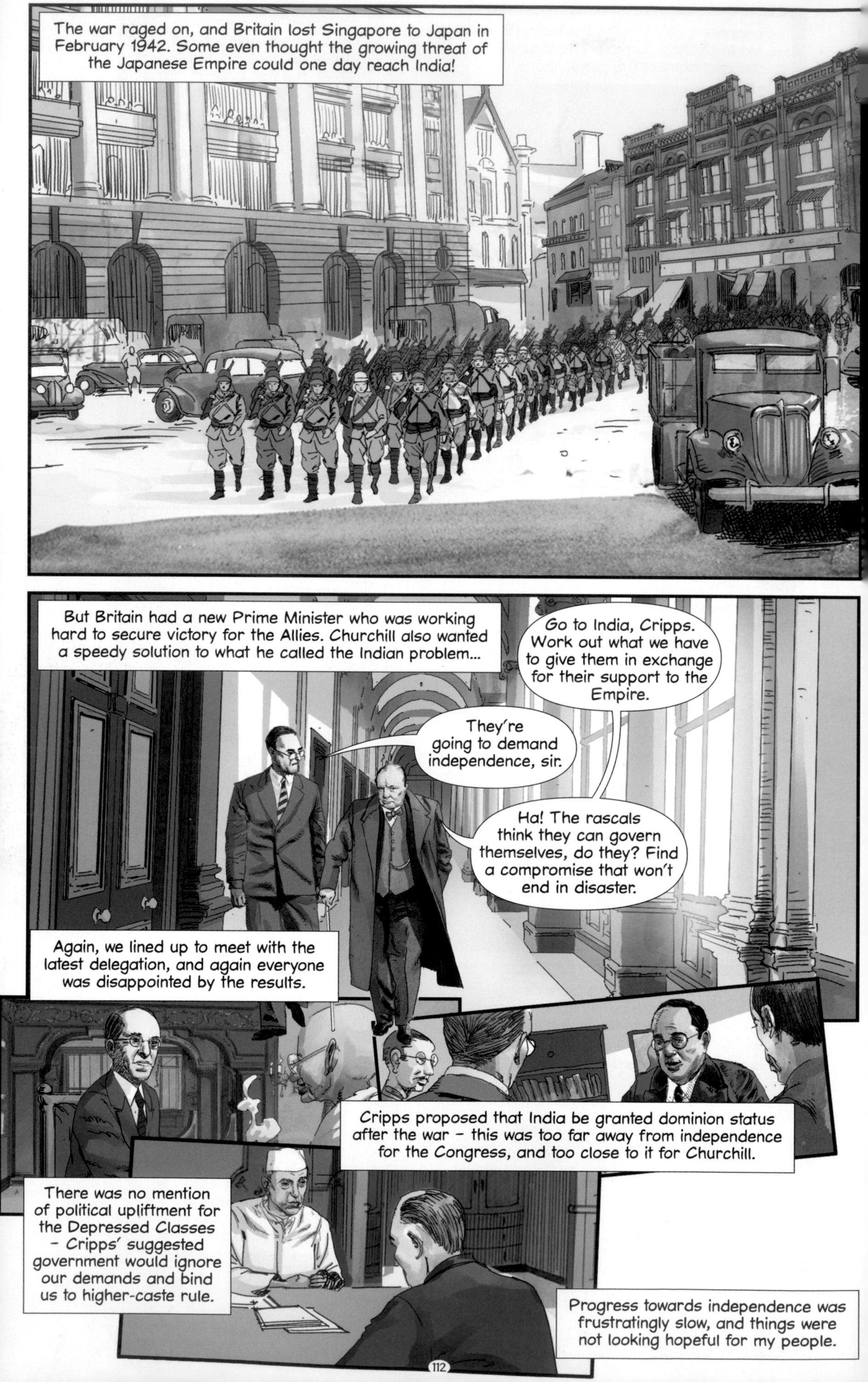
The war raged on, and Britain lost Singapore to Japan in February 1942. Some even thought the growing threat of the Japanese Empire could one day reach India!
But Britain had a new Prime Minister who was working hard to secure victory for the Allies. Churchill also wanted a speedy solution to what he called the Indian problem...
Go to India, Cripps. Work out what we have to give them in exchange for their support to the Empire.
They're going to demand independence, sir.
Ha! The rascals think they can govern themselves, do they? Find a compromise that won't end in disaster.
Again, we lined up to meet with the latest delegation, and again everyone was disappointed by the results.
Cripps proposed that India be granted dominion status after the war – this was too far away from independence for the Congress, and too close to it for Churchill.
There was no mention of political upliftment for the Depressed Classes – Cripps' suggested government would ignore our demands and bind us to higher-caste rule.
Progress towards independence was frustratingly slow, and things were not looking hopeful for my people.

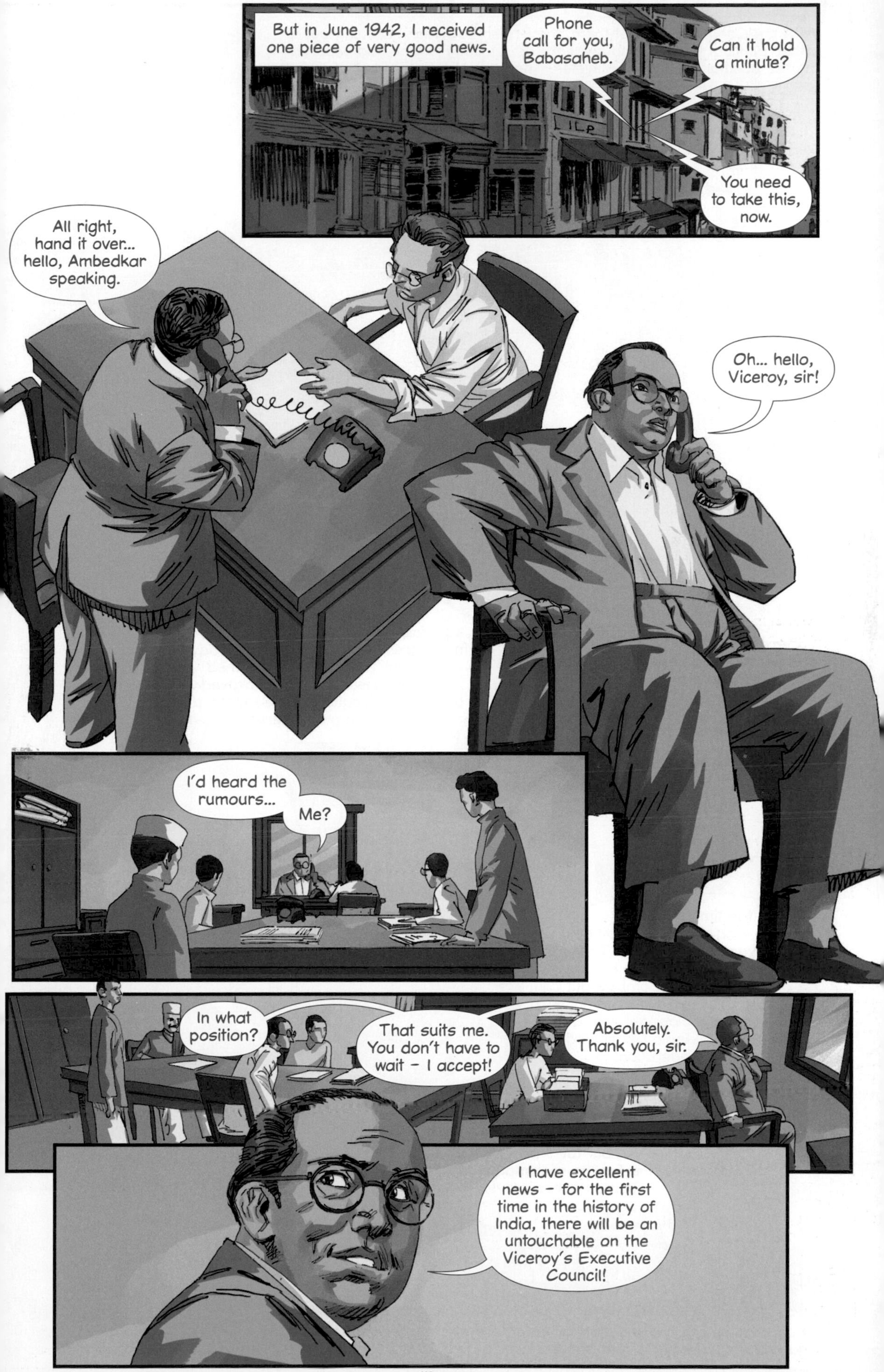
But in June 1942, I received one piece of very good news.
Phone call for you, Babasaheb.
Can it hold a minute?
You need to take this, now.
All right, hand it over... hello, Ambedkar speaking.
Oh... hello, Viceroy, sir!
I'd heard the rumours...
Me?
In what position?
That suits me. You don't have to wait - I accept!
Absolutely. Thank you, sir.
I have excellent news - for the first time in the history of India, there will be an untouchable on the Viceroy's Executive Council!

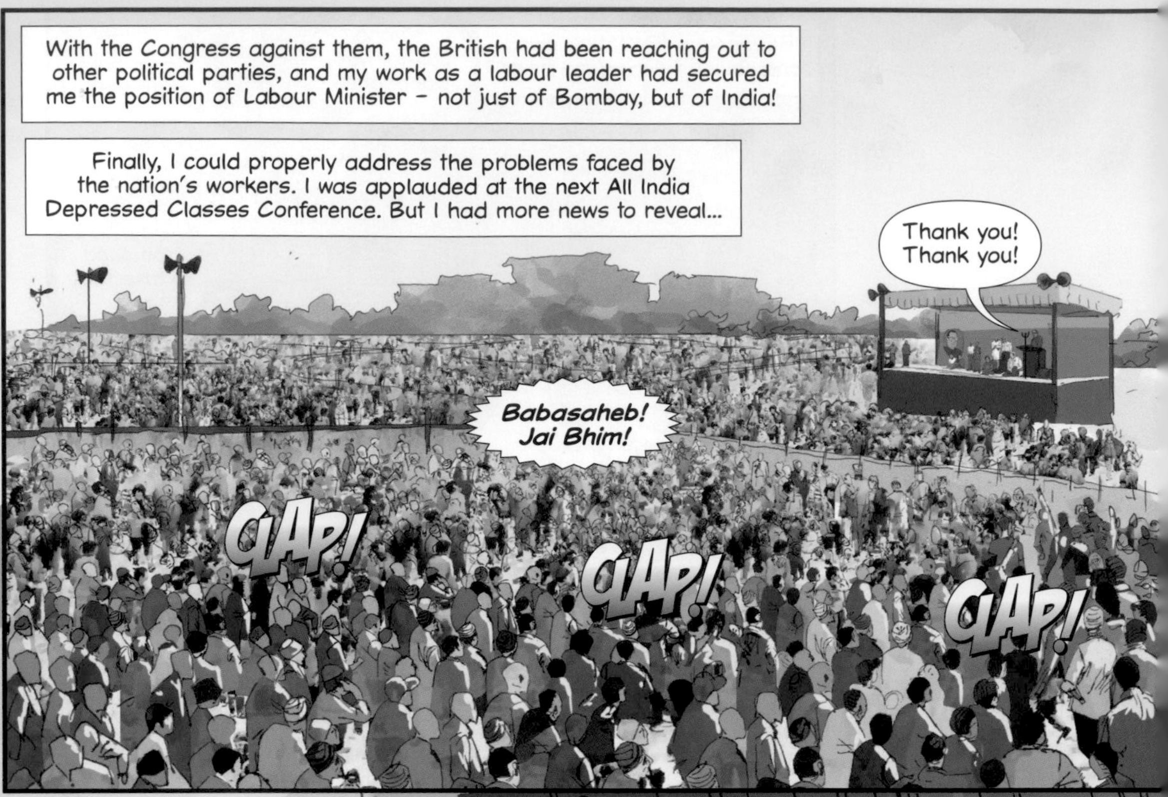
With the Congress against them, the British had been reaching out to other political parties, and my work as a labour leader had secured me the position of Labour Minister – not just of Bombay, but of India!
Finally, I could properly address the problems faced by the nation's workers. I was applauded at the next All India Depressed Classes Conference. But I had more news to reveal...
Thank you! Thank you!
Babasaheb! Jai Bhim!
CLAP!
CLAP!
CLAP!

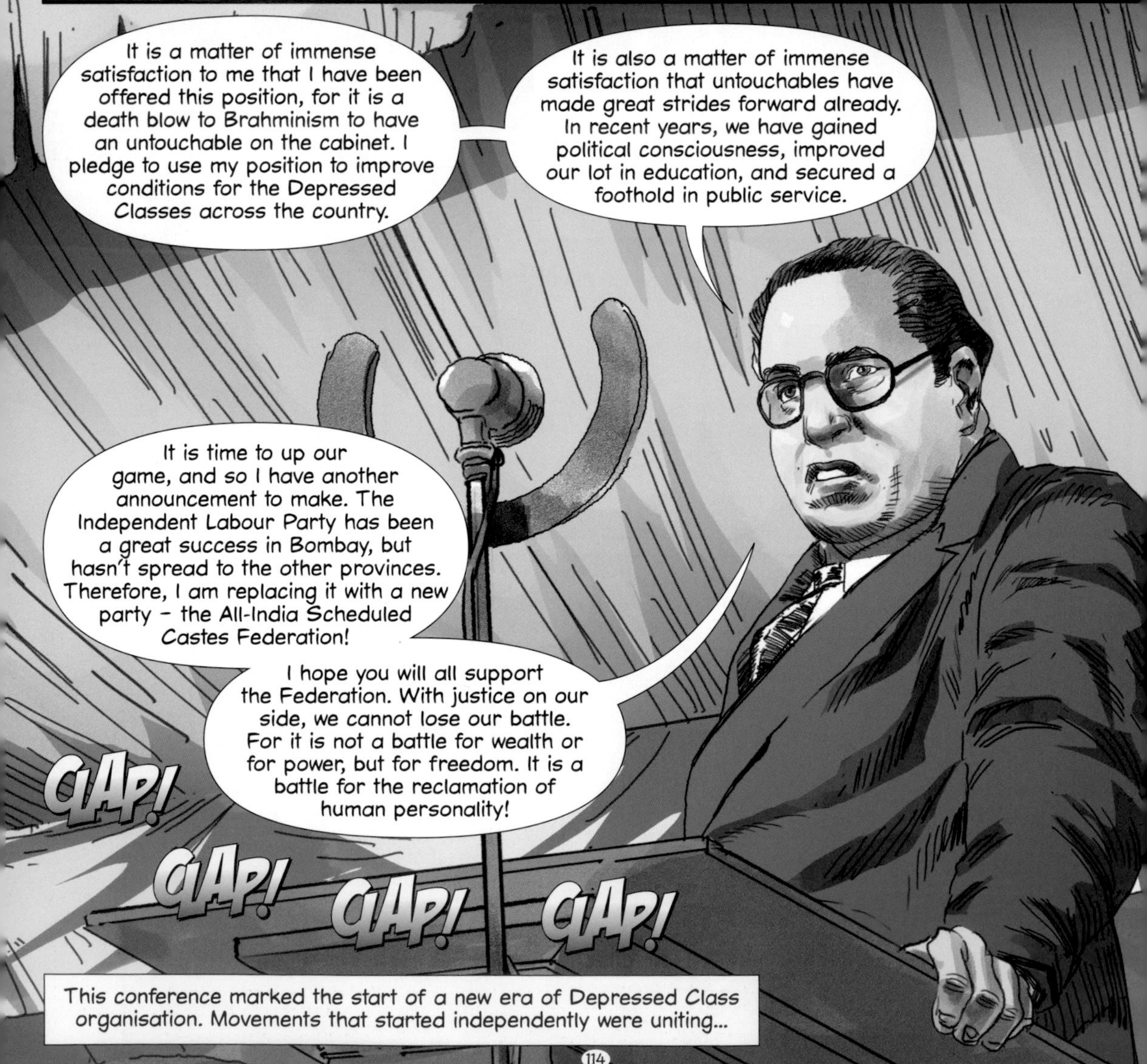
It is a matter of immense satisfaction to me that I have been offered this position, for it is a death blow to Brahminism to have an untouchable on the cabinet. I pledge to use my position to improve conditions for the Depressed Classes across the country.
It is also a matter of immense satisfaction that untouchables have made great strides forward already. In recent years, we have gained political consciousness, improved our lot in education, and secured a foothold in public service.
It is time to up our game, and so I have another announcement to make. The Independent Labour Party has been a great success in Bombay, but hasn't spread to the other provinces. Therefore, I am replacing it with a new party – the All-India Scheduled Castes Federation!
I hope you will all support the Federation. With justice on our side, we cannot lose our battle. For it is not a battle for wealth or for power, but for freedom. It is a battle for the reclamation of human personality!
CLAP!
CLAP!
CLAP!
CLAP!
This conference marked the start of a new era of Depressed Class organisation. Movements that started independently were uniting...

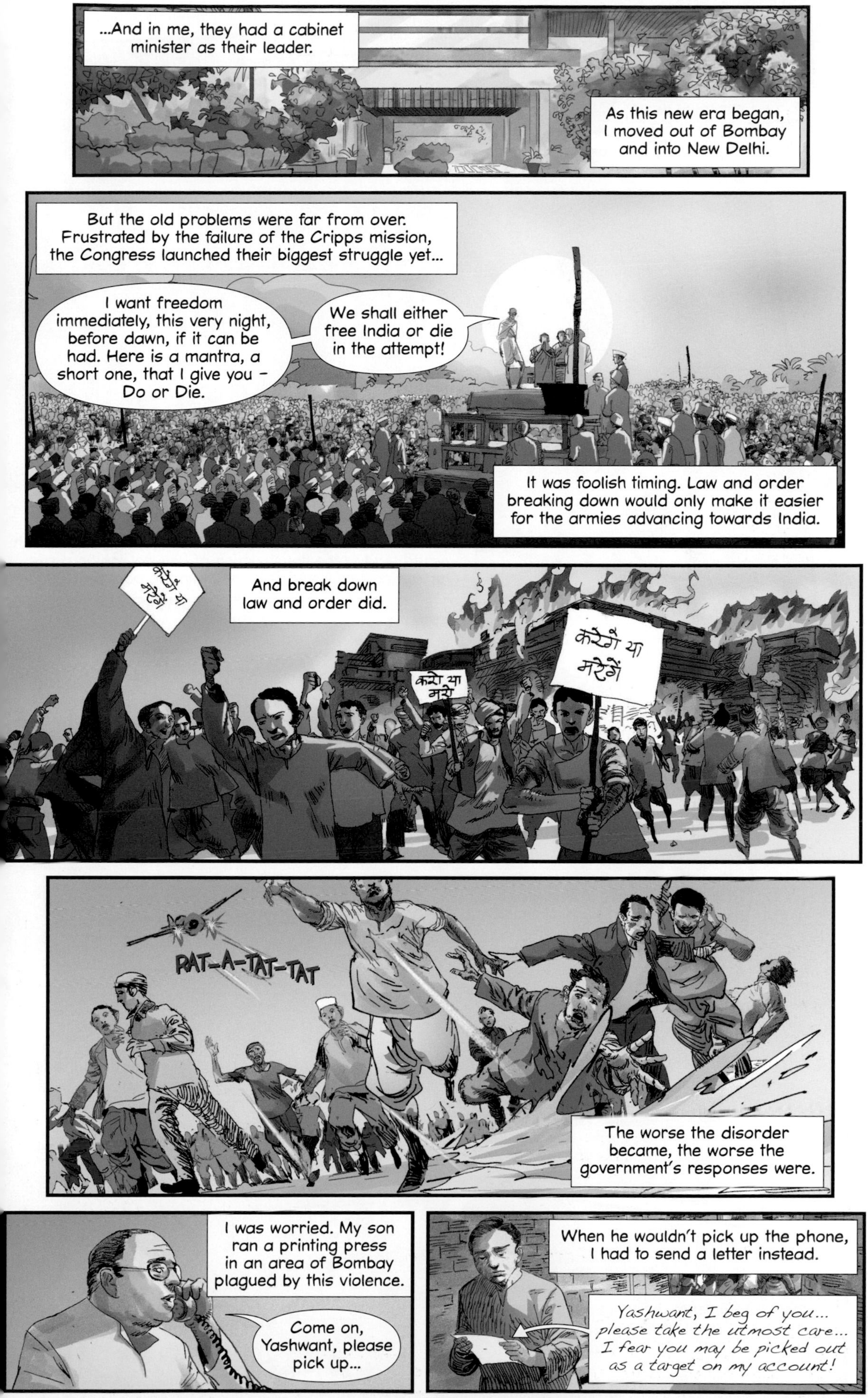
...And in me, they had a cabinet minister as their leader.
As this new era began, I moved out of Bombay and into New Delhi.
But the old problems were far from over. Frustrated by the failure of the Cripps mission, the Congress launched their biggest struggle yet...
I want freedom immediately, this very night, before dawn, if it can be had. Here is a mantra, a short one, that I give you – Do or Die.
We shall either free India or die in the attempt!
It was foolish timing. Law and order breaking down would only make it easier for the armies advancing towards India.
And break down law and order did.
करो या मरो
करेंगे या मरेंगे
RAT-A-TAT-TAT
The worse the disorder became, the worse the government's responses were.
I was worried. My son ran a printing press in an area of Bombay plagued by this violence.
Come on, Yashwant, please pick up...
When he wouldn't pick up the phone, I had to send a letter instead.
Yashwant, I beg of you... please take the utmost care... I fear you may be picked out as a target on my account!

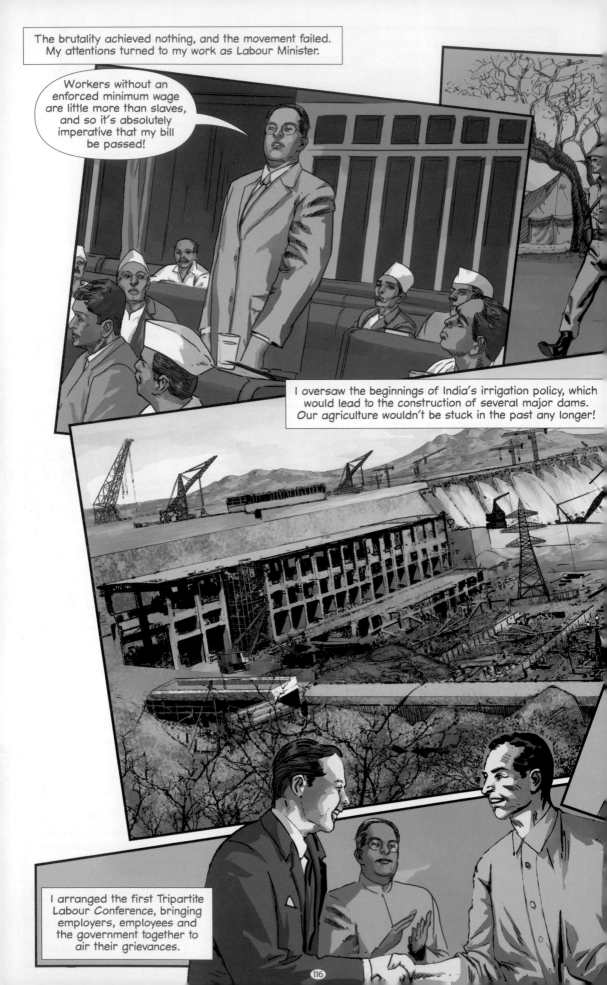

The brutality achieved nothing, and the movement failed. My attentions turned to my work as Labour Minister.

Workers without an enforced minimum wage are little more than slaves, and so it's absolutely imperative that my bill be passed!

I oversaw the beginnings of India's irrigation policy, which would lead to the construction of several major dams. Our agriculture wouldn't be stuck in the past any longer!

I arranged the first Tripartite Labour Conference, bringing employers, employees and the government together to air their grievances.

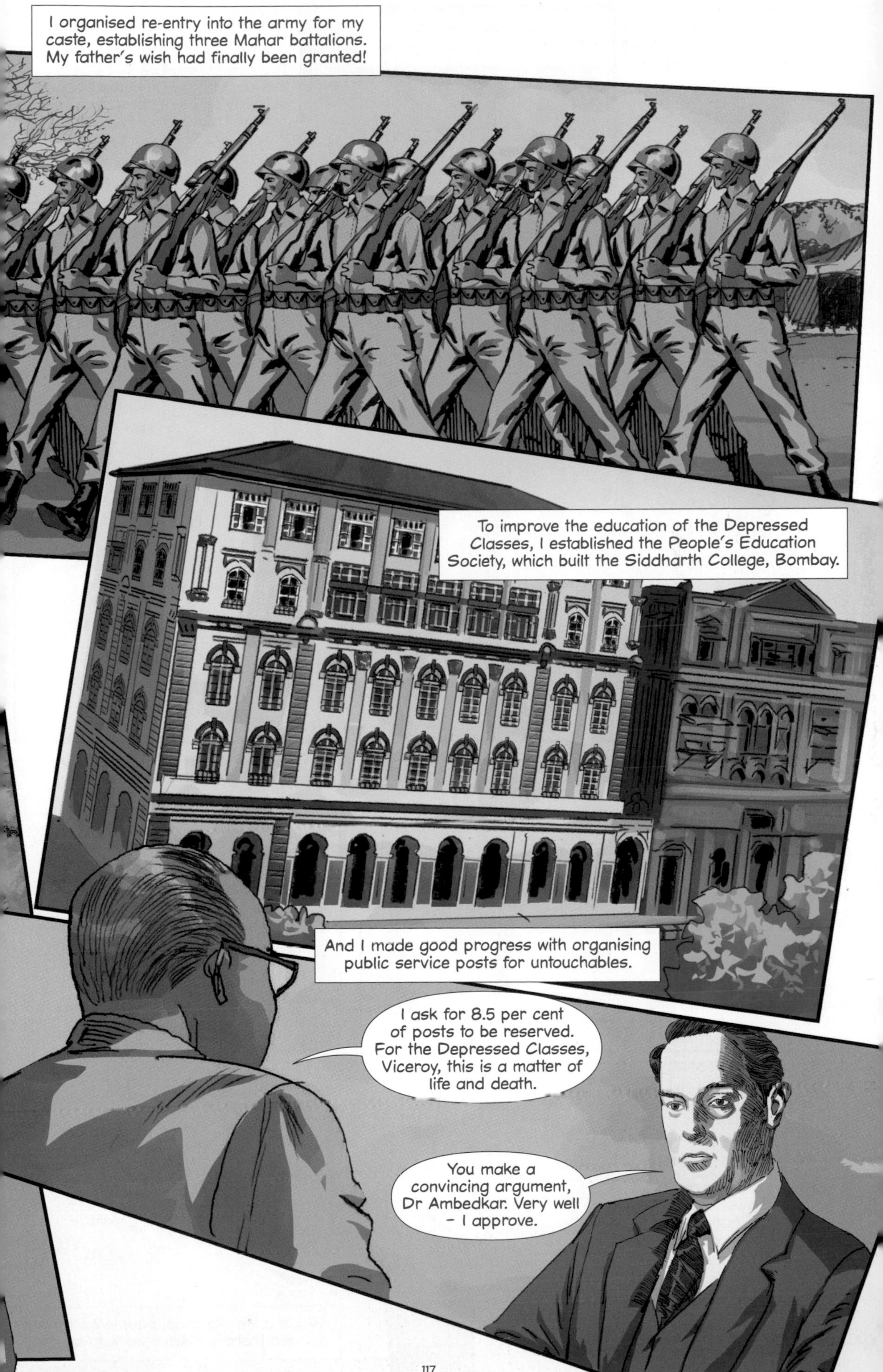
I organised re-entry into the army for my caste, establishing three Mahar battalions. My father's wish had finally been granted!
To improve the education of the Depressed Classes, I established the People's Education Society, which built the Siddharth College, Bombay.
And I made good progress with organising public service posts for untouchables.
I ask for 8.5 per cent of posts to be reserved. For the Depressed Classes, Viceroy, this is a matter of life and death.
You make a convincing argument, Dr Ambedkar. Very well – I approve.

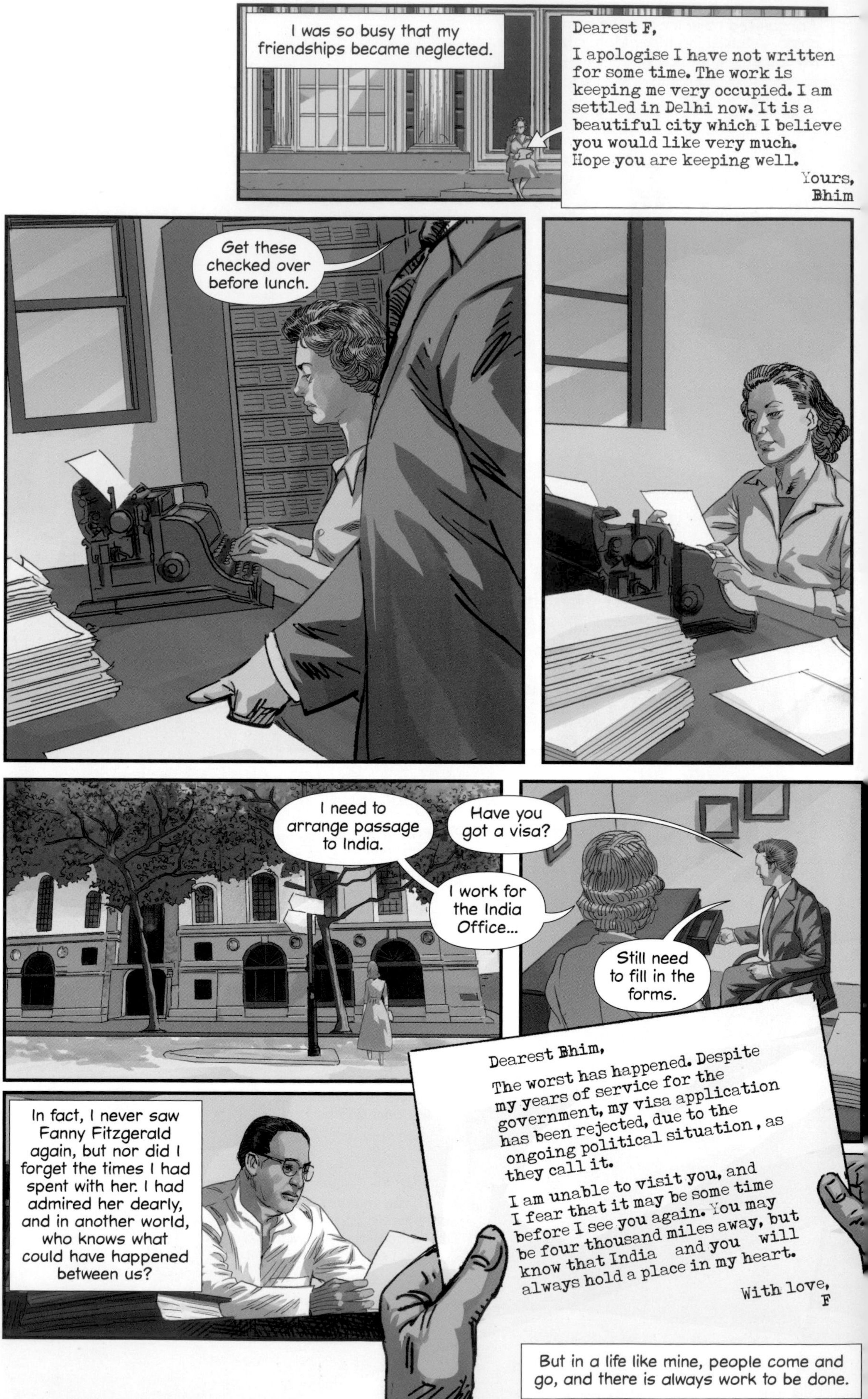

I was so busy that my friendships became neglected.
Dearest F,
I apologise I have not written for some time. The work is keeping me very occupied. I am settled in Delhi now. It is a beautiful city which I believe you would like very much. Hope you are keeping well.
Yours,
Bhim
Get these checked over before lunch.
I need to arrange passage to India.
Have you got a visa?
I work for the India Office...
Still need to fill in the forms.
In fact, I never saw Fanny Fitzgerald again, but nor did I forget the times I had spent with her. I had admired her dearly, and in another world, who knows what could have happened between us?
Dearest Bhim,
The worst has happened. Despite my years of service for the government, my visa application has been rejected, due to the ongoing political situation, as they call it.
I am unable to visit you, and I fear that it may be some time before I see you again. You may be four thousand miles away, but know that India and you will always hold a place in my heart.
With love,
F
But in a life like mine, people come and go, and there is always work to be done.

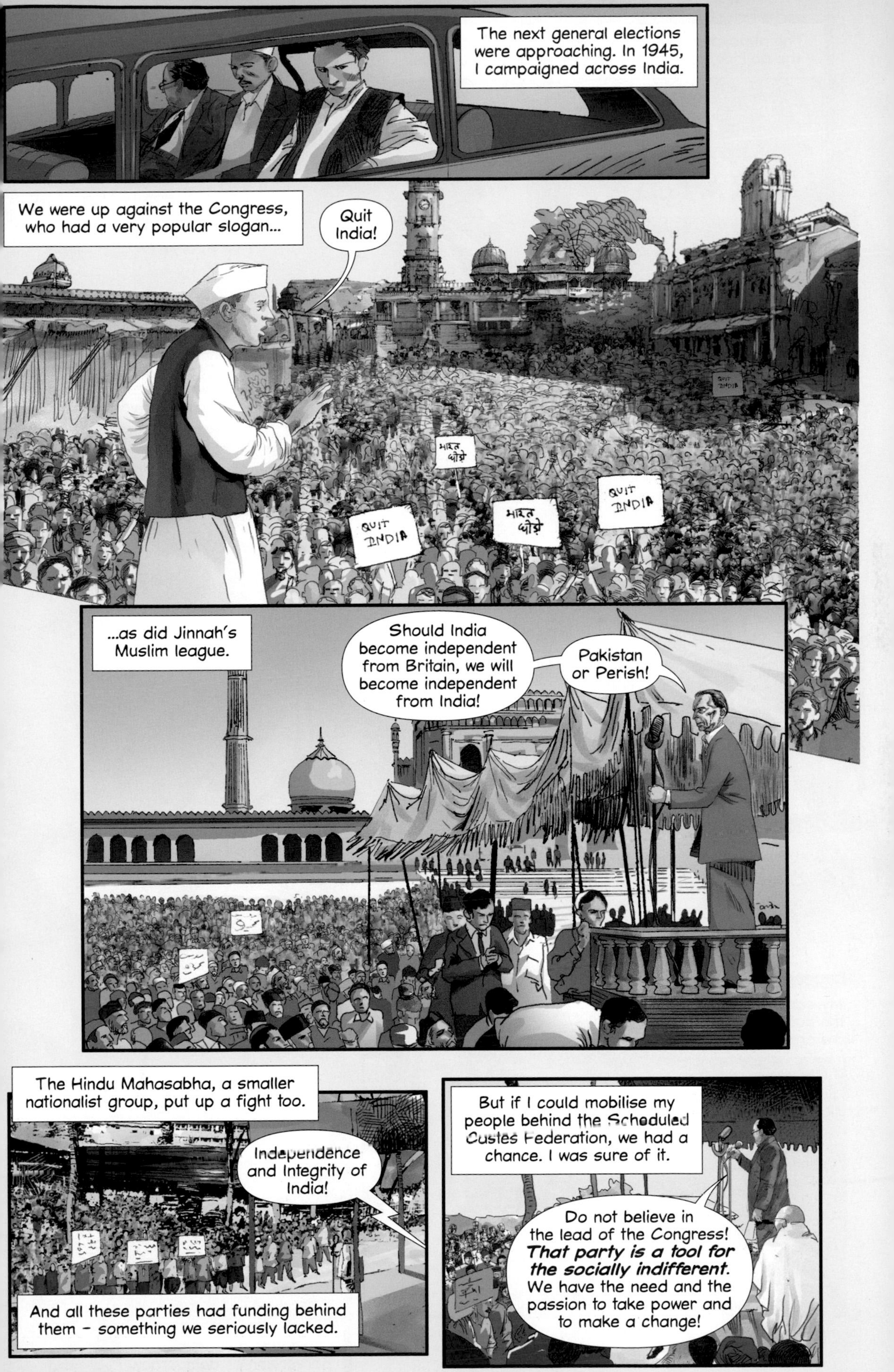
The next general elections were approaching. In 1945, I campaigned across India.
We were up against the Congress, who had a very popular slogan...
Quit India!
QUIT INDIA
QUIT INDIA
...as did Jinnah's Muslim league.
Should India become independent from Britain, we will become independent from India!
Pakistan or Perish!
The Hindu Mahasabha, a smaller nationalist group, put up a fight too.
Independence and Integrity of India!
And all these parties had funding behind them – something we seriously lacked.
But if I could mobilise my people behind the Scheduled Castes Federation, we had a chance. I was sure of it.
Do not believe in the lead of the Congress! ***That party is a tool for the socially indifferent***. We have the need and the passion to take power and to make a change!

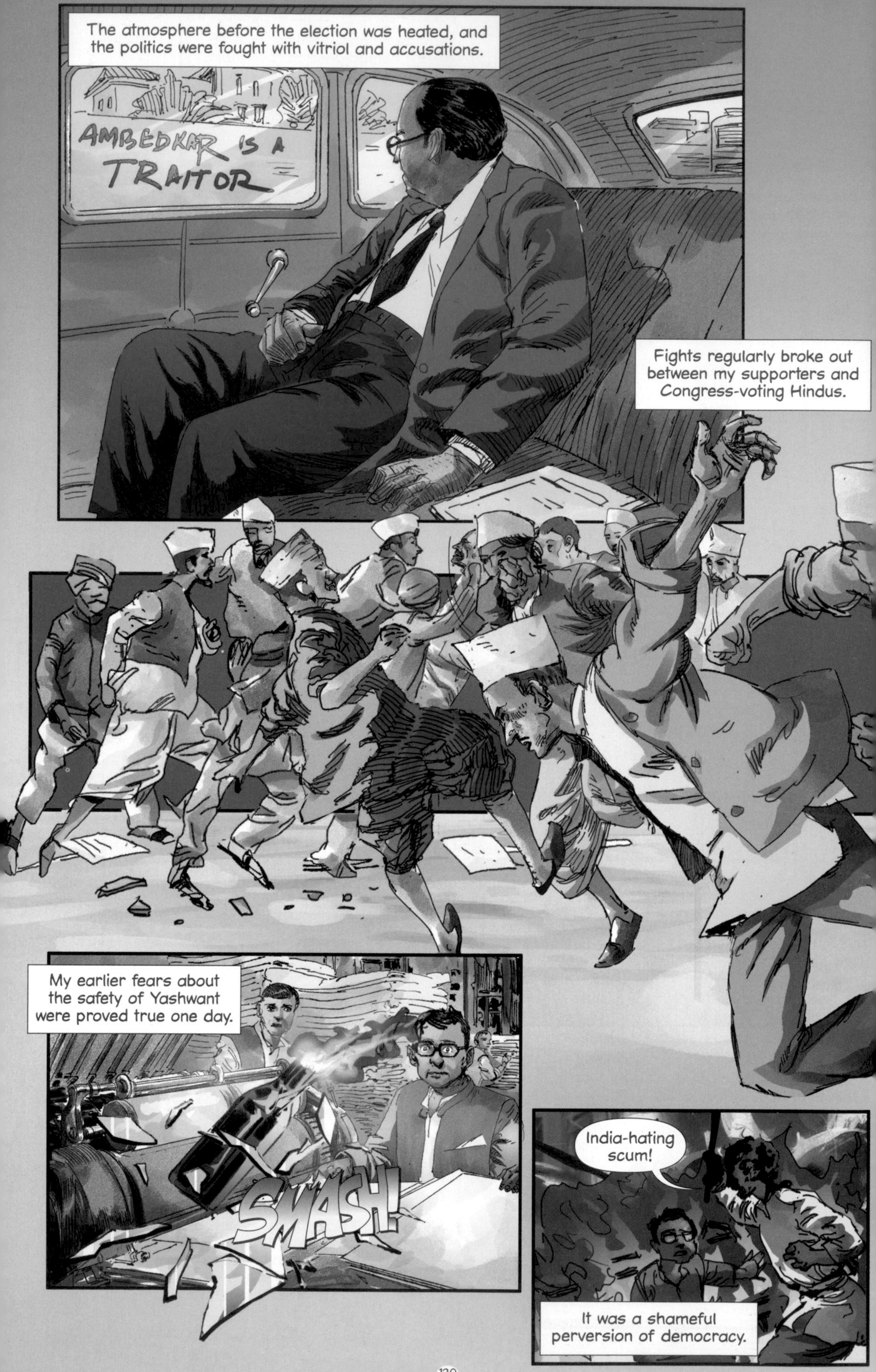
The atmosphere before the election was heated, and the politics were fought with vitriol and accusations.
AMBEDKAR IS A TRAITOR
Fights regularly broke out between my supporters and Congress-voting Hindus.
My earlier fears about the safety of Yashwant were proved true one day.
SMASH!
India-hating scum!
It was a shameful perversion of democracy.

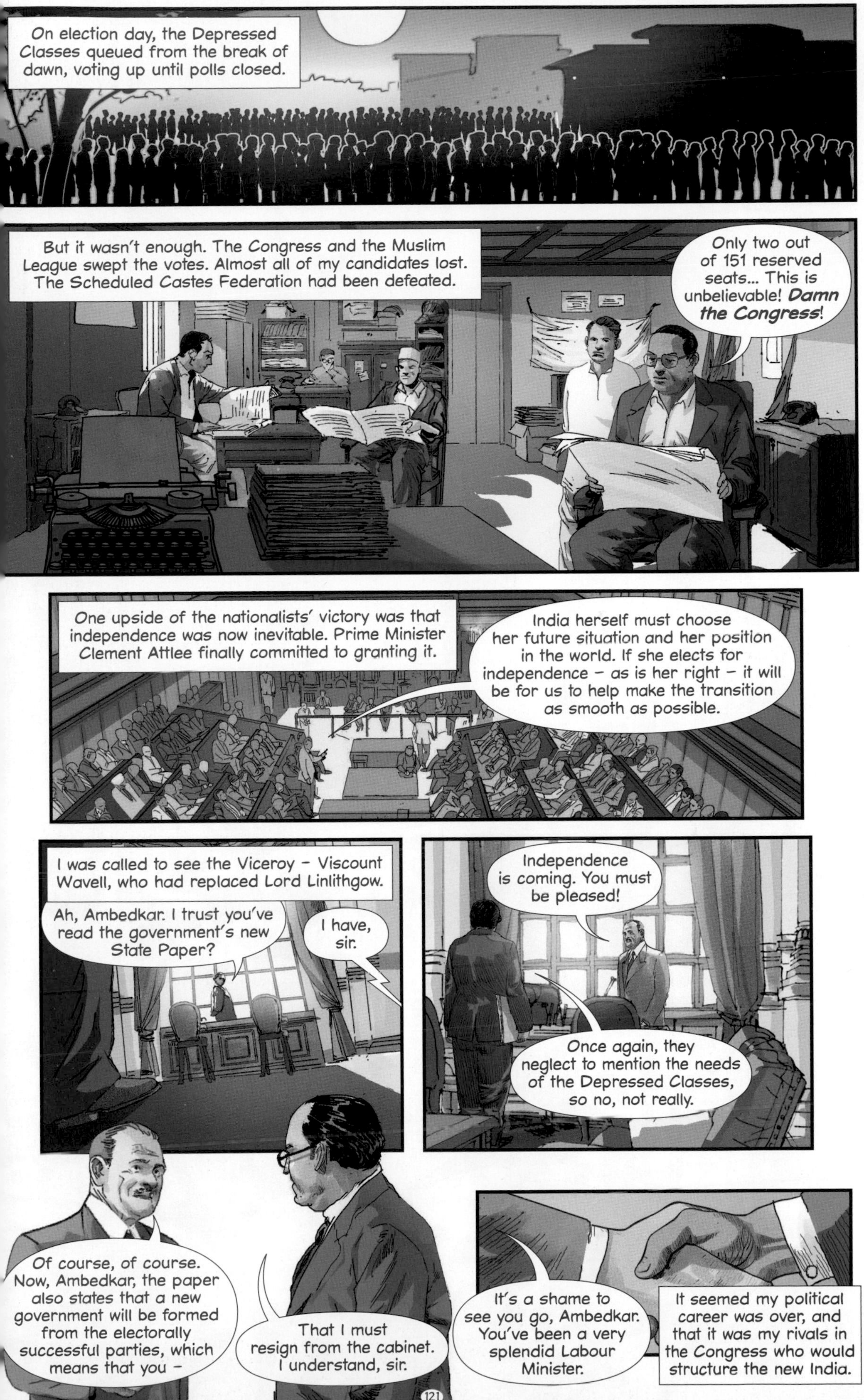
On election day, the Depressed Classes queued from the break of dawn, voting up until polls closed.
But it wasn't enough. The Congress and the Muslim League swept the votes. Almost all of my candidates lost. The Scheduled Castes Federation had been defeated.
Only two out of 151 reserved seats... This is unbelievable! ***Damn the Congress***!
One upside of the nationalists' victory was that independence was now inevitable. Prime Minister Clement Attlee finally committed to granting it.
India herself must choose her future situation and her position in the world. If she elects for independence – as is her right – it will be for us to help make the transition as smooth as possible.
I was called to see the Viceroy – Viscount Wavell, who had replaced Lord Linlithgow.
Ah, Ambedkar. I trust you've read the government's new State Paper?
I have, sir.
Independence is coming. You must be pleased!
Once again, they neglect to mention the needs of the Depressed Classes, so no, not really.
Of course, of course. Now, Ambedkar, the paper also states that a new government will be formed from the electorally successful parties, which means that you –
That I must resign from the cabinet. I understand, sir.
It's a shame to see you go, Ambedkar. You've been a very splendid Labour Minister.
It seemed my political career was over, and that it was my rivals in the Congress who would structure the new India.

7 AN INDEPENDENT INDIA

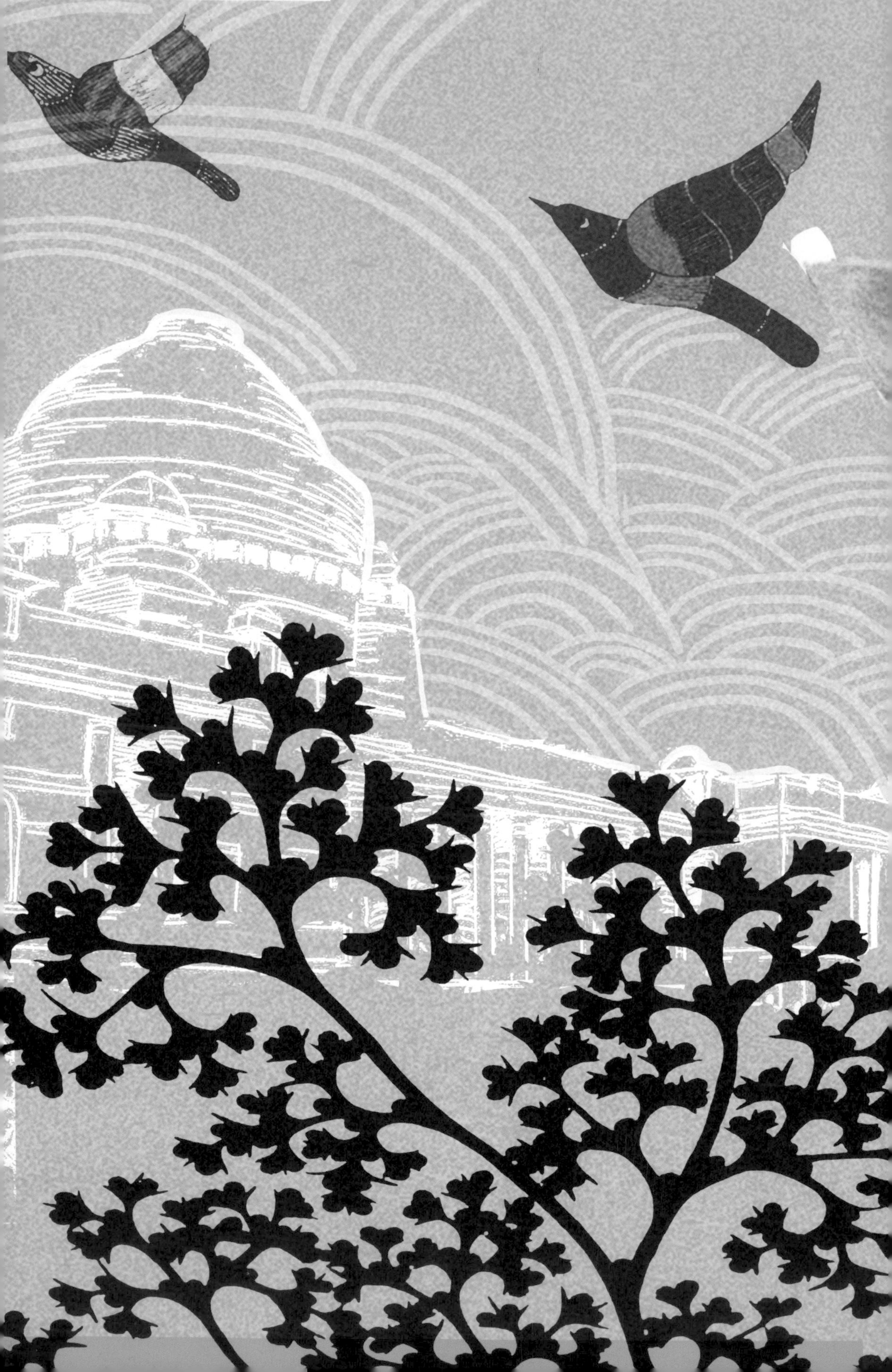

"Constitution is not a mere lawyer's document, it is a vehicle of Life, and its spirit is always the spirit of Age."

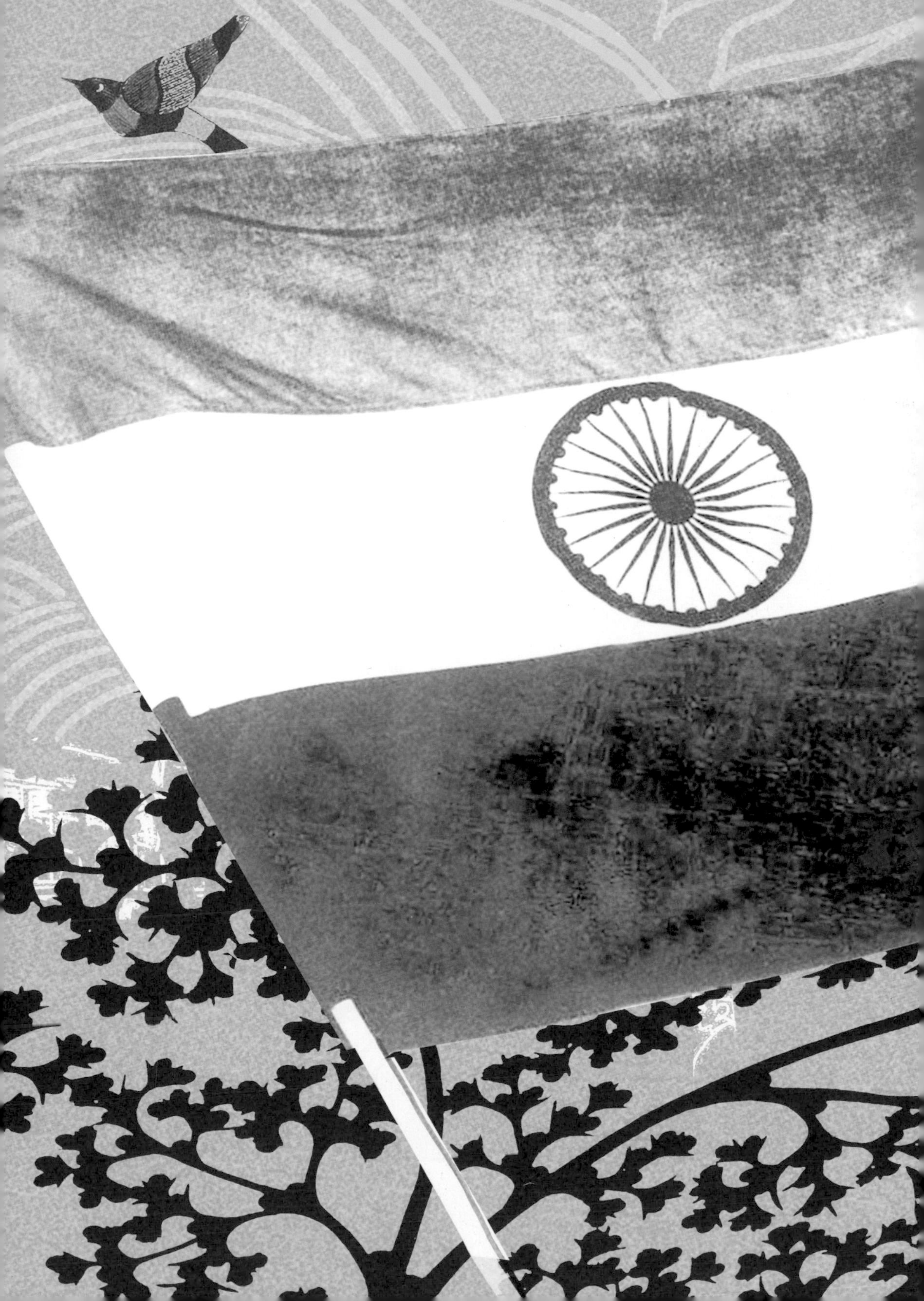

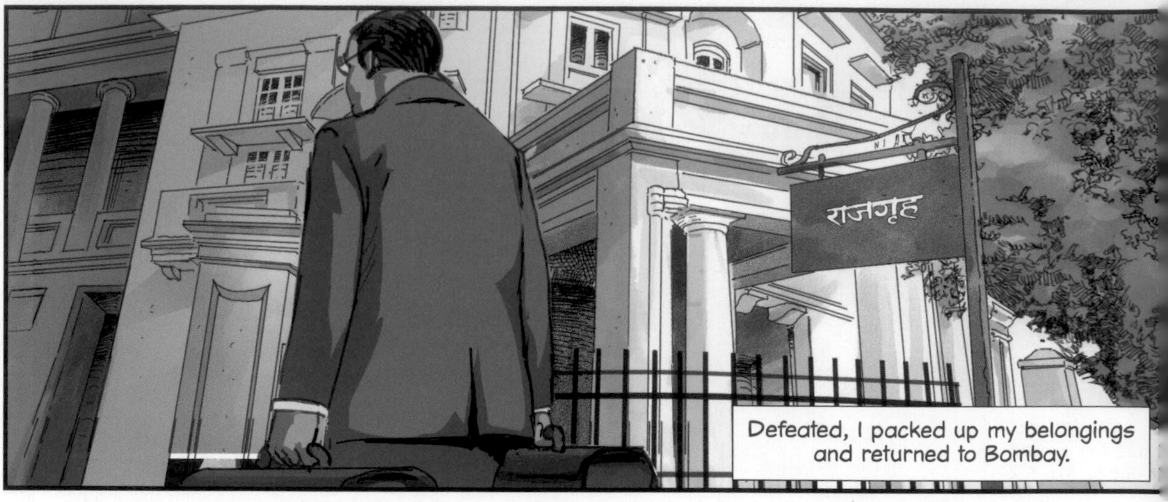
राजगृह
Defeated, I packed up my belongings and returned to Bombay.

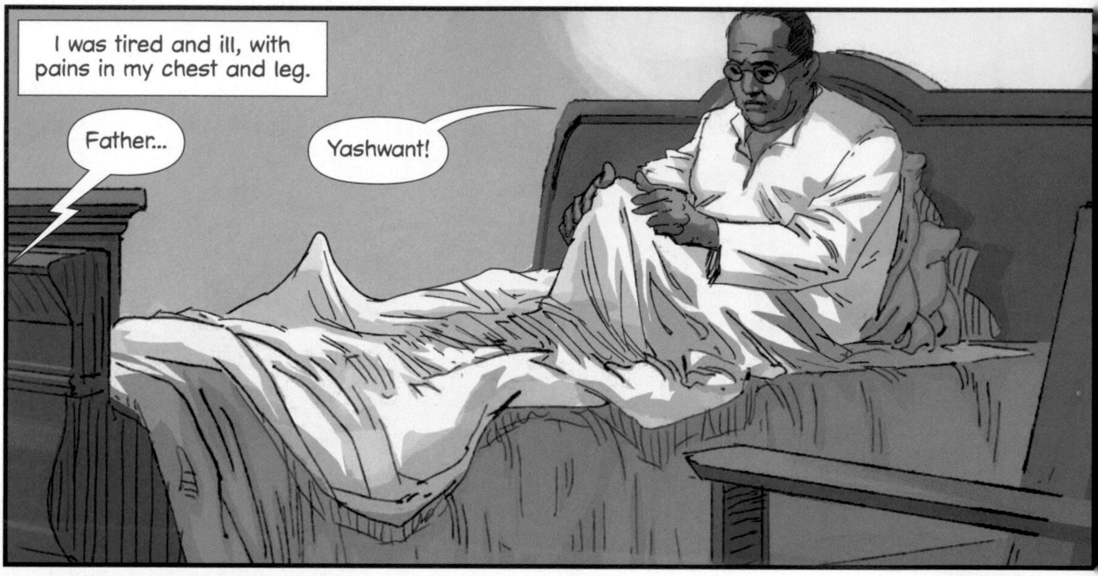
I was tired and ill, with pains in my chest and leg.
Father...
Yashwant!

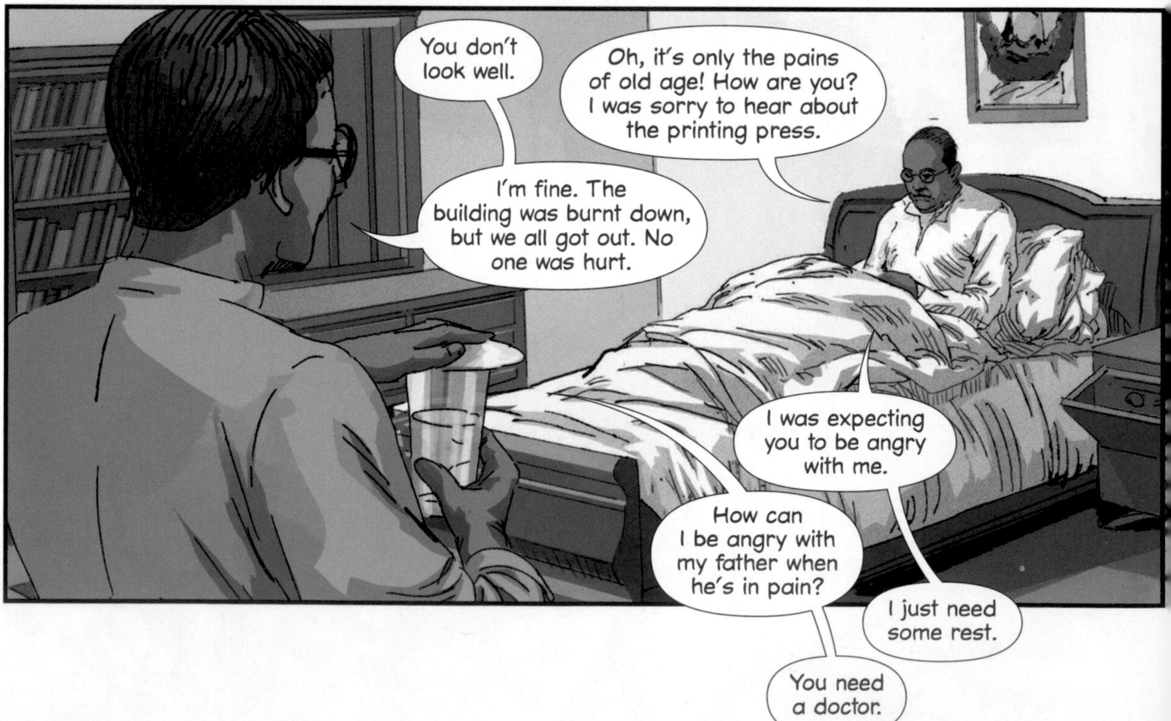
You don't look well.
Oh, it's only the pains of old age! How are you? I was sorry to hear about the printing press.
I'm fine. The building was burnt down, but we all got out. No one was hurt.
I was expecting you to be angry with me.
How can I be angry with my father when he's in pain?
I just need some rest.
You need a doctor.

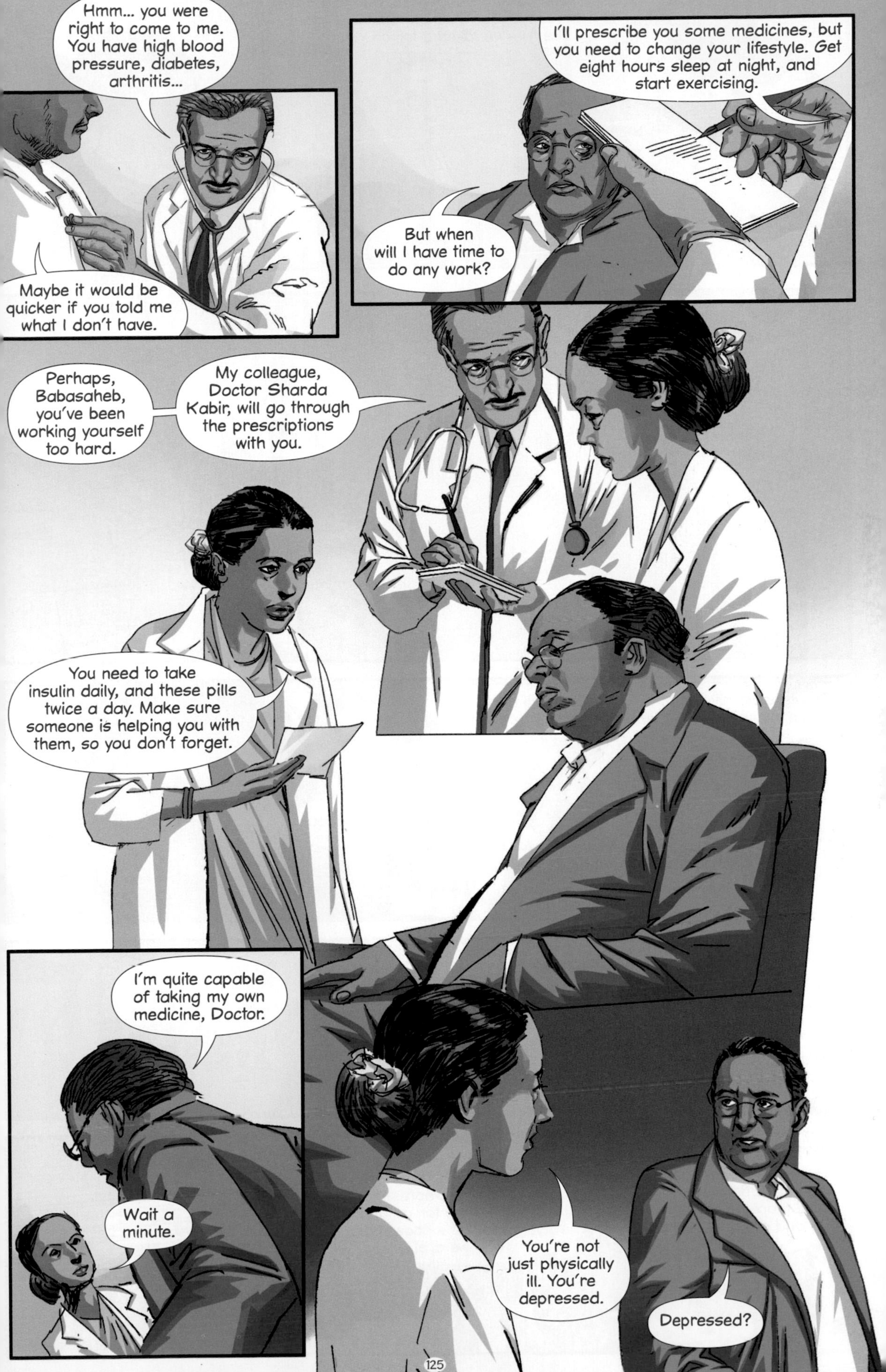
Hmm... you were right to come to me. You have high blood pressure, diabetes, arthritis...
Maybe it would be quicker if you told me what I don't have.
I'll prescribe you some medicines, but you need to change your lifestyle. Get eight hours sleep at night, and start exercising.
But when will I have time to do any work?
Perhaps, Babasaheb, you've been working yourself too hard.
My colleague, Doctor Sharda Kabir, will go through the prescriptions with you.
You need to take insulin daily, and these pills twice a day. Make sure someone is helping you with them, so you don't forget.
I'm quite capable of taking my own medicine, Doctor.
Wait a minute.
You're not just physically ill. You're depressed.
Depressed?

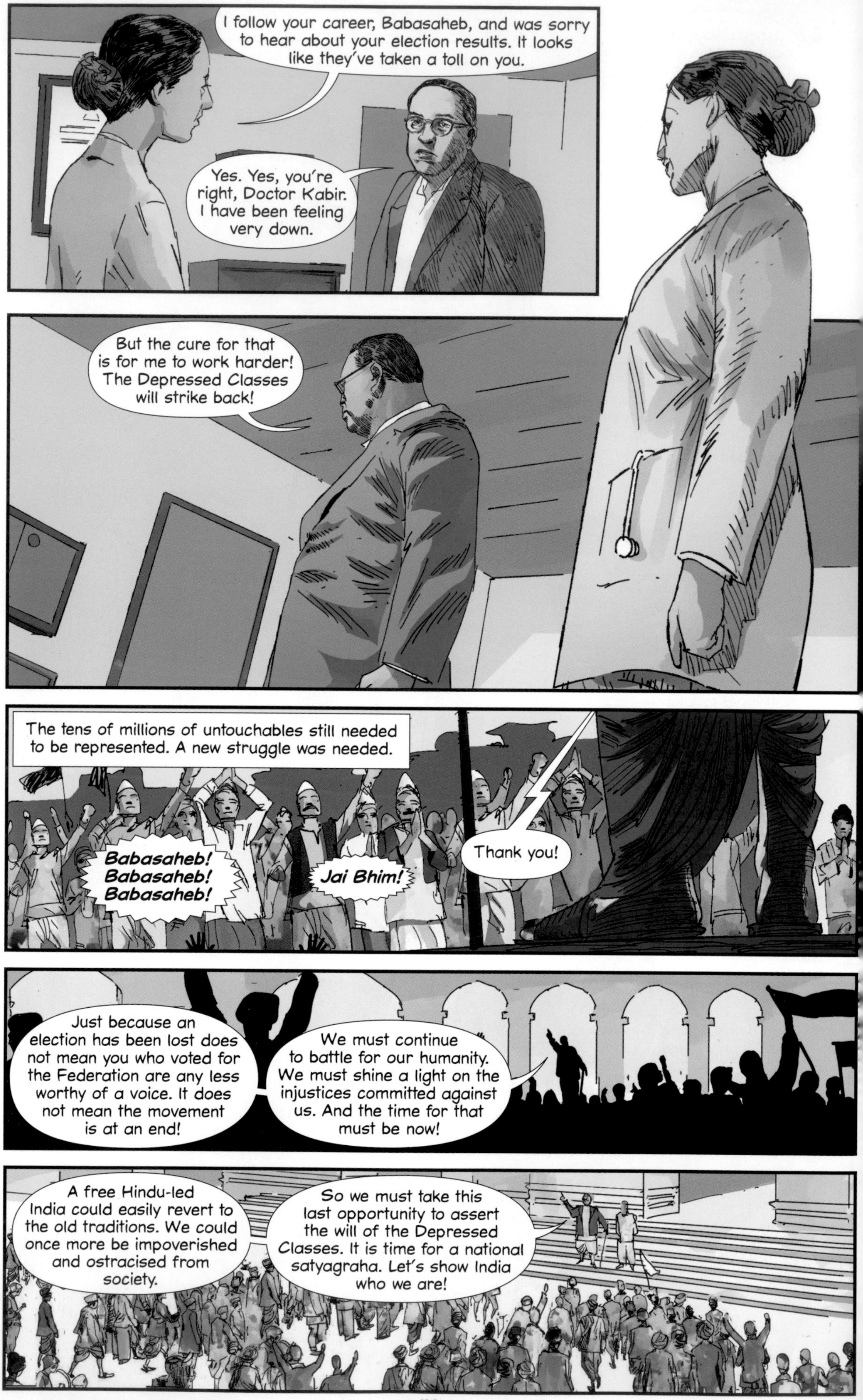
I follow your career, Babasaheb, and was sorry to hear about your election results. It looks like they've taken a toll on you.
Yes. Yes, you're right, Doctor Kabir. I have been feeling very down.
But the cure for that is for me to work harder! The Depressed Classes will strike back!
The tens of millions of untouchables still needed to be represented. A new struggle was needed.
Babasaheb! Babasaheb! Babasaheb!
Jai Bhim!
Thank you!
Just because an election has been lost does not mean you who voted for the Federation are any less worthy of a voice. It does not mean the movement is at an end!
We must continue to battle for our humanity. We must shine a light on the injustices committed against us. And the time for that must be now!
A free Hindu-led India could easily revert to the old traditions. We could once more be impoverished and ostracised from society.
So we must take this last opportunity to assert the will of the Depressed Classes. It is time for a national satyagraha. Let's show India who we are!

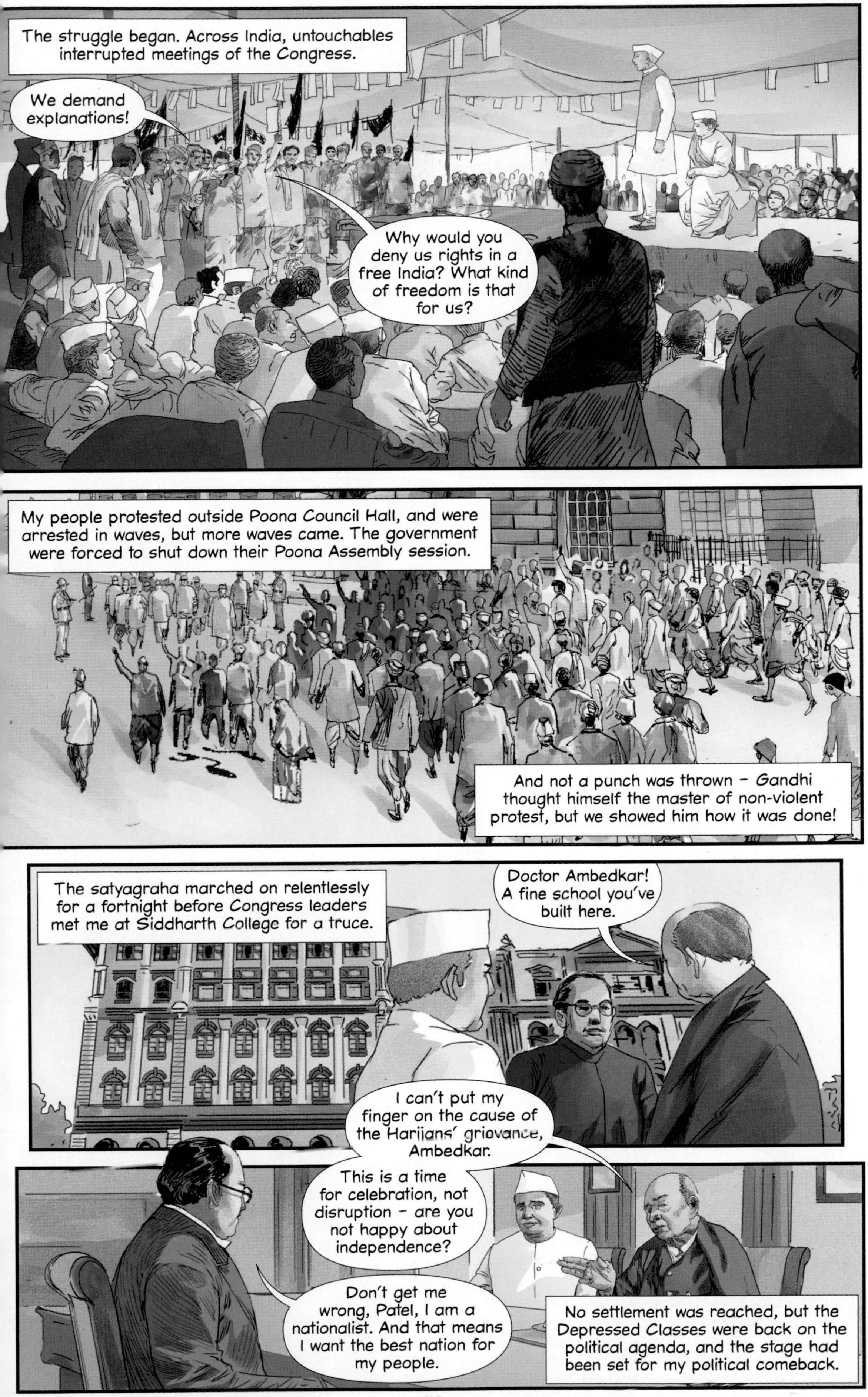
The struggle began. Across India, untouchables interrupted meetings of the Congress.
We demand explanations!
Why would you deny us rights in a free India? What kind of freedom is that for us?
My people protested outside Poona Council Hall, and were arrested in waves, but more waves came. The government were forced to shut down their Poona Assembly session.
And not a punch was thrown – Gandhi thought himself the master of non-violent protest, but we showed him how it was done!
The satyagraha marched on relentlessly for a fortnight before Congress leaders met me at Siddharth College for a truce.
Doctor Ambedkar! A fine school you've built here.
I can't put my finger on the cause of the Harijans' grievance, Ambedkar.
This is a time for celebration, not disruption – are you not happy about independence?
Don't get me wrong, Patel, I am a nationalist. And that means I want the best nation for my people.
No settlement was reached, but the Depressed Classes were back on the political agenda, and the stage had been set for my political comeback.

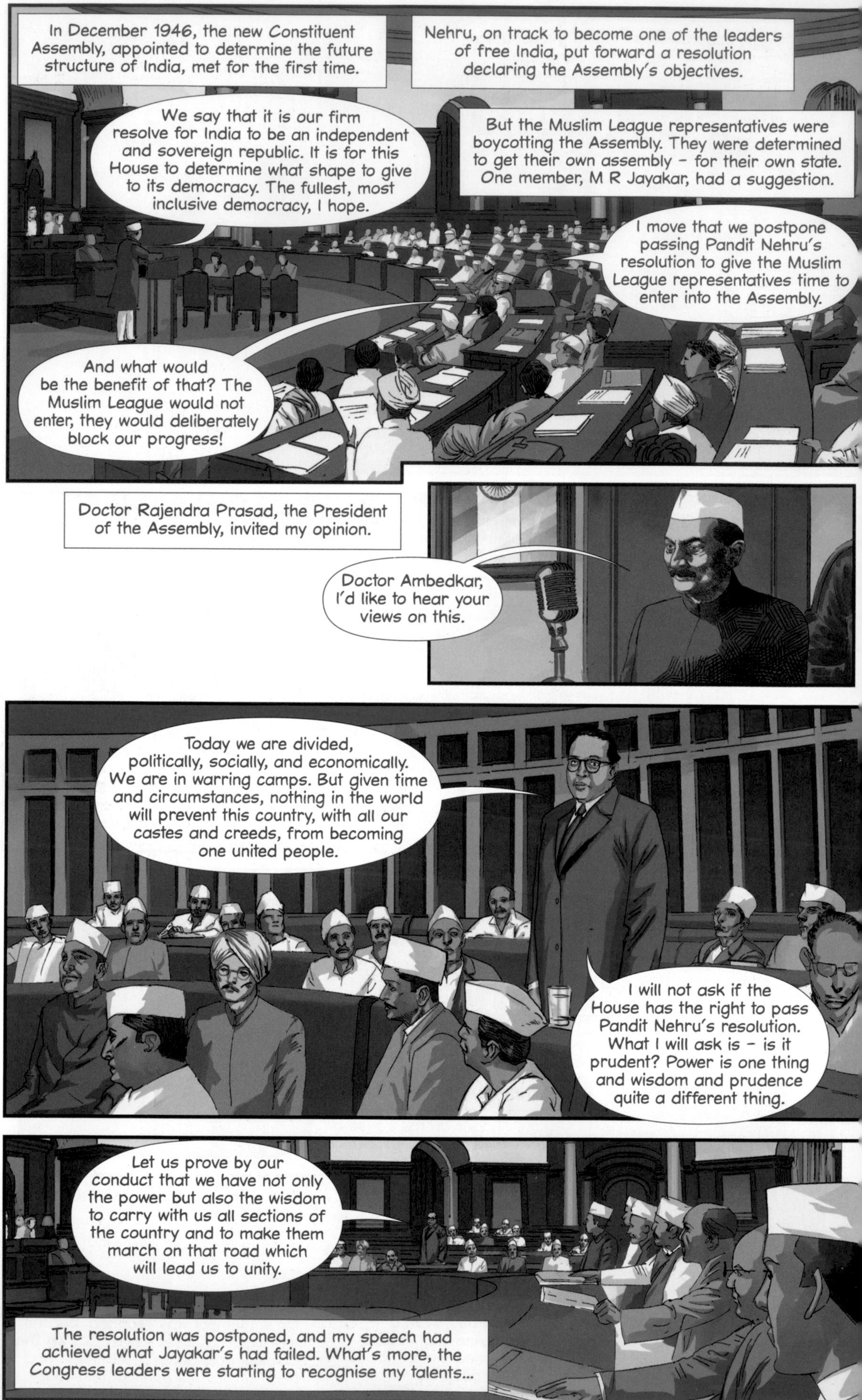
In December 1946, the new Constituent Assembly, appointed to determine the future structure of India, met for the first time.
Nehru, on track to become one of the leaders of free India, put forward a resolution declaring the Assembly's objectives.
We say that it is our firm resolve for India to be an independent and sovereign republic. It is for this House to determine what shape to give to its democracy. The fullest, most inclusive democracy, I hope.
But the Muslim League representatives were boycotting the Assembly. They were determined to get their own assembly – for their own state. One member, M R Jayakar, had a suggestion.
I move that we postpone passing Pandit Nehru's resolution to give the Muslim League representatives time to enter into the Assembly.
And what would be the benefit of that? The Muslim League would not enter, they would deliberately block our progress!
Doctor Rajendra Prasad, the President of the Assembly, invited my opinion.
Doctor Ambedkar, I'd like to hear your views on this.
Today we are divided, politically, socially, and economically. We are in warring camps. But given time and circumstances, nothing in the world will prevent this country, with all our castes and creeds, from becoming one united people.
I will not ask if the House has the right to pass Pandit Nehru's resolution. What I will ask is – is it prudent? Power is one thing and wisdom and prudence quite a different thing.
Let us prove by our conduct that we have not only the power but also the wisdom to carry with us all sections of the country and to make them march on that road which will lead us to unity.
The resolution was postponed, and my speech had achieved what Jayakar's had failed. What's more, the Congress leaders were starting to recognise my talents...

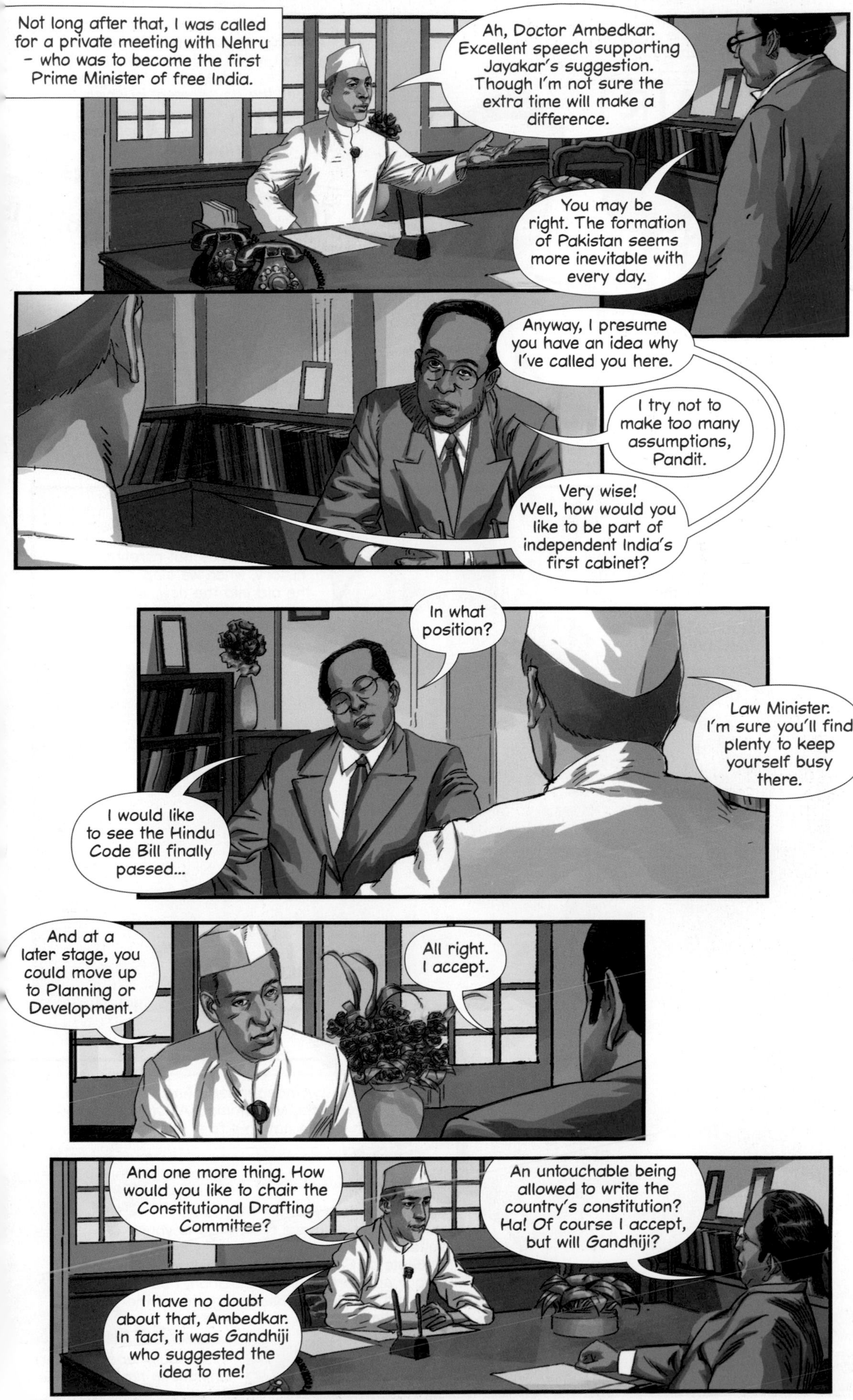
Not long after that, I was called for a private meeting with Nehru – who was to become the first Prime Minister of free India.
Ah, Doctor Ambedkar. Excellent speech supporting Jayakar's suggestion. Though I'm not sure the extra time will make a difference.
You may be right. The formation of Pakistan seems more inevitable with every day.
Anyway, I presume you have an idea why I've called you here.
I try not to make too many assumptions, Pandit.
Very wise! Well, how would you like to be part of independent India's first cabinet?
In what position?
Law Minister. I'm sure you'll find plenty to keep yourself busy there.
I would like to see the Hindu Code Bill finally passed...
And at a later stage, you could move up to Planning or Development.
All right. I accept.
And one more thing. How would you like to chair the Constitutional Drafting Committee?
An untouchable being allowed to write the country's constitution? Ha! Of course I accept, but will Gandhiji?
I have no doubt about that, Ambedkar. In fact, it was Gandhiji who suggested the idea to me!

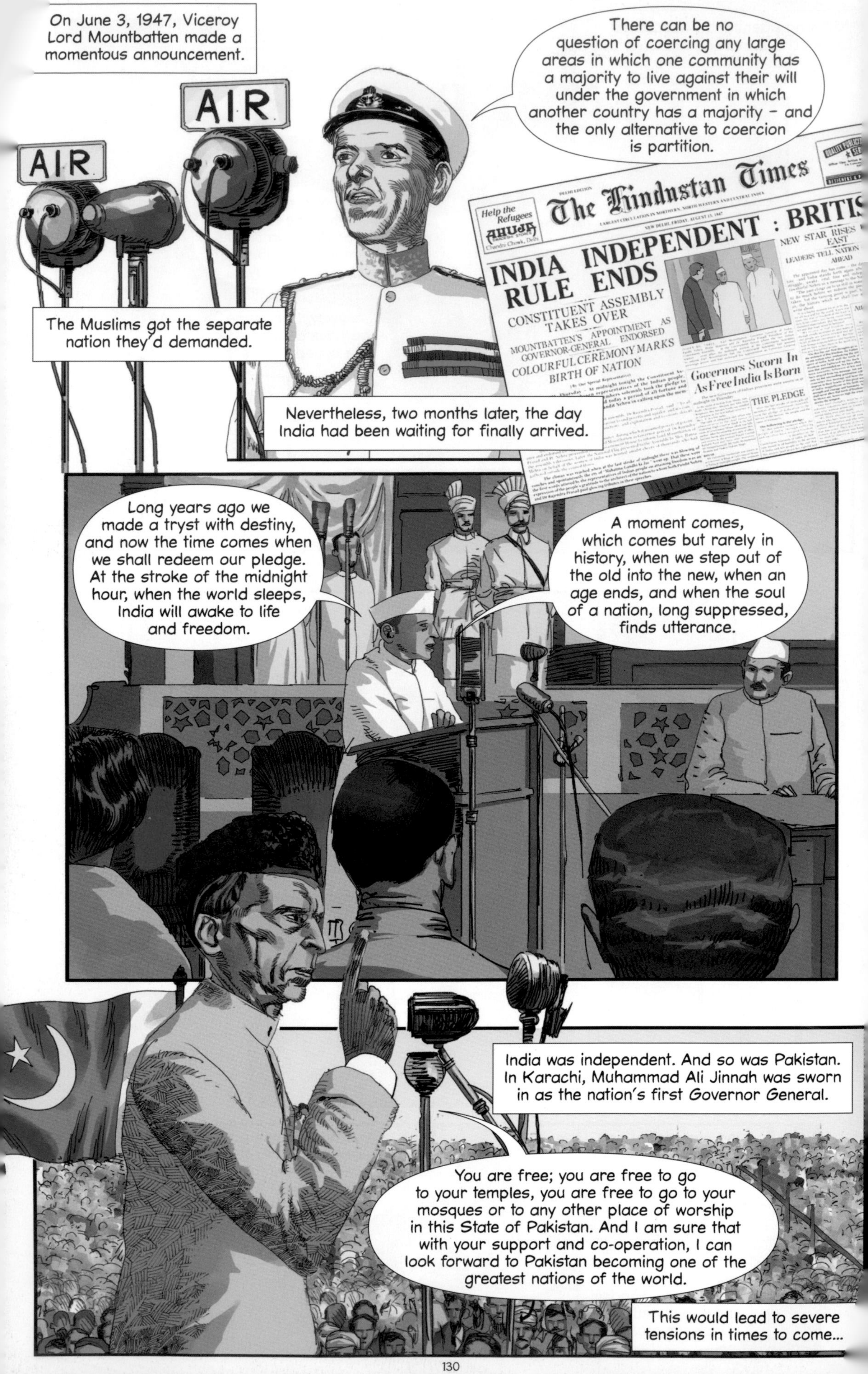
On June 3, 1947, Viceroy Lord Mountbatten made a momentous announcement.
AIR
AIR
There can be no question of coercing any large areas in which one community has a majority to live against their will under the government in which another country has a majority – and the only alternative to coercion is partition.
The Hindustan Times
Help the Refugees
INDIA INDEPENDENT : BRITIS
RULE ENDS
CONSTITUENT ASSEMBLY TAKES OVER
MOUNTBATTEN'S APPOINTMENT AS GOVERNOR-GENERAL ENDORSED
COLOURFUL CEREMONY MARKS BIRTH OF NATION
NEW STAR RISES EAST
Governors Sworn In As Free India Is Born
THE PLEDGE
The Muslims got the separate nation they'd demanded.
Nevertheless, two months later, the day India had been waiting for finally arrived.
Long years ago we made a tryst with destiny, and now the time comes when we shall redeem our pledge. At the stroke of the midnight hour, when the world sleeps, India will awake to life and freedom.
A moment comes, which comes but rarely in history, when we step out of the old into the new, when an age ends, and when the soul of a nation, long suppressed, finds utterance.
India was independent. And so was Pakistan. In Karachi, Muhammad Ali Jinnah was sworn in as the nation's first Governor General.
You are free; you are free to go to your temples, you are free to go to your mosques or to any other place of worship in this State of Pakistan. And I am sure that with your support and co-operation, I can look forward to Pakistan becoming one of the greatest nations of the world.
This would lead to severe tensions in times to come...

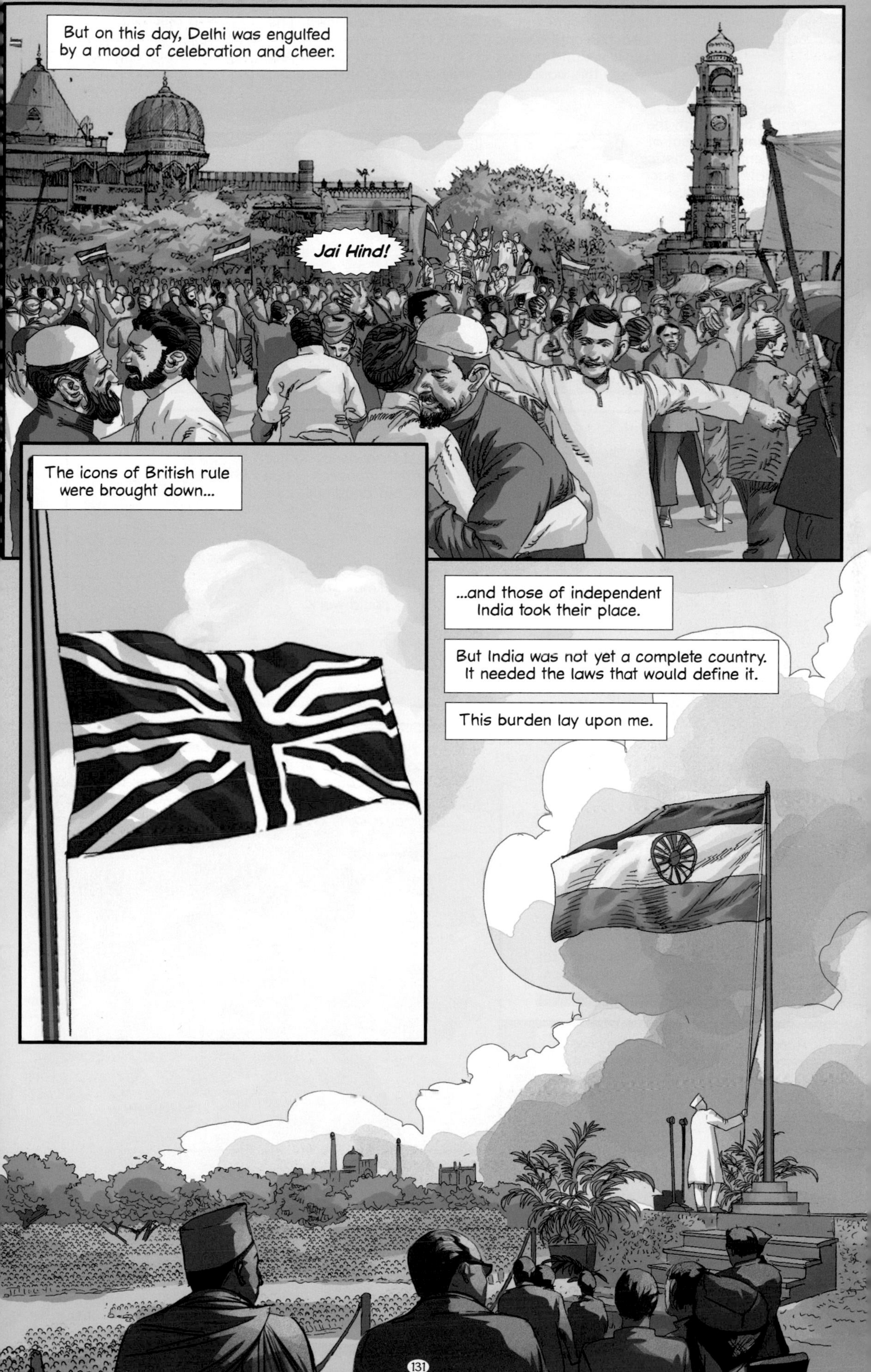
But on this day, Delhi was engulfed by a mood of celebration and cheer.
Jai Hind!
The icons of British rule were brought down...
...and those of independent India took their place.
But India was not yet a complete country. It needed the laws that would define it.
This burden lay upon me.

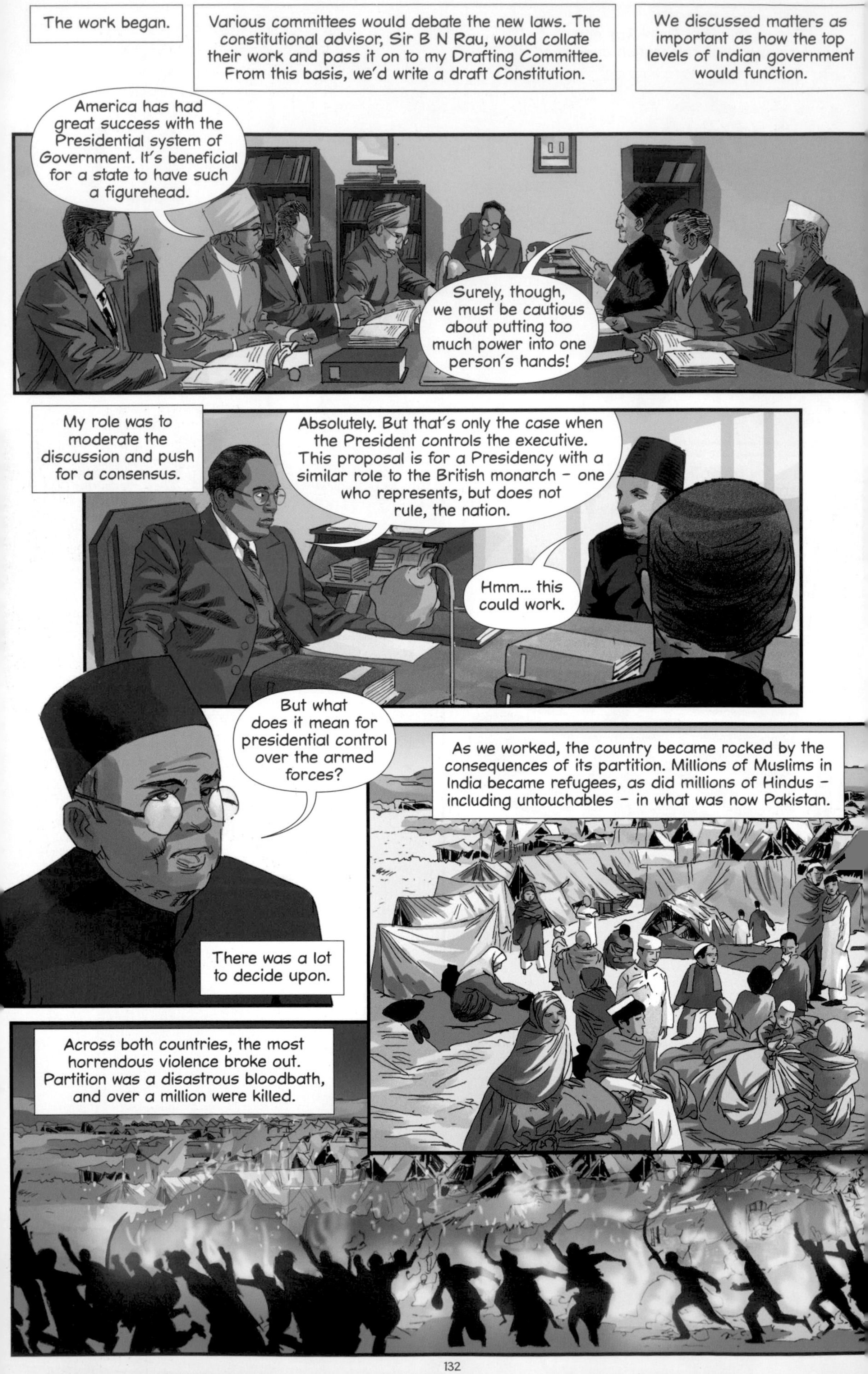
The work began.
Various committees would debate the new laws. The constitutional advisor, Sir B N Rau, would collate their work and pass it on to my Drafting Committee. From this basis, we'd write a draft Constitution.
We discussed matters as important as how the top levels of Indian government would function.
America has had great success with the Presidential system of Government. It's beneficial for a state to have such a figurehead.
Surely, though, we must be cautious about putting too much power into one person's hands!
My role was to moderate the discussion and push for a consensus.
Absolutely. But that's only the case when the President controls the executive. This proposal is for a Presidency with a similar role to the British monarch – one who represents, but does not rule, the nation.
Hmm... this could work.
But what does it mean for presidential control over the armed forces?
There was a lot to decide upon.
As we worked, the country became rocked by the consequences of its partition. Millions of Muslims in India became refugees, as did millions of Hindus – including untouchables – in what was now Pakistan.
Across both countries, the most horrendous violence broke out. Partition was a disastrous bloodbath, and over a million were killed.

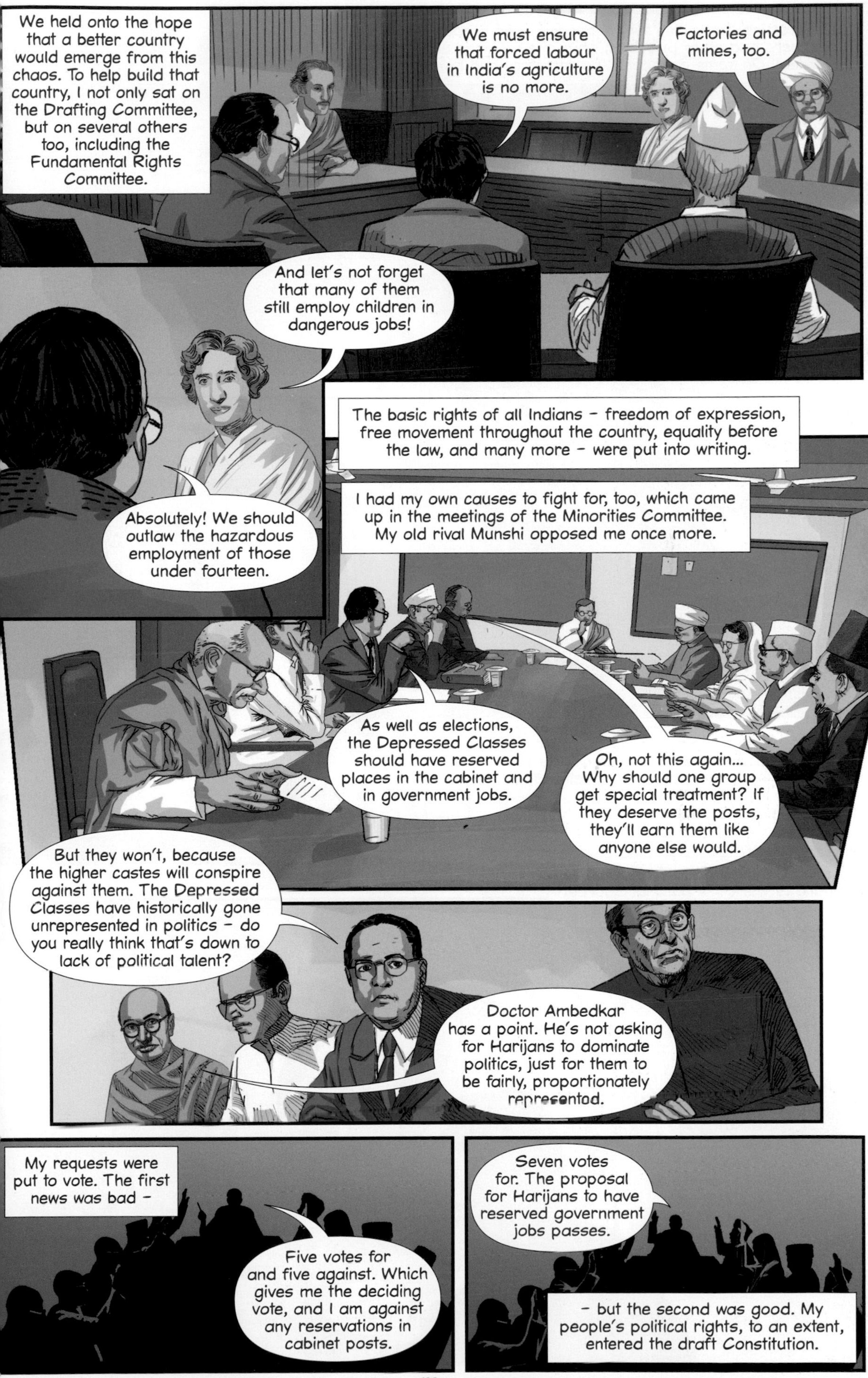
We held onto the hope that a better country would emerge from this chaos. To help build that country, I not only sat on the Drafting Committee, but on several others too, including the Fundamental Rights Committee.
We must ensure that forced labour in India's agriculture is no more.
Factories and mines, too.
And let's not forget that many of them still employ children in dangerous jobs!
Absolutely! We should outlaw the hazardous employment of those under fourteen.
The basic rights of all Indians – freedom of expression, free movement throughout the country, equality before the law, and many more – were put into writing.
I had my own causes to fight for, too, which came up in the meetings of the Minorities Committee. My old rival Munshi opposed me once more.
As well as elections, the Depressed Classes should have reserved places in the cabinet and in government jobs.
Oh, not this again... Why should one group get special treatment? If they deserve the posts, they'll earn them like anyone else would.
But they won't, because the higher castes will conspire against them. The Depressed Classes have historically gone unrepresented in politics – do you really think that's down to lack of political talent?
Doctor Ambedkar has a point. He's not asking for Harijans to dominate politics, just for them to be fairly, proportionately represented.
My requests were put to vote. The first news was bad –
Five votes for and five against. Which gives me the deciding vote, and I am against any reservations in cabinet posts.
Seven votes for. The proposal for Harijans to have reserved government jobs passes.
– but the second was good. My people's political rights, to an extent, entered the draft Constitution.

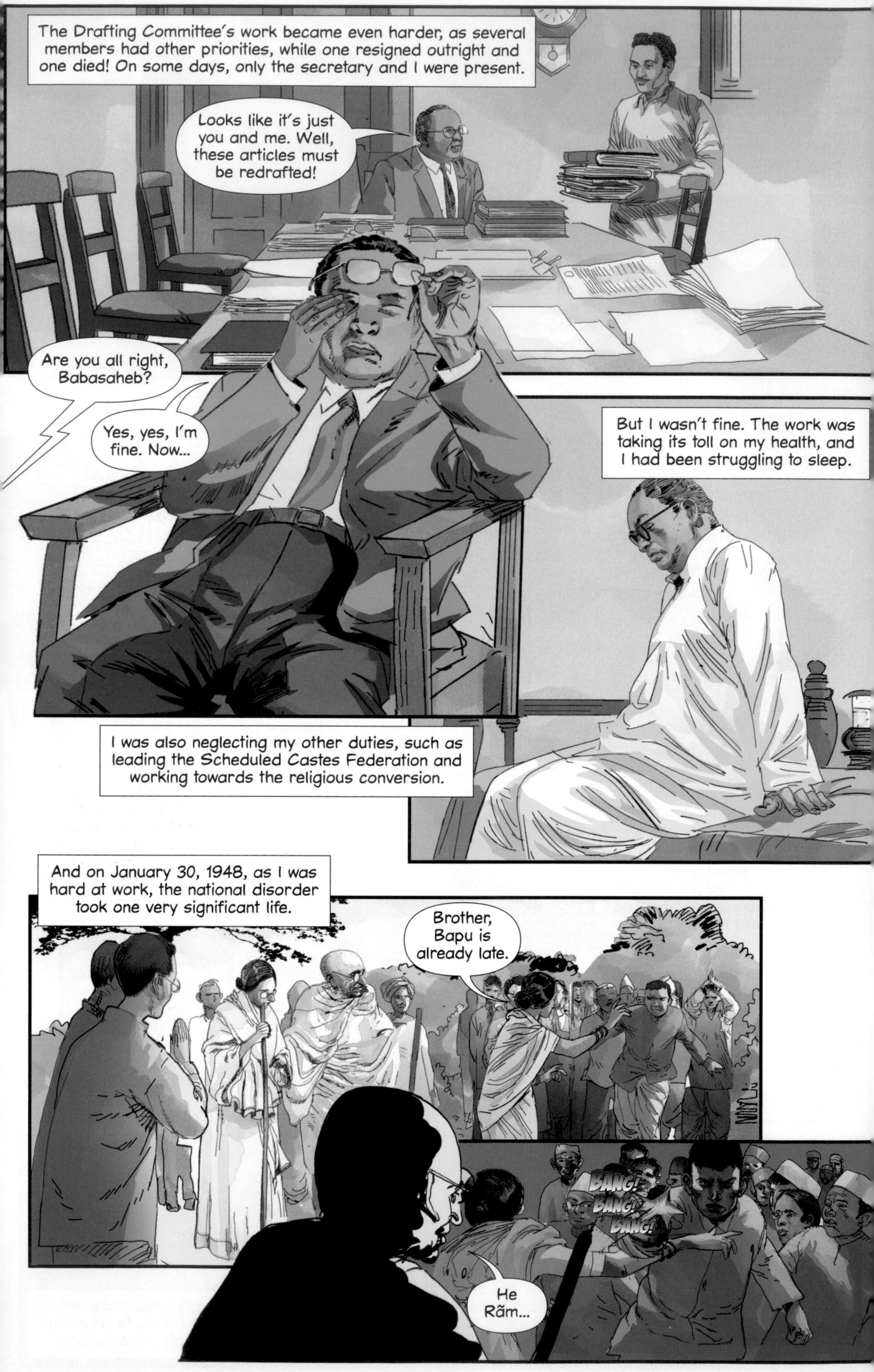

The Drafting Committee's work became even harder, as several members had other priorities, while one resigned outright and one died! On some days, only the secretary and I were present.
Looks like it's just you and me. Well, these articles must be redrafted!
Are you all right, Babasaheb?
Yes, yes, I'm fine. Now...
But I wasn't fine. The work was taking its toll on my health, and I had been struggling to sleep.
I was also neglecting my other duties, such as leading the Scheduled Castes Federation and working towards the religious conversion.
And on January 30, 1948, as I was hard at work, the national disorder took one very significant life.
Brother, Bapu is already late.
BANG! BANG! BANG!
He Rãm...

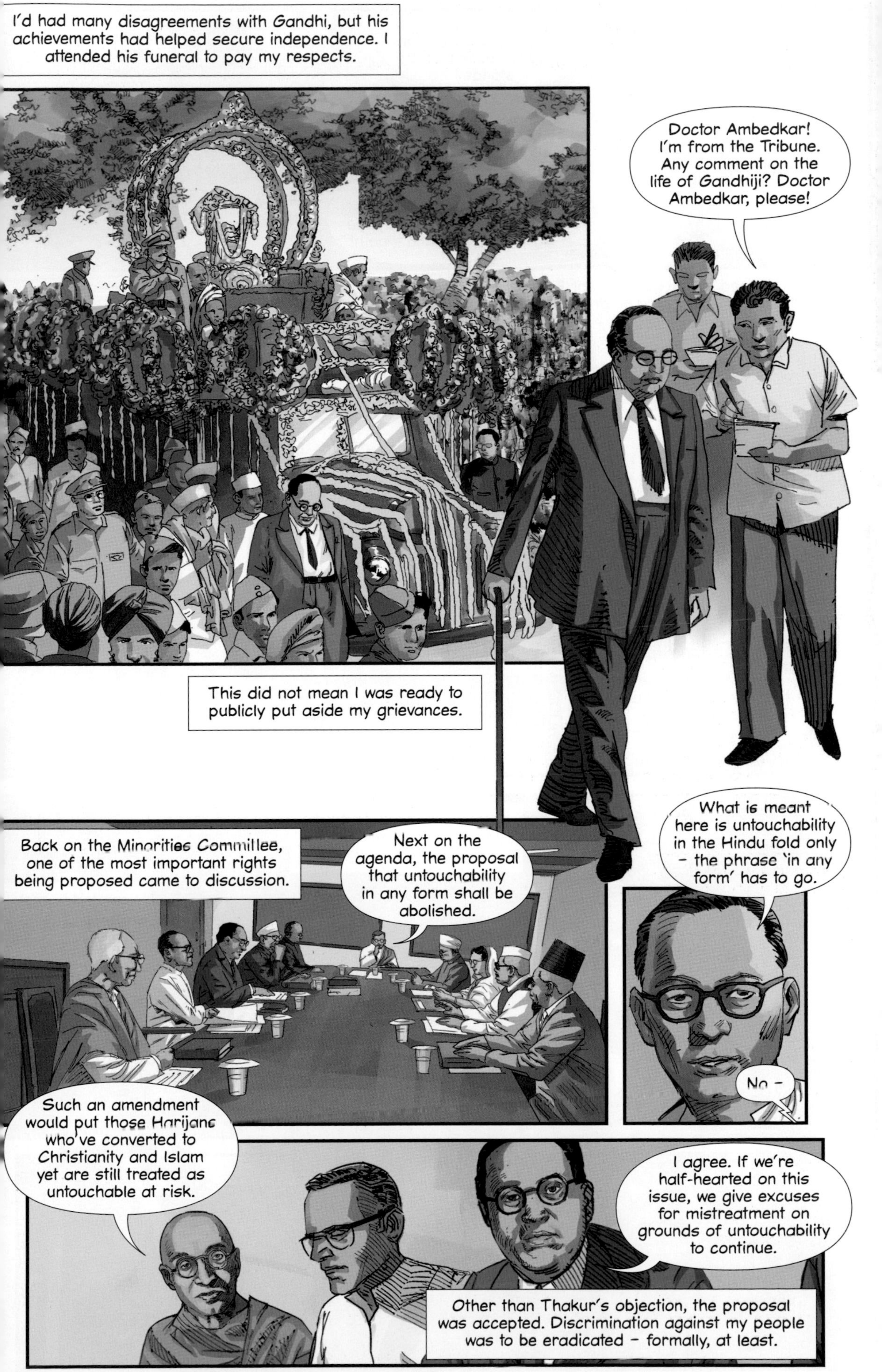
I'd had many disagreements with Gandhi, but his achievements had helped secure independence. I attended his funeral to pay my respects.
Doctor Ambedkar! I'm from the Tribune. Any comment on the life of Gandhiji? Doctor Ambedkar, please!
This did not mean I was ready to publicly put aside my grievances.
Back on the Minorities Committee, one of the most important rights being proposed came to discussion.
Next on the agenda, the proposal that untouchability in any form shall be abolished.
What is meant here is untouchability in the Hindu fold only – the phrase 'in any form' has to go.
No –
Such an amendment would put those Harijans who've converted to Christianity and Islam yet are still treated as untouchable at risk.
I agree. If we're half-hearted on this issue, we give excuses for mistreatment on grounds of untouchability to continue.
Other than Thakur's objection, the proposal was accepted. Discrimination against my people was to be eradicated – formally, at least.

The two Drafting Committee members who had left us were replaced, and the work neared its end.

So, are we all satisfied with the Fundamental Rights section as it stands?

Yes.

Finally, yes...

Excellent. We could have a draft Constitution by the end of the month!

And indeed, in the last week of February 1948, I submitted the first draft of the Constitution. It would now be presented for public review before redrafting could begin.

Splendid work, Ambedkar!

Thank you, sir, but I already have a few ideas for amendments. For example, the preamble uses the term 'republic', but I think 'state' would be more neutral, because...

Ambedkar. It'll take some time for the Constitution to go before the public. Take your rest. You deserve it.

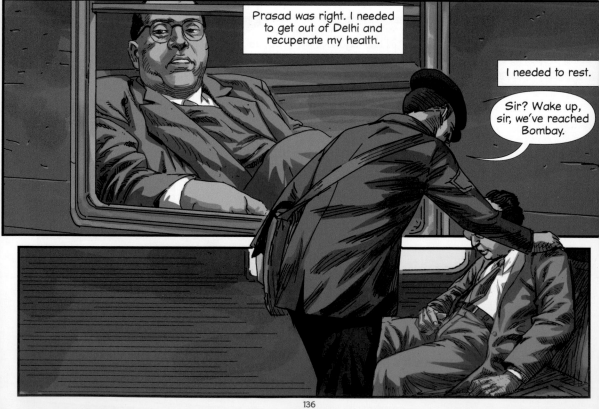

Prasad was right. I needed to get out of Delhi and recuperate my health.

I needed to rest.

Sir? Wake up, sir, we've reached Bombay.

136

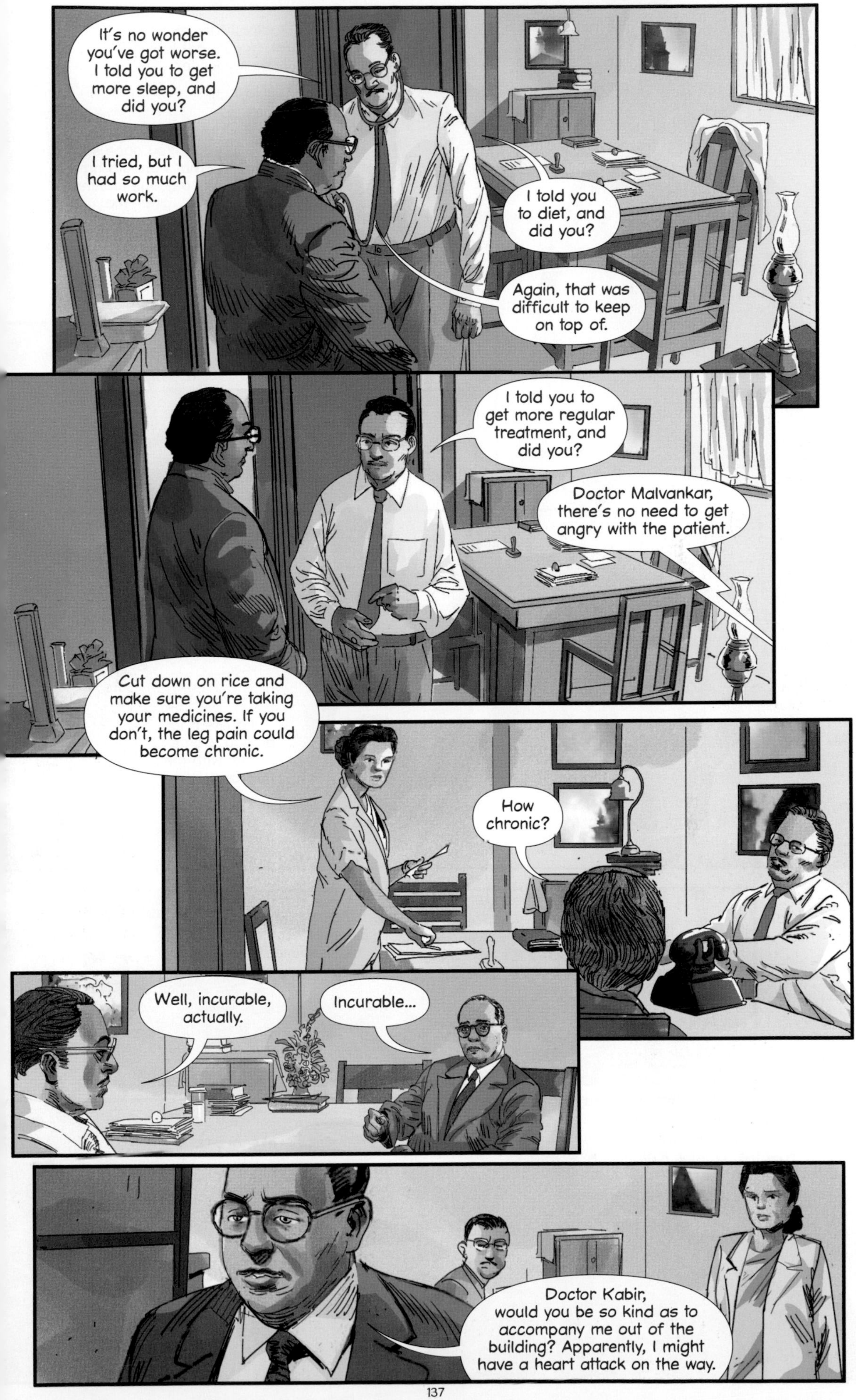
It's no wonder you've got worse. I told you to get more sleep, and did you?
I tried, but I had so much work.
I told you to diet, and did you?
Again, that was difficult to keep on top of.
I told you to get more regular treatment, and did you?
Doctor Malvankar, there's no need to get angry with the patient.
Cut down on rice and make sure you're taking your medicines. If you don't, the leg pain could become chronic.
How chronic?
Well, incurable, actually.
Incurable...
Doctor Kabir, would you be so kind as to accompany me out of the building? Apparently, I might have a heart attack on the way.

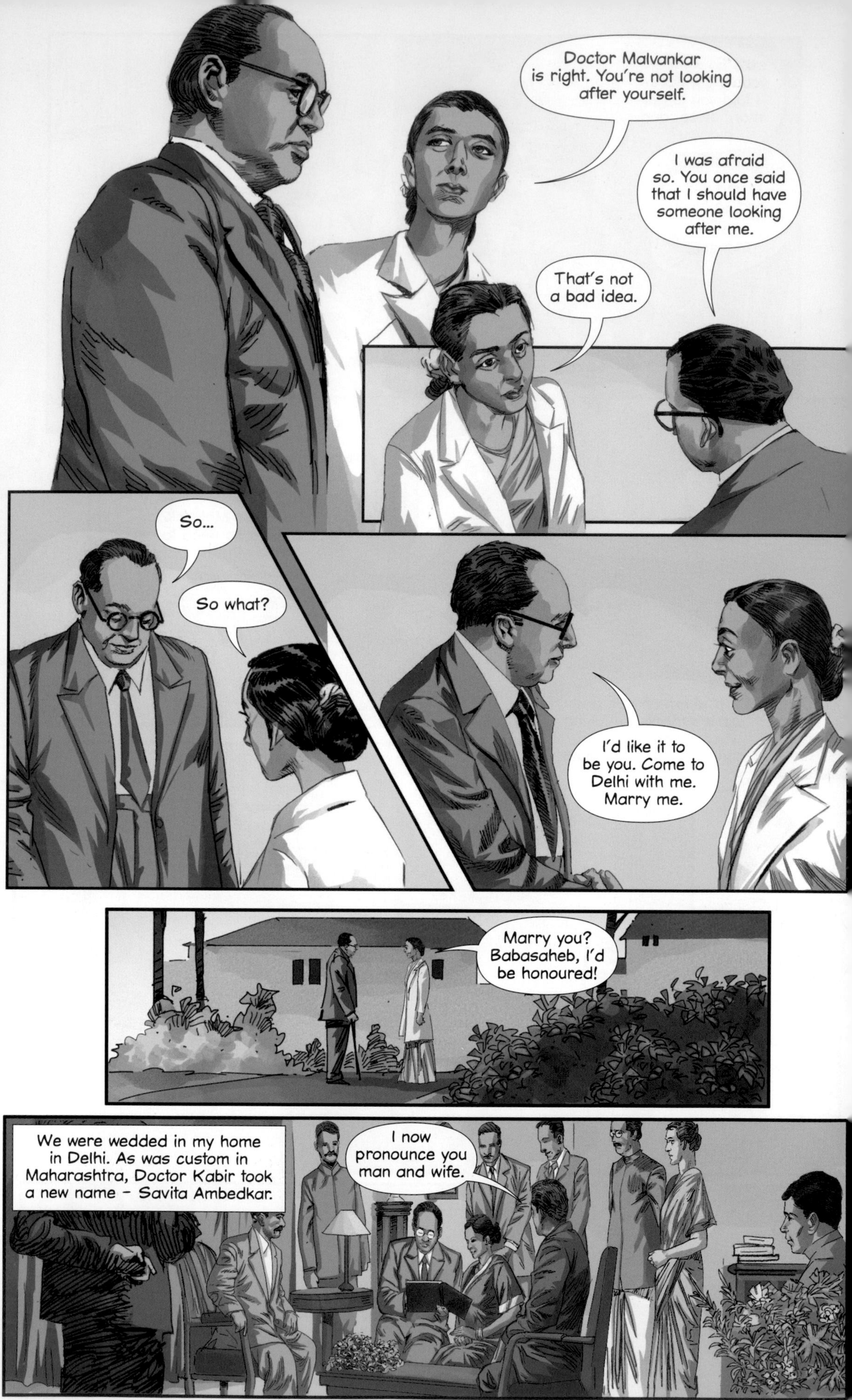
Doctor Malvankar is right. You're not looking after yourself.
I was afraid so. You once said that I should have someone looking after me.
That's not a bad idea.
So...
So what?
I'd like it to be you. Come to Delhi with me. Marry me.
Marry you? Babasaheb, I'd be honoured!
We were wedded in my home in Delhi. As was custom in Maharashtra, Doctor Kabir took a new name – Savita Ambedkar.
I now pronounce you man and wife.

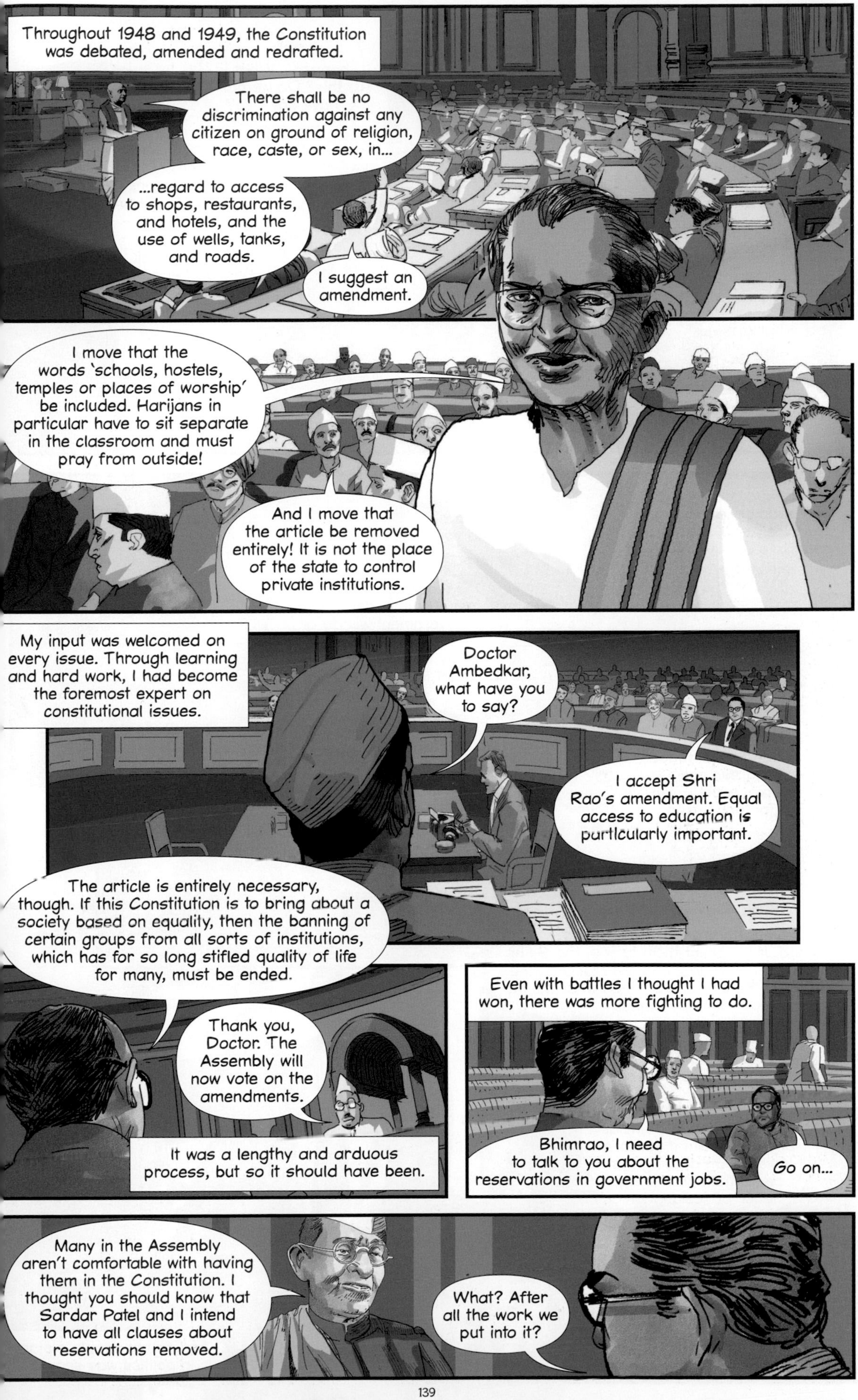
Throughout 1948 and 1949, the Constitution was debated, amended and redrafted.
There shall be no discrimination against any citizen on ground of religion, race, caste, or sex, in...
...regard to access to shops, restaurants, and hotels, and the use of wells, tanks, and roads.
I suggest an amendment.
I move that the words 'schools, hostels, temples or places of worship' be included. Harijans in particular have to sit separate in the classroom and must pray from outside!
And I move that the article be removed entirely! It is not the place of the state to control private institutions.
My input was welcomed on every issue. Through learning and hard work, I had become the foremost expert on constitutional issues.
Doctor Ambedkar, what have you to say?
I accept Shri Rao's amendment. Equal access to education is particularly important.
The article is entirely necessary, though. If this Constitution is to bring about a society based on equality, then the banning of certain groups from all sorts of institutions, which has for so long stifled quality of life for many, must be ended.
Thank you, Doctor. The Assembly will now vote on the amendments.
It was a lengthy and arduous process, but so it should have been.
Even with battles I thought I had won, there was more fighting to do.
Bhimrao, I need to talk to you about the reservations in government jobs.
Go on...
Many in the Assembly aren't comfortable with having them in the Constitution. I thought you should know that Sardar Patel and I intend to have all clauses about reservations removed.
What? After all the work we put into it?

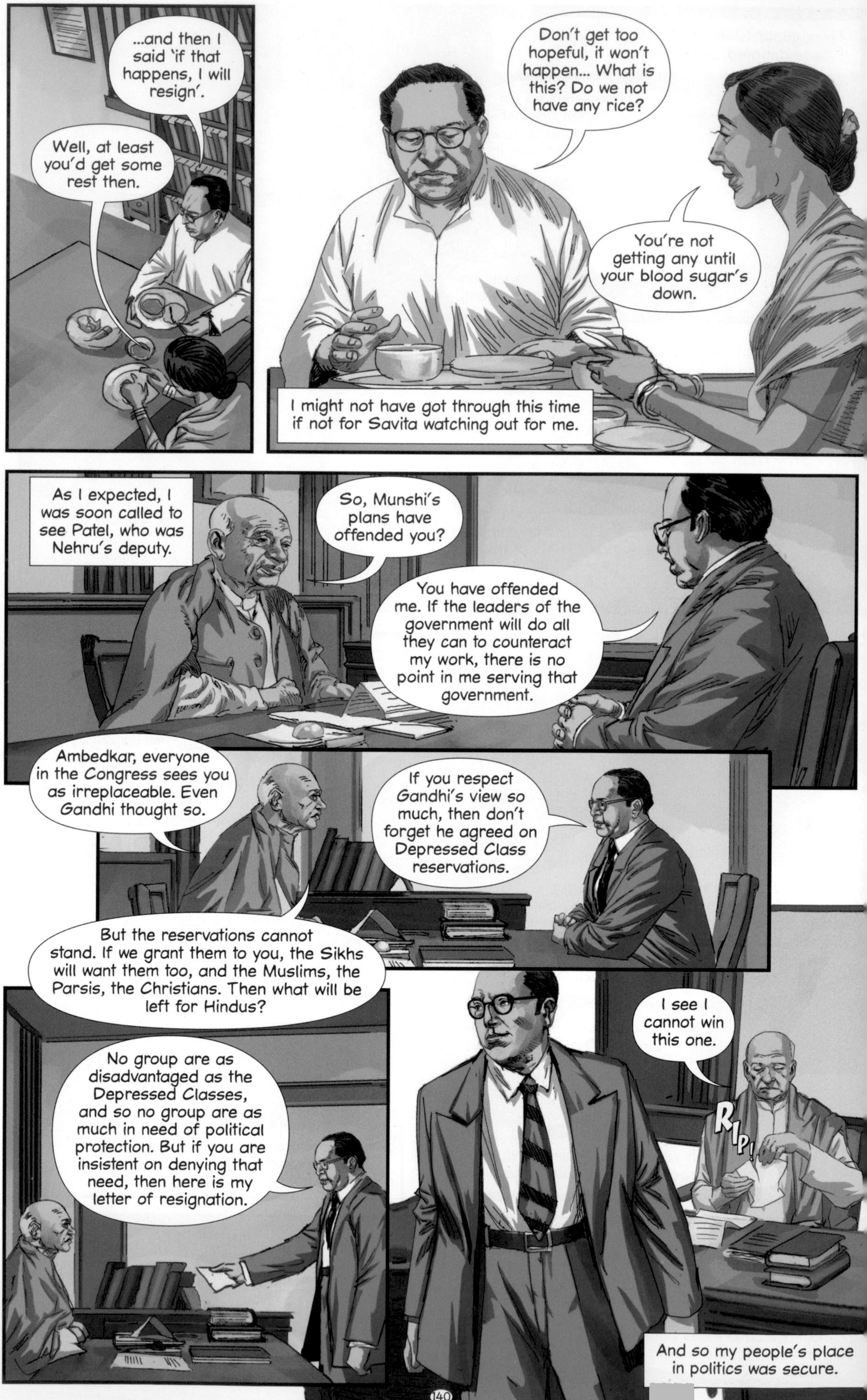

...and then I said 'if that happens, I will resign'.
Well, at least you'd get some rest then.
Don't get too hopeful, it won't happen... What is this? Do we not have any rice?
You're not getting any until your blood sugar's down.
I might not have got through this time if not for Savita watching out for me.
As I expected, I was soon called to see Patel, who was Nehru's deputy.
So, Munshi's plans have offended you?
You have offended me. If the leaders of the government will do all they can to counteract my work, there is no point in me serving that government.
Ambedkar, everyone in the Congress sees you as irreplaceable. Even Gandhi thought so.
If you respect Gandhi's view so much, then don't forget he agreed on Depressed Class reservations.
But the reservations cannot stand. If we grant them to you, the Sikhs will want them too, and the Muslims, the Parsis, the Christians. Then what will be left for Hindus?
No group are as disadvantaged as the Depressed Classes, and so no group are as much in need of political protection. But if you are insistent on denying that need, then here is my letter of resignation.
I see I cannot win this one.
RIP!
And so my people's place in politics was secure.

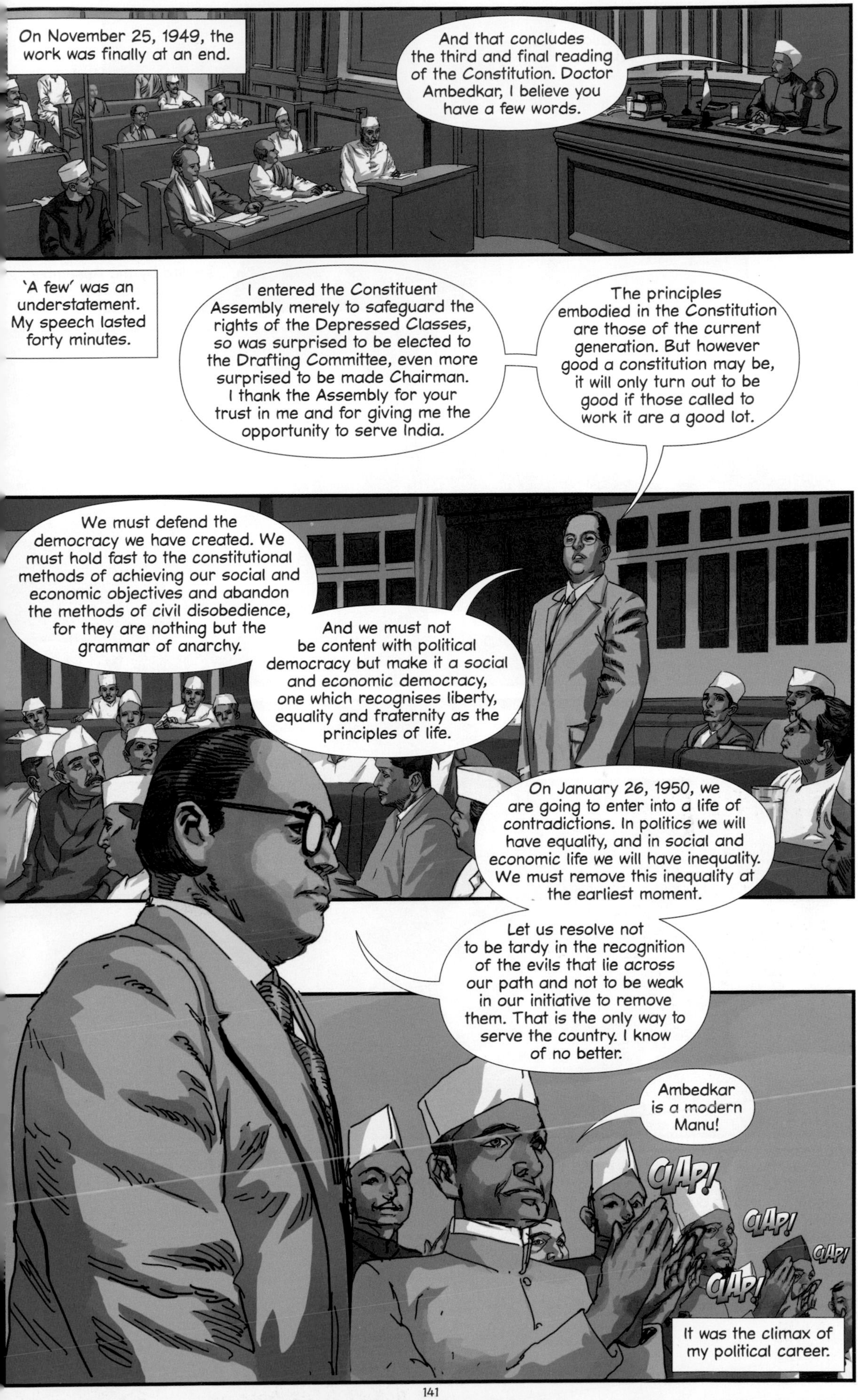
On November 25, 1949, the work was finally at an end.
And that concludes the third and final reading of the Constitution. Doctor Ambedkar, I believe you have a few words.
'A few' was an understatement. My speech lasted forty minutes.
I entered the Constituent Assembly merely to safeguard the rights of the Depressed Classes, so was surprised to be elected to the Drafting Committee, even more surprised to be made Chairman. I thank the Assembly for your trust in me and for giving me the opportunity to serve India.
The principles embodied in the Constitution are those of the current generation. But however good a constitution may be, it will only turn out to be good if those called to work it are a good lot.
We must defend the democracy we have created. We must hold fast to the constitutional methods of achieving our social and economic objectives and abandon the methods of civil disobedience, for they are nothing but the grammar of anarchy.
And we must not be content with political democracy but make it a social and economic democracy, one which recognises liberty, equality and fraternity as the principles of life.
On January 26, 1950, we are going to enter into a life of contradictions. In politics we will have equality, and in social and economic life we will have inequality. We must remove this inequality at the earliest moment.
Let us resolve not to be tardy in the recognition of the evils that lie across our path and not to be weak in our initiative to remove them. That is the only way to serve the country. I know of no better.
Ambedkar is a modern Manu!
CLAP!
CLAP!
CLAP!
CLAP!
It was the climax of my political career.

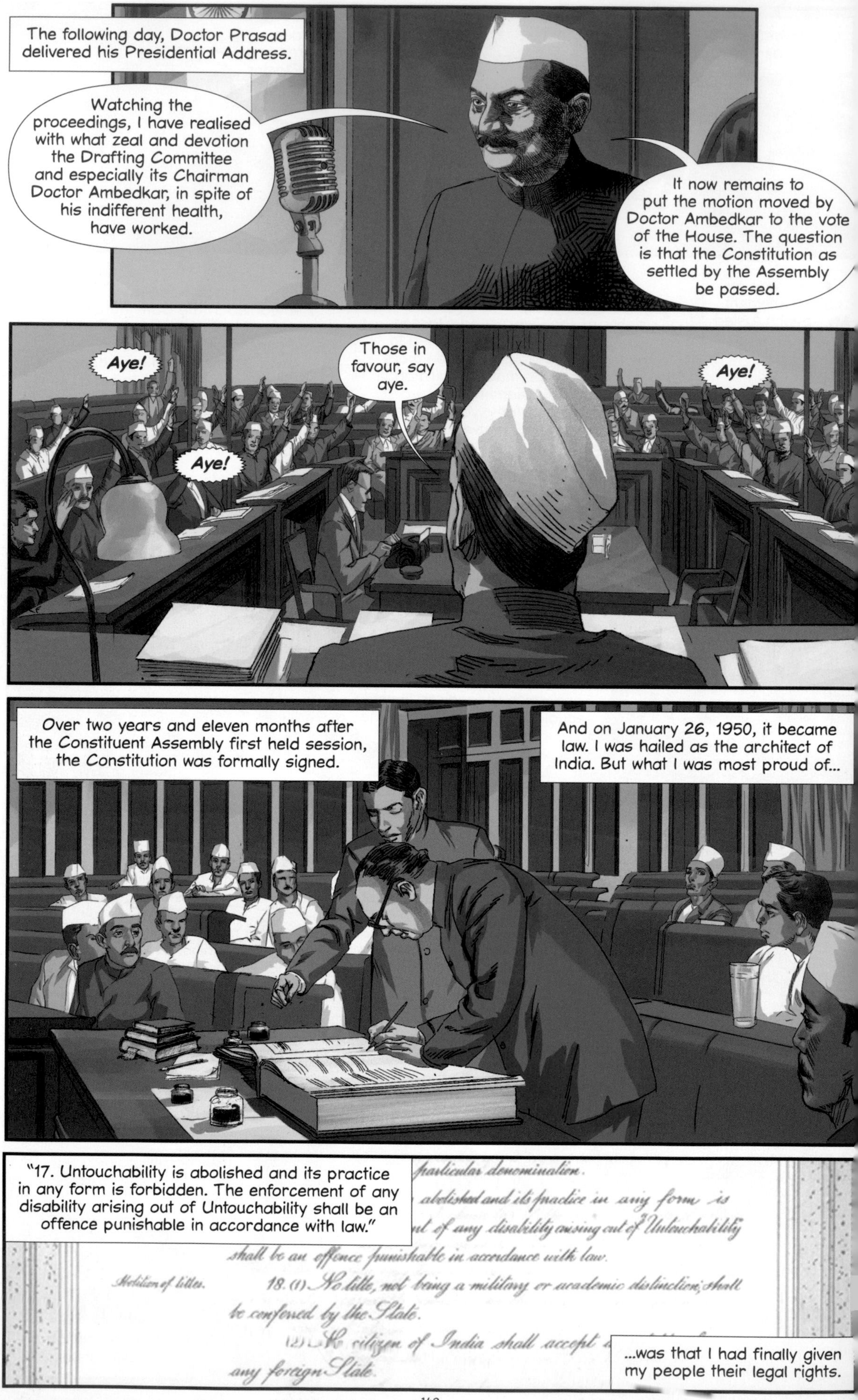
The following day, Doctor Prasad delivered his Presidential Address.
Watching the proceedings, I have realised with what zeal and devotion the Drafting Committee and especially its Chairman Doctor Ambedkar, in spite of his indifferent health, have worked.
It now remains to put the motion moved by Doctor Ambedkar to the vote of the House. The question is that the Constitution as settled by the Assembly be passed.
Aye!
Those in favour, say aye.
Aye!
Aye!
Over two years and eleven months after the Constituent Assembly first held session, the Constitution was formally signed.
And on January 26, 1950, it became law. I was hailed as the architect of India. But what I was most proud of...
"17. Untouchability is abolished and its practice in any form is forbidden. The enforcement of any disability arising out of Untouchability shall be an offence punishable in accordance with law."
shall be an offence punishable in accordance with law.
Abolition of titles.
18. (1) No title, not being a military or academic distinction, shall
be conferred by the State.
any foreign State.
...was that I had finally given my people their legal rights.

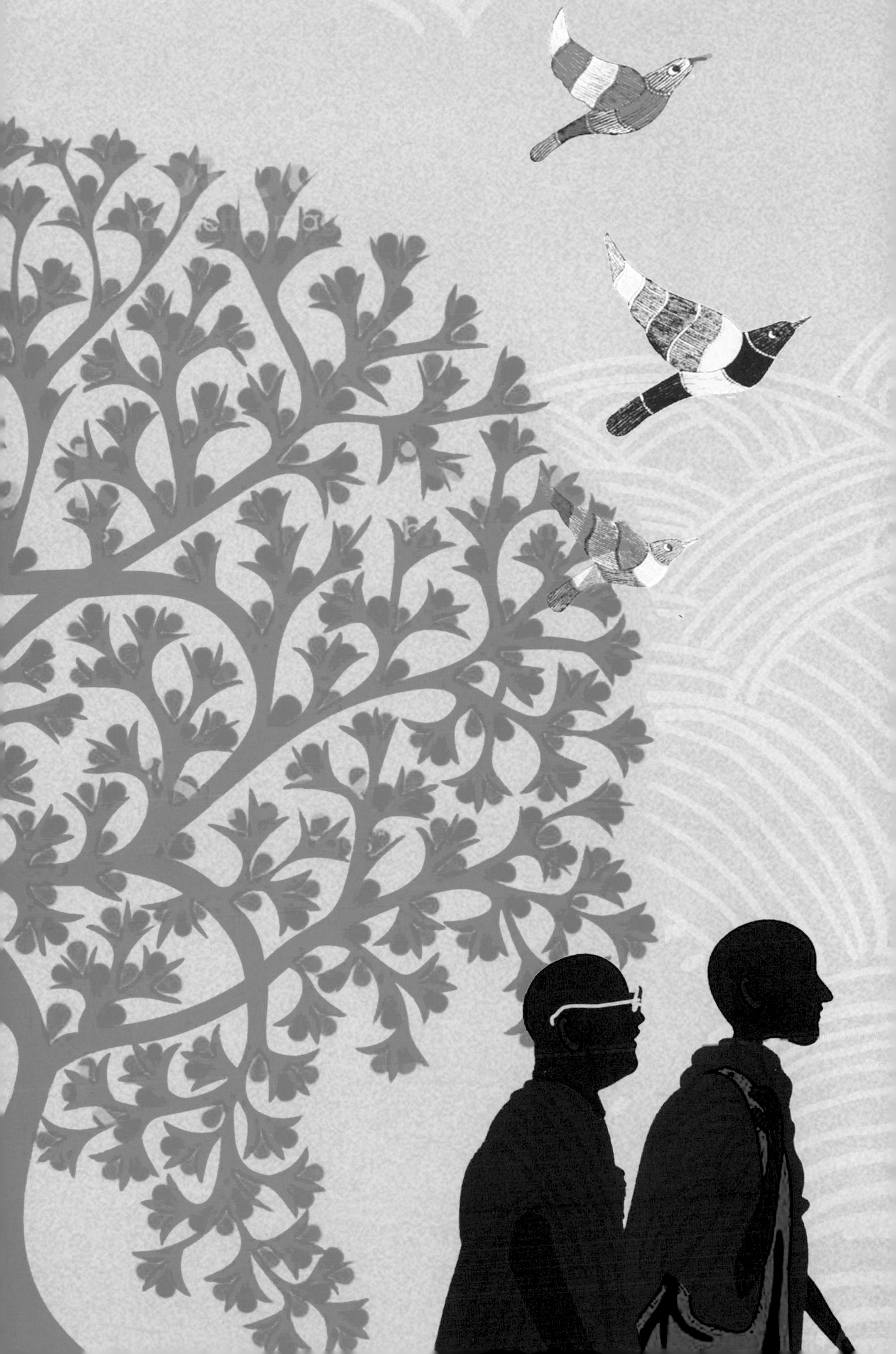

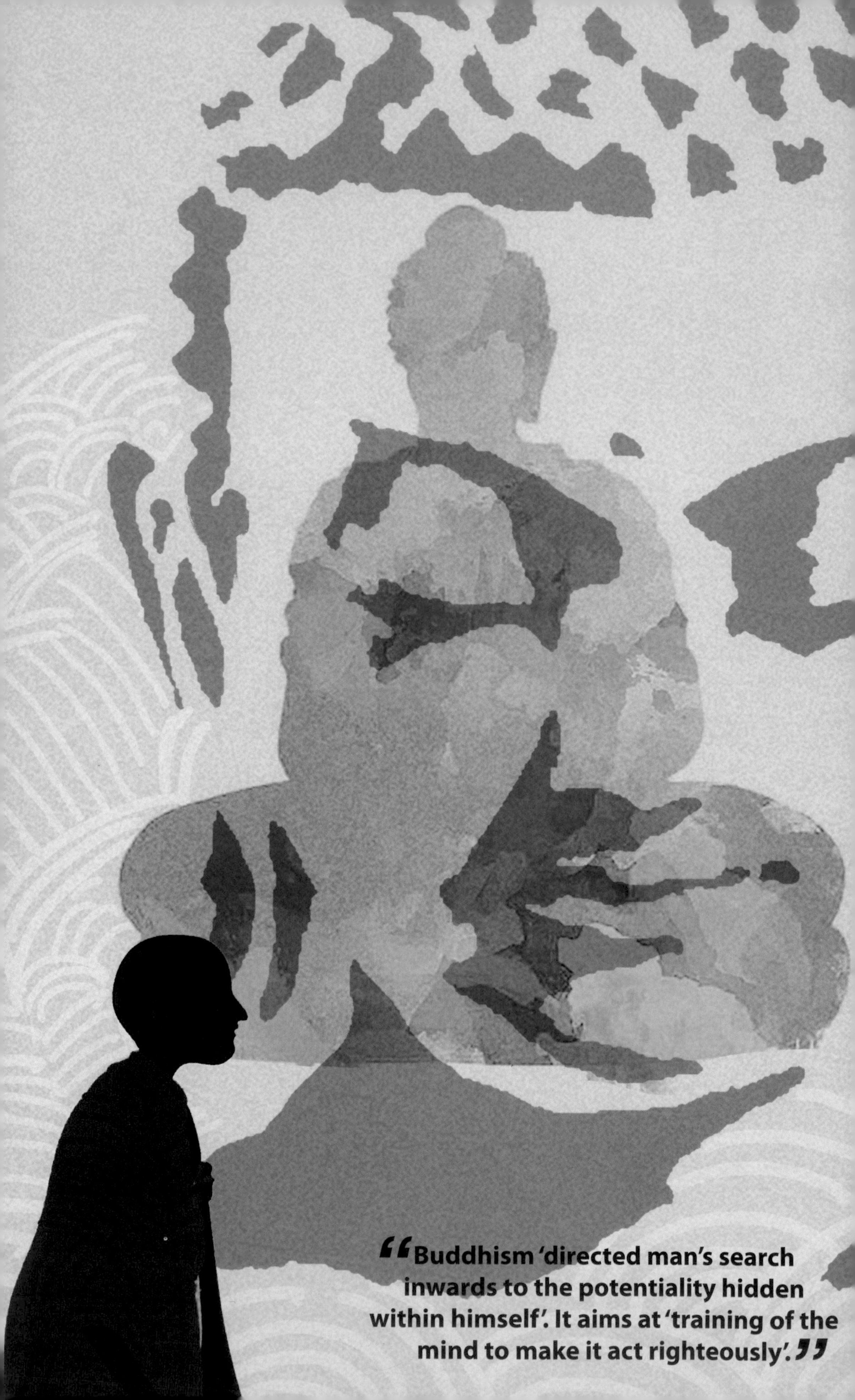

“Buddhism ‘directed man’s search inwards to the potentiality hidden within himself’. It aims at ‘training of the mind to make it act righteously’.”

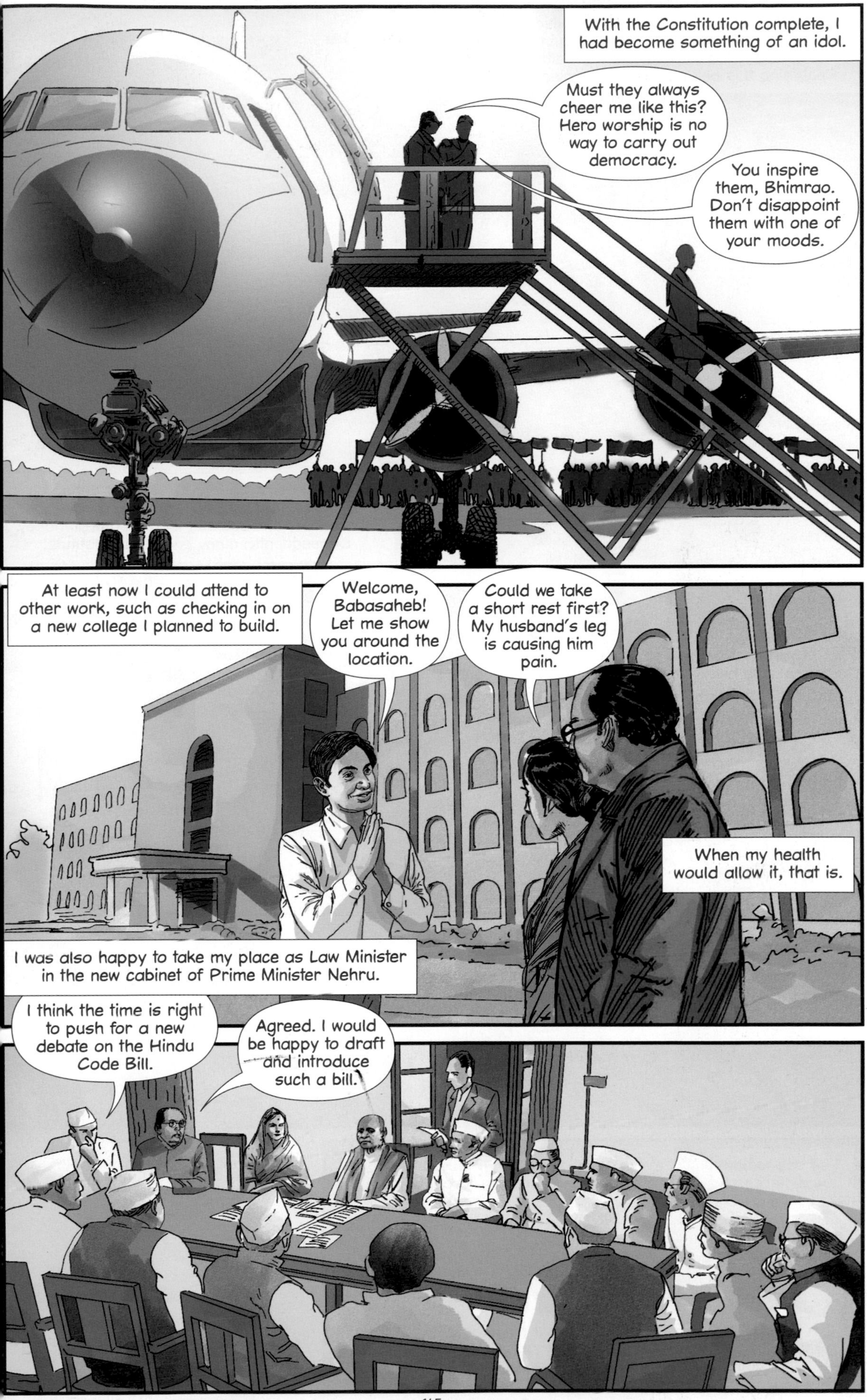
With the Constitution complete, I had become something of an idol.
Must they always cheer me like this? Hero worship is no way to carry out democracy.
You inspire them, Bhimrao. Don't disappoint them with one of your moods.
At least now I could attend to other work, such as checking in on a new college I planned to build.
Welcome, Babasaheb! Let me show you around the location.
Could we take a short rest first? My husband's leg is causing him pain.
When my health would allow it, that is.
I was also happy to take my place as Law Minister in the new cabinet of Prime Minister Nehru.
I think the time is right to push for a new debate on the Hindu Code Bill.
Agreed. I would be happy to draft and introduce such a bill.

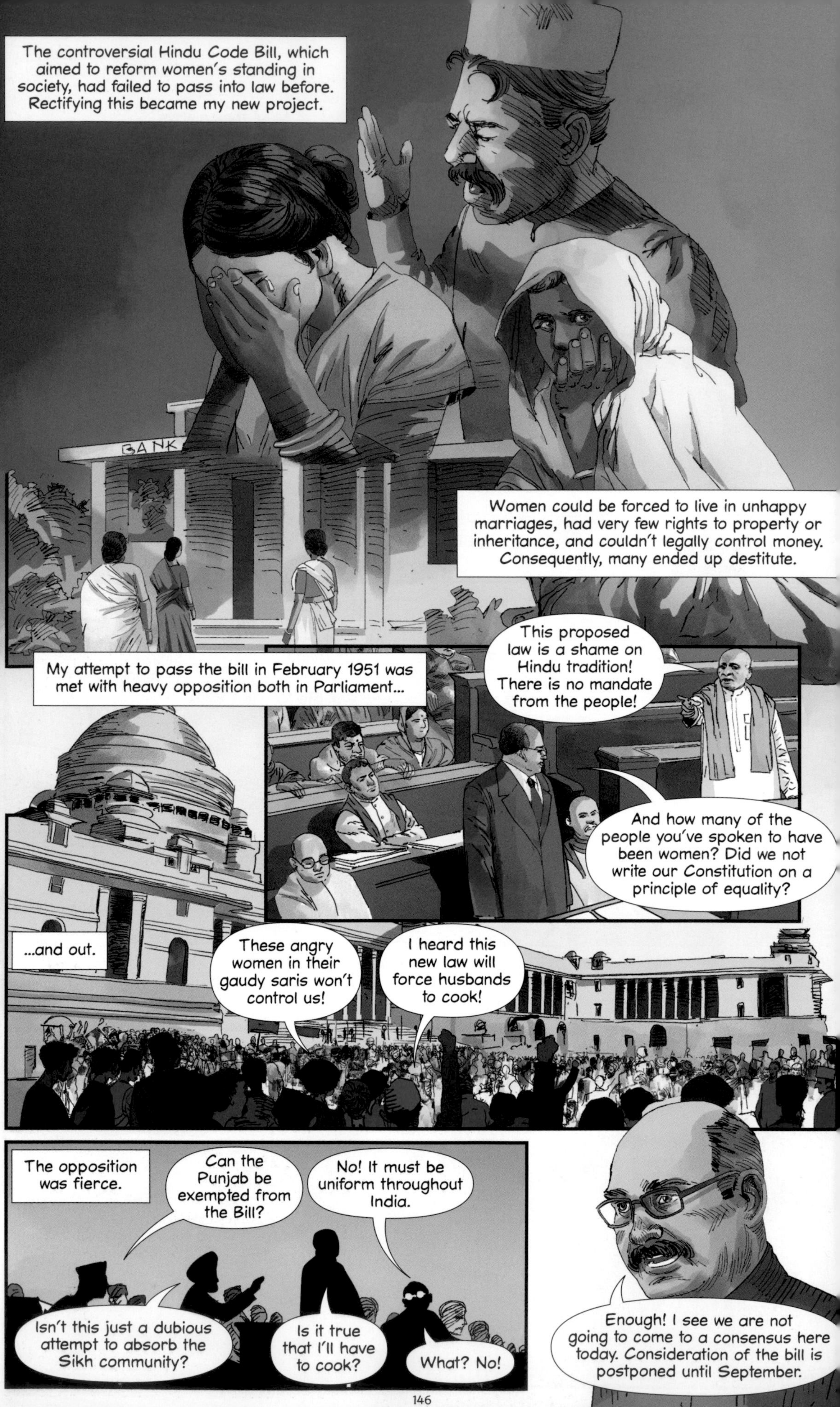
The controversial Hindu Code Bill, which aimed to reform women's standing in society, had failed to pass into law before. Rectifying this became my new project.
BANK
Women could be forced to live in unhappy marriages, had very few rights to property or inheritance, and couldn't legally control money. Consequently, many ended up destitute.
My attempt to pass the bill in February 1951 was met with heavy opposition both in Parliament...
This proposed law is a shame on Hindu tradition! There is no mandate from the people!
And how many of the people you've spoken to have been women? Did we not write our Constitution on a principle of equality?
...and out.
These angry women in their gaudy saris won't control us!
I heard this new law will force husbands to cook!
The opposition was fierce.
Can the Punjab be exempted from the Bill?
No! It must be uniform throughout India.
Isn't this just a dubious attempt to absorb the Sikh community?
Is it true that I'll have to cook?
What? No!
Enough! I see we are not going to come to a consensus here today. Consideration of the bill is postponed until September.

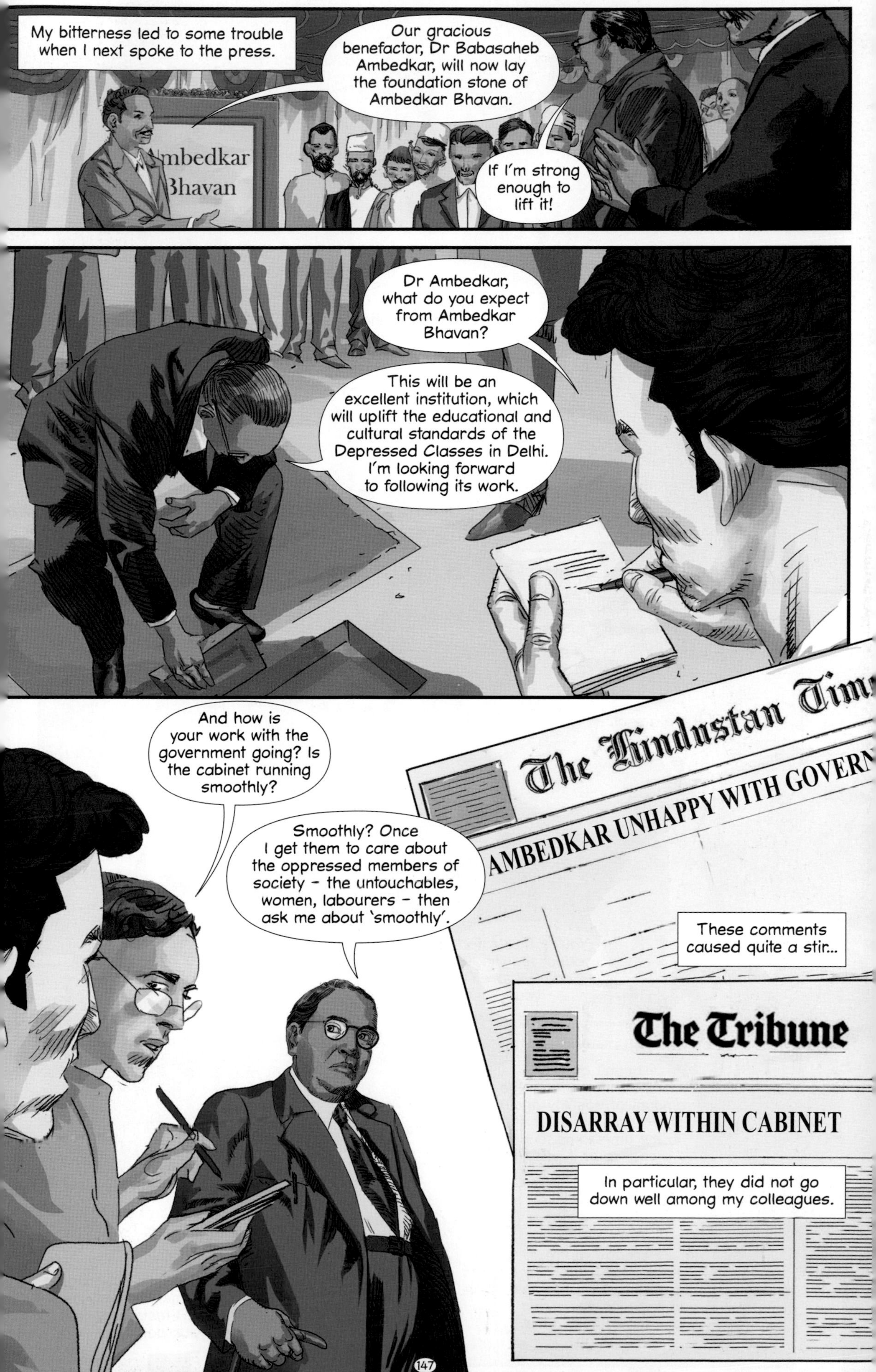
My bitterness led to some trouble when I next spoke to the press.
Our gracious benefactor, Dr Babasaheb Ambedkar, will now lay the foundation stone of Ambedkar Bhavan.
If I'm strong enough to lift it!
Ambedkar Bhavan
Dr Ambedkar, what do you expect from Ambedkar Bhavan?
This will be an excellent institution, which will uplift the educational and cultural standards of the Depressed Classes in Delhi. I'm looking forward to following its work.
And how is your work with the government going? Is the cabinet running smoothly?
Smoothly? Once I get them to care about the oppressed members of society – the untouchables, women, labourers – then ask me about 'smoothly'.
The Hindustan Tim
AMBEDKAR UNHAPPY WITH GOVERN
These comments caused quite a stir...
The Tribune
DISARRAY WITHIN CABINET
In particular, they did not go down well among my colleagues.

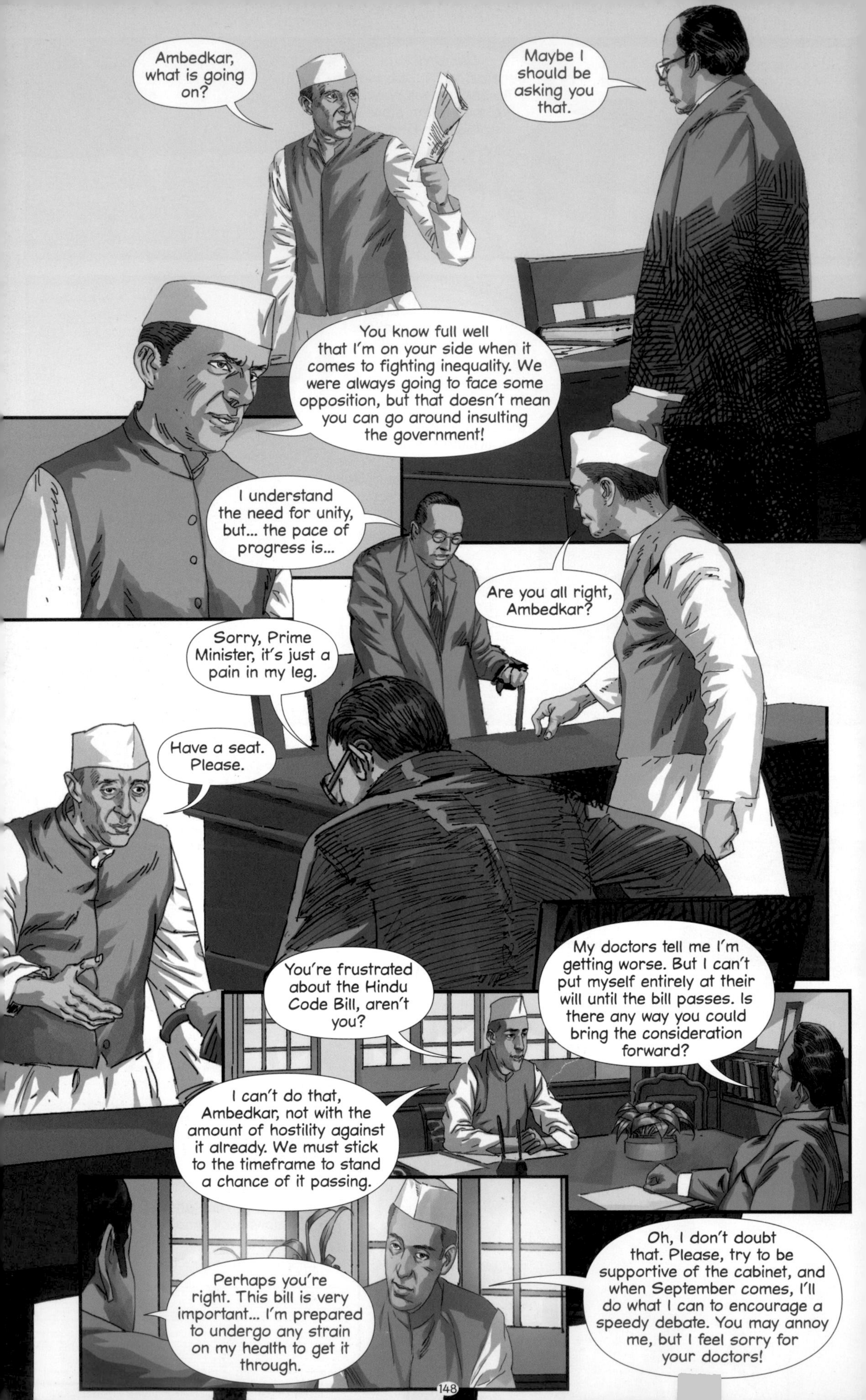
Ambedkar, what is going on?
Maybe I should be asking you that.
You know full well that I'm on your side when it comes to fighting inequality. We were always going to face some opposition, but that doesn't mean you can go around insulting the government!
I understand the need for unity, but... the pace of progress is...
Are you all right, Ambedkar?
Sorry, Prime Minister, it's just a pain in my leg.
Have a seat. Please.
You're frustrated about the Hindu Code Bill, aren't you?
My doctors tell me I'm getting worse. But I can't put myself entirely at their will until the bill passes. Is there any way you could bring the consideration forward?
I can't do that, Ambedkar, not with the amount of hostility against it already. We must stick to the timeframe to stand a chance of it passing.
Perhaps you're right. This bill is very important... I'm prepared to undergo any strain on my health to get it through.
Oh, I don't doubt that. Please, try to be supportive of the cabinet, and when September comes, I'll do what I can to encourage a speedy debate. You may annoy me, but I feel sorry for your doctors!

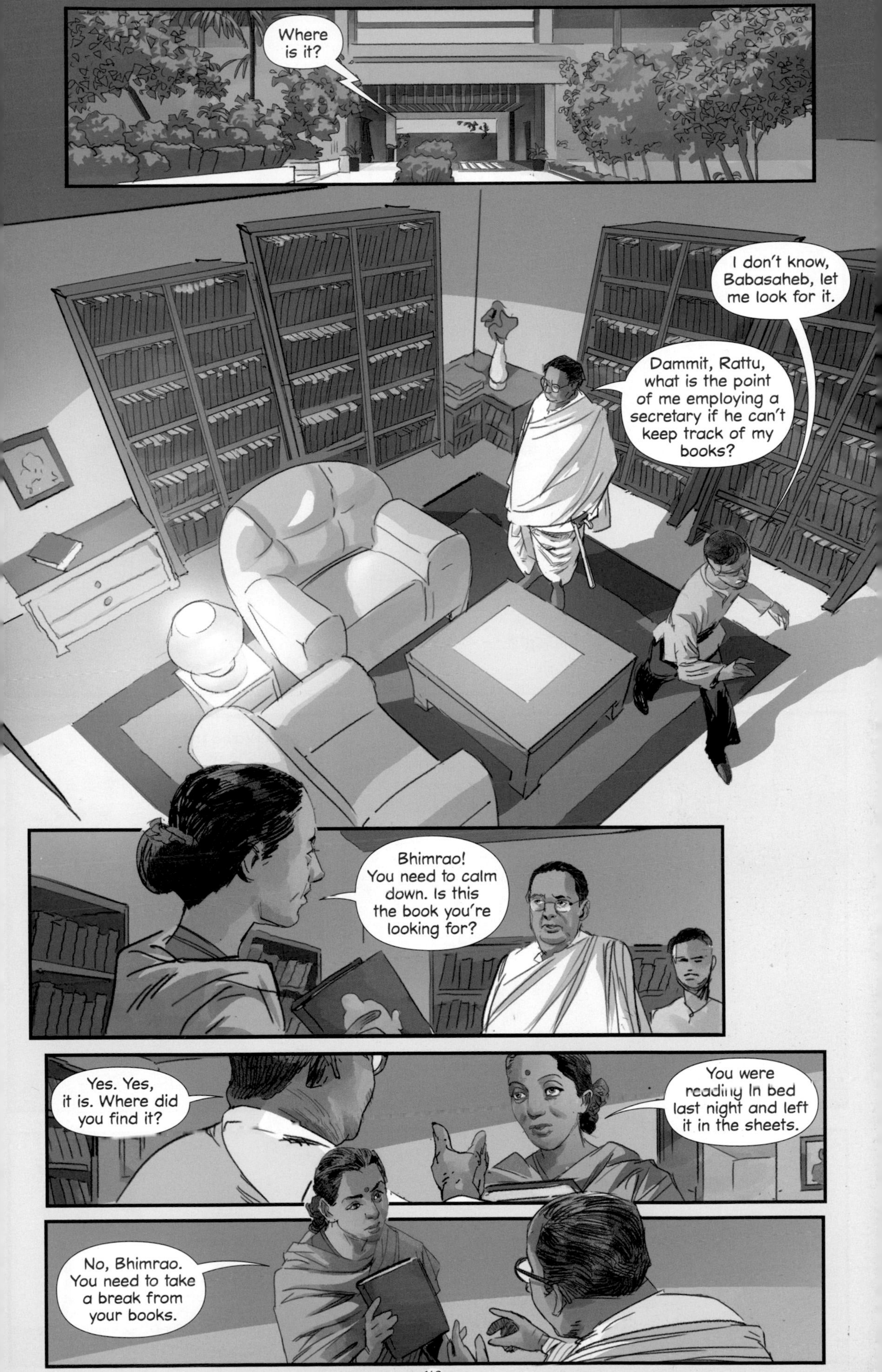
Where is it?
Dammit, Rattu, what is the point of me employing a secretary if he can't keep track of my books?
I don't know, Babasaheb, let me look for it.
Bhimrao! You need to calm down. Is this the book you're looking for?
Yes. Yes, it is. Where did you find it?
You were reading in bed last night and left it in the sheets.
No, Bhimrao. You need to take a break from your books.

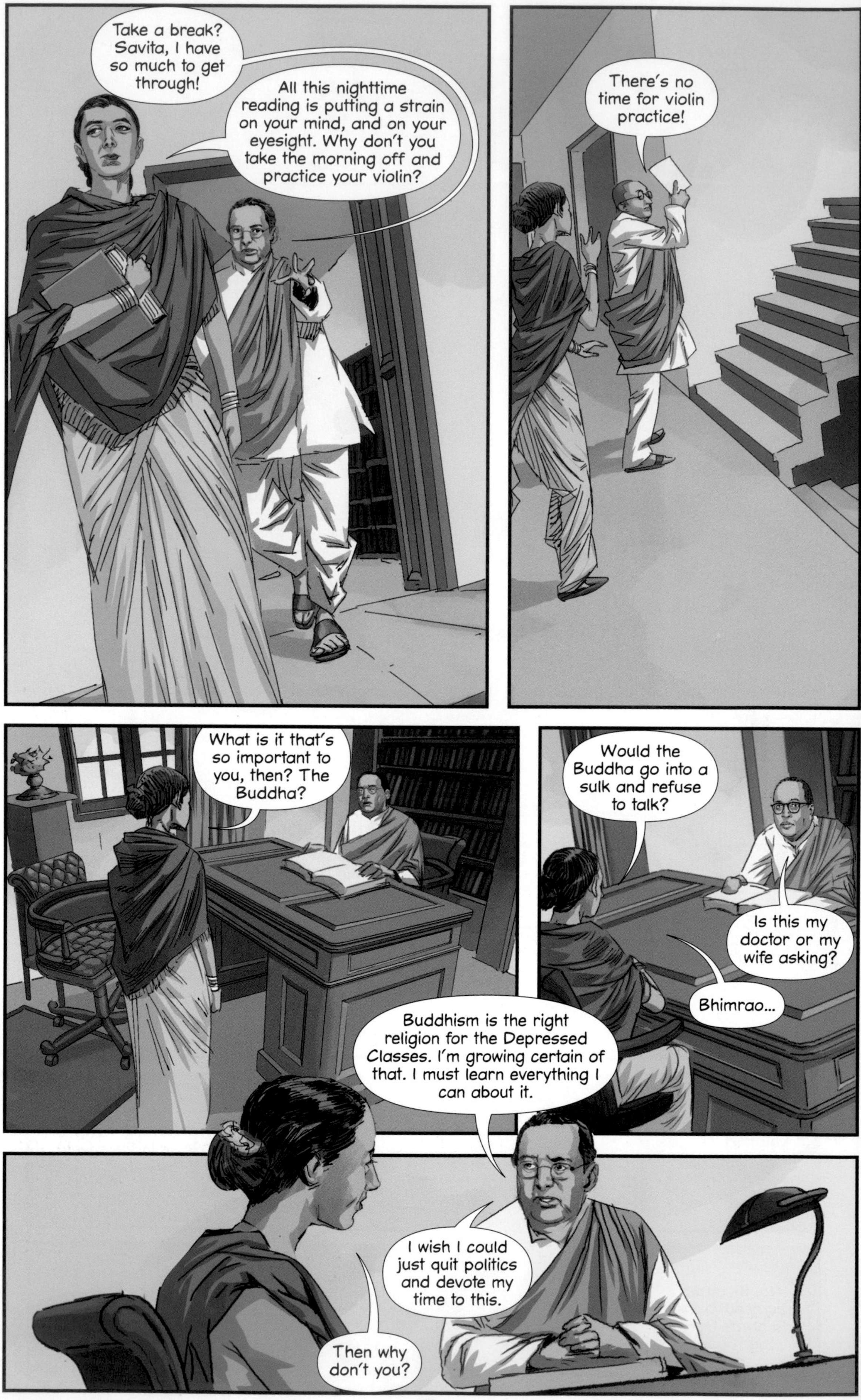
Take a break? Savita, I have so much to get through!
All this nighttime reading is putting a strain on your mind, and on your eyesight. Why don't you take the morning off and practice your violin?
There's no time for violin practice!
What is it that's so important to you, then? The Buddha?
Would the Buddha go into a sulk and refuse to talk?
Is this my doctor or my wife asking?
Bhimrao...
Buddhism is the right religion for the Depressed Classes. I'm growing certain of that. I must learn everything I can about it.
I wish I could just quit politics and devote my time to this.
Then why don't you?

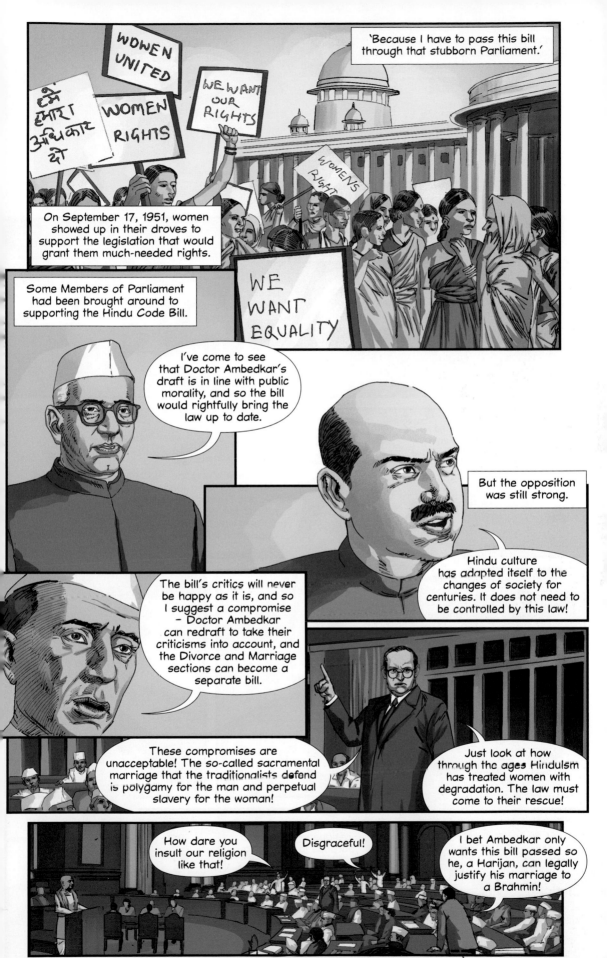

WOWEN UNITED

WOMEN RIGHTS

WE WANT OUR RIGHTS

छे हमारा अधिकार दो

WOMENS RIGHT

'Because I have to pass this bill through that stubborn Parliament.'

On September 17, 1951, women showed up in their droves to support the legislation that would grant them much-needed rights.

WE WANT EQUALITY

Some Members of Parliament had been brought around to supporting the Hindu Code Bill.

I've come to see that Doctor Ambedkar's draft is in line with public morality, and so the bill would rightfully bring the law up to date.

But the opposition was still strong.

Hindu culture has adapted itself to the changes of society for centuries. It does not need to be controlled by this law!

The bill's critics will never be happy as it is, and so I suggest a compromise – Doctor Ambedkar can redraft to take their criticisms into account, and the Divorce and Marriage sections can become a separate bill.

These compromises are unacceptable! The so-called sacramental marriage that the traditionalists defend is polygamy for the man and perpetual slavery for the woman!

Just look at how through the ages Hinduism has treated women with degradation. The law must come to their rescue!

How dare you insult our religion like that!

Disgraceful!

I bet Ambedkar only wants this bill passed so he, a Harijan, can legally justify his marriage to a Brahmin!

151

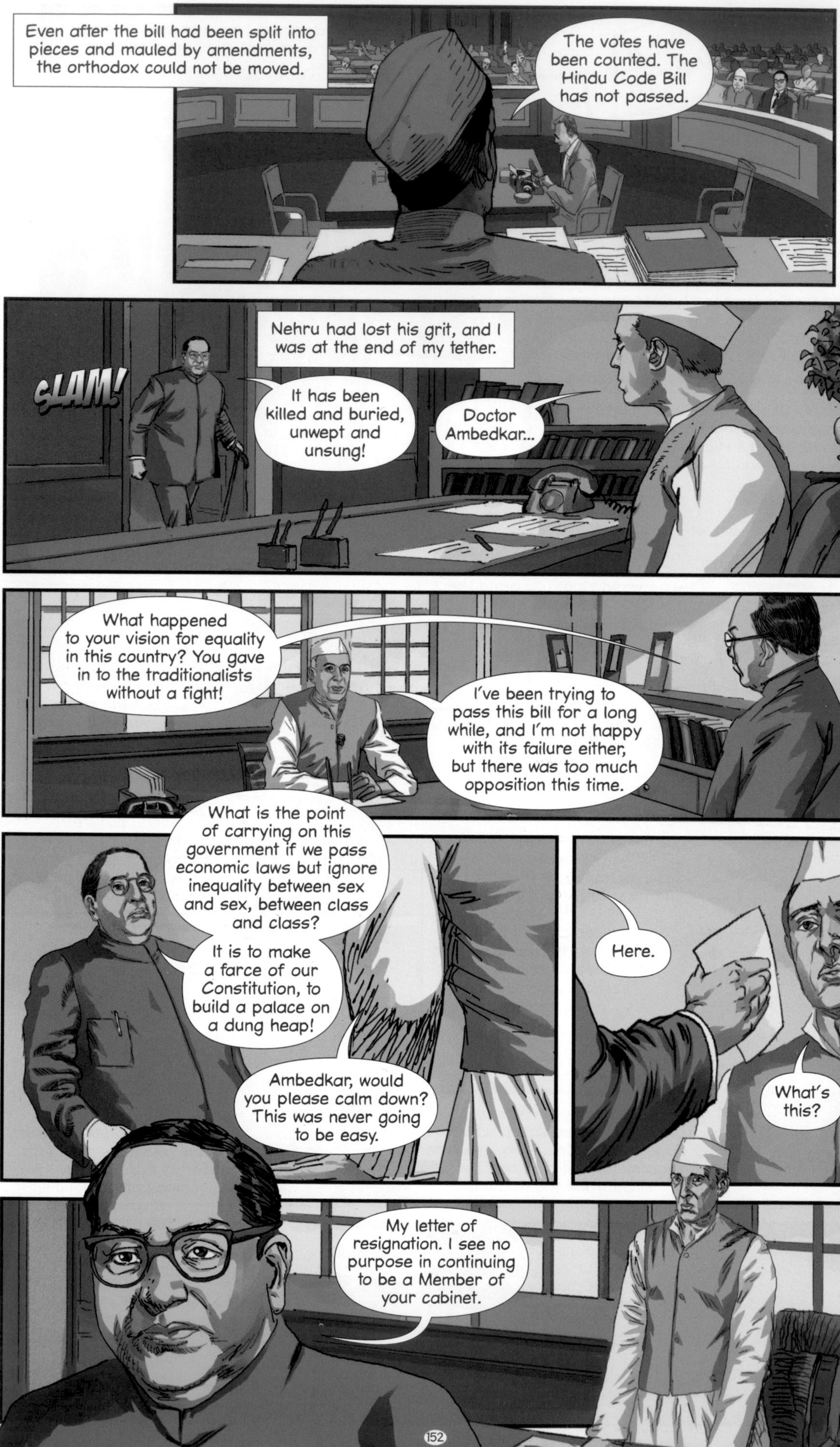

Even after the bill had been split into pieces and mauled by amendments, the orthodox could not be moved.
The votes have been counted. The Hindu Code Bill has not passed.
Nehru had lost his grit, and I was at the end of my tether.
SLAM!
It has been killed and buried, unwept and unsung!
Doctor Ambedkar...
What happened to your vision for equality in this country? You gave in to the traditionalists without a fight!
I've been trying to pass this bill for a long while, and I'm not happy with its failure either, but there was too much opposition this time.
What is the point of carrying on this government if we pass economic laws but ignore inequality between sex and sex, between class and class?
It is to make a farce of our Constitution, to build a palace on a dung heap!
Ambedkar, would you please calm down? This was never going to be easy.
Here.
What's this?
My letter of resignation. I see no purpose in continuing to be a Member of your cabinet.

With my responsibilities to the cabinet over, I could spend time thinking over the issue of religion.

As educational standards among the Depressed Classes had improved, the younger generation had begun to seek new teachers, and Buddhist thought was becoming popular.

Buddhism isn't about superstition or worship of gods. It is about looking into one's own self for insight and self-improvement.

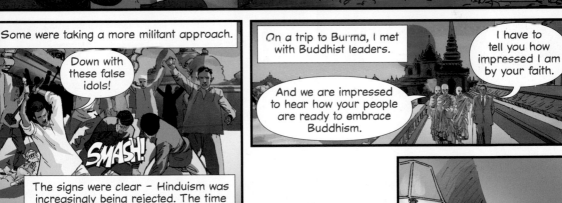

Some were taking a more militant approach.

Down with these false idols!

SMASH!

The signs were clear — Hinduism was increasingly being rejected. The time for conversion was nearing.

On a trip to Burma, I met with Buddhist leaders.

I have to tell you how impressed I am by your faith.

And we are impressed to hear how your people are ready to embrace Buddhism.

Absolutely. Buddhism will return to the land of its birth! Now, if you'd be willing to sponsor my campaign...

Ah... how much sponsorship are you looking for? We're hardly the wealthiest religion.

I began writing an accessible Buddhist gospel.

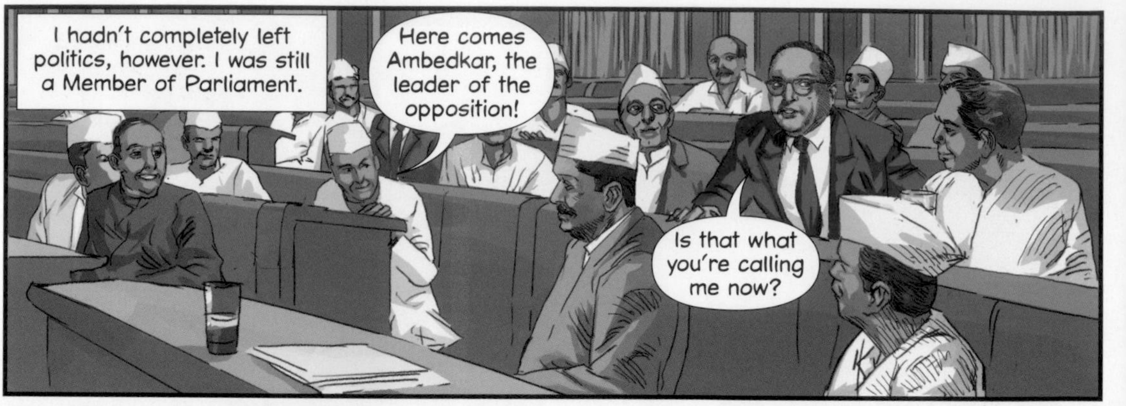
I hadn't completely left politics, however. I was still a Member of Parliament.
Here comes Ambedkar, the leader of the opposition!
Is that what you're calling me now?

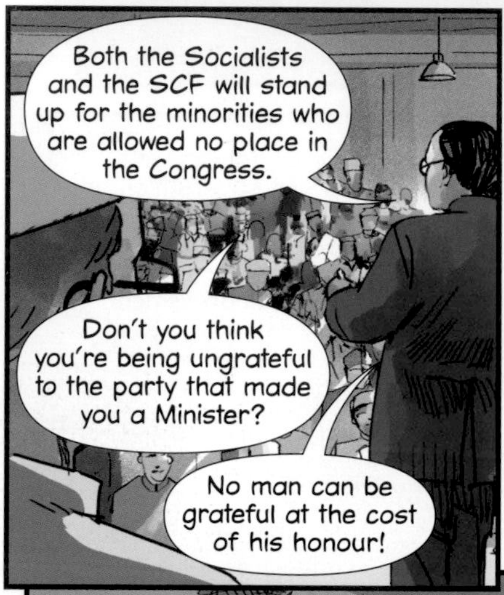
Both the Socialists and the SCF will stand up for the minorities who are allowed no place in the Congress.
Don't you think you're being ungrateful to the party that made you a Minister?
No man can be grateful at the cost of his honour!

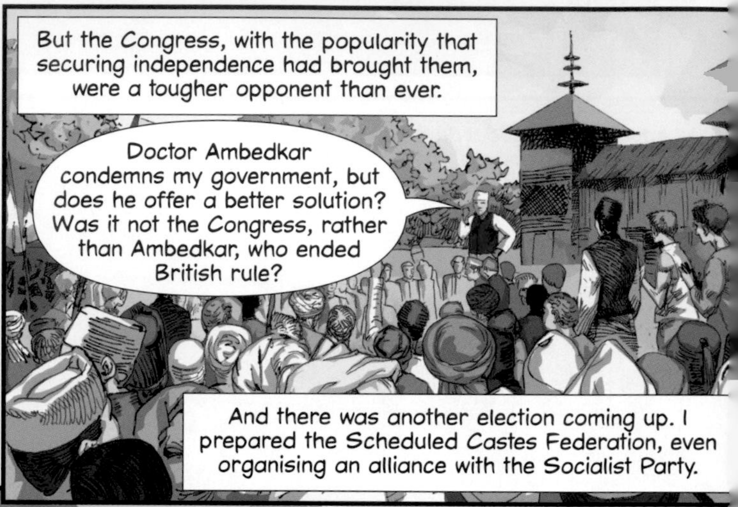
But the Congress, with the popularity that securing independence had brought them, were a tougher opponent than ever.
Doctor Ambedkar condemns my government, but does he offer a better solution? Was it not the Congress, rather than Ambedkar, who ended British rule?
And there was another election coming up. I prepared the Scheduled Castes Federation, even organising an alliance with the Socialist Party.

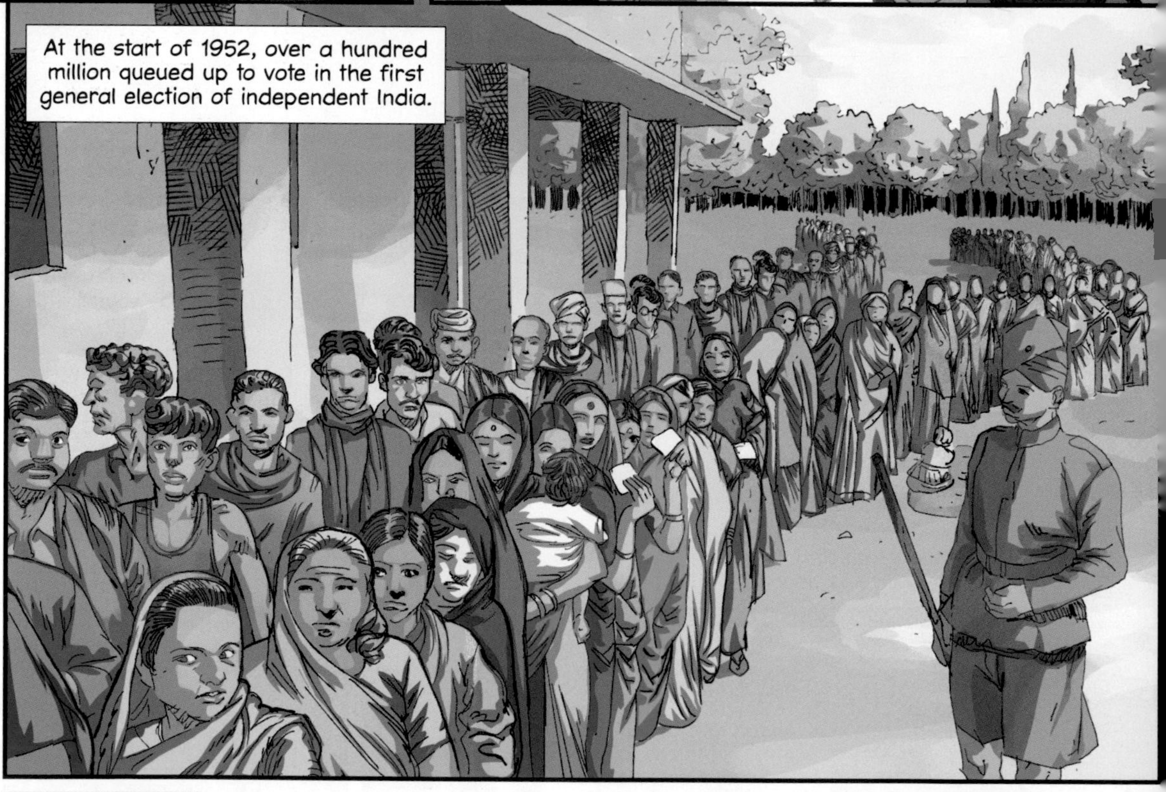
At the start of 1952, over a hundred million queued up to vote in the first general election of independent India.

It was a disaster.

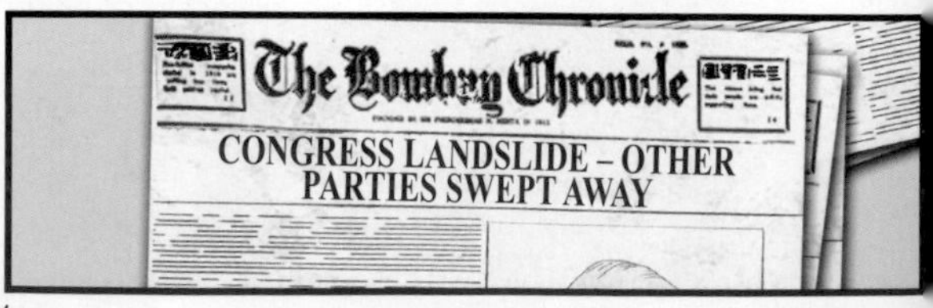
The Bombay Chronicle
CONGRESS LANDSLIDE – OTHER PARTIES SWEPT AWAY

The SCF were left with two seats, and I'd lost my place in the Parliament.

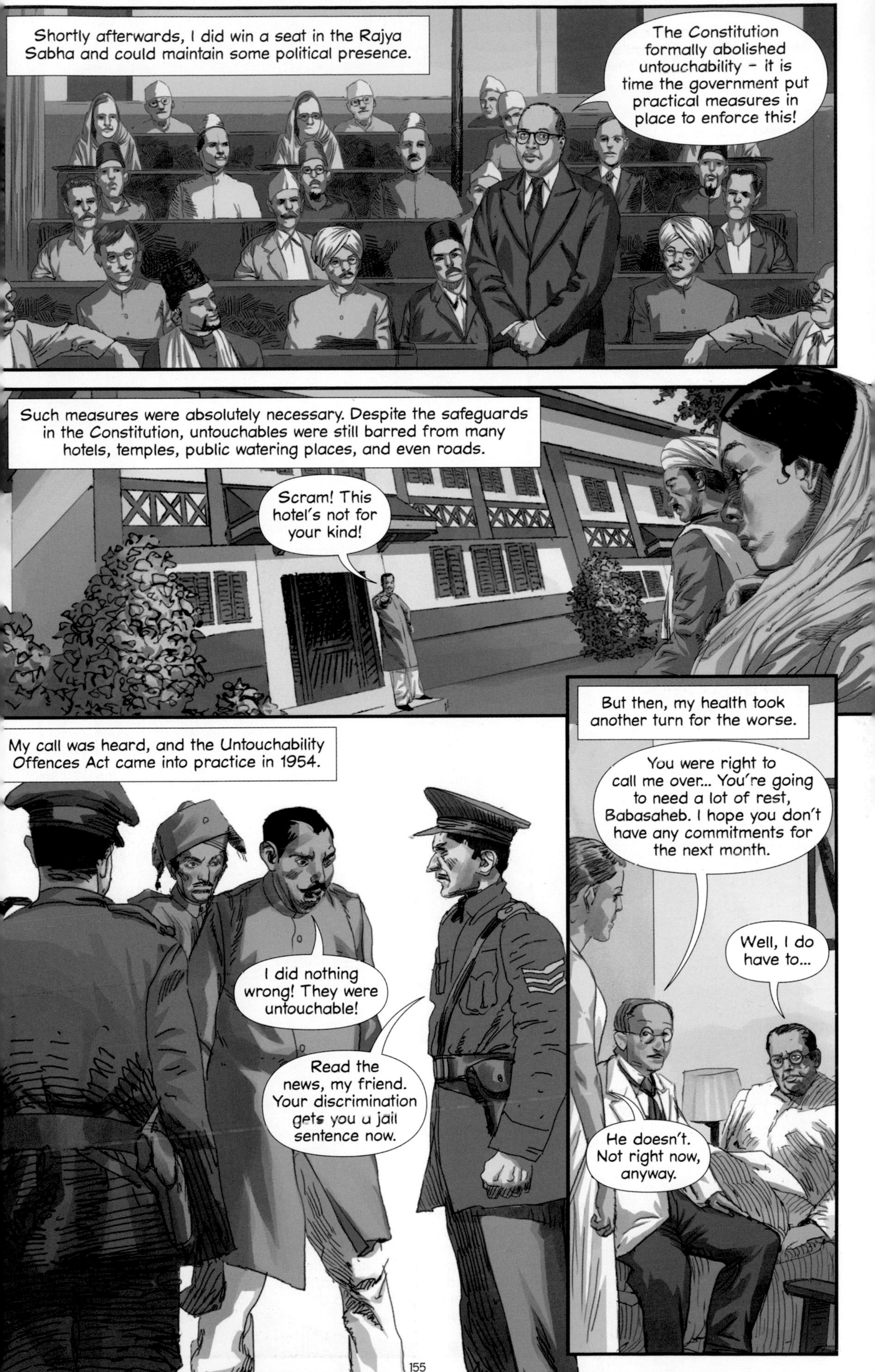
Shortly afterwards, I did win a seat in the Rajya Sabha and could maintain some political presence.
The Constitution formally abolished untouchability – it is time the government put practical measures in place to enforce this!
Such measures were absolutely necessary. Despite the safeguards in the Constitution, untouchables were still barred from many hotels, temples, public watering places, and even roads.
Scram! This hotel's not for your kind!
My call was heard, and the Untouchability Offences Act came into practice in 1954.
I did nothing wrong! They were untouchable!
Read the news, my friend. Your discrimination gets you a jail sentence now.
But then, my health took another turn for the worse.
You were right to call me over... You're going to need a lot of rest, Babasaheb. I hope you don't have any commitments for the next month.
Well, I do have to...
He doesn't. Not right now, anyway.

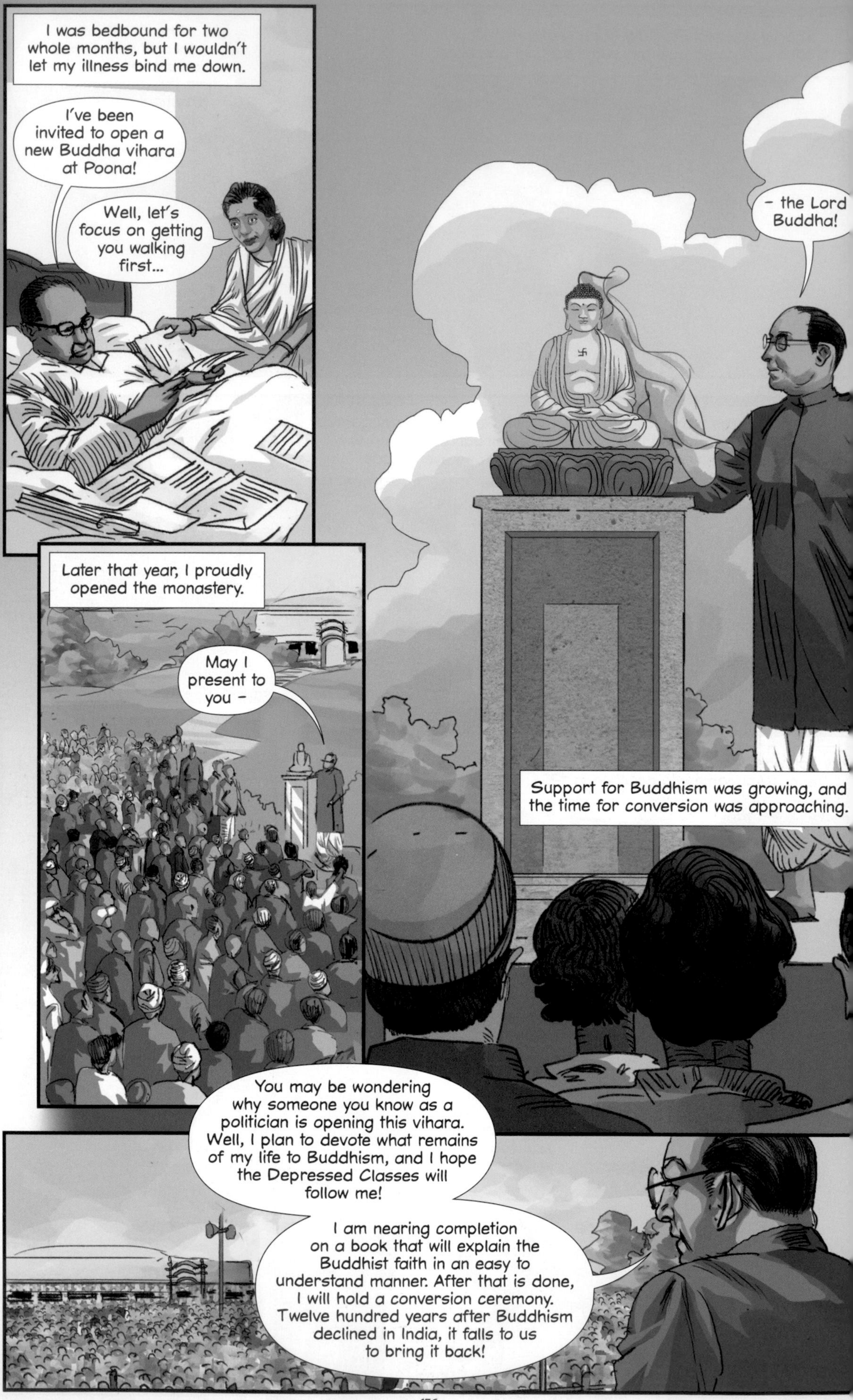

I was bedbound for two whole months, but I wouldn't let my illness bind me down.
I've been invited to open a new Buddha vihara at Poona!
Well, let's focus on getting you walking first...
Later that year, I proudly opened the monastery.
May I present to you –
– the Lord Buddha!
Support for Buddhism was growing, and the time for conversion was approaching.
You may be wondering why someone you know as a politician is opening this vihara. Well, I plan to devote what remains of my life to Buddhism, and I hope the Depressed Classes will follow me!
I am nearing completion on a book that will explain the Buddhist faith in an easy to understand manner. After that is done, I will hold a conversion ceremony. Twelve hundred years after Buddhism declined in India, it falls to us to bring it back!

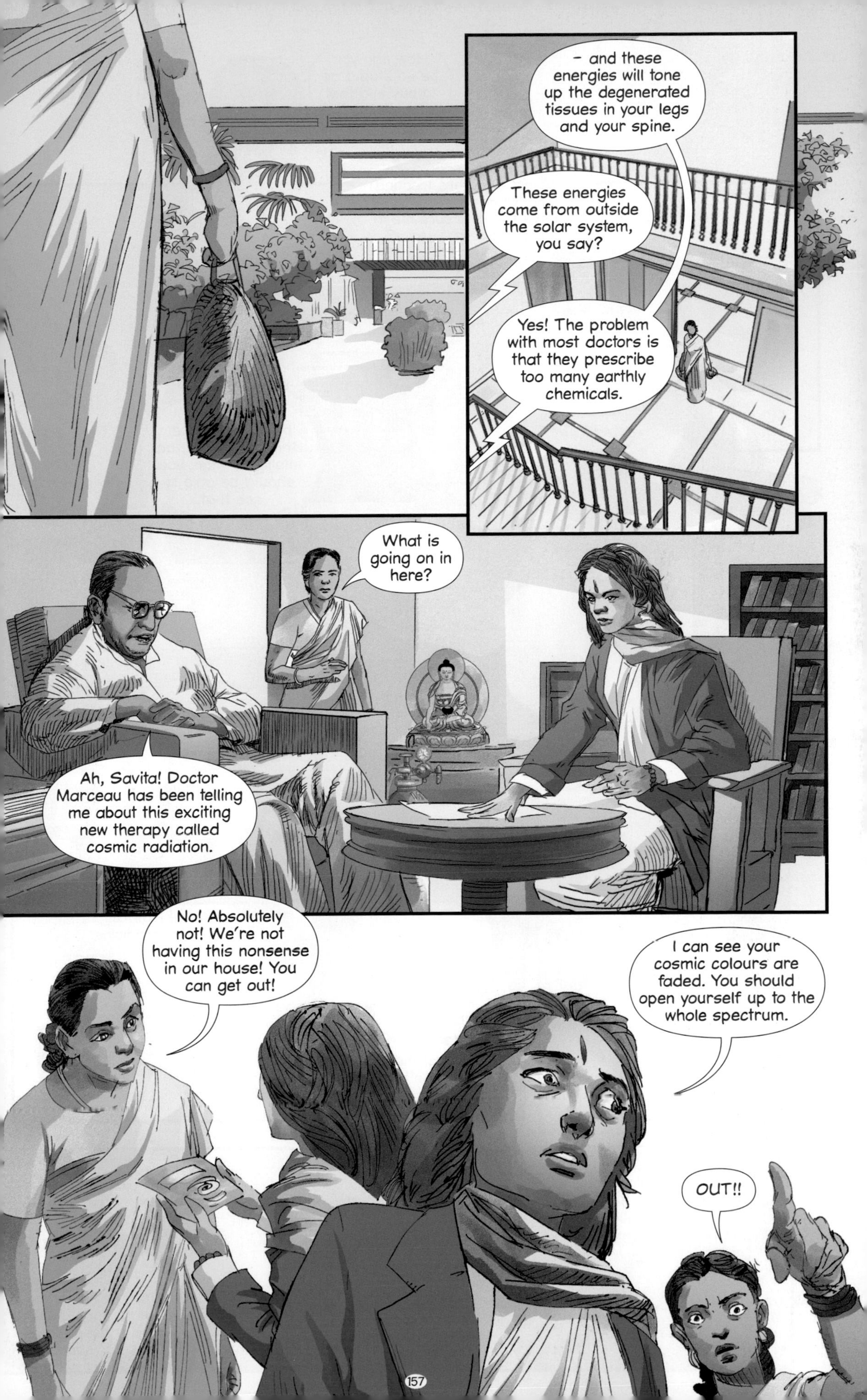

- and these energies will tone up the degenerated tissues in your legs and your spine.
These energies come from outside the solar system, you say?
Yes! The problem with most doctors is that they prescribe too many earthly chemicals.
What is going on in here?
Ah, Savita! Doctor Marceau has been telling me about this exciting new therapy called cosmic radiation.
No! Absolutely not! We're not having this nonsense in our house! You can get out!
I can see your cosmic colours are faded. You should open yourself up to the whole spectrum.
OUT!!

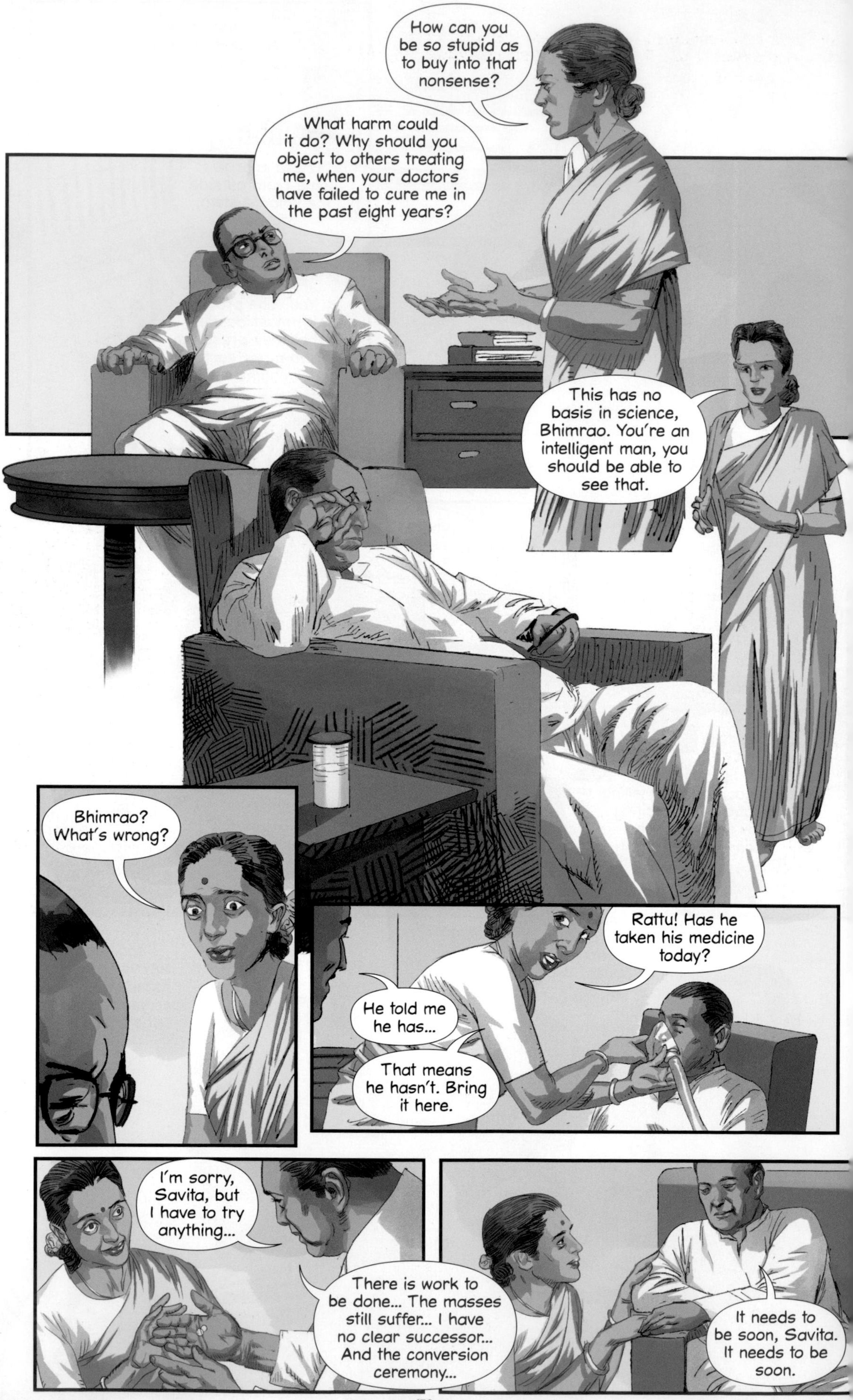
How can you be so stupid as to buy into that nonsense?
What harm could it do? Why should you object to others treating me, when your doctors have failed to cure me in the past eight years?
This has no basis in science, Bhimrao. You're an intelligent man, you should be able to see that.
Bhimrao? What's wrong?
Rattu! Has he taken his medicine today?
He told me he has...
That means he hasn't. Bring it here.
I'm sorry, Savita, but I have to try anything...
There is work to be done... The masses still suffer... I have no clear successor... And the conversion ceremony...
It needs to be soon, Savita. It needs to be soon.

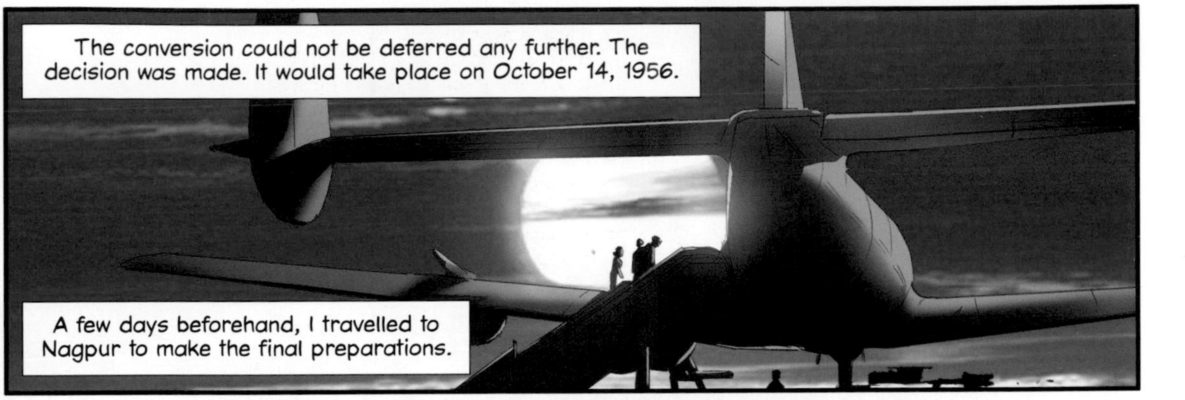
The conversion could not be deferred any further. The decision was made. It would take place on October 14, 1956.
A few days beforehand, I travelled to Nagpur to make the final preparations.

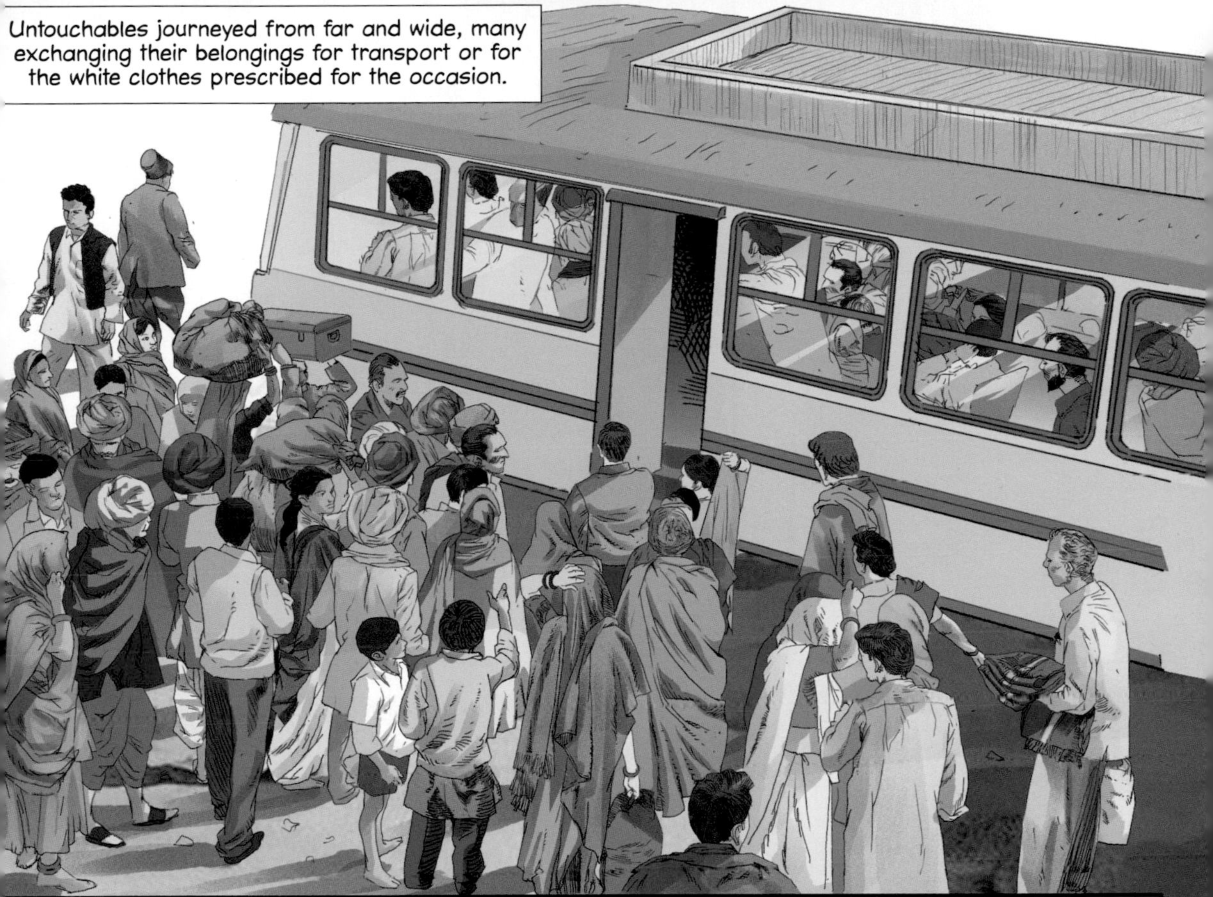
Untouchables journeyed from far and wide, many exchanging their belongings for transport or for the white clothes prescribed for the occasion.

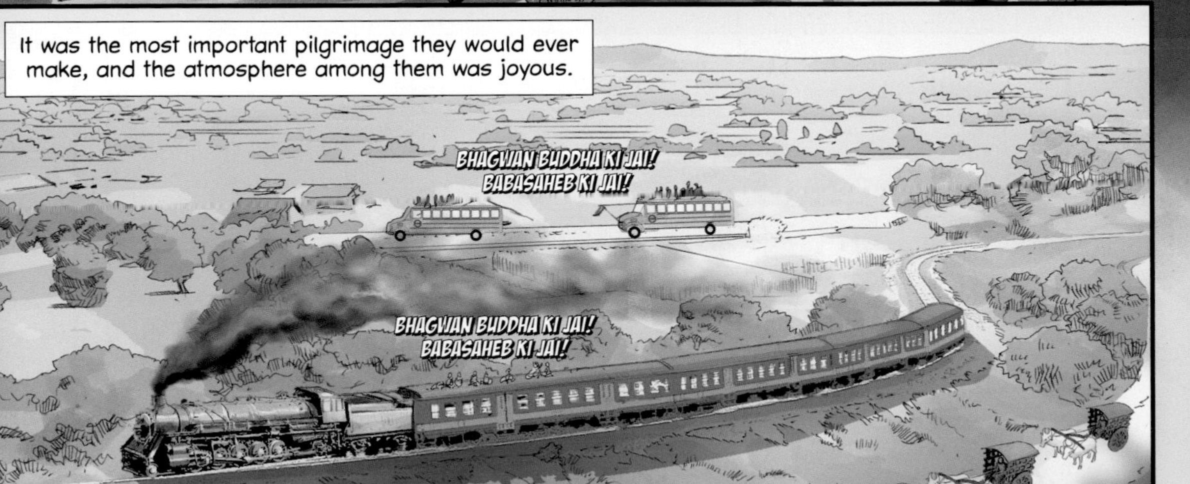
It was the most important pilgrimage they would ever make, and the atmosphere among them was joyous.
BHAGWAN BUDDHA KI JAI! BABASAHEB KI JAI!
BHAGWAN BUDDHA KI JAI! BABASAHEB KI JAI!

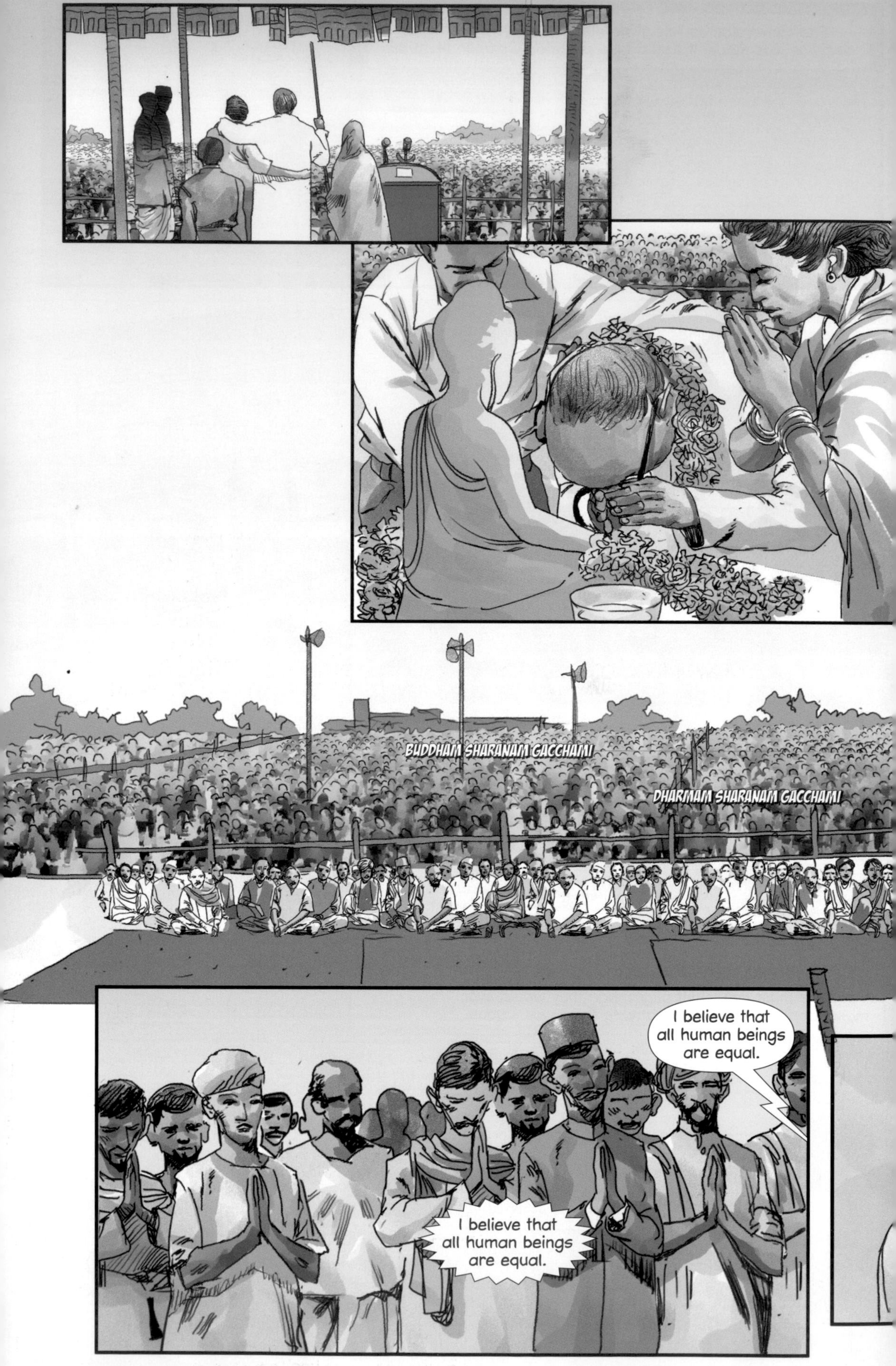
BUDDHAM SHARANAM GACCHAMI
DHARMAM SHARANAM GACCHAMI
I believe that all human beings are equal.
I believe that all human beings are equal.

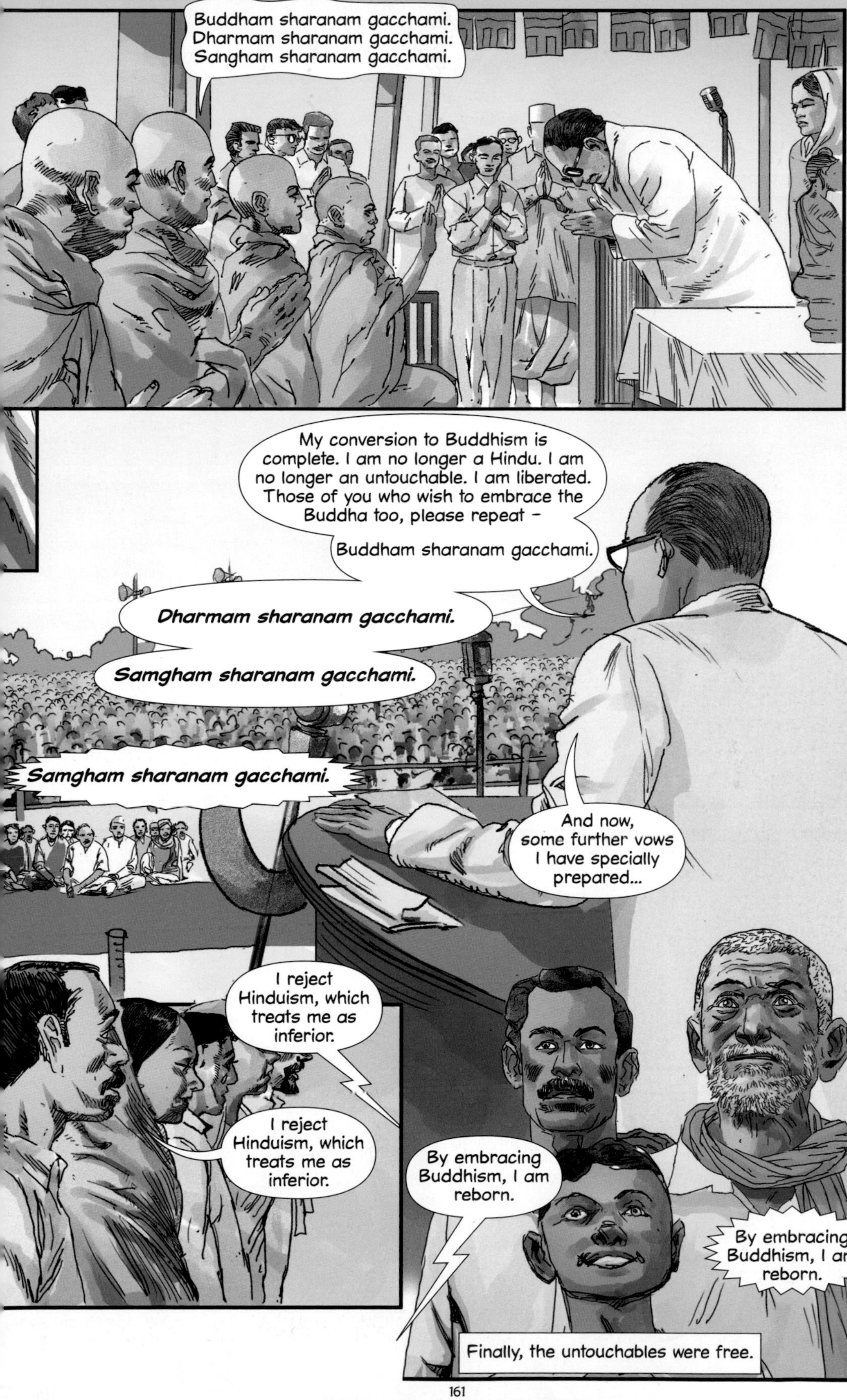
Buddham sharanam gacchami. Dharmam sharanam gacchami. Sangham sharanam gacchami.
My conversion to Buddhism is complete. I am no longer a Hindu. I am no longer an untouchable. I am liberated. Those of you who wish to embrace the Buddha too, please repeat –
Buddham sharanam gacchami.
Dharmam sharanam gacchami.
Samgham sharanam gacchami.
Samgham sharanam gacchami.
And now, some further vows I have specially prepared...
I reject Hinduism, which treats me as inferior.
I reject Hinduism, which treats me as inferior.
By embracing Buddhism, I am reborn.
By embracing Buddhism, I am reborn.
Finally, the untouchables were free.

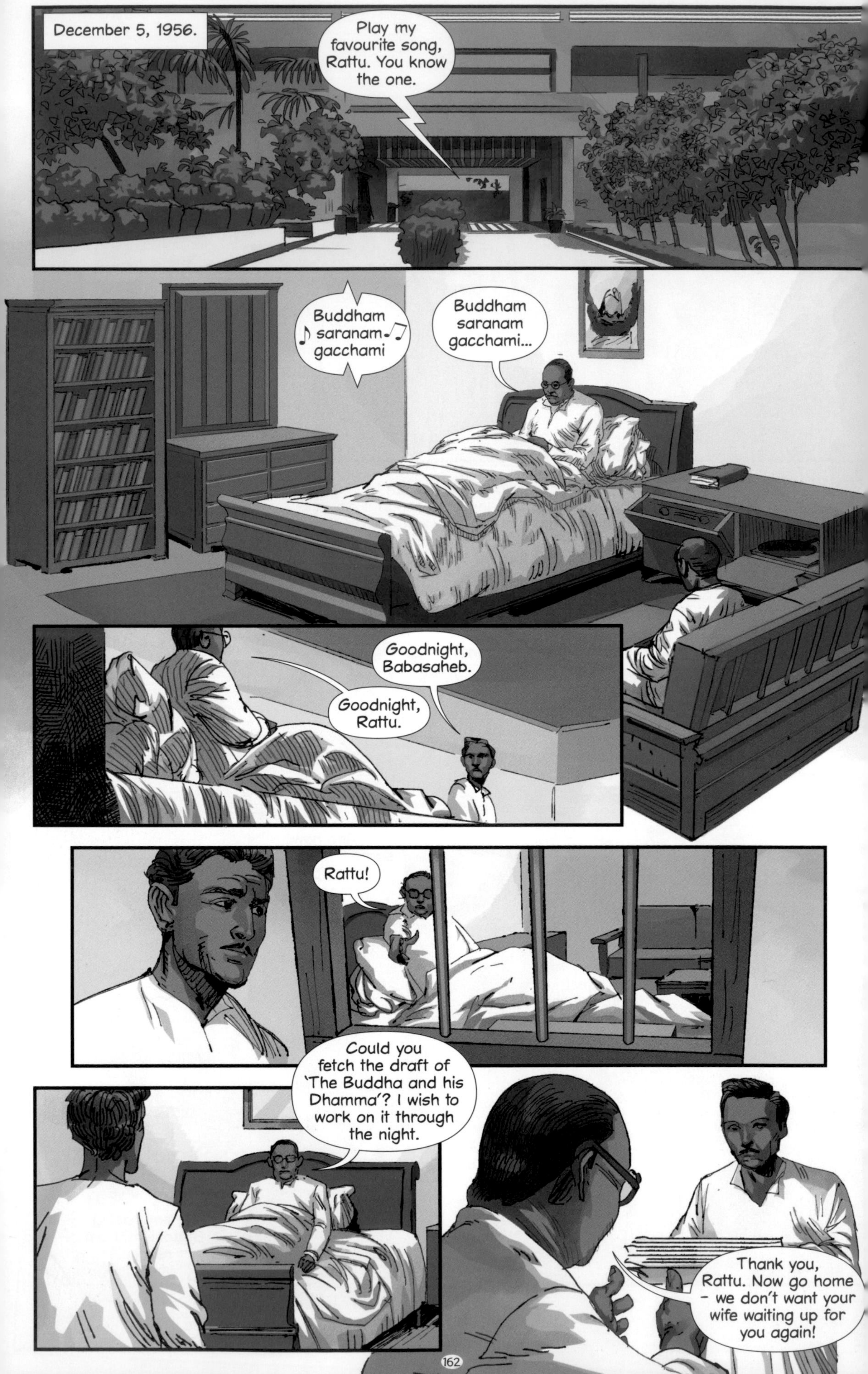

December 5, 1956.
Play my favourite song, Rattu. You know the one.
Buddham saranam gacchami
Buddham saranam gacchami...
Goodnight, Babasaheb.
Goodnight, Rattu.
Rattu!
Could you fetch the draft of 'The Buddha and his Dhamma'? I wish to work on it through the night.
Thank you, Rattu. Now go home – we don't want your wife waiting up for you again!

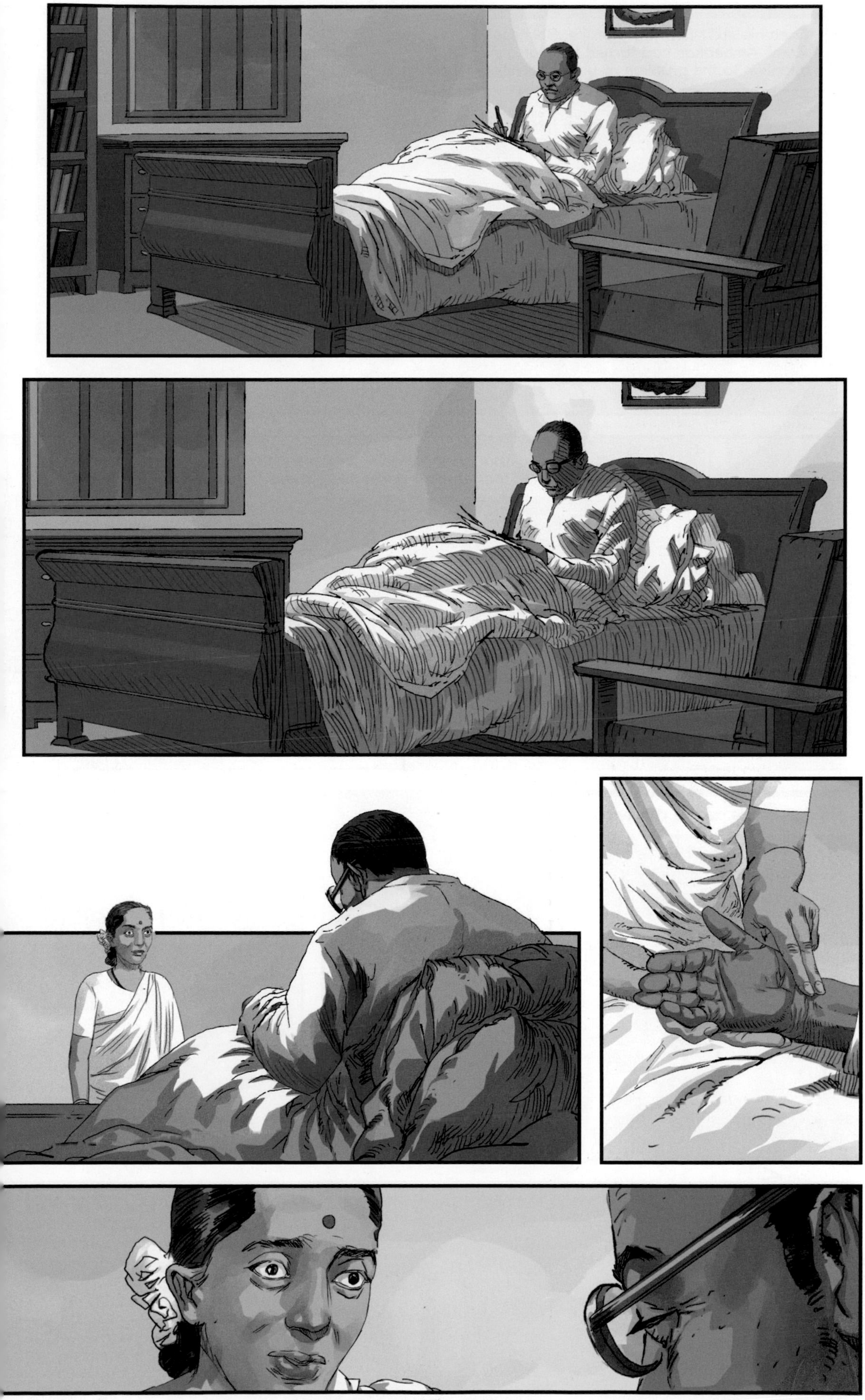

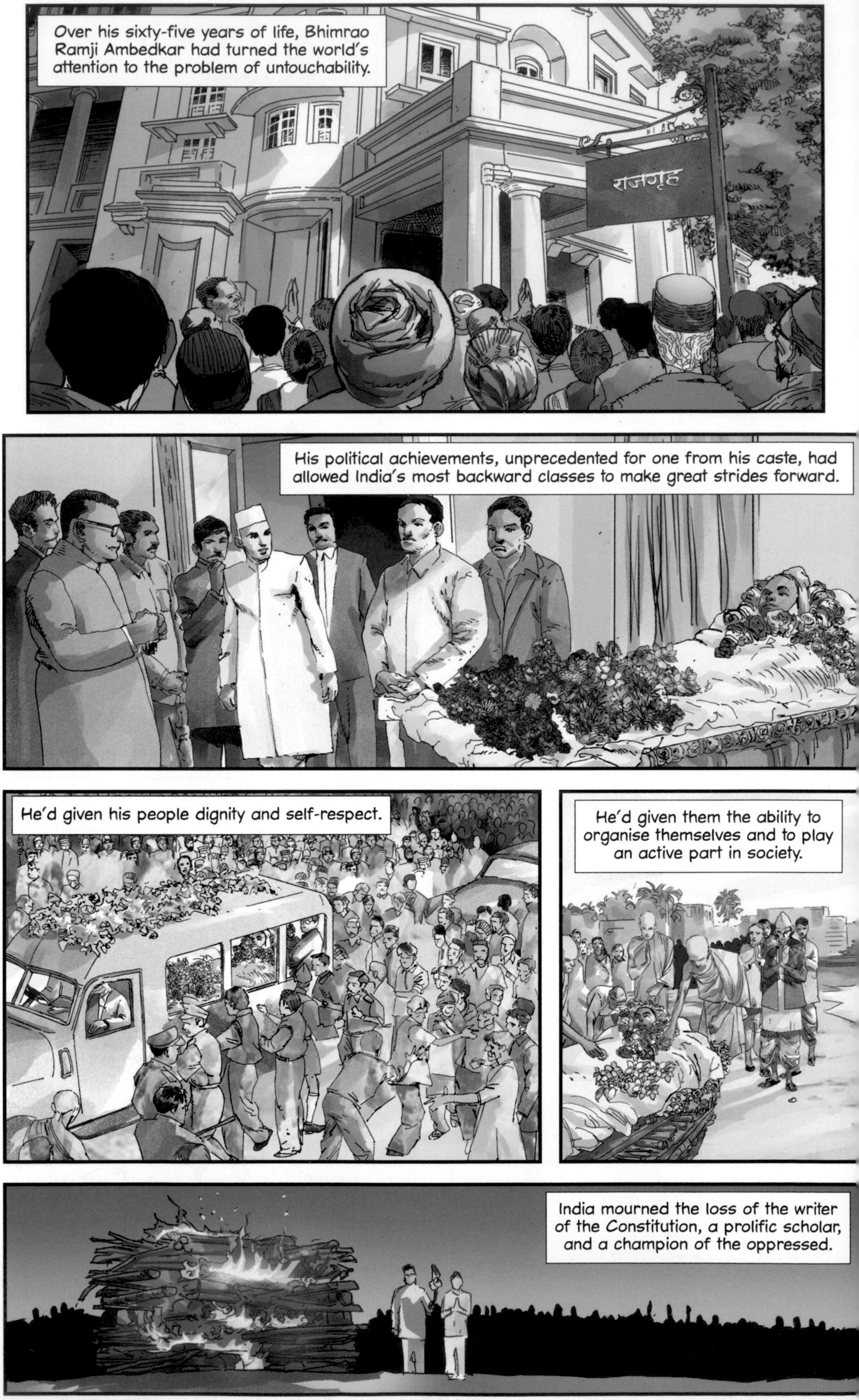
Over his sixty-five years of life, Bhimrao Ramji Ambedkar had turned the world's attention to the problem of untouchability.
राजगृह
His political achievements, unprecedented for one from his caste, had allowed India's most backward classes to make great strides forward.
He'd given his people dignity and self-respect.
He'd given them the ability to organise themselves and to play an active part in society.
India mourned the loss of the writer of the Constitution, a prolific scholar, and a champion of the oppressed.

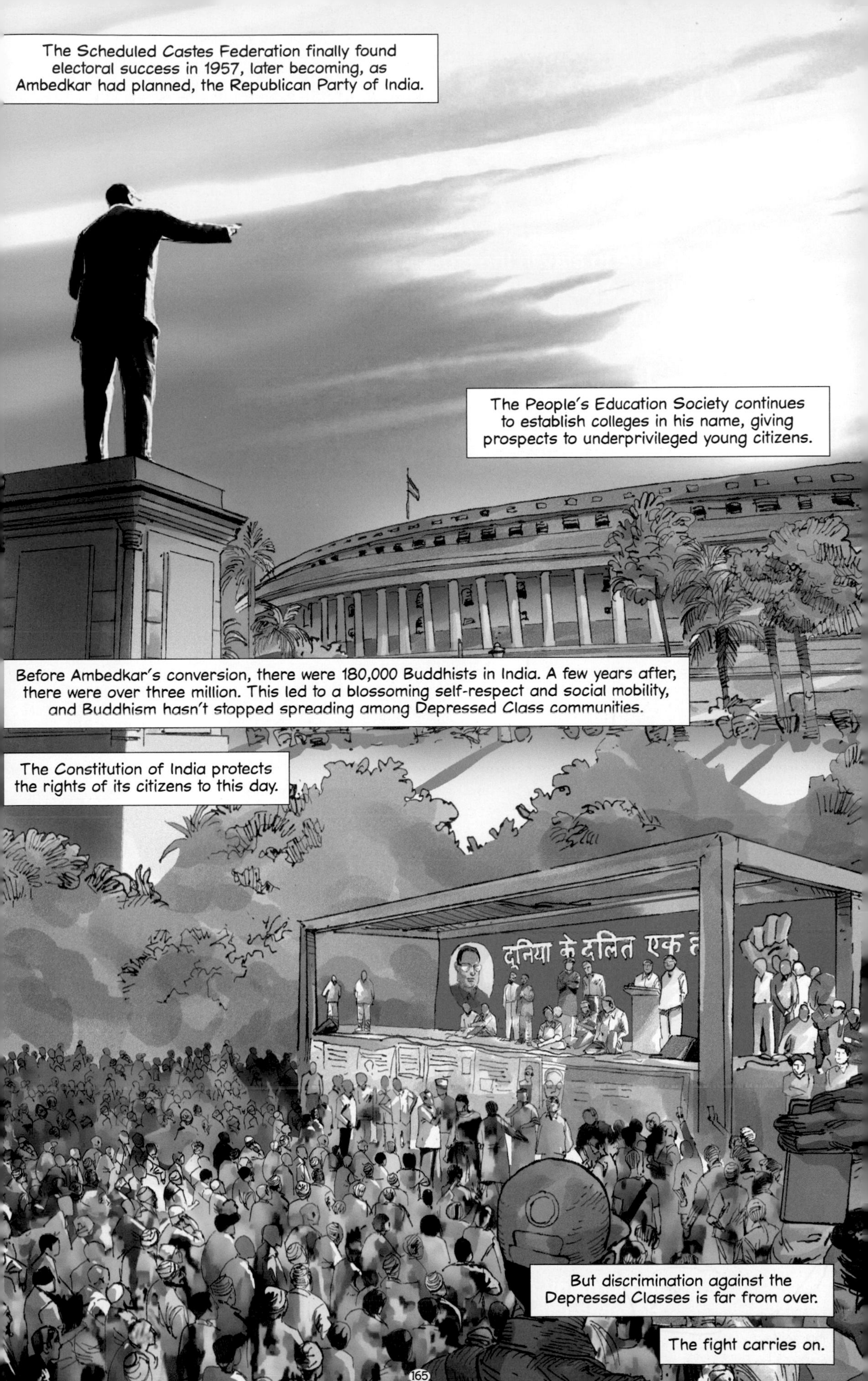
The Scheduled Castes Federation finally found electoral success in 1957, later becoming, as Ambedkar had planned, the Republican Party of India.
The People's Education Society continues to establish colleges in his name, giving prospects to underprivileged young citizens.
Before Ambedkar's conversion, there were 180,000 Buddhists in India. A few years after, there were over three million. This led to a blossoming self-respect and social mobility, and Buddhism hasn't stopped spreading among Depressed Class communities.
The Constitution of India protects the rights of its citizens to this day.
दुनिया के दलित एक
But discrimination against the Depressed Classes is far from over.
The fight carries on.

Toward a modern and enlightened India

Ambedkar was a man ahead of his times. His visionary ideas had an instrumental role to play in the creation of a secular and modern India. His ideas did face resistance at the time, but his proposals have been enshrined in Indian law.

Social Reforms

Equal rights: The Constitution of India guarantees civil liberties and fundamental rights to all Indian citizens. Ambedkar championed the cause of the Dalits, who were treated as untouchables and lacked access to justice, education and jobs.

Women's rights: The Hindu Code Bill debates of 1946-1952, and subsequent implementation of much-needed acts, secured the position of women in daily life regarding employment, maternity, marriage, guardianship, adoption and divorce at a time when Indian society was still dominated by a traditional, patriarchal mindset. Ambedkar's views faced great opposition from conservative politicians but they eventually became law, such as the Maternity Benefit Act, Women Labour and Welfare Fund, Women and Child Labour Protection Act, a ban on employment of women in underground work in coal mines, and equal pay for equal work.

Safeguards for minorities and disadvantaged: Ambedkar favoured reservation in education and jobs for communities that were socially backward and disadvantaged. As a visionary, he proposed that some reservations be limited to 20 years.

Modernism: Ambedkar's thoughts were contemporary and modern. He propagated a modern Western lifestyle and displayed it by wearing a suit and a tie.

Political Reforms

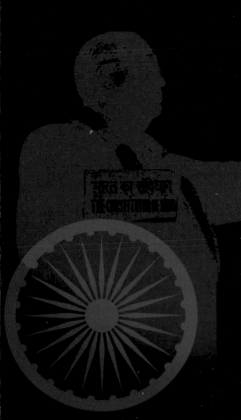

Universal adult franchise: Ambedkar believed that all citizens had a right to vote, irrespective of class, race, religion, gender or caste. He propounded this to be a basic principle of a democracy.

Parliamentary democracy: Ambedkar advocated the parliamentary form of government and a social democracy, which he believed would ensure equality for all.

Article 370: Ambedkar opposed the insertion of Article 370 in the Constitution, which confers special status upon the state of Jammu and Kashmir.

Economic Reforms

Reserve Bank of India: The Reserve Bank of India was set up in 1935 to monitor the Indian rupee based on the principles presented by Ambedkar in his PhD thesis *The Problem of the Rupee: Its Origins and its Solutions*. He emphasised a free economy with a stable rupee as the pillar of a functioning economy. To commemorate Ambedkar's work on the Indian currency, the Prime Minister of India, Narendra Modi, launched a mobile app for cashless payments named BHIM, in honour of Bhimrao Ambedkar. The app was linked with Aadhar (India's unique biometric identity number) on Ambedkar's 126th birth anniversary on April 14, 2017.

Land reforms: The 1927 land reforms in the Bombay Legislative Council declared that 'Smallness or largeness of an agricultural land holding is not determined by its physical extent alone but by the intensity of cultivation as reflected in the amounts of productive investment made on the land and the amounts of all other inputs used, including labour.'

Labour reform: As Labour Minister in the Viceroy's Council, Ambedkar forced the British to reduce working hours from twelve to eight in 1942.

Agriculture: Ambedkar was a strong proponent of investment in agriculture, which he believed would alleviate food shortages in India.

What is a constitution?

A constitution is a set of fundamental principles or established precedents according to which a state is governed. Such sets of laws laying out the rights of citizens have their precedents in ancient Mesopotamia, such as the Codes of Hammurabi. The Magna Carta, established in England in 1215, prevented the king from illegally imprisoning or murdering citizens of the state, and laid the groundwork for the rights and liberties enjoyed by all citizens of a sovereign state today.

STATES PROVISIONS POWER CONSTITUTION
PARLIAMENT LAW ARTICLE RIGHTS PROVISIONS ARTICLE LAW
POWER SOCIETY EVERYONE PARLIAMENT
PROTECTION SOCIETY
EVERYONE PROTECTION LAW LEGISLATURE
LEGISLATURE ARTICLE PROVISIONS

The Constitution of India

The Constitution of India is the longest written constitution of a sovereign state. It came into effect on 26 January 1950. B R Ambedkar, as chairman of its Drafting Commitee, was the chief architect of the Indian Constitution.

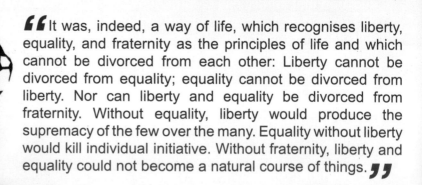

❝ It was, indeed, a way of life, which recognises liberty, equality, and fraternity as the principles of life and which cannot be divorced from each other: Liberty cannot be divorced from equality; equality cannot be divorced from liberty. Nor can liberty and equality be divorced from fraternity. Without equality, liberty would produce the supremacy of the few over the many. Equality without liberty would kill individual initiative. Without fraternity, liberty and equality could not become a natural course of things. **❞**

- B R Ambedkar

PREAMBLE TO THE CONSTITUTION OF INDIA

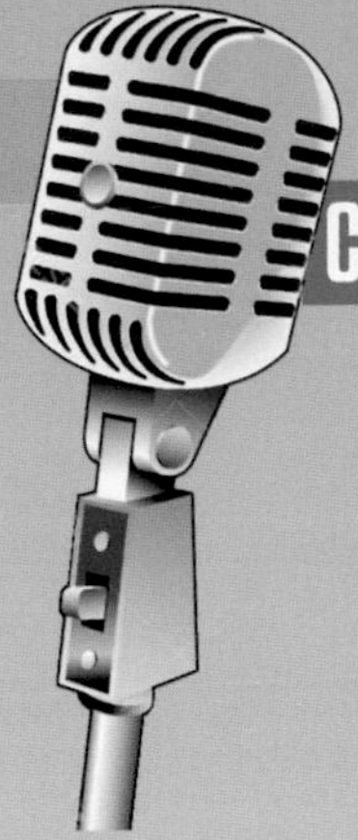

The Preamble to the Constitution of India declares India a sovereign, socialist, secular, democratic republic, assuring its citizens of justice, equality, and liberty, and endeavours to promote fraternity among them

"WE, THE PEOPLE OF INDIA, having solemnly resolved to constitute India into a **SOVEREIGN, SOCIALIST, SECULAR, DEMOCRATIC REPUBLIC** and to secure to all its citizens:

JUSTICE, social, economic and political;

LIBERTY of thought, expression, belief, faith and worship;

EQUALITY of status and of opportunity; and to promote among them all

FRATERNITY assuring the dignity of the individual and the unity and integrity of the Nation;

IN OUR CONSTITUENT ASSEMBLY this twenty-sixth day of November, 1949, do HEREBY ADOPT, ENACT AND GIVE TO OURSELVES THIS CONSTITUTION."

THE CONSTITUTION OF INDIA

WE, THE PEOPLE OF INDIA, having solemnly resolved to constitute India into a SOVEREIGN DEMOCRATIC REPUBLIC and to secure to all its citizens:

JUSTICE, social, economic and political;

LIBERTY of thought, expression, belief, faith and worship;

EQUALITY of status and of opportunity; and to promote among them all

FRATERNITY assuring the dignity of the individual and the unity of the Nation;

IN OUR CONSTITUENT ASSEMBLY this twenty-sixth day of November, 1949, do HEREBY ADOPT, ENACT AND GIVE TO OURSELVES THIS CONSTITUTION.

CONSTITUTION
OF
INDIA

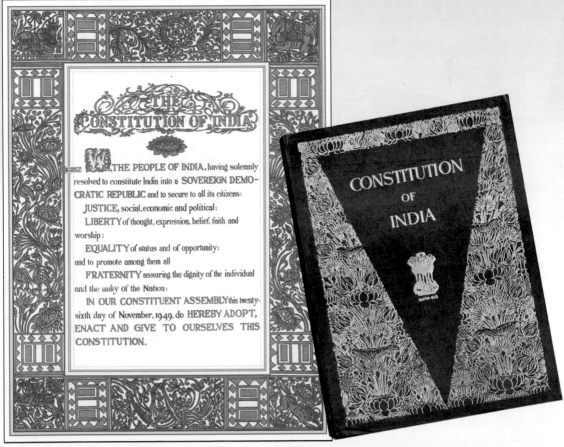

Source: https://www.wdl.org/en/item/2672/view/1/1/

The Constitution of India is also a work of art

The Constitution of India, with its handwritten calligraphy and accompanying illustrations, can be considered to be a great work of art. The entire manuscript was handwritten by Prem Behari Narain Raizada, with accompanying illustrations by the Bengal School artist Nandalal Bose and his students. The illustrations depict the richness of Indian history, starting with the Indus Valley civilisation, right up to the present day. The Constitution of India is the only constitution of a state that has illustrations.

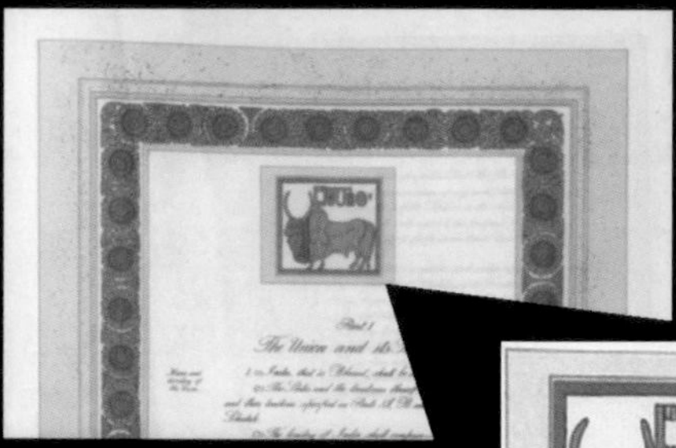
Part I
The Union and its

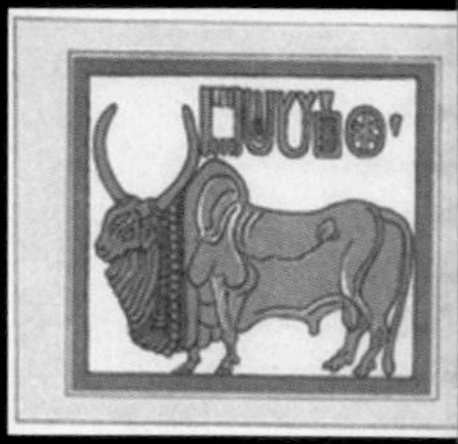

Bull from an Indus Valley seal at the beginning of Part I of the Constitution of India.

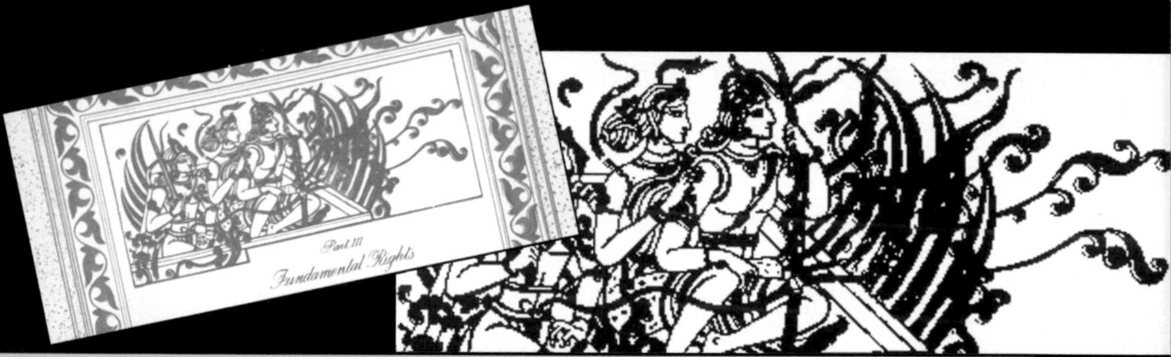
Part III
Fundamental Rights

Rama, Lakshmana and Sita depicted at the beginning of Part III of the Constitution of India.

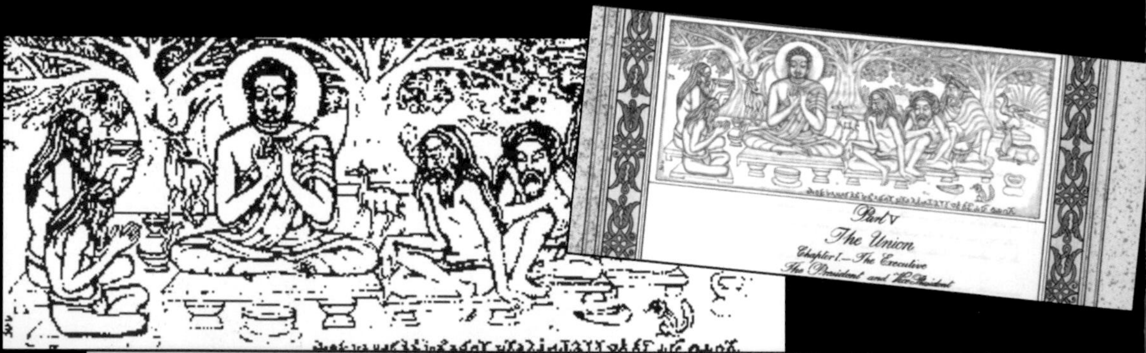
Part V
The Union
Chapter I.—The Executive

The enlightenment of Buddha, depicted at the beginning of Part V of the Constitution of India.

All Images are sourced from https://www.wdl.org/en/item/2672/view/1/1/

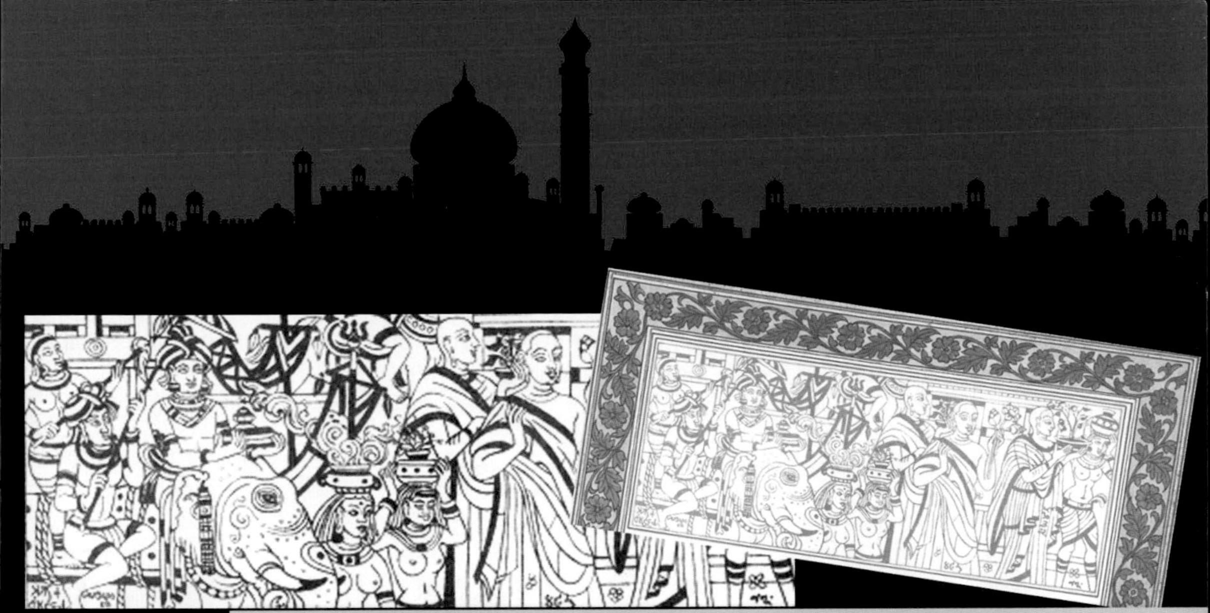

Life of Ashoka as depicted at the beginning of Part VII of the Constitution of India.

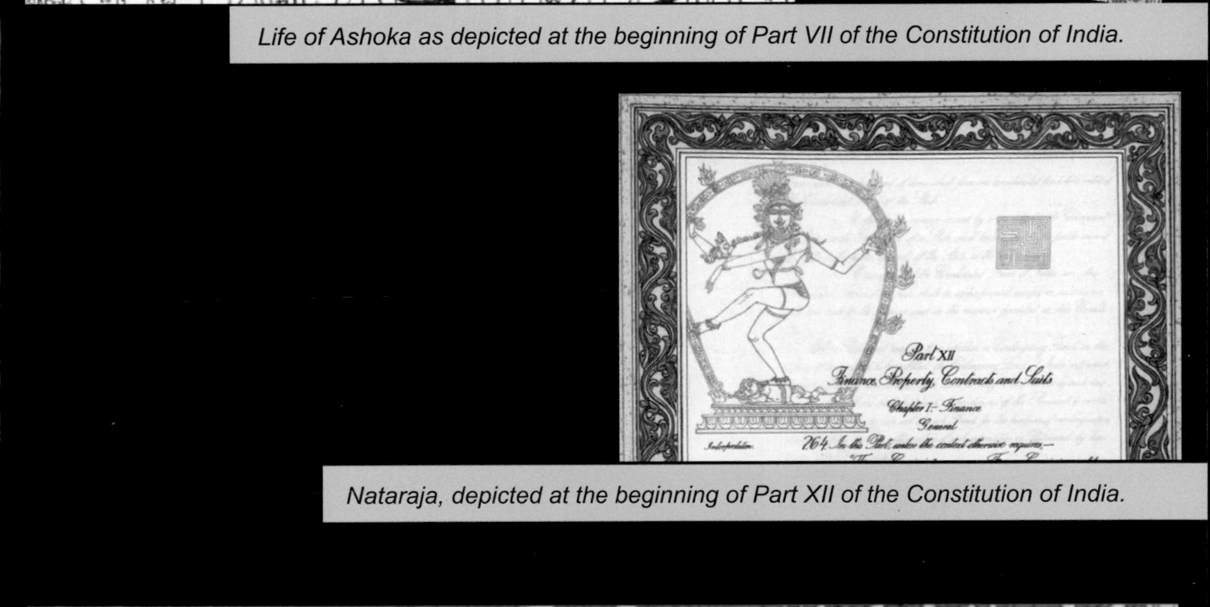

Part XII
Finance, Property, Contracts and Suits
Chapter I.- Finance
General
264. In this Part, unless the context otherwise requires,—

Nataraja, depicted at the beginning of Part XII of the Constitution of India.

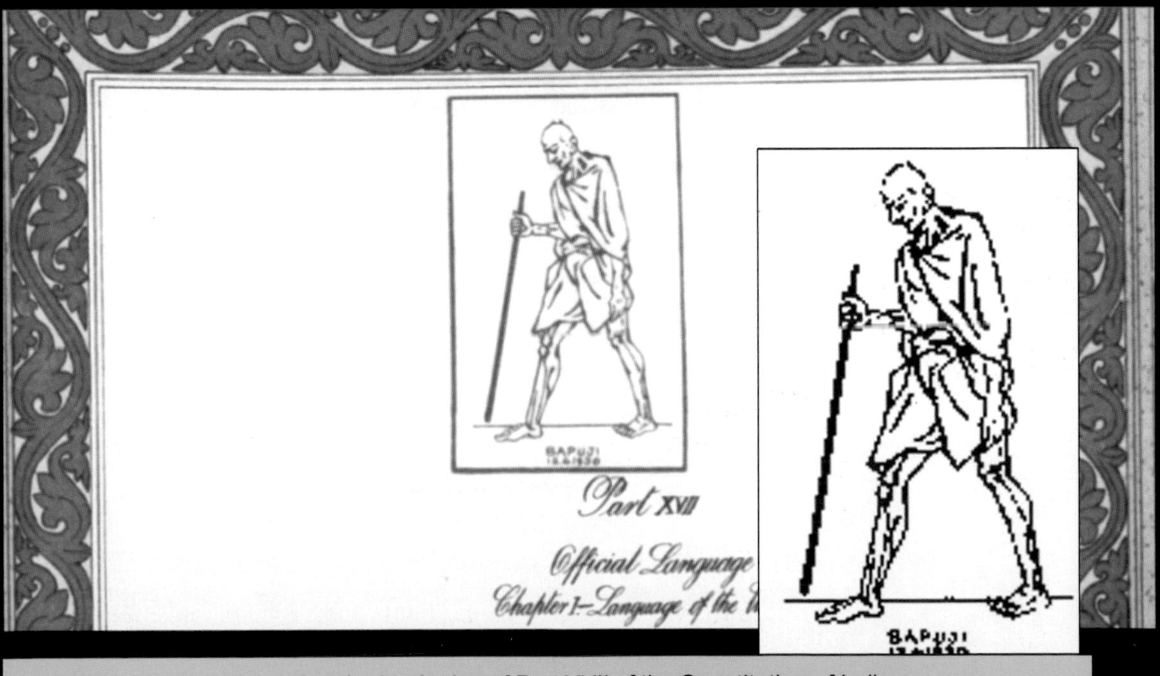

BAPUJI
Part XVII
Official Language
BAPUJI

Mahatma Gandhi, depicted at the beginning of Part XVII of the Constitution of India.

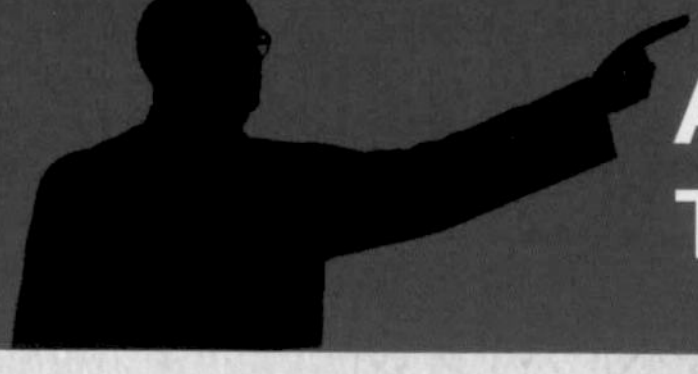

Ambedkar in the United States
The Birth of a Future Leader

Ambedkar spent some of his most formative years (1913-1916) in the United States of America as he attended Columbia University in New York. It was here that he picked up some of his most influential ideas, and while brief, his stay in New York proved to be momentous in the shaping of his thoughts and ideals, both social and economic.

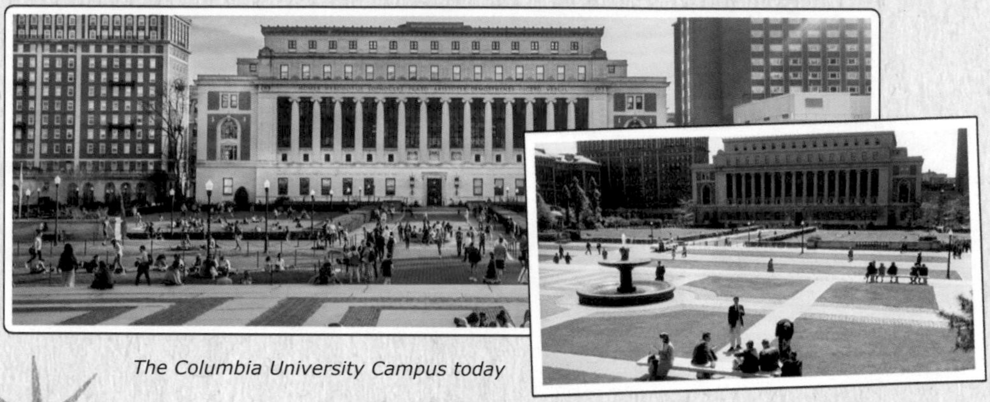

The Columbia University Campus today

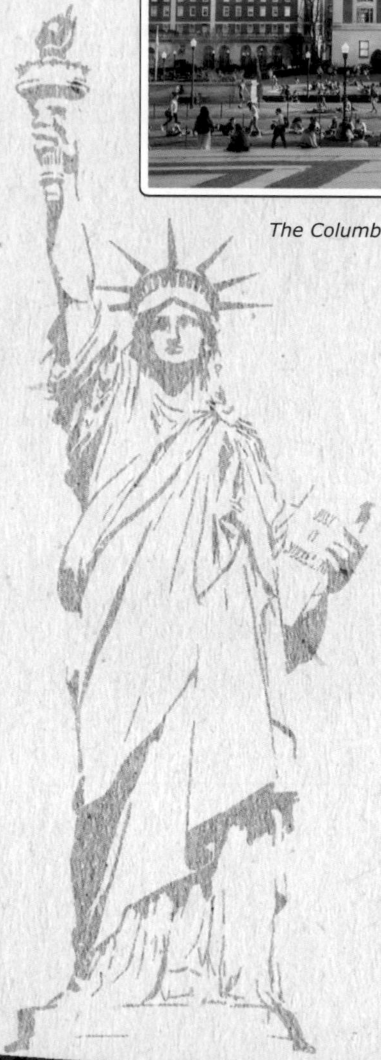

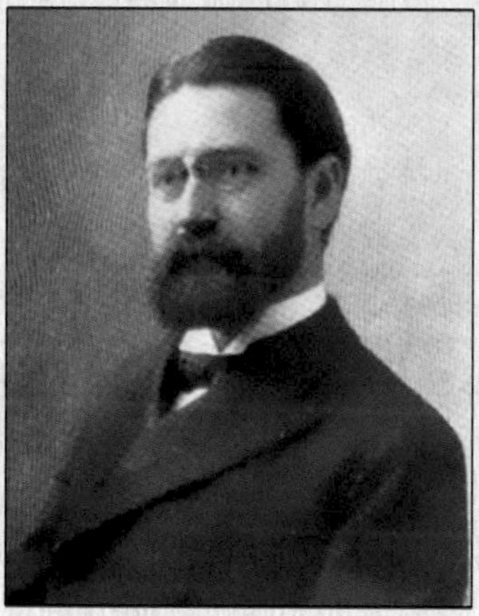

Edwin Seligman, a friend and mentor

Economic Views

It was at Columbia that he met noted economist Professor Edwin Seligman. (See pp 27-29 of this book) Under his influence, he wrote two theses, 'Ancient Indian Commerce' and 'National Dividend of India: A Historic and Analytical Study'. Ambedkar's work on economics, specifically related to India, would later find shape in his final PhD thesis, 'The Problem of the Rupee' at the University of London in 1923.

Women's Rights

Ambedkar's stay in the United States also coincided with the suffrage movement demanding equal voting rights for women. Ambedkar was a supporter of women's rights. He personally taught his first wife Ramabai to read and write, and later, during the framing of the Constitution of India, he did his best to ensure that women had the same rights as men such as equal voting.

Civil Rights

W E B Du Bois, US civil rights activist

Ambedkar's stay in New York also coincided with the reawakening of African American consciousness, which was to lead to the well-known Harlem Renaissance a few years later. The similarities in the conditions and treatment of Blacks in America and the Dalits in India could not have escaped Ambedkar, and he likely picked up a few ideas and inspiration from African American civil rights activists and intellectuals who fought against racism and advocated equal rights. One such civil rights activist was W E B Du Bois, who was one of the founders of the National Association for the Advancement of Colored People. Du Bois was an ardent supporter of India's struggle for freedom against the British, and he knew Indian nationalist leader Lajpat Rai, who was in America between 1914 and 1919. (See pp 28-29 of this book) While Ambedkar had not met Du Bois during this time, they did exchange letters much later in the 1940s.

In his letter to Du Bois, Ambedkar wrote, *"Although I have not met you personally, I know you by name as everyone does who is working in the cause of securing liberty to the oppressed people. I belong to the Untouchables of India and perhaps you might have heard my name. I have been a student of the Negro problem and have read your writings throughout. There is so much similarity between the position of the Untouchables in India and of the position of the Negroes in America that the study of the latter is not only natural but necessary. I was very much interested to read that the Negroes of America have filed a petition to the U.N.O. The Untouchables of India are also thinking of following suit. Will you be so good as to secure for me two or three copies of this representation by the Negroes and send them to my address. I need hardly say how grateful I shall be for your troubles in this behalf."*

In his reply on 31 July, 1946, Du Bois wrote, *"I have your letter concerning the case of the Negroes of America and the Untouchables in India before the United Nations. As you say a small organization of American Negroes, the National Negro Congress has already made statement which I am enclosing. I think however, that a much more comprehensive statement well documented will eventually be laid before the United Nations by the National Association for the Advancement of Colored people. If this is done, I shall be glad to send you a copy. I have often heard of your name and work and of course have every sympathy with the Untouchables of India. I shall be glad to be of any service I can render if possible in the future."*

While in Columbia, Ambedkar also wrote a paper on the caste system in India titled 'Castes in India: Their Mechanism, Genesis and Development'. This paper was to lay down the basis of Ambedkar's views on the origin of the caste system in India.

WOMEN'S RIGHTS

CASTES IN INDIA.

Their mechanism, genesis and development.[1]

BY BHIMRAO R. AMBEDKAR, M.A.

MANY of us, I dare say, have witnessed local, national, or international expositions of material objects that make up the sum total of human civilization. But few can entertain the idea of there being such a thing as an exposition of human institutions. Exhibition of human institutions is a strange idea; some might call it the wildest of ideas. But as students of Ethnology I hope you will not be hard on this innovation, for it is not so, and to you at least it should not be strange.

You all have visited, I believe, some historic place like the ruins of Pompeii, and listened with curiosity to the history of the remains as it flowed from the glib tongue of the guide. In my opinion a student of Ethnology, in one sense at least, is much like the guide. Like his prototype, he holds up (perhaps with more seriousness and desire of self-instruction) the social institutions to view, with all the objectiveness humanly possible, and inquires into their origin and function.

Most of our fellow students in this Seminar, which concerns itself with Primitive *versus* Modern Society, have ably acquitted themselves along these lines by giving lucid expositions of the various institutions, modern or primitive, in which they are interested. It is my turn now, this evening, to entertain you, as best I can, with a paper on "Castes in India: their mechanism, genesis and development."

I need hardly remind you of the complexity of the subject I intend to handle. Subtler minds and abler pens than mine have been brought to the task of unravelling the mysteries of Caste; but unfortunately it still remains in the domain of the "unexplained," not to say of the "un-understood." I am quite alive to the complex intricacies of a hoary institution like Caste, but I am not so pessimistic as to relegate it to the region of the unknowable, for I believe it can be known. The caste problem is a vast one, both theoretically and practically. Practically, it is an institution that portends tremendous consequences. It is a local problem, but one capable of much wider mischief, for "as long as caste in India does exist, Hindus will hardly intermarry or have any social intercourse with outsiders; and if Hindus migrate to other regions on earth, Indian caste would become a world problem."[2] Theoretically, it has defied a great many scholars who have taken upon themselves, as a labour of love, to dig into its origin. Such being the case, I cannot treat the problem in its entirety. Time, space and acumen, I am afraid, would all fail me, if I attempted to do otherwise than limit myself to a phase of it, namely, the genesis, mechanism and spread of the caste system. I will strictly observe this rule, and will dwell on extraneous matters only when it is necessary to clarify or support a point in my thesis.

To proceed with the subject. According to well-known ethnologists, the population of India is a mixture of Aryans, Dravidians, Mongolians and Scythians. All these stocks of people came into India from various directions and with various cultures, centuries ago, when they were in a tribal state. They all in turn elbowed their entry into the country by fighting with their predecessors, and after a stomachful of it settled down as peaceful neighbours. Through constant contact and mutual intercourse they evolved a common

---

[1] **A paper read before the Anthropology Seminar (9th May 1916) of Dr. A. A. Goldenweiser, Columbia University, New York.**

[2] **Ketkar, *Caste*, p. 4.**

First page of Ambedkar's paper 'Castes in India' as published in the Indian Antiquary, May 1917.

A Towering Personality - What others have said

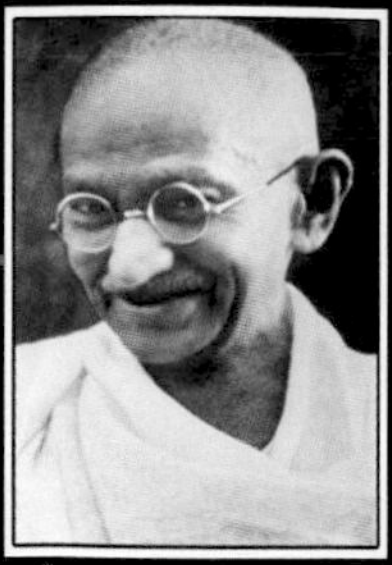

“Dr Ambedkar is such an intelligent and clever lawyer that he puts to shame many othe[redacted]he magnitude of his sacrifice is grea[redacted]He is capable of earning [redacted] to two thousand rupees every month. [redacted] is also in a position to settle down in Europe if he so desires. But he does not want to stay there. He is only concerned about the welfare of the [depressed people].”

- Mahatma Gandhi

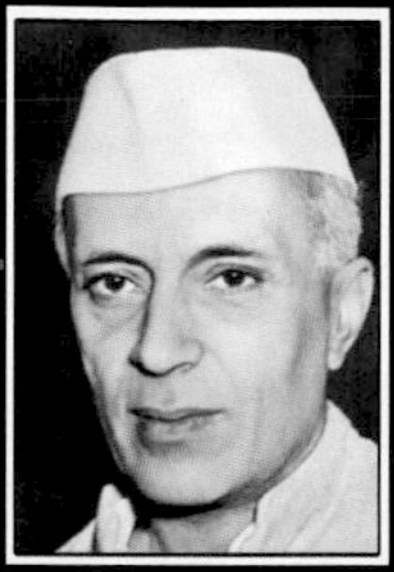

“Dr Ambedkar for many many years had been a very controversial figure in Indian public affairs, but there can be no doubt about his outstanding quality, his scholarship, and the intensity with which he pursed his convictions, sometimes rather with greater intensity than perhaps required by the particular subject, which sometimes reacted in a contrary way. But he was the symbol of that intense feeling which we must always remember, the intense feeling of the suppressed classed in India who have suffered for ages past under our previous social systems, and it is as well that we recognise this burden that all of us should carry and should always remember.”

- Then Prime Minister Jawaharlal Nehru
on the death of Ambedkar, as spoken in the Rajya Sabha

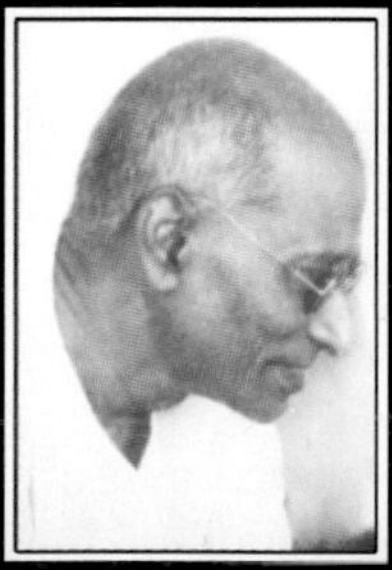

“Ambedkar was a thoroughly upright person and a man with keen jurist sense, a proud and irreconcilable heart, a great learning and when approached in the right spirit, full of friendliness.”

- C Rajagopalachari, former Governor General of India

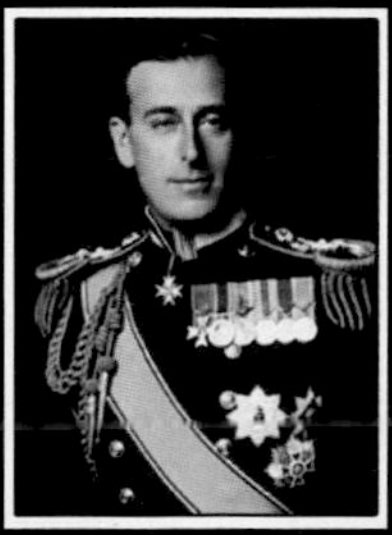

“Dr Ambedkar was a man of courage, a clear sighted brave fighter who has created an immortal niche for himself in the history of India.”

- Lord Mountbatten, last Viceroy of India

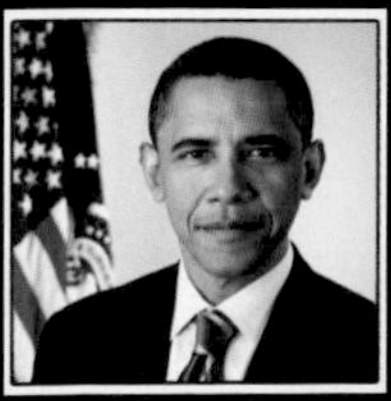

“We believe that no matter who you are or where you come from, every person can fulfil his God given potential; just as a Dalit like Dr Ambedkar could lift himself up and pen the words of the Constitution that protects the rights of all Indians.”

-Barack Obama, former US President

ABOUT
THE AUTHOR

Kieron Moore grew up in Lancashire, northern England. He studied at the University of York, and has worked as a freelance writer, journalist, and filmmaker. He has previously written *Buddha: An Enlightened Life* for Campfire and is passionate about using the medium of comics to bring interesting stories to life.

ABOUT
THE ARTIST

Sachin Nagar has worked on many of Campfire's most successful books, including the award-winning *Gandhi: My Life is My Message*, *Sundarkaand: The Triumph of Hanuman*, *Mother Teresa: Angel of the Slums*, *Ravana: Roar of the Demon King*, the *Kaurava Empire* series, and most recently, *Karna: Victory in Death*. Sachin is one of the most versatile artists in the industry today, and he likes to push the boundaries and try something new in every project he works on.